Eucharist & Ministry

Lutherans and Catholics in Dialogue IV

Edited by Paul C. Empie and T. Austin Murphy

AUGSBURG Publishing House • Minneapolis

EUCHARIST AND MINISTRY
Lutherans and Catholics in Dialogue IV

1979 Augsburg Publishing House edition
International Standard Book No. 0-8066-1781-0

Published by Augsburg Publishing House for
Lutheran World Ministries and the Bishops' Commission
on Ecumenical and Interreligious Affairs

For information address Augsburg Publishing House,
426 South Fifth Street, Minneapolis, Minnesota 55415.

FOREWORD

This volume is the fourth in a series designed to share with interested clergy and laity the progress made in the course of theological conversations between representatives of the Lutheran and the Roman Catholic traditions. The first volume, published in 1965, dealt with the subject "The Status of the Nicene Creed as Dogma of the Church." The second series of conversations dealt with the topic "One Baptism for the Remission of Sins." In both of these areas of theological concern the participants from the two communions found themselves in general agreement, a fact which they had anticipated but which added substantially to mutual understanding regarding the ways according to which each group proceeds theologically, and also indicated to some extent that consideration of future scheduled topics would require intensified research within the perspective of the astonishing ecclesiastical developments of the last decade.

Therefore it came as no surprise that the discussions on "The Eucharist as Sacrifice," a controversial issue which has estranged Lutherans from Roman Catholics for four centuries, required a much longer period of dialogue and uncovered more knotty problems than could be solved in that series of conversations. Nevertheless, the joint statement approved unanimously by participants on both sides represented a remarkable advance in convergence toward a common understanding on this critical theological point, something for which we can only acknowledge with humility and thanks the effective working of the Holy Spirit among us.

It seemed natural to take up as the next point the question of intercommunion. A weekend of conversations on this subject quickly revealed that one could not even discuss the matter without considering the key question of a valid Ministry in relation to the administration of the eucharist. Therefore the question of intercommunion was set aside until the groups could concentrate on the subject "Eucharist and Ministry." Over two years was spent in the preparation of studies, in conversations and drafting, the results of which are reflected in this volume. Again, while some points of importance remain unresolved, the common statement of the group, adopted unanimously, together with the separate statements of the representatives of the two traditions represent a forward step of immense significance. Those who have participated in this series of conversations again bear testimony to their awareness of the workings of the Holy Spirit in their midst and trust that the readers of this volume will find it as stimulating and instructive in the furthering of their concerns toward Christian unity as did those who are responsible for the studies and statements which are here reported.

It must again be emphasized that the studies and position papers contained herein represent the views of the authors and of the dialogue groups, and do not constitute official statements by any of the churches of which they are members.

It is anticipated that the dialogues will continue with the consideration of at least two or three additional theological issues which have been stumbling-blocks to mutual understanding between Lutherans and Roman Catholics in the past. We hope fervently that these efforts will make at least a modest contribution toward the ultimate outward realization of the oneness which all Christians have in Jesus Christ.

Paul C. Empie
✠ T. Austin Murphy

CONTENTS

EUCHARIST AND MINISTRY: A LUTHERAN-ROMAN CATHOLIC STATEMENT

CHAPTER ONE

Common Observations on Eucharistic Ministry

INTRODUCTION

1. The problem of the Ministry [1] is an inevitable item on any agenda of doctrinal discussion between Roman Catholics and Lutherans. In each of our other discussions, we have found ourselves confronted by it.

2. In our treatment of the Nicene creed and the significance of dogmatic statements we saw the necessary connection between dogma (i. e., authoritative creeds and confessions) and the teaching authority of the church. [2] Our dialogue on baptism made it possible for us to confess together our faith that this sacrament is an act of Christ by which God calls his church into being. At the same time we recognized that differences of interpretation of this sacramental act have frequently been rooted in differing understandings of the Ministry of the church. [3]

---

[1] For the distinction between *M*inistry and *m*inistry, see paragraph 9 below.

[2] *The Status of the Nicene Creed as Dogma of the Church.* Published Jointly by Representatives of the U. S. A. National Committee of the Lutheran World Federation and the Bishops' Commission for Ecumenical Affairs. 1965.

[3] *Lutherans and Catholics in Dialogue II: One Baptism for the Remission of Sins.* Edited by Paul C. Empie and William W. Baum. Published jointly by Representatives of the U. S. A. National Committee of the Lutheran World Federation and the Bishops' Commission for Ecumenical Affairs. 1966.

7

3. Sessions devoted to the problems of the eucharist as sacrifice and of the presence of Christ in the sacrament showed again a remarkable agreement in these much controverted topics, but also showed us how many matters could be cleared up only by discussion of the question of the Minister of the eucharist.[4] This became even more clear when we devoted one meeting to the problems of receiving communion in each other's eucharistic celebrations. There we recognized that a solution was not possible until the problems of the Ministry were squarely faced.

4. In our sessions dealing with the Ministry, as in our other discussions, we have attempted to clear away misunderstandings, to clarify to each other the theological concerns of our traditions, and to see what common affirmations we can make about the reality of the Ministry. Neither Catholic nor Lutheran participants came to this dialogue with a complete doctrine of this Ministry and we have not formulated one in our discussions. We have found certain areas that we judge are central to this reality and critical for the unity of the church. In these areas we make common affirmations. We gratefully acknowledge the contribution of the ongoing discussion of the Ministry in the ecumenical movement, both for its clarification of the theological issues and for its service in prodding us to do our thinking about the Ministry in a responsibly ecumenical context.[5]

5. Again we have noted that in our use of the same terms, we have not always meant the same things, and that differing theological language has sometimes masked theological concerns which are similar if not identical. We are convinced that in spite of differing vocabularies and problematics we are both approaching greater agreement on what God is doing in his church, as is evidenced in the following paragraphs.

I. THE MINISTRY IN THE CONTEXT OF GOD'S ACT IN CHRIST

6. Both the Catholic and the Lutheran traditions confess that God fulfills his promise to his people and definitively reveals his saving love

---

[4] *Lutherans and Catholics in Dialogue III: The Eucharist as Sacrifice.* Published jointly by Representatives of the U. S. A. National Committee of the Lutheran World Federation and the Bishops' Committee for Ecumenical and Interreligious Affairs. 1967.

[5] *Faith and Order Findings,* Montreal, 1963 (Minneapolis: Augsburg Publishing House, 1963).

for the world in the life, death, resurrection, and coming again of Jesus Christ. The God of Israel acts and speaks in the deeds and words of his Son.

7. Scripture attests that it was through the work of the Holy Spirit that Jews and Gentiles alike repented, believed, and were baptized. Thus were men united by Christ into the unique community called the church.

8. The Lord of the church, through the Holy Spirit, continues to act sacramentally and to proclaim his teaching through the men whom he has united with himself. The words and acts of Jesus in which the God of Israel has revealed his love for all mankind are the "good news." Under the guidance of the Spirit the first believers proclaimed by deed and word this gospel of the saving presence, activity, and teaching of the Lord.

9. The church has, then, the task of proclaiming the gospel to all, believers and unbelievers. This task or service of the whole church is spoken of as "ministry" *(diakonia)*. In the course of this statement, we employ the term ministry (lower case *m*, with or without the definite article) in this sense. The ministry of the church, thus defined, will be distinguished from the (or a) Ministry, a particular form of service — a specific order, function or gift (charism) within and for the sake of Christ's church in its mission to the world. The term Minister in this document refers to the person to whom this Ministry has been entrusted. We are convinced that the special Ministry must not be discussed in isolation but in the context of the ministry of the whole people of God.

II. THE MINISTRY IN THE CONTEXT OF THE CHURCH

A. The Ministry of the People of God

10. The ministry which devolves upon the whole church can rightly be described as a priestly service (*hierateuma,* cf. I Peter 2: 5, 9), such as that of ancient Israel, whom Yahweh fashioned into "a kingdom of priests and a holy nation" among all peoples (Exodus 19:5-6). We are agreed that in Jesus Christ God has provided his people with a high priest and sacrifice (cf. Hebrews 4:14ff.). All who are united with Jesus as Christ and Lord by baptism and faith are also united with, and share, his priesthood. We recognize therefore that the whole church has a priesthood in Christ, i. e., a ministry or service from God to men, that "they may see your good deeds and glorify

9

God on the day of visitation" (I Peter 2:12). They are thus privileged and obliged to represent the concerns of God to men and those of men to God.

11. To enable the church to be what God intends it to be in and for the world, God bestows within this priesthood various gifts for ministering. In particular, "God has appointed . . . apostles, prophets, teachers," etc. (I Corinthians 12:28-30; cf. Romans 12:6-8, Ephesians 4:7-12). While no single Ministry mentioned in the New Testament corresponds exactly to the special Ministry of the later church,[6] many of the specialized tasks of which we hear in the New Testament are entrusted to that later Ministry: preaching the gospel, administering what the church came to call sacraments, caring for the faithful. We turn now to what we can say in common of this special Ministry in the church (keeping in mind the particular aspect of our study — valid Ministry in relation to the eucharist).

B. The Special Ministry

12. Just as the church is to be seen in the light of God's love, his act in Christ, and the work of the Spirit, so also the Ministry is to be

---

[6] Development of the Ministry of the Christian church is difficult to trace and much controverted. Cf. Jerome D. Quinn, "Ministry in the New Testament," pp. 69-100. The passages cited in the text above list the following varieties of ministering:

I Corinthians 12: apostles, prophets, teachers, miracle-workers, healers, administrators, those who speak in tongues;

Romans 12: prophecy, serving *(diakonia),* teaching, exhorting, liberality in giving, zeal in aid, acts of mercy;

Ephesians 4: apostles, prophets, evangelists, pastors, teachers.

Everyone would agree that some of these categories belong in the special Ministry of the church (e. g., apostles, prophets, teachers), and that others reflect the ministry of the people of God (acts of mercy, aid and helping), and that some are hard to categorize (healing, teaching). Of particular interest, in any sketch of the development, would be the Ministry of "the Twelve," the Ministry of the apostles in a broader sense, the Ministry of the presbyter-bishop, the Ministry of those who baptized, and the Ministry of those who presided at the eucharist. Information, however, is incomplete. Neither the Twelve nor the apostles in the Pauline writings seem to have limited their Ministry to a local church as the later presbyter-bishop normally did, nor do we have much evidence of their administering sacraments. In fact, we are told very little in the New Testament about those who did preside at the eucharist. Thus the Ministry in the later church involving evangelism, preaching, sacraments, pastoral care, and administration in a community, combines functions that were not always united in the early church.

seen in light of the love of God, his saving act in Jesus Christ, and the ongoing activity of the Holy Spirit. This Ministry has the twofold task of proclaiming the gospel to the world — evangelizing, witnessing, serving — and of building up in Christ those who already believe — teaching, exhorting, reproving, and sanctifying, by word and sacrament. For this twofold work, the Spirit endows the Ministry with varieties of gifts, and thus helps the church to meet new situations in its pilgrimage. Through proclamation of the word and administration of the sacraments, this Ministry serves to unify and order the church in a special way for its ministry.[7]

13. The Ministry stands with the people of God under Christ but also speaks in the name of Christ to his people. On the one hand, the Ministry as part of the church's ministry stands under the Word and the Spirit, under judgment as well as under grace. But it also has a special role within the ministry of the people of God, proclaiming God's Word, administering the sacraments, exhorting and reproving.[8]

14. This Ministry is "apostolic." The term "apostolic" has had a variety of references: it has been applied for instance to doctrine, practices, authority.[9] Indeed, the *variety* of ways in which the gospel is expressed in the early church may be recognized as a feature of apostolicity.[10]

---

[7] Cf. the paper given at the Catholic-Lutheran conversations in Nemi, Italy, May, 1969, by George A. Lindbeck, "The Lutheran Doctrine of the Ministry: Catholic and Reformed," in *Theological Studies* 30 (1969), 588-612; also the Common Statement of the Nemi meeting.

[8] Warren A. Quanbeck, "A Contemporary View of Apostolic Succession," pp. 185-187.

[9] James F. McCue, "Apostles and Apostolic Succession in the Patristic Era," pp. 138-171; and Walter J. Burghardt, "Apostolic Succession: Notes on the Early Patristic Era," pp. 173-177.

[10] The variety of ways in which the term "apostolic" is applied is not startling when we note that the New Testament authors employ the term "apostle" to designate persons with a variety of roles in the earliest Christian generations (cf. R. Schnackenburg, *"L'apostolicité: état de la recherche,"* in *Istina* 14 (1969), 5-32, a paper originally prepared for the Vatican — World Council of Churches discussions on "Apostolicity and Catholicity."

The Second Vatican Council Decree on Ecumenism twice adverts to the fact that variety is itself an element in apostolicity. "While preserving unity in essentials, let all members of the Church, according to the office entrusted to each, preserve a proper freedom in the various forms of spiritual life and discipline, in the variety of liturgical rites, and even in the theological elaboration of revealed truth. In all things let charity be exercised.

15. Apostolicity has usually implied some sort of succession in what is apostolic. For many Catholics the phrase "apostolic succession" has meant succession in the ministerial office as a sign of unbroken transmission from the apostles. The stress for Lutherans has been on succession in apostolic doctrine. Historical studies have shown that in the New Testament and patristic periods there was stress on doctrinal succession; there also arose an emphasis on succession in apostolic office as a very important way of ensuring doctrinal succession and thus providing a sign of unity and a defense against heresy.[11]

16. Entry into the Ministry has been designated by both Catholics and Lutherans as "ordination." This term too has had a variety of meanings. Catholics have seen in ordination a sacramental act, involving a gift of the Holy Spirit, a charism for the service of the church and the world, the designation to a special service in the church, and the quality of permanence and unrepeatability. Lutherans, using a different (and more restricted) definition of sacrament, have generally been reluctant to use "sacrament" with reference to ordination, although the Apology of the Augsburg Confession is willing to do so (13, 9-13). Because of post-Reformation polemics, Lutherans became even more reluctant to use the term. Their consistent practice, however, shows a conviction concerning the sacramental reality of ordination to the Ministry. Lutherans too invoke the Holy Spirit for the gifts of the Ministry, see ordination as the setting apart for a specific service in the church and for the world, and regard the act as having a once-for-all significance.[12] Thus there is considerable convergence

---

If the faithful are true to this course of action, they will be giving ever richer expression to the authentic catholicity of the Church, and, at the same time, to her apostolicity" (4).

This principle finds its first and obvious application in relation to the churches of the East and the council fathers emphatically reaffirmed it when they said, ". . . this Sacred Synod declares that this entire heritage of (Eastern) spirituality and liturgy, of discipline and theology, in their various traditions, belongs to the full catholic and apostolic character of the Church" (17).

Our Lutheran-Catholic dialogue has been conscious of and attempted to implement this principle as we sorted out our answers to the question, "How is the Ministry apostolic?"

11 Burghardt, *op. cit.*

12 Cf. the Lutheran replies to Catholic questions, Baltimore sessions, given by George A. Lindbeck and Warren A. Quanbeck, pp. 53-60.

between the Catholic and the Lutheran understandings of ordination.

17. The expressions "character" and "indelible" have been used by Catholics with reference to ordination to describe the aspects of gift, charism, designation, and the qualities of permanence and unrepeatability.[13] Lutherans have objected to these terms because of the metaphysical implications they understand to be involved in them. However, historical studies and the renewal of liturgical and sacramental theology have brought into our discussions an emphasis upon the functional aspect of character and upon the gift of the Spirit.[14] These factors may help us to overcome traditional disagreements and open the way to a common approach to this complex of problems.

18. Having discussed the terms "apostolic," "ordination," and "character," we now affirm together that entry into this apostolic and God-given Ministry is by ordination. No man ordains himself or can claim this office as his right, but he is called by God and designated in and through the church. In reference to what has been called "character," we are agreed that ordination to the Ministry is for a lifetime of service and is not to be repeated.

C. The Structuring of the Special Ministry

19. Although we agree that Christ has given his church a special order of Ministry, we must also acknowledge the diverse ways in which this Ministry has been structured and implemented in the Catholic and Lutheran traditions.

20. In Catholicism, the Ministry of order has been apportioned among three Ministries or major orders: deacon, priest *(presbyter),* and bishop. All are conferred by a rite of ordination that includes the laying on of hands. The distribution of ministerial functions among these orders varies and has varied. In the present discipline, all three are appointed to baptize and proclaim the gospel; only priests and bishops celebrate the eucharist; only bishops ordain to major orders. Without prejudice to their belief that it is the bishop who possesses

---

13 Denzinger-Schönmetzer, *Enchiridion Symbolorum,* 33rd ed. (Hereafter cited as DS) (Freiburg: Herder, 1965), 1609; cf. 1313.
14 Lindbeck, "The Lutheran Doctrine of the Ministry: Catholic and Reformed," cited above, note 7; article *"Ordo"* by Piet Fransen, in *Lexikon für Theologie und Kirche* (Freiburg: Herder), vol. 7 (1962), columns 1215, 1216; article "Orders and Ordination" by Piet Fransen, in *Sacramentum Mundi* (New York: Herder and Herder), vol. 4 (1969), pp. 305-327.

the fullness of the Ministry conferred by ordination,[15] Catholics note that it is both historically and theologically significant that priests have ordained others as priests.[16]

21. The Lutheran tradition has one order of ordained Ministers, usually called pastors, which combines features of the episcopate and the presbyterate. This Ministry is also conferred by a rite of ordination that includes the laying on of hands. The pastor who has received this Ministry possesses the fullness of that which ordination confers and in general he corresponds in his functions with the bishop in the Catholic tradition.[17] In the Lutheran churches represented in this dialogue, the ordination of pastors is reserved to the district or synodical president or a pastor designated by him. The ordination of pastors in these churches goes back historically to priests ordained in the Catholic tradition who, on becoming Lutherans and lacking Catholic bishops who would impose hands on successors, themselves imposed hands for the ordination of co-workers and successors in the Ministry. From the Lutheran standpoint, such an ordination in presbyteral succession

---

[15] The Dogmatic Constitution on the Church (*Lumen Gentium*) of Vatican II states, "This sacred Synod teaches that by episcopal consecration is conferred the fullness of the sacrament of orders (*plenitudinem conferri sacramenti Ordinis*), that fullness which in the church's liturgical practice and in the language of the holy Fathers of the Church is undoubtedly called the high priesthood, the apex of the sacred ministry" (21). The council fathers were first asked whether they wished to say that episcopal consecration constituted the *summum gradum sacramenti Ordinis*. After agreeing upon this, the precise terminology for expressing it was debated. As the *Relatio* of 1964 puts it, "*Potius autem quam supremus gradus sacramenti Ordinis, Episcopatus dicendus est eius plenitudo seu totalitas, omnes partes includens . . . ; plenitudo sacerdotii cui presbyteri deinde participant . . . ; plenitudo sacramenti Ordinis, vel ipsum sacramentum Ordinis*" (Rather than the highest degree of the sacrament of orders, the episcopate should be called its fullness or totality, embracing all its parts . . . ; the fullness of priesthood in which priests then participate . . . ; the fullness of the sacrament of orders, or the sacrament of orders itself).

[16] DS 1145-1146, 1290. Cf. Fransen, "Orders and Ordination," in *Sacramentum Mundi*, vol. 4, esp. p. 316; Kilian McDonnell, "Ways of Validating Ministry," *Journal of Ecumenical Studies* 7 (1970), 209-265; Arthur Carl Piepkorn, "The Sacred Ministry and Holy Ordination in the Symbolical Books of the Lutheran Church," pp. 116-117.

[17] In Lutheran churches, for pastoral and administrative reasons, one pastor is designated "pastor of pastors," president of district or synod, or bishop. See Piepkorn, *op. cit.* See also the "Reflections of the Lutheran Participants" below.

designates and qualifies the Lutheran pastor for all the functions that the Catholic priest *(presbyter)* exercises, including that of celebrating a eucharist which would be called (in Catholic terminology) valid. It is to be noted, however, that the Lutheran confessions indicate a preference for retaining the traditional episcopal order and discipline of the church, and express regret that no bishop was willing to ordain priests for evangelical congregations.[18]

22. These ways in which the Ministry has been structured and implemented in our two traditions appear to us to be consonant with apostolic teaching and practice. We are agreed that the basic reality of the apostolic Ministry can be preserved amid variations in structure and implementation, in rites of ordination and in theological explanation. As we learn more of the complex history of the Ministry, we begin to grasp the ways in which this gift of God to his church is able to assimilate valuable elements from different ages and cultures without losing its authentic apostolic character. In this context we find that the present moment speaks persuasively to us, urging both the renewal of what is basic in our apostolic heritage as well as openness to the variants that our Christian witness to the world requires. In presenting these common observations on the eucharistic Ministry we are aware of the difficulties implied therein for both of our traditions,[19] as our respective reflections in the following two chapters in-

----

[18] Apology of the Augsburg Confession, Article 14. The critical edition of the Lutheran confessions is *Die Bekenntnisschriften der evangelisch-lutherischen Kirche* (Göttingen: Vandenhoeck & Ruprecht, 6th ed., 1967). The standard English edition is *The Book of Concord: The Confessions of the Evangelical Lutheran Church,* edited by Theodore G. Tappert (Philadelphia: Fortress Press, 1959). Cf. below the Lutheran answer to the Catholic question at the Baltimore sessions, "How do Lutherans evaluate, theologically and practically, episcopally structured churches?" pp. 53-56. Cf. also no. 28 of the Lutheran "Reflections" below.

[19] Other aspects of matters treated need further discussion and many other topics are not touched in these common observations. Among the latter might be mentioned the apostolic Ministry and succession of the bishop of Rome and its relationship to the apostleship of Peter and Paul; infallibility, especially as applied to papal infallibility; the distinction between matters that are of divine law and those which are of human law *(jure divino et humano);* the question of a purely charismatic ministry; questions of eucharistic sharing; the specific relations of a presbyterally ordained Ministry to an episcopally oriented Ministry; and finally, the practical problems of mutual recognition of Ministries, including psychological, canonical, and administrative factors.

dicate. That we have not found these difficulties insuperable is indicated by the recommendations which each group has been able to make. We rejoice together at the future prospect of Christian recognition and reconciliation opened by these recommendations.

CHAPTER TWO

Reflections of the Lutheran
Participants

23. Lutherans approach the questions dealt with in this common statement on the basis of the conviction that their churches belong to the one, holy, catholic, and apostolic church. They regard their ordained clergymen as persons validly set apart for the Ministry of the gospel and of the sacraments in the church of Christ. They hold that the sacraments that these ordained clergymen administer in their midst are valid sacraments. In their confessional writings, the Lutherans claim to stand in the authentic catholic tradition.[1]

24. On the basis of their confessional writings, Lutherans also affirm the churchly character of the Roman Catholic community and the validity of the Roman Catholic church's Ministry and sacraments. For Lutherans the church exists wherever there is a community of believers among whom the gospel of God's grace in Christ is responsibly proclaimed and applied and the sacraments are administered in accordance with our Lord's intention.[2] The responsible proclaiming and applying of the gospel and the administering of the sacraments require that persons be set aside for this office and function.[3]

25. Some Lutherans have had misgivings in the area of Roman Catholic commitment to the gospel. Nevertheless, Lutherans have always held that as long as the gospel is proclaimed in any Christian

---

[1] Augsburg Confession, Epilogue to Article 21, 1-5; Preface to Article 22, 1; Postscript to Article 28. See also Apology of the Augsburg Confession, 2, 32; 10, 2-3.

[2] "Sacraments" in this connection include at least baptism, absolution — conceived of either as implied in baptism or as an independent sacrament — and the sacrament of the altar.

[3] Augsburg Confession, 5, 1-3; 7, 1-4; 14; 28, 5-9, 21-22; Apology, 28, 13.

community in such a way that it remains the gospel and as long as the sacraments are administered in that community in such a way that they are channels of the Holy Spirit, human beings are through these means reborn to everlasting life and the church continues to subsist in these communities. We believe that the Roman Catholic church meets these criteria.

26. Noteworthy in this connection is the insistence of the Lutheran symbolical books that the church never ceased to exist down to their own time. Concretely they declare that St. Bernard of Clairvaux (1090-1153), the most famous son of the Cistercian Order, St. Dominic Guzman (1170-1221), founder of the Order of Preachers, and St. Francis of Assisi (1181?-1226), founder of the Order of Friars Minor, are "holy fathers" *(sancti patres)*.[4] As evidence of the persistence of the church and of the communication of the Holy Spirit within it through baptism, the Book of Concord cites not only St. Bernard, but also, bracketed with him, two late medieval churchmen of quite diverse theological views, John le Charlier de Gerson (1363-1429) of the University of Paris and John Hus (1369?-1415) of Prague.[5]

27. There is no doubt in Lutheran minds that the Roman Catholic church subscribes to the fundamental Trinitarian and Christological dogmas, "the high articles of the divine majesty" (Smalcald Articles, Part One). Lutherans must take seriously the Roman Catholic church's profession of the catholic creeds — including the "for us men and for our salvation" and the "was crucified also for us" of the creed of Constantinople ("Nicene Creed") and the "suffered for our salvation" of the Symbol *Quicumque vult* ("Athanasian Creed"). The Roman Catholic church affirms its kinship with "those Christians who openly confess Jesus Christ as God and Lord and as the sole Mediator between God and man to the glory of one God, Father, Son, and Holy Spirit." [6] Lutherans are well aware that Roman Catholics pray the same Sunday collects that Lutherans pray (including those that stress man's helplessness and salvation by grace alone, such as those for Sexagesima Sunday, the Second Sunday in Lent, Laetare Sunday, Easter Day, and the First, Third, Eighth, Twelfth, Fourteenth, Sixteenth, and Eighteenth Sundays after Trinity). They know too that the Roman Catholic church affirms the gospel in unmistakable terms

---

4 Apology, 4, 211.

5 Large Catechism, Baptism, 50.

6 Decree on Ecumenism, 20.

in many other places of its liturgy — for example, the *Exsultet* in the Easter Eve office and the *Veni, Sancte Spiritus,* in Whitsuntide.[7]

28. The episcopal structure and polity of the Roman Catholic church does not in itself constitute a problem for Lutherans. Indeed, the Book of Concord itself affirms the desire of the Lutheran reformers to preserve, if possible, the episcopal polity that they had inherited from the past.[8] As long as the ordained Ministry is retained, any form of polity which serves the proclamation of the gospel is acceptable. Within their own community some Lutherans have episcopacy with a formal "apostolic succession"[9] (e. g., Sweden, Finland, and some Asian and African churches). Other Lutherans have episcopacy without the "apostolic succession" (e. g., Norway, Denmark, Iceland, and Germany). Lutherans also have or have had churches governed by synods, by consistories, and by ministeria.

29. Even with the misgivings that sixteenth-century Lutherans had about the papacy,[10] the Lutheran symbolical books recognize the

---

[7] Augsburg Confession, 20, 40, recalls that "the church sings: *'Sine tuo numine / Nihil est in homine, / Nihil est innoxium'* " (Without [the action of] your godhead, there is nothing in a human being, there is nothing that is not destructive), from the *Veni, Sancte Spiritus.*

[8] Apology, 14, 1.5.

[9] In the technical sense of an unbroken personal succession of members of the episcopal order theoretically going back to the apostles, with each bishop consecrated to the episcopal order by one or more persons already in the order.

[10] The focus of Lutheran concern in the sixteenth century (Smalcald Articles, Part Two, 4, 4. 10-12) was the concluding definition of *Unam Sanctam: "Porro subesse Romano Pontifici omni humanae creaturae declaramus, dicimus, diffinimus omnino esse de necessitate salutis"* (Further, we declare, state [and] define that for every human being it is absolutely necessary for salvation to be under the bishop of Rome) (DS 875). We have not discussed the papacy with our Roman Catholic partners-in-dialogue, but we look forward to an examination of this issue at an early date. In the meantime, however, it may be observed that, however widely the cited thesis of Boniface VIII may have been held during the three centuries following its promulgation in 1302, it runs counter to twentieth century Roman Catholic thought (see, for instance, the letter of the Holy Office to the cardinal archbishop of Boston dated August 8, 1949, of which DS 3866-3873 reproduces the essential portions). Similarly, the recognition sanctioned by Vatican II that the "churches and ecclesial communities" that are not in communion with the Roman see are not without "significance and importance in the mystery of salvation," that the Holy Spirit uses these churches and ecclesial communities "as means of salvation," and that Roman Catholics are to re-

bishop of Rome as the lawful pastor of the church in that city.[11] In fact, the confessional writings do not exclude the possibility that the papacy might have a symbolic or functional value in a wider area as long as its primacy is seen as being of human right.[12]

30. We have no basis in the Book of Concord for denying that Roman Catholic priests are competent Ministers of the gospel and the sacraments. While some Lutherans in times past have doubted that the Ministry of Roman Catholic clergymen is really a Ministry of the gospel, the fact that Vatican II has called the proclamation of the gospel of God to all a "primary duty" of priests in the Roman Catholic church [13] should remove these uncertainties.

31. Within this context, we see no reason for doubting the validity of the sacrament of the altar within the Roman Catholic church.[14] In conformity with the Lutheran confessional writings, we

---

gard "all those justified by faith through baptism [as] incorporated into Christ" and as "brothers in the Lord" may be read as a kind of modern modification of the passage in *Unam Sanctam* that Lutherans have found so disconcerting (Decree on Ecumenism, 3). We also note that in the Dogmatic Constitution on the Church, 15, "communion with the successor of Peter" is not a necessary prerequisite in the case of baptized persons for being "honored with the name of Christian," for being "united with Christ," and for receiving "other sacraments." Again, the entire section on "The Separated Churches and Ecclesial Communities in the West" in the Decree on Ecumenism (19-23) nowhere mentions the papacy as such. At most it speaks of "the churches and ecclesial communities which were separated from the Apostolic See of Rome" and "the ecclesial communities separated from us." Also relevant to this issue is the fact that the Roman Catholic church recognizes as authentic churches the Eastern Orthodox bodies that have consistently refused to acknowledge a divine-right universal jurisdiction of the pope (Decree on Ecumenism, 14-18).

11 Smalcald Articles, Part Two, 4, 1, *"Dass der Bapst nicht sei* jure divino *oder aus Gottes Wort das Häupt der ganzen Christenheit (denn das gehoret einem allein zu, der heisst Jesus Christus), sondern allein Bischof oder Pfarrherr der Kirchen zu Rom. . . ."* (The pope is not the head of all Christendom by divine right or according to God's Word, for this position belongs only to one, namely, to Jesus Christ. The pope is only the bishop and pastor of the churches in Rome . . .).

12 *Ibid.,* 7-8. We have as yet not had the opportunity to discuss with our Roman Catholic counterparts the full significance of the terms *jure divino* and *jure humano.*

13 For example, in the Decree on the Ministry and Life of Priests, 4.

14 In this dialogue (but cf. *Lutherans and Catholics in Dialogue III: The Eucharist as Sacrifice,* p. 191) we have not discussed the matter of "private masses," which Lutherans have regarded as an abuse (cf. Smalcald Articles,

20

hold that the distribution and reception of the sacrament in one kind only, conflicts with the biblical injunction, but we do not hold that this invalidates the sacrament that Roman Catholic communicants receive. We note that Eastern Catholics in union with Rome have always received holy communion under both kinds. We likewise observe with joy the increasing frequency with which members of Roman-rite congregations are communicated under both kinds in the Roman Catholic church since Vatican II.

32. There are Lutherans who do not find it easy to overcome their concerns about the inferences that they have heard drawn from the Roman Catholic teaching of transubstantiation, about some of the language in which the sacrificial aspect of the sacrament of the altar has been popularly described, and about some of the attitudes and practices involving the reserved sacrament. But we observe that, in terms of the Lutheran theology of consecration, these things do not affect the *validity* of the sacrament of the altar as Roman Catholic priests celebrate and dispense it. At the same time, we have taken cognizance elsewhere of the official Roman Catholic instruction on eucharistic worship (1967) which asserts that the "primary and original purpose of the reservation of the sacrament is the communication of the sick" and that "the adoration of Christ present in the reserved sacrament is of later origin and is a secondary end." [15] In the same connection we have gratefully recorded the increasing measure of agreement between Lutherans and Roman Catholics on the sacrificial aspects of the sacrament of the altar. We have likewise stated that today "when Lutheran theologians read contemporary (Roman) Catholic expositions, it becomes clear to them that the dogma of transubstantiation intends to affirm the fact of Christ's presence and of the change which takes place and is not an attempt to explain how Christ becomes present." [16]

33. Although we see our common statement as removing some of the obstacles that separate Roman Catholics and Lutherans, there

Part Two, 2, 8). We rejoice that current Roman Catholic theology emphasizes the communal aspects of the eucharist.

[15] Instruction on Eucharistic Worship (May 25, 1967), p. 49, cited in *Lutherans and Catholics in Dialogue III: The Eucharist as Sacrifice*, p. 194.

[16] *Ibid.*, pp. 188-198 (the quotation is from p. 196). This sentence from the conclusion is particularly apposite (p. 198): "Despite all remaining differences in the ways we speak and think of the eucharistic sacrifice and our Lord's presence in his supper, we are no longer able to regard ourselves as divided in the one holy catholic and apostolic faith on these two points."

are still problems to be discussed before we can recommend pulpit and altar fellowship. The common statement that precedes these reflections does not provide an adequate basis for the establishment of such fellowship. Nor does it constitute approval by either community of every practice fostered or tolerated by the other community.

34. We Lutherans are conscious of the real and imagined differences that centuries of mutual separation have built up between us and Roman Catholics. We are sensitive to the canonical, traditional, and psychological barriers to eucharistic sharing that are present in both communities. We are aware of the many doctrinal discussions with other churches that both the Roman Catholic and the Lutheran churches in the United States are conducting, and recognize the magnitude of the theological work that still needs to be done.[17]

35. **As Lutherans, we joyfully witness that in theological dialogue with our Roman Catholic partners we have again seen clearly a fidelity to the proclamation of the gospel and the administration of the sacraments which confirms our historic conviction that the Roman Catholic church is an authentic church of our Lord Jesus Christ. For this reason we recommend to those who have appointed us that through appropriate channels the participating Lutheran churches be urged to declare formally their judgment that the ordained Ministers of the Roman Catholic church are engaged in a valid Ministry of the gospel, announcing the gospel of Christ and administering the sacraments of faith [18] as their chief responsibilities, and that the body and blood of our Lord Jesus Christ are truly present in their celebrations of the sacrament of the altar.**

---

[17] For example, the examination of what the anathemas of Trent and of Vatican I (DS 3055, 3058, 3064, and 3075) and the exceedingly severe judgments on dissenters from the definitions of 1854 (DS 2804) and 1950 (DS 3904) really imply. These are occasions of concern to Lutherans, since they apparently exclude large numbers of sincere believers from the church. Indeed, they exclude so many believers that they seem to some Lutherans to call into question the churchly character of the community that pronounces them. We anticipate a thorough discussion of this problem with our Roman Catholic colleagues.

[18] See the Decree on the Bishops' Pastoral Office in the Church, 12, and the Dogmatic Constitution on the Church, 21.

CHAPTER THREE

Reflections of the Roman Catholic Participants

INTRODUCTION

36. At first glance the Roman Catholic attitude toward the Lutheran eucharistic Ministry would seem easily determinable. A simplified expression of the traditional Roman Catholic outlook is that those who preside at the eucharist do so in virtue of being ordained by a bishop who stands in succession to the apostles who received from Christ the commission, "Do this in commemoration of me." Without such ordination a man can make no claim to a valid eucharistic Ministry. Now, at the time of the Reformation in Germany the bishops did not ordain Ministers for the congregations that professed to follow Martin Luther; and so it came about that priests who had adopted Lutheran beliefs ordained other men to preside at the eucharist,[1] thus perpetuating a presbyteral rather than an episcopal succession. Among most Lutherans there is no claim to an episcopate in historical succession to the apostles.[2] Thus the Lutheran eucharistic Ministry would seem to be deficient in what Catholics have hitherto regarded as essential elements.

37. Yet, as we Catholics in this dialogue have examined the

---

[1] See the Lutheran answers given to Catholic questions at the Baltimore sessions, pp. 53-61. Cf. no. 21 above.

[2] We do not wish to discuss here or elsewhere in this document the preservation of pre-Reformation episcopal structure in the Lutheran church of Sweden, Finland, and some missionary churches. See the Lutheran answer at the Baltimore sessions, question 1, section 3, p. 55. In general, what we say in this document of the Lutherans or the Lutheran communities refers to those Lutheran communities with whose representatives we have been in dialogue. Cf. no. 28 above.

problem, our traditional objections to the Lutheran eucharistic Ministry were seen to be of less force today, and reasons emerged for a positive reappraisal. We may group our reflections below under the headings of historical arguments and theological arguments.

I. HISTORICAL ARGUMENTS

38. It is impossible to prove from the New Testament that the only Ministers of the eucharist were the apostles, their appointed successors, and those ordained by their successors. Modern biblical investigations have shown that there were several different concepts of "apostle" in the New Testament.[3] While Luke-Acts is representative of a strain of New Testament thought that would equate the apostles with the Twelve and hence with those whom Jesus commanded, "Do this in commemoration of me," Paul is representative of a wider (and perhaps earlier) view whereby men, like himself, could be apostles even though they had not been disciples of Jesus during his lifetime. There is no clear biblical evidence that the Twelve were the exclusive Ministers of the eucharist in New Testament times or that they appointed men to preside at the eucharist. (On the other hand, we may add that neither is there evidence that all Christians were eligible Ministers of the eucharist.) While in the local churches, founded by apostles like Paul, there were leaders or persons in authority, we are told very little about how such men were appointed and nothing about their presiding at the eucharist. Even in the Pastoral Epistles (which are of uncertain date), in which there is described a church order featuring bishop-presbyters, we are not told that such figures had a eucharistic Ministry. Of course, this argument drawn from the silence of the New Testament has serious limitations, and the eucharistic practice may have been far more definite than the limited evidence proves. We must insist, however, in face of this silence, how difficult it is to make affirmations about what is necessary in the eucharistic Ministry.

39. At the beginning of the second century (but perhaps even earlier), as attested by Ignatius of Antioch, the bishop had emerged as the highest authority in the local church, and either he or his appointee presided at the eucharist. However, we are not certain how the Ignatian bishop was appointed or that he stood in a chain of

---

[3] Cf. R. Schnackenburg, *"L'apostolicité,"* as cited above, Chapter One, note 10.

historical succession to the apostles by means of ordination or even that the pattern described by Ignatius was universal in the church. Some find in *Didache* 10:7 evidence that wandering charismatic prophets could preside at the eucharist.[4]

40. When the episcopate and the presbyterate had become a general pattern in the church, the historical picture still presents uncertainties that affect judgment on the Minister of the eucharist. For instance, is the difference between a bishop and a priest of divine ordination? St. Jerome maintained that it was not;[5] and the Council of Trent, wishing to respect Jerome's opinion, did not undertake to define that the preeminence of the bishop over presbyters was by divine law.[6] If the difference is not of divine ordination, the reservation to the bishop of the power of ordaining Ministers of the eucharist would be a church decision. In fact, in the history of the church there are instances of priests (i. e., presbyters) ordaining other priests, and there is evidence that the church accepted and recognized the Ministry of priests so ordained.[7]

41. By way of summation, we find from the historical evidence that by the sixteenth century there had been a long and almost exclusive practice whereby the only Minister of the eucharist was one ordained by a bishop who had been consecrated as heir to a chain of episcopal predecessors. Yet, in this long history there are lacunae, along with exceptions that offer some precedent for the practice adopted by the Lutherans.

---

[4] The *Didache* is a work of uncertain date, perhaps even first century. James F. McCue, "Apostles and Apostolic Succession in the Patristic Era," pp. 163-164, interprets Tertullian, *De exh. cast.* 7 (early third century) to mean that in cases of necessity the eucharist might be celebrated by an unordained layman.

[5] Arthur Carl Piepkorn, "A Lutheran View of the Validity of Lutheran Orders," pp. 217-219.

[6] Session XXIII, canon 7; DS 1777. See Piepkorn, *op. cit.*, p. 220.

[7] Piepkorn, *op. cit.*, pp. 220-226; Corrado Baisi, *Il Ministro Straordinario degli Ordini Sacramentali* (Rome: Anonima Libreria Cattolica Italiana, 1935); Yves Congar, *"Faits, problèmes et réflexions à propos du pouvoir d'ordre et des rapports entre le presbytérat et l'épiscopat,"* in *La Maison-Dieu* 14 (1948), 107-128; Piet Fransen, "Orders and Ordination," *Sacramentum Mundi* (New York: Herder and Herder), vol. 4 (1969), p. 316; the full texts of the bulls may be found in H. Lennerz, *De Sacramento Ordinis, editio secunda* (Rome: Pontificia Universitas Gregoriana, 1953).

II. THEOLOGICAL ARGUMENTS

42. The negative appraisal of the Lutheran eucharistic Ministry that has been traditional among Catholics was not based solely or even chiefly on an analysis of the historical evidence favoring episcopal ordination. Theological factors entered prominently into this appraisal. Here again, however, as we Catholic participants in the dialogue examined the difficulties, we found that they no longer seemed insuperable.

43. A. The question of an authentic eucharistic Ministry in a worshipping community is intimately related to an evaluation of that community as part of the church. The unity that is signified and realized by the reception of the eucharistic body of Christ is related to the unity of the body of Christ which is the church. Formerly the Roman Catholic church did not speak of the Christian denominations that resulted from the Reformation as churches; but in the Second Vatican Council these groups were spoken of as "churches or ecclesial communities," [8] a change that seems to have theological implications.[9] Not all Catholic theologians would conclude that because a Christian community possesses "ecclesial reality," its table fellowship is necessarily graced by the presence of the body and blood of the Lord. Nevertheless, our ability to recognize the Lutheran communities as churches removes a barrier to our favorable understanding of the Lutheran sacred Ministry. We are now obliged to reassess whether the Lutheran communities may not be churches that truly celebrate the holy eucharist.[10]

44. B. It may be objected that while the Lutheran communities do constitute churches, they are defective churches in an essential note that has ramifications for the eucharistic Ministry, namely, apostolicity. This charge is true if apostolicity is defined so as necessarily to include apostolic succession through episcopal consecration.[11] However, it is dubious that apostolicity should be so defined. In the first two centuries of Christianity apostolic succession in doctrine (fidelity to the

---

[8] Constitution on the Church (*Lumen Gentium*), 15; Decree on Ecumenism, 3.

[9] Kilian McDonnell, "The Concept of 'Church' in the Documents of Vatican II as Applied to Protestant Denominations," pp. 307-324.

[10] Constitution on the Church, 15. Speaking of Christian churches that do not preserve the unity of communion with the successor of Peter, Vatican II states, "Many of them . . . celebrate the Holy Eucharist."

[11] Cf. note 2, above.

gospel) was considered more important than simple succession in office or orders.[12] The lists of bishops that appeared late in the second century were intended to demonstrate more a line of legitimatized teachers than a line of sacramental validity.[13] Undoubtedly apostolic succession through episcopal consecration is a valuable sign and aspect of apostolicity, for in church history there is a mutual interplay between doctrinal integrity and the succession of those who are its official teachers. Yet, despite the lack of episcopal succession, the Lutheran church by its devotion to gospel, creed, and sacrament has preserved a form of doctrinal apostolicity.[14]

45. C. In the past, Catholics commonly assumed that Lutherans did not believe in the real presence of Christ's body and blood, sacramentally offered in the eucharistic sacrifice, and consequently were presumably not ordaining a eucharistic Ministry in the sense in which Catholics understood eucharist. This assumption of defective intent now appears to us unfounded; for in our joint statement on the eucharist, we Catholics and Lutherans affirmed our agreement on the real presence and on the sacrificial character of the Lord's supper.[15]

46. D. Still another Catholic difficulty about the Lutheran eucharistic Ministry arose from a fear that the Lutheran understanding of the sacred Ministry was defective. In examining a number of points discussed below, we found that, while there are differences of emphasis and phrasing in the theologies of our respective churches, there is also a gratifying degree of agreement as to the essentials of the sacred Ministry.

47. 1) Do Lutherans recognize that the sacred Ministry is of divine institution? We find the Lutheran affirmation: "God instituted the sacred Ministry of teaching the gospel and administering the sacraments." [16] Also, "The church institutes clergymen by divine com-

---

[12] Walter J. Burghardt, "Apostolic Succession: Notes on the Early Patristic Era," pp. 173-177.

[13] *Ibid.;* see also McCue, *op. cit.,* pp. 156-157.

[14] In the joint Lutheran-Roman Catholic document, *The Status of the Nicene Creed as Dogma of the Church* (1965), p. 32, both sides confess that "the Nicene Faith possesses a unique status in the hierarchy of dogmas," and it is that creed which proclaims the church as one, holy, catholic, and *apostolic.*

[15] *Lutherans and Catholics in Dialogue III: The Eucharist as Sacrifice,* pp. 192, 188.

[16] Cf. Piepkorn, "The Sacred Ministry and Holy Ordination in the Symbolical Books of the Lutheran Church," p. 102, section 4.

mand," so that "ordination performed by a pastor in his own church is valid by divine right." [17]

48. 2) Do Lutherans conceive of the sacred Ministry as simply or primarily a Ministry of the word (preaching) rather than of sacrament? We have found a frequent joining of word and sacrament in the Lutheran writings on the subject. It is true that in the sixteenth century the Lutherans gave emphasis to a Ministry of the word in reaction to what they saw as a danger of a purely ritualistic Ministry. In response, Catholics tended to give emphasis to the dispensation of the sacraments lest the importance of that factor in Ministry be denigrated. In the less apologetic atmosphere currently prevailing, both groups see that the task of the Ministry includes both word and sacrament.

49. 3) Do Lutherans see the sacred Ministry as something beyond or distinct from the general ministry of all believers? It is quite clear that the Lutherans have a concept of a *special* Ministry in the church. "The symbolical books see the sacred ministry both as an office *(ministerium; Amt)* and as an order or estate *(ordo; Stand)* within the church." [18] There have been disagreements among Lutheran theologians about the relation of the special Ministry to the universal priesthood of believers.[19] Catholic theologians too have been unable to state this relationship with complete accord; yet we do find the statement made by the Second Vatican Council that the common priesthood of the faithful and the ministerial priesthood differ from one another in essence and not only in degree.[20] On the Lutheran side there is the affirmation: "We say that no one should be allowed to administer the word and the sacraments in the church unless he is duly called." [21] Theologians of both churches need to clarify further

---

[17] Cf. *ibid.*, p. 116, section 25.

[18] *Ibid.*, p. 105, section 8; cf. pp. 107-108, section 12.

[19] John Reumann, "Ordained Minister and Layman in Lutheranism," sections 16-18, 28-30, 44, pp. 235, 239-240, 247-248.

[20] Constitution on the Church, 10: *"Essentia enim et non gradu tantum inter se differunt"* (Though they differ from one another in essence and not only in degree); for discussions of these, see *Commentary on the Documents of Vatican II*, Herbert Vorgrimler, editor (New York: Herder and Herder, 1967), pp. 156-159, and John F. Hotchkin, "The Christian Priesthood: Episcopate, Presbyterate and People in the Light of Vatican II," pp. 202-206.

[21] Augsburg Confession, 14: *"De ordine ecclesiastico docent, quod nemo debeat in ecclesia publice docere aut sacramenta administrare nisi rite vocatus"* (Our churches teach that nobody in the church should publicly

the relation between clergy and laity and to analyze the biblical concept of the royal priesthood of God's people in order to see if that concept really tells us anything about eucharistic Ministry.[22]

50. 4) Do Lutherans recognize the sacramentality of ordination to the sacred Ministry? Actually on one occasion in the Lutheran confessional documents,[23] the term "sacrament" is deemed applicable to ordination, but such language is not common in Lutheran theology. This question is obviously affected by the sixteenth century dispute about the number of Christian sacraments, a dispute which reflected differences in sacramental theology and in the criteria for defining the term, sacrament. Despite the difference of terminology in reference to the sacramentality of ordination, we have heard our Lutheran partners in the dialogue affirming what to us would be the essentials of Catholic teaching on this subject, namely, that ordination to a sacred Ministry in the church derives from Christ and confers the enduring power to sanctify. We heard the affirmation that "The church has the command to appoint Ministers . . . God approves the Ministry and is present in it." [24] "All three American Lutheran churches understand the Ministry of clergymen to be rooted in *the Gospel.*" [25] "Like the Roman Catholic, the Lutheran too sees ordination as conferring a spiritual authority on the recipient in a once-for-all fashion — namely, the power to sanctify through proclamation . . . of the word of God and the administration of the sacraments." [26]

---

preach or administer the sacraments unless he is regularly called); Apology, 14, 1: *"Dicimus nemini nisi rite vocato concedendam esse administrationem sacramentorum et verbi in ecclesia"* (We say that no one should be allowed to administer the word and the sacraments in the church unless he is duly called); see Piepkorn, *op. cit.,* pp. 113-116, section 23, for a discussion of *rite vocatus.*

22 The concept of royal priesthood is found in Exodus 19:6; I Peter 2:9; Revelation 5:9-10. A recent Lutheran work, John H. Elliott, *The Elect and the Holy,* Supplements to *Novum Testamentum* 12 (Leiden: Brill, 1966), has examined I Peter 2:9 carefully and finds no evidence that the author of that biblical book related this priesthood to the eucharistic Ministry. The Constitution on the Church, 10, says: "The faithful join in the offering of the Eucharist by virtue of their royal priesthood."

23 Apology, 13, 9-13; see Reumann, *op. cit.,* sections 25-26, p. 238; Piepkorn, *op. cit.,* p. 112, section 21.

24 Cf. Reumann, section 26, p. 238.

25 Cf. *ibid,* section 73, p. 265.

26 Arthur Carl Piepkorn, "A Lutheran View of the Validity of Lutheran Orders," p. 215. It should be noted that one who resigns from the Lutheran

51. E. Perhaps the most serious obstacle standing in the way of a favorable Catholic evaluation of the Lutheran eucharistic Ministry has been the doctrine of the Council of Trent pertinent to sacred orders. In particular, canon 10 of Session VII (A. D. 1547; DS 1610) denied that all Christians have the power of administering all the sacraments; and canon 7 of Session XXIII (A. D. 1563; DS 1777) said that those who had not been ordained or commissioned by ecclesiastical or canonical power were not legitimate Ministers of the word and the sacraments. It would seem, *prima facie,* that in Trent's judgment Lutheran Ministers, since they have not been ordained by bishops, would not have the power of presiding at the eucharist, and that the Catholic church could not change its stance on this question since the doctrine of Trent is permanently binding.[27] Yet cautions are in order. The Council of Trent was not concerned primarily with passing judgment on the sacred orders of the Reformed communities but with defending the legitimacy of the Catholic priesthood against Protestant attacks.[28] The Tridentine assessment of Protestant ideas about the Ministry is detected chiefly through the implications of its condemnations of anti-Catholic theories. In the anathemas formulated against "Those who say . . ." there is no indication of whether Lutherans are meant in distinction from Calvinists, Zwinglians, Anabaptists, etc. Because of these difficulties, it is not easy to determine Trent's attitude toward the Lutheran eucharistic Ministry and the permanent value of that attitude.

52. One approach to the problem is the contention that the Tridentine attitude was not so absolutely negative as has been thought. Some are not sure that the council meant that a Minister "not ordained by ecclesiastical or canonical power" [29] was really incapable of celebrating the eucharist. They emphasize that all that the council

---

Ministry and then seeks readmission to the exercise of the Ministry is not re-ordained. Cf. Piepkorn, "The Sacred Ministry . . ." p. 117, section 26.

[27] For a variety of possible Catholic reactions to the Tridentine and Counter-Reformation positions, see George H. Tavard, "Roman Catholic Theology and 'Recognition of Ministry,'" pp. 301-305.

[28] It argues on behalf of a visible and sacramental priesthood that has a perpetual character, on behalf of an episcopate and the pope's right to appoint bishops, and on behalf of the validity of ordination by a bishop.

[29] DS 1777. Note the wording; it is significant that Trent ignored a proposal which stated that only those ordained *by bishops* are legitimate Ministers of the eucharist.

said was that this was not a "lawful" Ministry.[30] They further point out that the term "power" is vague in the Tridentine teaching that all Christians do not have the power to celebrate the eucharist, for that word need mean no more than ecclesial authority or authorization.[31]

53. Another approach to the Tridentine position reckons with the likelihood that the council really did mean implicitly to declare invalid Lutheran orders in the sixteenth century but wonders whether the present situation is not so changed that the Tridentine attitude is now only partially applicable.[32] If Trent rejected the Lutheran Ministry, it did so in the context of what it considered the defective Reformation theology of the church, the sacraments, and the eucharist. (While we may admit that the Tridentine assessment of these Reformation attitudes was not entirely adequate or correct, we should point out that some of the polemic of the Reformers against the legitimacy of Catholic practices likewise had its share of inadequacies and incorrect assessments — there were weaknesses on both sides.) As is evident from the theological arguments already discussed, we have found in the course of our dialogue with the Lutherans that in the twentieth century there is a much broader agreement on theological questions related to the eucharist than there seems to have been in the sixteenth. Thus the whole context of the discussion of Lutheran Ministry has changed. There is indeed something of permanent value for the church in Trent's rejection of abuses; but, without settling the question of the past, one might well conclude that the abuses Trent rejected are not present now.

54. The historical and theological reflections made above move us to doubt whether Roman Catholics should continue to question the eucharistic presence of the Lord in the midst of the Lutherans when they meet to celebrate the Lord's supper. And so we make the following statement:

As Roman Catholic theologians, we acknowledge in the spirit

---

[30] Harry J. McSorley, "Trent and the Question: Can Protestant Ministers Consecrate the Eucharist?" especially pp. 291-293. On p. 293, he contends, "It seems to us that Trent is asserting the canonical or juridical illegitimacy (illiceity) of Lutheran ordinations — not their invalidity in a widely held modern sense."

[31] *Ibid.,* pp. 283-285, 294-295. It should be noted that there was disagreement among the Catholic participants in regard to this position.

[32] Particularly involved here is the question of hermeneutics, and the nature of the church's grasp of truth in any era.

of Vatican II that the Lutheran communities with which we have been in dialogue are truly Christian churches, possessing the elements of holiness and truth that mark them as organs of grace and salvation.[33] Furthermore, in our study we have found serious defects in the arguments customarily used against the validity of the eucharistic Ministry of the Lutheran churches. In fact, we see no persuasive reason to deny the possibility of the Roman Catholic church recognizing the validity of this Ministry. Accordingly we ask the authorities of the Roman Catholic church whether the ecumenical urgency flowing from Christ's will for unity [34] may not dictate that the Roman Catholic church recognize the validity of the Lutheran Ministry and, correspondingly, the presence of the body and blood of Christ in the eucharistic celebrations of the Lutheran churches.

55. Lest we be misunderstood, we wish to add the following clarifications:

a. While this statement has implications for the question of Lutheran orders in the past, we have not made that question the focus of our discussions, and we do not think it necessary to solve that problem in order to make the present statement. Nor do we attempt to decide whether recognition by the Roman Catholic church would be constitutive of validity or merely confirmatory of existing validity.

56. b. By appealing for *church* action we stress our belief that the problem should be resolved by the respective churches and not on the level of private action by Ministers and priests, for such private action may jeopardize a larger solution.

57. c. In speaking of the recognition of a Lutheran Ministry not ordained by bishops, we are not in any way challenging the age-old insistence on ordination by a bishop within our own church or covertly suggesting that it be changed. While we believe that the church of Jesus Christ is free to adapt the structure of the divinely instituted Ministry in the way she sees fit (so long as the essential meaning and

---

[33] See the Constitution on the Church, 8 and 15 (with the *relatio specialis* to 15), and the Decree on Ecumenism, 19-23.

[34] Our intention here echoes the assurance of Cardinal Willebrands, President of the Vatican Secretariat for Christian Unity, when, in speaking of the divisions which still remain, he declares ". . . our firm resolve to do everything possible to overcome them" (*The Position of the Catholic Church concerning a Common Eucharist between Christians of Different Confessions,* January 7, 1970, see *One in Christ* 6 (1970), p. 201, no. 10).

function of apostolic Ministry is retained), we affirm explicitly that the apostolic Ministry is retained in a preeminent way in the episcopate, the presbyterate, and the diaconate. We would rejoice if episcopacy in apostolic succession, functioning as the effective sign of church unity, were acceptable to all;[35] but we have envisaged a practical and immediate solution in a *de facto* situation where episcopacy is not yet seen in that light.

58. d. We do not wish our statement (no. 54) concerning the Lutherans to be thought applicable to others without further and careful consideration, i. e., to other churches, communities, or movements that have the practice of ordination by priests, or where the congregation ordains, or where there is a spontaneous charismatic ministry. Our outlook on the possibilities of accepting the Lutheran eucharistic Ministry has been greatly determined by our increasing awareness that so much of Lutheran doctrine, practice, and piety is sound from the Catholic viewpoint, particularly in the areas of church, Ministry, and eucharist. Other churches and communities would have to be studied from a similar perspective before one could make a recommendation concerning their Ministries and eucharistic celebrations.

59. e. We caution that we have not discussed the implications that a recognition of valid Ministry would have for intercommunion or eucharistic sharing. Obviously recognition of valid Ministry and sharing the eucharistic table are intimately related, but we are not in a position to affirm that the one must or should lead to the other. At the same time, we note that the *Ecumenical Directory,* promulgated by the Vatican Secretariat for Christian Unity, states that Catholics in circumstances involving sufficient reason or urgent cause may receive the sacraments of the holy eucharist, penance, and the anointing of the sick from one who has been "validly ordained." [36]

---

[35] See the Lutheran answer to a Catholic question, given at the Baltimore sessions. pp. 56-60.

[36] *Directory for the Application of the Decisions of the Second Ecumenical Council of the Vatican Concerning Ecumenical Matters,* published by the Secretariat for Promoting Christian Unity (Washington, D. C.: United States Catholic Conference, 1967), 55.

STAGES IN QUESTIONS AND DEVELOPMENT

By Maurice C. Duchaine

The above statement on "Eucharist and Ministry," divided into three chapters of common observations, reflections on the part of the Lutheran and then of the Roman Catholic participants, represents over two years' work by this consultation group. Study began after the March, 1968, meeting on intercommunion or eucharistic sharing (see Foreword above) and continued to the drafting committee sessions that ran through the spring of 1970. Four full meetings were held from September, 1968, to February, 1970.[1] We would like to give highlights of the papers given and of some of the questions raised during these meetings.

I. THE WILLIAMSBURG SESSIONS

The first paper at the Williamsburg meeting, Jerome D. Quinn's "Ministry in the New Testament,"[2] touched off critical questions that the consultation group was to continue discussing in one way or another up to the final drafting sessions. For the Roman Catholic participants the *points névralgiques* in the scriptural and early apostolic evidence were the recognition of the diversity of the structure or order in the early churches, the paucity of information on the minister of the eucharist, and the consideration of the emphasis on apostolic succession in terms of doctrinal faithfulness rather than in terms of apostolic succession by office.

The Lutheran participants were asked to express their understanding of the place of order and ministry in the New Testament; what it

---

[1] These meetings were held at Williamsburg, Virginia, September 27—29, 1968; San Francisco, California, February 21—23, 1969; Baltimore, Maryland, September 26—29, 1969; and St. George, Bermuda, February 20—23, 1970.

[2] Included in this volume. An unpublished paper by John Reumann on *"Diakonia:* Scriptural Foundation," was also circulated.

meant to them that the term "apostle" could be viewed as functional, and in what way they viewed the New Testament as the ground for the theology of the sacred ministry and ordination in their confessions (as given in Arthur Carl Piepkorn's paper; see below).

Much of the discussion centered on the scriptural problems of the value of Acts as a source, either in whole or in part, in relationship to the dating and value of the Pauline writings, as well as the interpretation of the diversity indicated in the Pauline material. The scripture men went into caucus to see upon which points they could agree and came up with the following summary: [3]

1. What Paul and other Christian leaders left behind in the churches they planted (cf. Reumann, *Diakonia,* pp. 9 f.), included leaders of various sorts, some persons charged with authority.

2. These patterns of leadership varied, not only in the churches of Paul as compared with that of Matthew, or Luke-Acts, or the Apocalypse, but also among the churches founded by Paul; e.g., Philippi, Corinth, let alone the situation in the Pastorals.

3. The term "apostle" can be viewed as functional, and does refer to more than "the Twelve" in Paul; Luke seems to equate it with "the Twelve" (except perhaps for Barnabas, Acts 14). However, the apostles in these New Testament references are not tied to a local church, administratively, as a bishop later is. Apostles are not involved in "administration" in the narrow sense of the term.

4. "The Seven" in Acts, while seemingly appointed by "the (twelve) apostles" (and traditionally but wrongly called "deacons"), carry out the same functions as the twelve apostles in Acts, and may have been a parallel structure in the Jerusalem church.

5. Ministry *(diakonia)* is something committed to the entire church.

6. Since there is variety in the structure of the early Christian churches (see 1 and 2 above), the presiding official in the church's ministry at eucharistic celebrations varied; certainly the title varies; e. g., in the *Didache,* wandering charismatics; in Ignatius, a local bishop; in Paul, and other churches described in the New Testament documents, authorities of varying titles (though some authority seems regularly involved).

---

[3] We point out that the papers submitted in our summary article are working papers only, written with particular discussions in mind and as practical steps for continued study and for refinement toward the final statement.

In the discussion that ensued, the question arose as to the weight attached to the argument from silence. As one member asked, can we conclude from the fact that Paul does not indicate an *episcopos* in Corinth that there is no *episcopos* in any of the other churches? There was also the question of the normative value of this diversity found in the New Testament in relation to the normative value of a particular structure that developed later in the Spirit-inspired church. Is the narrowing down of the diversity in functional leadership, which can be seen even in the time of the Pastorals, merely a practical phenomenon from which one can change or is this process an evidence of divine providence; does the specification that developed belong to the *ad esse* or only the *bene esse* of the church? Point was then made on the need for principles of interpretation as regards the use of New Testament material. John Reumann gave the following summary of his position on the relevance of New Testament evidence on ministry:

1. Historically examined, the New Testament (and other early Christian documents) indicate a variety of structures of organization for ministry.

2. Between the New Testament period and present-day questions there are intervening centuries of history and development which must be considered; the New Testament cannot be brought up into the twentieth century apart from consideration of this later history, and it will not give answers on all questions we can raise.

3. While the New Testament does present a variety of structures for ministry and is separated from us by intervening centuries, it still does provide some norms and guidance for current questions.

The next two papers presented to the consultation group centered around confessional material: Arthur Carl Piepkorn's "The Sacred Ministry and Holy Ordination in the Symbolical Books of the Lutheran Church," and Harry J. McSorley's "The Roman Catholic Doctrine of the Competent Minister of the Eucharist in Ecumenical Perspective." [4]

Arthur Carl Piepkorn's paper gave to the Catholic group an idea of how similar were much of the concerns and theology of the symboli-

---

[4] Both papers are included in this volume. Portions of this paper by Arthur Carl Piepkorn and of his other contribution to this volume, "A Lutheran View of the Validity of Lutheran Orders," were published as a single article under the present title in *Concordia Theological Monthly* 40 (1969), 552—573. The essay by Harry J. McSorley is a slightly revised version of the article as published in *One in Christ* (1969), 405—422.

cal books to traditional Roman Catholic theology on the ministry and ordination. Although the primary concern of the symbolical books was to present ministry in functional terms, they did not do so exclusively. Sacred ministry was considered not only as an office *(ministerium; Amt)*, but also as an order *(ordo; Stand)*. The main questions posed by the Catholics were to what degree were the symbolical books considered "binding Lutheran doctrine," does Lutheran theology view the ordained ministry merely as part of the universal priesthood, and in what way do Lutherans view the necessity of ordination.

Harry J. McSorley's paper was the focus of much discussion among the Catholic participants, especially as regards the methodology, the sufficiency of information for the conclusions offered, and the difficulty of clarifying, and thereby drawing conclusions from, the meaning of such terms as *potestas, debet* and *potest, ordinarie,* etc. Attention was called to the distinction between what Trent might have meant and what the church might judge to determine in the future because of changed circumstances. Two major conclusions rose more clearly as a result of this stimulating discussion: (1) both sides agreed that only a priest can preside over the eucharist; the question before us was whether episcopal consecration was necessary for making a priest, or in Roman Catholic terminology, for the valid ordination of a priest and (2) the Roman Catholics now had a broader theological context in which to view the question as a result of the recent affirmation of Vatican II as regards the ecclesial reality of non-Roman churches or communities.

Both groups then met separately to prepare questions to pose to the other confession in light of the discussions that had taken place.[5] Thomas E. Ambrogi presented the following questions from the Roman Catholic group:

1. To what extent can the Piepkorn interpretation of the Lu-

_____

[5] These questions were given at the Williamsburg meeting and the responses were presented and discussed at the San Francisco meeting. Each group then raised at the end of the San Francisco meeting a second set of questions, whose responses were presented and discussed at the Baltimore sessions. We have included a report of these responses in this article under the meeting in which they were discussed.

It is from the material of these responses that gradually developed the schema and text for the joint statement on eucharist and ministry given above. First outlined at the Baltimore meeting, the statement was prepared by drafting committees for review and revision at the St. George meeting.

theran symbols be said to describe a commonly held doctrine on the ministry within contemporary Lutheranism? [6]

2. We would like some clarification on the sacraments as "means by which God gives the Holy Spirit . . ." (Piepkorn paper, no. 4).

3. What is the theological basis on which Lutherans practically and unofficially recognize the validity of ministry in some Christian communions and are hesitant to recognize it in others?

4. How important in Lutheran ecclesiology is presbyteral succession in the ordination of ministers?

Warren A. Quanbeck presented a positive position statement on the part of the Lutheran participants and then a set of questions.

A. We can affirm that

1. The ministry is of the essence (or *esse*) of the church.

2. The ministry is a means of exercising authority in the church.

3. There is a succession in the ministry, whether episcopal or presbyteral.

4. One of the chief duties of the ministry is to preside at the eucharist.

B. We pose the following questions to the Roman Catholics:

1. Inasmuch as our discussion has shown that the New Testament presents a variety of patterns of ministry and that no one structure was demonstrably normative in the New Testament period, is the later developed Roman Catholic view of ministry based on revelation, development, or canon law; i. e., is it *de jure divino* or *de jure humano?*

2. In the Roman Catholic view, is the validity of the eucharist so essentially related to an episcopally ordained ministry that Lutherans, because they do not require episcopal ordination, cannot be said to have a valid ministry and a valid eucharist?

3. If the answer to the above is affirmative, what are the grounds for this judgment?

II. THE SAN FRANCISCO SESSIONS

The first paper to be discussed was Raymond E. Brown's "Observations in Answer to a Question," [7] containing his personal reaction

---

[6] We note that the distinction between Ministry (upper case *M*) as a specific order, and ministry (lower case *m*) as the service of the whole church (see the Common Observations above, no. 9) had not as yet been agreed upon.

[7] Not published.

to a Lutheran query of the previous meeting: given the fact that there may have been a variety of patterns of church structure in the first and early second centuries and that there was insufficient evidence that any one pattern was normative, why has the Roman Catholic church insisted that only a man ordained by a bishop can be minister of the eucharist? Brown pointed out that our modern change in understanding the New Testament situation would not necessarily be enough in itself to demand a change in the position adopted at Trent for there is also the element of church practice of many centuries upon which Trent also based itself. Brown's observations on his reactions to the Tridentine position became the basis for the Roman Catholic response given at the end of this meeting to Lutheran question no. 2 (q. v).

In the discussion, the question on the principles for the development of dogma arose. If one is not satisfied with the idea of a homogeneous development, what are the principles for a heterogeneous process and to what degree would the Roman Catholics allow heterogeneity? It was also asked whether the church had a right to exclude groups that set up their own ministry, such as sects. On the Lutheran side, it was noted that Lutherans are not accustomed to begin with ministry. Where God's grace is at work, there ministry is to be found, at least in some sense.

In the second paper, "Apostles and Apostolic Succession in the Patristic Era," [8] James F. McCue highlighted 1 Clement 42, 44 and especially the material on Irenaeus to convey his position that apostolicity was more than simply faithfulness to apostolic preaching. At a time when both Gnostics and orthodox were laying claim to apostolic succession, Irenaeus was arguing for public, historically ascertainable succession of teachers in a direct line. Visible fidelity to apostolic preaching was one way only of certifying faithful apostolic succession.

The discussion then centered on the question of apostolicity and the criteria for apostolicity. The Lutherans raised the question whether the paper was not too strong a representation of the Luke-Acts tradition at the expense of other New Testament writings such as the Pastorals. Whereas the Lutherans emphasized faithfulness to the gospel as the most important, although not exclusive, criteria for apostolicity, the Roman Catholic representatives tended to emphasize the importance of commission and appointment. The question then came down to "by whom" was the commission given. All agreed that

---

[8] Included in this volume.

self-appointment was not sufficient, therefore recognition was also an important factor.

Rather than the word "appointment," Lutherans would tend to use the term "call" to the ministry, which would include both an internal prompting and a call by the church. The word "valid" also caused problems. The Lutherans pointed out that validity is not necessarily determined by recognition, so that something may be valid even without being recognized (or in technical language and as regards this dialogue, the *res* of apostolicity can be present even when the *signum* of episcopal succession is absent — see the Lutheran questions on ministry to the Roman Catholics, 3 a-b, submitted at the end of this meeting). The Lutherans asked the Roman Catholics if they could acknowledge that Lutheran ministry achieves what Christ intended ministry to achieve, however imperfectly (i. e., do they have the body and blood of Christ). In response, the Roman Catholics brought up the question of the need for church recognition and the place of the authority of the church in this recognition. The point was not in considering a defective eucharistic theology on the part of the Lutherans, the previous joint statement on the eucharist had clarified that point, but rather the validity of ministry which would have to be assured before one can judge on the eucharist. In this process of thinking by the Roman Catholics, therefore, church recognition was vital for considering a valid ministry. It was suggested that we might do better if we spoke of "authentic" instead of "valid" ministry.

In his presentation of "A Contemporary View of Apostolic Succession," [9] Warren A. Quanbeck noted the complexity in describing the apostolic tradition (involving mission, liturgy, the pneumatic element, etc.), and the interaction of call and response. The Lutherans were in general agreement that episcopal succession is highly desirable, but that it is not a guarantee of a valid ministry. Also, episcopal ordination is a sign of the apostolic tradition of faith and life, but it is possible to have apostolic succession without it. In following the position of Edmund Schlink, the episcopal succession may be seen as a sign of fullness or unity towards which the church is working. For Schlink, reality must become visible and signs make things visible. One Lutheran member noted that there is a sense of New Testament development in which episcopal succession has become a symbol of transmission.

On their part, the Roman Catholic participants were impressed

---

[9] Included in this volume.

by the sheer weight of history behind the practice of episcopal laying of hands and by the value of this rite as a sign of unity. Some pointed out that the Lutherans do have a laying on of hands, even if in the presbyteral sense. The sign may be lacking, but this does not necessarily mean that the *res* is absent. One member spoke of the double conferring of the Holy Spirit: on Pentecost to the whole church and on Easter to the apostles. The key point is appointing, and whether this takes place by laying on of hands or some other way is secondary.

John F. Hotchkin led the discussion on the material in Vatican II with his paper, "The Christian Priesthood: Episcopate, Presbyterate and People in the Light of Vatican II." [10] Differing opinions among the Roman Catholics as regards the precise relationship between the priesthood of believers and of the ministry touched off a number of points. Some felt that the scriptural exegesis evident in Vatican II on this point of priestly nation left much to be desired. It was also noted that Vatican II was both dependent on and independent of Vatican I as regards The Constitution on the Church, chapter III, where it treats of the hierarchy. As regards a contemporary theology of the priesthood, there is a change of emphasis from the cultic to the pastoral function of the priest. This type of theology sees more easily the unity between priest and laity, priest and bishop, and more difficulty in specifying the difference. The implications of this type of theology still have to be worked out as regards ministry, eucharist, and ecclesiology.

This should not mean, however, that one should minimize the centrality of the cultic event. The celebration is more complete as a sign of the Christ event when there is a congregation; still more complete when a bishop is there. It would seem the Vatican II documents refer to many elements as central to the church's life without presenting any one as exclusively so; e. g., they speak of the word of God as well as the eucharist as the source and sign of unity.

One Lutheran summarized what he heard the Catholics saying. One should speak of the priesthood in communal and functional categories rather than in generic, universal, individualistic properties. The starting point should be the community as subject of priestly power. There is a role differentiation, and one should not attempt to say that one is more or less important than the other.

The communal-functional way is not fully identical with much of traditional Lutheranism. Lutherans have talked too individualisti-

---

[10] Included in this volume.

cally as well. Many Lutherans would find the communal-functional categories better than the terms many Lutherans and Catholics have traditionally used.

George H. Tavard, in his presentation of "Notes on Medieval Theology and Apostolic Succession," [11] offered the tentative conclusion that, as far as the material which he studied was concerned, the church could accept presbyteral ordination. This would not seem to contradict the medieval theology of sacraments, although a developed hylomorphic interpretation lends itself less easily to change. The problem in the sixteenth century was the lack of universal recognition of Lutheran ordinations, due to the change of method of ordination without consensus. The way is now open and possible, however.

The final paper was given by Arthur Carl Piepkorn, "A Lutheran View of the Validity of Lutheran Orders," [12] in which he pointed out, among other things, that laying on of hands for the Lutherans designates that the individual is being set aside for the ministry of word and sacrament. Convinced of the basic compatibility of Lutheran understanding of orders with the Roman Catholic theology affirmed in The Constitution on the Church (Lumen Gentium), 28, of Vatican II, the author felt that "the substantive matter at issue is the question of the minister of the sacrament of ordination." [13] Most of the discussion involved the Roman Catholic participants who discussed the principle that sign belongs to the church. Signs can be changed by the church except where Christ specifically instituted them. Piepkorn pointed out that Lutheran formulas start with the principle, what does Christ want in his ministry, and it is to this that Lutherans then proceed to ordain.

The group then turned to the responses that had been prepared for the questions submitted at the previous (Williamsburg) meeting.

A. LUTHERAN RESPONSES TO THE ROMAN CATHOLIC QUESTIONS

Question No. 1 (presented by Warren A. Quanbeck):

> To what extent can the Piepkorn interpretation of the Lutheran symbols be said to describe a commonly held doctrine on the ministry within contemporary Lutheranism?

---

[11] Not published.

[12] Included in this volume. See note 4 above.

[13] See p. 211 below.

Quanbeck stated that although there are varying views among Lutherans, Piepkorn's interpretation can be said to be commonly held and pretty well accepted. Moreover, it is an interpretation which is coming to the fore within Lutheranism, and is being substantiated more and more in the practice of the church.

Question No. 2 (presented by Arthur Carl Piepkorn):

> *We would like some clarification on the sacraments as "means by which God gives the Holy Spirit . . ."*

Piepkorn stated that he had used this term in preference to "means of grace" because the latter term has come into use in Lutheran theology only at a relatively recent point in time. For us Lutherans the "means by which God gives the Holy Spirit" are primarily the gospel, baptism, eucharist, absolution (and orders). The basic reference is Article 5 of the Augsburg Confession, which says that in order to enable human beings to obtain saving faith God gave the ministry, the gospel, and the sacraments through which "as through means the Holy Spirit is given who works faith." To be sure, there are echoes of Lombard identifying grace and the Holy Spirit, but the author would disassociate himself from Lombard's theories.

Question No. 3 (presented by Kent S. Knutson):

> *What is the theological basis on which Lutherans practically and unofficially recognize the validity of ministry in some Christian communions and are hesitant to recognize it in others?*

Knutson suggested that the best way to answer this would be to give a description of how a Lutheran would react to the question.

1. Lutherans have no policy and methodology by which they proceed, either by custom or writing. Some might assume that all ministry outside of Lutheranism is valid; others might assume no such ministry is valid; either position would be too extreme.

2. Lutherans are more prone to make specific rather than general judgments. If asked about a particular ministry in a given church, Lutherans might proceed as follows: (a) has Christ acted through his chosen means to create a community, and has the word of God been communicated here for the forgiveness of sins; (b) are other signs present, e. g., baptism, eucharist; (c) is there evidence of confession of faith, awareness that it is church; is there trinitarian faith, though the confession need not be a written one; (d) has the minister been

designated to be a leader in some way acceptable to the church so that there is some kind of appointment or ordination; (e) have the signs produced a believing congregation?

3. With their background, Lutherans are more comfortable with the idea of Christendom as a family of churches. We tend to think historically, internationally. Lutherans do distinguish among ministries and know how to deal better with some families (e. g., the Roman Catholic, German and Swiss Reformed churches) than with others (e. g., American free churches present certain problems).

4. With regard to the question of reordination, we have no precedent. Baptism might be a model, i. e., we would be hesitant to reordain. We have no rubrics. Is there any tradition that does not have laying on of hands? We would want to leave room for the charismatic element.

5. We might note that we are more at home in bilateral dialogue with such churches as the Reformed and Roman Catholic, but we are not in the Consultation on Church Union, which is another methodology and style.

6. As regards our attitude towards ministries in other churches in relation to the eucharist, we begin first with God's action and are wary of trying to judge on this. Where there is the people of God, where they remember Christ's institution and repeat it, where there is bread and wine, consecration, eating and drinking, there is sacrament. We would want to leave room for emergencies, and would sometimes simply not be able to decide. We might say that we have not assumed that wherever people claim a sacrament, it is a sacrament; nor is the reverse true. I assume that Lutherans assume that where a leader does preside at a eucharistic assembly and is properly designated, that the eucharist is valid. We would want to make room for charismatic appeal and extraordinary cases.

As regards intercommunion, we are very cautious, feeling that included here is a proper understanding of the Lord's supper. There is no clear-cut policy regarding individuals. Despite seeming latitude, there *is* church discipline for Lutherans. Pastoral concern for a communicant's need can be a compensating factor for intercommunion, even for the most orthodox Lutheran.

Question No. 4 (presented by John Reumann):

> *How important in Lutheran ecclesiology is presbyteral succession in the ordination of ministers?*

Reumann replied that in this, of all the questions, Lutherans can be most clear and emphatic: they do consider "presbyteral succession" as important, though they might not customarily employ the term.

1. For Lutherans "succession" is first of all succession in the gospel (*successio evangelii,* as used by Edmund Schlink), but there is also regularly a succession of ministers to ministers, priests to priests.

2. For Lutherans, "presbyter" equals priest or clergy or minister; the terms are used as equivalents.

3. Clergy are regularly ordained by clergy. Although it can be added as a footnote that there is now some interest in having laymen participate in the service of ordination, laying on of hands is regularly by clergy.

4. The regular practice is that the president of the synod or district himself ordains or authorizes the dean or some other clergyman to do so. It is not simply local clergy, but designated leadership that is responsible for authorizing and conducting the service of ordination.

B. ROMAN CATHOLIC RESPONSES TO THE LUTHERAN QUESTIONS

The following responses were the result of a group meeting by the Roman Catholic participants and were presented by Maurice C. Duchaine.

Question No. 1:

> *Inasmuch as our discussion has shown that the New Testament presents a variety of patterns of ministry and that no one structure was demonstrably normative in the New Testament period, is the later developed Roman Catholic view of ministry based on revelation, development, or canon law, i. e., is it* de jure divino *or* de jure humano?

We recognize the unique importance of the New Testament data in this question as in other questions. However, in instances where the New Testament does not speak with one voice about a theological problem, the Roman Catholic church has recognized that there are clarifying post-biblical developments that can be and have been normative for its life. Our precise problem here is to determine which post-biblical developments in the question of ministry are normative for Christians today.[14]

Question No. 2:

> *In the Roman Catholic view, is the validity of the eucharist so essentially related to an episcopally ordained ministry that Lutherans, because they do not require episcopal ordination, cannot be said to have a valid ministry and a valid eucharist?*

1. As Regards the Past

Trent's use of the word, "illegitimate," is not synonymous with the technical understanding of "invalid" (null and void) that is used by many today. The following three reactions are found among Catholics.

a. Certainly some Catholic theologians would regard the Tridentine answer as correct and permanently binding in the church.

b. Some theologians would be inclined to ask whether we can say that Trent was wrong.

c. Others prefer a more nuanced answer, stemming from a modern hermeneutical stance in regard to the church's grasp of truth in any era. While they recognize inadequacies and even elements of error in Trent's response, they insist that there was truth of permanent value for the church in Trent's reaction to the problem it saw. However, precisely because of this mixture they do not think that the Tridentine answer is the total Catholic answer to the very different problem that faces us today in considering the Lutheran ministry.

2. As Regards the Present

As far as the present is concerned, we have asked ourselves what we can say about the possibility of accepting Lutheran orders now, if we think that the distinction should be made. In the broader theological context, the following were seen as major elements.

a. There is the statement of Vatican II that there are other communities having ecclesial realities; therefore there are implications with regard to valid ministry in these ecclesial communities.

b. There is the realization that the New Testament does not

---

[14] Reference was made to the discussion on Raymond E. Brown's "Observations in Answer to a Question" at the beginning of this San Francisco meeting (q. v.). See pp. 38-39 above.

46

present clear evidence of a single ecclesiastical structure, in particular as regards the ministry of the eucharist. Although we would not necessarily feel that the New Testament is normative as regards these points, this realization certainly liberalizes our possible position.

c. There is the realization of a Lutheran understanding and theology of the eucharist and the ministry not in opposition to, but compatible with, basic Roman Catholic understanding and theology.

d. There is the placing of the understanding of the ministry and eucharist in a broader theological context, that is, a broader ecclesial and sacramental theology.

e. There is the question of the historical evidence, that priests did ordain in the church.

After the above responses were presented and discussed, each group met separately once again to prepare another set of questions. The Lutherans asked the following questions of the Roman Catholic participants:

1. Did we understand you rightly to say that you see no reasons for denying that the body and blood of Christ are present in the eucharist celebrated in the Lutheran community?

2. If so, in what way would you describe the inadequacy, if any, in the Lutheran orders?

3. Would you be inclined to agree with these two points (Quanbeck-Schlink):

a. That the *res* of apostolicity may be absent even when the *signum* of episcopal succession is present;

b. That the *res* of apostolicity may be present even when the *signum* of episcopal succession is absent?

A certain amount of discussion ensued, as the Roman Catholics found themselves uneasy with the wording of the first question. It was not for them to judge on the presence of the body and blood of Christ; the discussion was more on the validity of ministry as it had been handed down. One Lutheran noted the difference in approach: for the Roman Catholics, ministry came first, then the question of eucharistic reality; the Lutherans were asking the Catholics to look first at the Real Presence, then answer the ministry question. Both sides then accepted the following Lutheran wording of the question to which the Catholics were asked to respond at the following meeting:

We, as Roman Catholic theologians, see no persuasive reason

to deny the possibility of the Roman Catholic church recognizing the validity of the present Lutheran ministry in its presbyteral succession and the presence of the body and blood of Christ in the eucharistic celebrations in Lutheran churches.

How would the Roman Catholic participants react to this statement?

The Roman Catholics then asked the Lutherans to discuss the following questions:

1. How do Lutherans evaluate, theologically and practically, episcopally structured churches: (a) their own, e. g., Swedish; (b) the Roman Catholic, as presented by Vatican II? How do they evaluate synod or district presidents?

2. If the Roman Catholic church were to recognize the presbyterally ordained ministry in the Lutheran church, would Lutherans be inclined to go back to the normal pre-Reformation situation of episcopal succession and ordination? The context in which this question is asked includes (a) the Consultation on Church Union, (b) Eastern Orthodox insistence on episcopal ordination, (c) anti-episcopalian feelings within Lutheranism, (d) lack of bishops in Germany as the historical context of presbyteral succession within Lutheranism.

3. What difference does Lutheranism see between the ordained Lutheran minister and the Lutheran layman?

4. Do Lutherans, with their understanding of sacraments, have serious difficulty in recognizing orders (episcopate, presbyterate) as a sacrament?

III. THE BALTIMORE SESSIONS

At this meeting each group met separately at first to review the responses to the questions of the previous meeting. They then came together to present the responses, to discuss a number of papers and finally to focus their attention on the drafting of a future joint statement.

Warren A. Quanbeck and Jerome D. Quinn had already met previously to discuss the matter for the possible joint statement. Quinn gave the following report of their conversations. He felt that Quanbeck and he had reached substantial agreement on the following points:

1. God first established a church and to the church gave a ministry; this ministry belongs to the *esse* of the church.

2. The ministry is part of the gospel and is the means God has chosen to make the body and blood of Christ present in the eucharist.

3. The ministry is conferred by a visible sign of ecclesial appointment to a task; the sign is unrepeatable. All admit ordination by a bishop constitutes such a sign. The Catholic group is willing to admit that theologically priestly ordination could constitute such a sign (Lutherans do acknowledge it in practice).

4. The church is ordered to the world and the ministry to the church.

The following were still outstanding problems:

1. A viable mutual statement on sacramentality of order (or ministry).

2. Ecclesial recognition of presbyter ordination of the ministry and the sacraments administered by this ministry.

3. Precisely in what does apostolicity consist (a viable mutual statement on this)?

4. Sacramental vs. non-sacramental apostolicity or ministry.

After having met separately, the groups came together to discuss the responses. Due to the length of these responses, we shall first report on the papers that were given and the plans for drafting a joint statement.

Harry J. McSorley presented a second paper on Tridentine theology, "Trent and the Question: Can Protestant Ministers Consecrate the Eucharist?" [15] McSorley again pointed out there was the historical question of a lack of clear distinction between *potestas ordinis* and *potestas jurisdictionis* (the power of orders and the power of jurisdiction) and that the study of the ambiguous use of the word power from *exousia* to *potestas* warrants our interpreting Trent in terms of what we would today call power of jurisdiction and not power of orders. One would then conclude that Tridentine theology was not making judgment on what we would call today the invalidity of Lutheran orders. Trent was heir, rather, to a tradition that had a strong concept of jurisdiction in the church's care of its people. Discussion also cen-

---

[15] Included in this volume. This is a slightly revised version of the essay as published in *Worship* 43 (1969), 574—589.

tered on the question to what extent the lack of *potestas jurisdictionis* had an effect on the validity of different sacraments.

There was again among the Roman Catholic participants a strong reaction to McSorley's position: one can not necessarily conclude from the evidence that Trent did not mean the power of orders and thereby the validity of orders.

Kilian McDonnell then presented his paper on "The Concept of 'Church' in the Documents of Vatican II as Applied to Protestant Denominations." [16] Two phrases in Vatican II stood out: the recognition of ecclesial realities in others (see the Decree on Ecumenism, 19) and the theology behind the phrase the church of Christ "subsists" in the Catholic church (Constitution on the Church, 8). Is it possible to have true manifestations of the church without a valid ministry? [17] McDonnell was careful to point out that the Vatican II fathers did not wish any conclusion be drawn as regards the relationship between the churches and the validity of their ministry or eucharist.

A lively discussion followed on the question to what extent one can hold a council responsible for the logical conclusions of its remarks. Some felt speaking of communities in which is the work of the Spirit of Christ, such as The Constitution on the Church, 8, describes, necessarily involves some sort of recognition of the validity of ministry. Some of the Roman Catholics reacted strongly against drawing such conclusions. It was suggested that one might draw some conclusion on the ministry from the theology behind the word "subsists" but not from the use of "ecclesial reality."

There was general agreement that involved here was the very problem of the mystery of the church itself, a component of its inner mystery of the power and love of Christ and the understanding of this in terms of a concrete society, which itself is composed of sinners. The Lutherans indicated that they could more easily understand "subsist" in terms of the spirit of Christ than in terms of something concrete. All churches are in darkness and in fullness. One Lutheran suggested that the eschatological approach might be a differentiating element between Roman Catholics and Lutherans. One has to be clear on the direction towards which the church points. The Roman Catholic

---

[16] Included in this volume. This essay appeared in *Worship* 44 (1970), 332—349.

[17] E. Schillebeeckx seems to conclude to the necessary relationship in his Nemi paper on "Catholic Understanding of Office"; see an indication of this in *Theological Studies* 30 (1969), 569.

speaks in terms of a dynamism towards catholic unity, the fullness of unity towards the Roman Catholic church; in that view, other churches can be seen as having less ecclesial reality. The Lutheran, on the other hand, might see ecclesial realities more in terms of the boundedness of the eschatological disclosure of redemption and the work of the Spirit; limitations, then, would be in terms of the clarification of this disclosure or the work of the Spirit.

George H. Tavard presented the last paper of the session, "Roman Catholic Theology and 'Recognition of Ministry', " [18] in which he described his own reaction to the Lutheran questions on the possibility of Catholic recognition of Lutheran ministry. The Lutherans were particularly interested in Tavard's response to Question No. 2 [19] and the view that lack of unity with the Roman Catholic church was the source of the inadequacy of Lutheran ministry today. Some Roman Catholics were prepared to agree with Tavard, others were more insistent that a major point of deficiency in Lutheran orders is that they do not have the bishops to identify the presence of unity among themselves. They may have other forms of unity, but not the episcopacy. In reaction to this latter emphasis, the Lutherans spoke of unity of faith or unity in the gospel, while one of the Catholic participants suggested that the *res* of apostolicity is expansive, the *signum* of episcopacy is limited in the sense that it is only one of the elements in the church's evaluation of the sacrament of orders. He felt uneasy in speaking of the unitive sign of the episcopacy unless it is done in the context of doctrine and the liturgy. Historical realism shows that bishops can also be signs of disunity in the church.

In general the Lutherans agreed that their tradition had taken for granted an emergency situation. It was suggested that they might even have a hang-up along these lines — they consider exceptional cases and write their theology in terms of these exceptions.

The Catholics returned the discussion to the topic of apostolic succession. In summary, there have been two different emphases. In the Lutheran confessions the emphasis seems more strongly on succession in fidelity to the gospel, without denying other elements. The Roman Catholic tradition has placed more emphasis on juridical succession without denying doctrinal, or fidelity to the gospel, succession.

---

[18] Included in this volume. This essay appeared in *Journal of Ecumenical Studies* 6 (1969), 623—628.
[19] See below.

It was also said that even if there is juridical succession but not faithfulness to the gospel, one cannot really speak of succeeding.

The Catholics pointed out that in the use of the technical terms of *res* and *signum* in the question of the validity of orders one should not lose sight of the fact that the decisive element in all this is the power of the Lord and the working of the Spirit. In technical terms, the *res et sacramentum* context must be retained.

At the close of the discussions one Lutheran participant felt that he could accept the explanation of apostolic succession, but he did not see that the sign of episcopal succession guarantees apostolicity. Paul C. Empie suggested that the Roman Catholics would have to dispel the Lutheran caricature of the Catholic understanding of episcopal succession in terms of merely a physical laying on of hands. Bishop T. Austin Murphy assured the group that in the ordination rite of a bishop, in which he has had some experience, fidelity to faith, the gospel, the commandments, the working of the Spirit — all those things which have been mentioned in the discussions and hoped for — are present.

The final session of the Baltimore meeting treated of the forthcoming joint statement. Warren A. Quanbeck, in consultation with Jerome D. Quinn, had come up with a possible schema in the form of affirmations:

1. Awareness of our common mission to the world.

2. All Christians share in this mission, but there is a special ministry with the task of directing and renewing.

3. The church is the context for understanding ministry.

4. Ministry is conferred by a visible sign.

5. Apostolicity is directed to the world and not itself; the apostolicity of the ministry is ordered to the church.

In view of the discussions which had taken place, a number of suggestions were made: apostolicity and ministry should be first instead of last; it should be noted that the sign of conferral should not be repeated; the sacramental nature of the priesthood should be brought in. In the course of these suggestions, which represented to a great extent points of convergence between the Lutheran and Roman Catholic groups, the recommendation was made to have each group address a statement to its own constituency, in addition to the common statement. For the Lutherans, it would be a case of attempting to dispel reactions that have stemmed from Reformation days; the

Catholics would explain how they see the possibility of accepting a line of presbyteral orders.

A discussion arose from the Lutheran side as regards the expression "church is ministry" or "church is mission." In a sense the church is a means of grace, something of herself, and therefore not to be judged absolutely in instrumental terms. The ministry, on the other hand, is wholly instrumental. As a precaution, note was made that the Latin language has no article, but that care must be taken to include one in an English translation. *"Ecclesia est missio"* makes sense in Latin but not in English.

The importance of making clear our understanding of apostolicity was again emphasized. If we recognize each other's ministry, it will be because of the connection of the existence of apostolicity of ministry and doctrine. Also, the Catholics asked for emphasis upon the relationship between church and ministry, since Lutheran church understanding had made great impression upon them during the course of the conversations.

The following seemed to be an acceptable working plan for the drafters: we should just state briefly that we are aware that the special ministry should be seen in light of the world, the church, the general ministry, etc.; we should then write on what we have found in our conversations with each other and on what we can contribute or recommend; lastly, we should indicate the questions we still have to consider. Some might criticize us for not treating of the other problems, but historically this is the way we proceeded.

As the final documents of the Baltimore meeting, we present the responses to the questions each group addressed to the other at the previous meeting (San Francisco).

A. LUTHERAN RESPONSES TO THE ROMAN CATHOLIC QUESTIONS

Question No. 1 (presented by Warren A. Quanbeck):

> How do Lutherans evaluate, theologically and practically, episcopally structured churches: (a) their own, e. g., Swedish; (b) the Roman Catholic, as presented by Vatican II? How do they evaluate synod or district presidents?

1. The answer is given quite clearly in the Lutheran confessions:

a. Apology of the Augsburg Confession, on Ecclesiastical Order: ". . . We have given frequent testimony in the assembly to our deep desire to maintain the church polity and various ranks of the ecclesiastical hierarchy, although they were created by human authority. We know that the Fathers had good and useful reasons for instituting ecclesiastical discipline in the manner described by the ancient canons" (14, 1).

"Thus the cruelty of the bishops is the reason for the abolition of canonical government in some places, despite our earnest desire to keep it" (14, 2).

"Furthermore, we want at this point to declare our willingness to keep the ecclesiastical and canonical polity, provided that the bishops stop raging against our churches. This willingness will be our defense, both before God and among all nations, present and future, against the charge that we have undermined the authority of the bishops" (14, 5).

b. Smalcald Articles: "If the bishops were true bishops and were concerned about the church and the Gospel, they might be permitted (for the sake of love and unity, but not of necessity) to ordain and confirm us and our preachers" (Part Three, 10, 1).

c. Apology: "Those who are now bishops do not perform the duties of bishops according to the Gospel, though they may well be bishops according to canonical polity, to which we do not object" (28, 12).

2. From these statements one may draw the following conclusions:

a. The Reformers favored the retention of episcopal structure and traditional canonical polity. They objected to the misuse of episcopal authority, especially in the condemnation of a doctrine and practice rooted in scriptures.

b. They regard episcopacy as good and useful, but not necessary. Bishop and priest have the same authority by divine right. The reservation of ordination to bishops is of human authority (see Treatise on the Power and Primacy of the Pope, 61, 62). For the sake of love and unity, but not of necessity, retention of episcopal authority is desirable in the church.

c. Episcopal structure is lacking among some Lutherans at the time of the Reformation, not because they rejected it, but because they were deprived of it by the opposition of the bishops. They endured this situation because they were convinced that presbyters had the same powers as bishops by divine law and that ordination by presbyters, if exceptional, was nevertheless valid.

3. The preservation of the pre-Reformation episcopal structure in the church of Sweden can therefore be regarded as a fortunate historical development, meaningful in practical and ecumenical dimensions but not of especial theological significance. Where non-episcopal ordination is regarded as defective, whether by Orthodox, Anglicans, or occasional Lutherans, most Lutherans react by insisting on the sufficiency of presbyteral ordination, even though they may acknowledge the value of episcopal ordination as a sign of historical continuity.

4. Most Lutherans regard the development of Roman Catholic ecclesiology in the Second Vatican Council as an achievement to be admired and perhaps even envied. They can appreciate the effective interpretation of the scriptures, the development of patristic insights, and the adoption of a new theological posture which turns away from the polemics of the post-Reformation period to a new openness to other churches and to the discussions of the ecumenical movement. The new stress on the church as the mystery of God's redeeming activity and as the people of God, on the collegiality of bishops, on the priesthood of all believers, and on the universal call to holiness can be regarded as the development of a new theological and ecclesiastical situation. Other features of the council's work could be mentioned as contributing to this new theological situation: the understanding of liturgy, of missions, of the relationship of the church to the world, as well as the development of new relationships to other churches, to the world religions and to atheists.

But far ranging as the council was in its exploration of theological possibilities, the question of episcopal authority was not scrutinized either from the point of view of history or from that of theology. One frequently heard the assertion that bishops have the authority of teaching and of jurisdiction by divine right. A Lutheran sees this as the kind of theological assertion which needs examination. The study of the scriptures does not seem to produce such a doctrine. The study of the church's history seems to indicate that episcopally structured church government is not present in the first century but emerges in second or early third century. No generally accepted theology of development has yet emerged to explain how second or third century historical developments are to be treated as of divine authority. Lutherans accordingly hold that the form of church government is not given by divine authority and that the church can adopt whatever structures serve the gospel most effectively in a given time.

5. The Lutheran confessions affirm that bishops and priests have the same authority by divine right and that the reservation of confirmation and ordination to bishops is of human right. All who preside over the churches have a common authority by divine right, whether they are called pastors, presbyters, or bishops (Treatise, 61, 62). The synod president therefore differs from the pastor only in the kind of responsibility assigned to him. He has oversight of pastors and congregations, responsibility for the peace and harmony of the district or synod, and in practice ordinations are reserved to him or to persons designated by him.

It should be noted that Lutherans are in a period of theological re-examination of the doctrine of the ministry, partly because of the growth of biblical studies and ecumenical discussions, partly because of dissatisfaction with existing administrative arrangements. A new openness exists among many Lutherans to consider alternative structures of church government. Opposition to episcopacy, rooted in the controversies of the past, seems to be in decline.

Question No. 2 (presented by George A. Lindbeck):[20]

> *If the Roman Catholic church were to recognize the presbyterally ordained ministry in the Lutheran church, would Lutherans be inclined to go back to the normal pre-Reformation situation of episcopal succession and ordination? The context in which this question is asked includes (a) the Consultation on Church Union, (b) Eastern Orthodox insistence on episcopal ordination, (c) anti-episcopalian feelings within Lutheranism, (d) lack of bishops in Germany as the historical context of presbyteral succession within Lutheranism.*

The two parts of this answer, (1) explain two contrary effects that "recognition" might have, and (2) assess their relative importance.

1. The two contrary effects of recognition are (a) a weakening of certain arguments in favor of the re-establishment of the historic episcopacy, and (b) a simultaneous weakening of certain objections against such re-establishment.

---

[20] Arthur Carl Piepkorn submitted his own response to this question. We have not included this paper, however, since it was basically in accord with and complementary to Lindbeck's response.

a. The arguments which would be weakened might be called "pragmatically ecumenical" ones. These invoke the fact that most Christians consider episcopacy necessary. Non-episcopal churches must therefore come to terms with it if large scale re-union is to occur. But greater visible unity belongs to the *bene esse* of the church, and therefore so also does episcopacy, which is a precondition for this. Obviously the force of such considerations in favor of re-establishing episcopacy would be attenuated if the Roman Catholic half of Christendom were by recognition of presbyterally ordained ministries to modify its insistence on the absolute necessity of the historic succession.

This kind of pragmatically ecumenical pro-episcopalianism exists, though perhaps more often as an unarticulated mood than as an explicit argument. Gerald Brauer suggests that it will grow in the future (in *Episcopacy in the Lutheran Church?* edited by Ivar Asheim and Victor R. Gold [Philadelphia: Fortress, 1970], pp. 209—211). As he develops the argument, it claims no intrinsic or abiding advantages for the historic episcopacy over other forms of ecclesiastical polity, but simply affirms that if it can be made acceptable, it would also be desirable because of its value in the present situation (where most Christians insist on it) in promoting unity.

The implicit assumption, of course, is that the historic episcopacy is totally an *adiaphoron* from the point of view of what belongs to the unchanging constitution of the church. It is for this reason that pragmatic considerations are decisive, either for or against it. Many of those who take this line are not in the least indifferent to questions of theological principle. They would insist on the South India approach in which those who adopted episcopacy were left free to understand it theologically in whatever way they wished.

While it is true, as we have said, that these pragmatic pressures towards episcopacy would decline if Roman Catholics were to recognize presbyterally ordained ministries, they would not be entirely eliminated. The problem of the Orthodox would remain. Further, those interested in joining COCU can argue on pragmatic ecumenical grounds for accepting its proposals on episcopacy (for these basically follow the South Indian line). Nevertheless, apart from Roman Catholic insistence on episcopacy, such grounds would not operate except in the actual implementation of union schemes. They would no longer contribute to a mood favorable to the re-establishment of episcopacy in the absence of re-union with episcopal churches.

b. On the other hand, however, Roman Catholic recognition of presbyteral orders would not only weaken, but would also, from another point of view, strengthen pressures towards episcopacy. It would do so by removing what are, in the Lutheran perspective, the most serious objections to it. These objections have been well stated by W. Joest:

> ". . . solange die bischöfliche Sukzession von anderen Kirchen als dogmatisch notwendig und im Sinne der Garantie der Erhaltung in der Einheit wahrer Lehre verstanden und gefordert wird, wäre das Bemühen um den Anschluss an diese Sukzession ein so zweideutiges Zeichen, dass wir besser daran tun, es zu unterlassen. Wo die formale Sukzession der Bischöfe durch die Reformation der Kirche hindurch erhalten blieb, mag man sich dessen ohne allzu grosses dogmatisches Pathos freuen. Wo sie — wie bei uns — gerade über der Reformation der Kirche verlorenging, wird es richtig sein, durch den Verzicht auf Wiederanschluss an sie dafür ein Zeichen zu geben, dass die wahre Einheit der Kirche ihre Einheit im Zeugnis und Glauben des apostolischen Evangeliums von Christus ist . . ." (from "Das Amt und die Einheit der Kirche," in Die Autorität der Freiheit, ed. by J. C. Hampe [Munich: Kösel-Verlag, 1967], vol. 2, p. 467).

This objection involves a higher evaluation of the historic episcopacy than is necessary for the pragmatic ecumenical argument which we have already considered. Joest is here commenting on Edmund Schlink's contention that the adoption of the apostolic succession is desirable, not simply because it may facilitate re-union, but because of its intrinsic importance as a sign (efficacious when properly exercised) of the apostolic continuity and unity of the Church (see E. Schlink, "Apostolic Succession," in The Coming Christ and the Coming Church [Philadelphia: Fortress Press, 1967], pp. 186—233, esp. p. 232). The sign value of the succession is in itself permanent. It is not merely a function of accidental historical situations to the extent that purely pragmatic considerations allow. Episcopacy is therefore the normal polity of the church. Yet it is a subordinate, instrumental, and fallible sign of apostolicity which may be misused by being made superordinate and constitutive. A part of the church which through unfavorable historical circumstances loses the episcopate does not necessarily for that reason lose apostolicity. (This may differ from the Roman Catholic position as presented in Tavard's memorandum, which denies that "the res of apostolicity may be absent even when the signum of episcopal succession is present.") Lutherans, of course, believe that this happened in the sixteenth century. And many of them, like Joest, think that this exceptional situation is not yet ended. The errors which justified the Reformation discontinuance of episcopacy are still prevalent. It is still often viewed as *"dogmatisch notwendig und im Sinne der Garantie der Erhaltung in der Einheit wahrer Lehre"* and this involves a failure sufficiently to recognize that *"die wahre Einheit der Kirche ihre Einheit im Zeugnis und Glauben des apostolischen Evangeliums von Christus ist."* In short, these Lutherans regard the historic episcopacy as still so widely "absolutized" that it remains unacceptable even though it is in itself normal and desirable.

This objection would be largely removed by Roman Catholic admission of the possibility of full recognition of presbyteral orders. It would not, to be sure, be entirely removed. Lutherans would still insist that the *signum* of succession can exist where the *res* of apostolicity is absent (or, at any rate, so seriously distorted and obscured that the presence of the *signum* is misleading rather than helpful). Still, recognition of presbyteral orders would help "de-absolutize" episcopacy by making clear its subordinate and instrumental role. It would help eliminate the ambiguities which now make episcopacy unacceptable to many. This would be true even if the Orthodox continued to be — from the Lutheran viewpoint — "recalcitrant."

2. In assessing these two contrary effects of Roman Catholic recognition of presbyteral orders, my guess is that the second would preponderate. Anti-episcopal sentiments feed on many sources, but in a Lutheran context, the theological justifications for these sentiments all converge in one way or another on objections to "absolutization." To the degree it becomes clear that "episcopalianism" does not involve the view that the historic succession is essential to fully valid ministry and sacraments, the theological basis for anti-episcopalianism will be eliminated. This would leave the theological field in the possession of a position like Schlink's or Joest's and, to the extent theological considerations are influential — which is, of course, variable — this will incline Lutherans towards episcopacy.

This, I would suppose, would be likely to more than compensate for the loss of a "pragmatically ecumenical" impetus towards episcopacy which I described under 1-a. My impression is that this impetus has not been strong and is not likely to become strong within Lutheranism. On balance, therefore, my answer to the question is that "recognition" would increase such Lutheran inclinations as now exist "to go back to the normal pre-Reformation situation of episcopal succession and ordination."

Needless to say, it is impossible to predict how effective or pervasive these inclinations would be. The contemporary mood in all denominations seems increasingly disinclined to take the question of episcopacy seriously. It is not that there is an increase in anti-episcopalianism. Rather, much of what passes for progressivism is so anti-institutional that it says, in effect, "a plague on both your houses." Both episcopacy and non-episcopacy are irrelevant. Problems of "participatory democracy" and "morphological fundamentalism" are central. From the point of view of these questions, it is widely thought that it makes no difference whether a given church is or is not in the succession. The tendency, therefore, is to leave churches as they are on the question of episcopacy, and to get on with what are conceived as more important structural problems.

While these developments do have their positive side, they may also have the dangerous and unintended consequence of reinforcing the institutional *status quo*. Institutional forms when ignored have a disconcerting habit of persisting unchanged. Be that as it may, the main point of these final comments is that, given the current anti-institutional mood, it seems unlikely that Roman Catholic recognition of presbyteral orders would make much practical difference. Whatever influence it had, however, would be more *pro* than *con*.

Question No. 3 (presented by John Reumann):

> What difference does Lutheranism see between the ordained minister and the Lutheran layman?

The answer to this question was given by John Reumann in his paper, "Ordained Minister and Layman in Lutheranism," which is printed in this volume.

Question No. 4 (presented by George A. Lindbeck):

> Do Lutherans, with their understanding of sacraments, have serious difficulty in recognizing orders (episcopate, presbyterate) as a sacrament?

"If *ordo* is interpreted in relation to the ministry of the Word, we have no objection to calling it a sacrament" because "it is commanded by God and has great promises attached to it." The rite of laying on of hands can also be termed a sacrament in view of the fact that "the Church has the command to appoint ministers, to this we must subscribe wholeheartedly, for we know that God approves this ministry and is present in it" (Apology, 13, 11—12).

To be sure, the ministry and ordination should not be placed on the same level as the "three sacraments of salvation," baptism, the Lord's supper, and absolution (*ibid.*, 3-4). Sacraments in the strict sense are (a) rites "which have the command of God," (b) "to which the promise of grace has been added," and in which (c) the grace conferred is that of the "New Testament," i. e., "salvation" or "the forgiveness of sins" (*ibid.*, 3, 4, and 14). In the case of the ministry, the last condition is lacking. Grace is given the minister in the words of Luther, *"nicht für sich selbs noch für seine Person, sondern für das Ampt"* (WA 28, 468, 2 ff.). It is therefore only in a broader or secondary sense that the ministry is sacramental.

B. ROMAN CATHOLIC RESPONSES TO THE LUTHERAN QUESTIONS

In considering the Lutheran questions posed at the end of the San Francisco meeting, the Roman Catholics focused on what they considered the most basic question, especially as it had been rephrased in statement form:

> We, as Roman Catholic theologians, see no persuasive reason to deny the possibility of the Roman Catholic church recognizing the validity of the present Lutheran ministry in its presbyteral succession and the presence of the body and blood of Christ in the eucharistic celebrations in Lutheran churches.

If they were to make such a statement, the Roman Catholics felt they should list the difficulties that had been found in times past about the validity of Lutheran orders and to explain to themselves why they felt these reasons were no longer persuasive. It was thought that the results might form the basis of at least part of the final statement that might be issued by the joint group. The following four difficulties were listed and four corresponding responses submitted:

> 1. The objection to Lutheran orders based on the presumably false Lutheran concept of the eucharist.

> 2. The objection to Lutheran orders based on historical data showing that the church has always insisted upon episcopal ordination for the minister of the eucharist. Related to this would be the data pertinent to the necessary apostolic succession of the episcopate.

3. The objection that Lutheran orders had already been ruled as invalid by binding statements of the magisterium.

4. The objection that Lutheran orders are not valid because the Lutheran concept of ministry is not properly related to a concept of the church and sacraments.

Response No. 1: Doctrine of the Eucharist (presented by Joseph W. Baker and John F. Hotchkin)

One reason some Catholics have denied the authenticity of the eucharist celebrated in Lutheran communities is the assumption that Lutherans do not believe in the real presence of Christ's body and blood sacramentally offered in the eucharistic sacrifice. Hence they would not intend to raise up ministers to serve the eucharist thus understood. Neither would their ministers intend to act in such a role. This would reveal a clear discrepancy between the Lutheran understanding of the minister and the Catholic understanding of the priest, a discrepancy which Catholics would regard as a defect that invalidates the Lutheran eucharistic ministry.

Such an assumption of defective intention now appears to us to be unfounded. In our St. Louis statement Catholics and Lutherans jointly affirmed their agreement on:

The real presence:

> "We affirm that in the sacrament of the Lord's supper Jesus Christ, true God and true man, is present wholly and entirely, in his body and blood, under the signs of bread and wine" (*Lutherans and Catholics in Dialogue III: The Eucharist as Sacrifice*, 1967, p. 192).

The sacrificial character of the eucharist:

> "Lutherans and Roman Catholics alike acknowledge that in the Lord's supper 'Christ is present as the Crucified who died for our sins and who rose again for our justification, as the once-for-all sacrifice for the sins of the world who gives himself to the faithful.' On this Lutherans insist as much as Catholics, although, for various reasons, Lutherans have been reticent about speaking of the eucharist as a sacrifice" (*ibid.*, p. 188).

It was further affirmed that this sacramental reality "is meant to be celebrated in the midst of the believing community" and that the presence of Christ comes about "by the power of the Holy Spirit through the word" (*ibid.*, p. 198).

Thus no reason appears for doubting that Lutherans do intend to raise up ministers for this service.

Response No. 2: Historical Data Pertinent to the Eucharistic Ministry (presented by James F. McCue, Walter J. Burghardt, Jerome D. Quinn, and Raymond E. Brown)

1. Sacred Scripture on Eucharistic Ministry

The New Testament offers very little information about the ministry of the eucharist, and the information that it does offer does not settle the question of who is the minister of the eucharist.

a. The saying of Jesus, "Do this in commemoration of me," reported in Luke and Paul indicates an early Christian belief that certain men had been directly appointed by Jesus to celebrate the eucharist. There is no further New Testament evidence about the role of the Twelve in relation to the celebration of the eucharist, nor is there evidence that the Twelve appointed others to celebrate the eucharist. The idea that the Twelve and their appointees were the exclusive ministers of the eucharist cannot be proved from the New Testament.

b. Luke-Acts appears to equate "the Twelve" with the apostles. But certainly for Paul, "apostle" is a wider term. In neither case is the activity of an "apostle" limited to a local church. We have no information in the Pauline letters about the relation of the Pauline "apostle" to the eucharist.

c. In the churches founded by Paul and the others, we find leaders or persons charged with authority; there seem to be various patterns or models of authority. We are not told, however, who presided at the eucharist. This is true even in the Pastorals which speak at length about church order.

d. On the other hand, while I Peter 2:9 designates Christians as a (royal) priesthood, there is no evidence that the author of this passage related this priesthood to the eucharistic ministry.

2. Earliest Non-Scriptural Christian Writings

The earliest Christian non-scriptural writings supplying more information about the minister of the eucharist do not attest to a single pattern of (eucharistic) ministry. Some would see in the *Didache* evidence that wandering charismatic prophets could preside at the eucharist. 1 Clement 42.4 suggests that the *episkopoi-presbyteroi* of the Corinthian church presided at the eucharist. Some read Tertullian (*De exh. cast.,* 7; see in this volume James F. McCue's paper, "Apostolic Succession in the Patristic Era") as supposing that in cases of necessity, the eucharist may be celebrated by the unordained Christian.[21]

Response No. 3: Magisterial Pronouncements (presented by Harry J. McSorley and George H. Tavard)

Modern historical researches have brought about a new awareness of the difficulty of being absolutely certain of the exact meaning of the texts of the magisterium, especially when these are written in Greek or Latin and conceived in categories that are no longer familiar to us. Accordingly the pronouncements of the magisterium can be read today in two different perspectives.

1. Read from a predominantly historical point of view, the documents are often ambiguous, for their vocabulary can no longer be understood with certainty.

For instance:

a. As early as the first ecumenical council at Nicaea (325) the church referred to the question of the competent minister of the eucharist. In Canon 18 it was stated parenthetically that deacons do not have the *exousia* to offer the body and blood of Christ. Nicaea does not tell us how this lack of "power" in the deacon is to be understood. Does it mean that he is utterly (absolutely) incapable in any circumstances of offering the eucharist, or that he lacks the ecclesial authorization to do so?

b. Magisterial statements of the middle ages leave us with basically the same ambiguity when they refer to the inability *(non potest nec debet)* of a minister to celebrate the eucharist if he has not been "episcopally" or "properly" ordained (see Denziger-Schönmetzer, 784, 802, 1084).

c. The Council of Trent devoted practically no attention to the question of the status of the ministry in the Reformation churches since it was largely concerned with defending the authenticity of the Catholic ministry under attack. The council does teach that those who are "neither properly ordained nor sent by ecclesiastical and canonical power" are not "legitimate" ministers of word and sacrament (see Denziger-Schönmetzer, 1777, Canon 7 in the Sacrament of Orders). Once again this leaves us with the ambiguity: is Trent teaching that

_____

[21] For a more complete response, see Walter J. Burghardt, "Apostolic Succession in the Early Patristic Era," included in this volume.

such improperly ordained ministers are totally unable to celebrate the eucharist, or simply that they do so in a canonically illicit manner? It is a fact that post-Tridentine theologians commonly understood Trent in the former sense. Modern study of Trent, however, shows that the other interpretation is compatible with the text of the council.

Nearer to us in time and mentality, Vatican II speaks only of a "defect" of the sacrament of orders among some of the ministries of the separated churches of the West (see the Decree on Ecumenism, 22). Two things are to be noted in this connection:

a. The council does not say that the sacrament of orders is absent or non-existent in the separated communities of the West, but that it is defective;

b. The council does not say that such a defect in the sacrament of orders makes it impossible for such ministers to be the celebrants of the eucharistic mystery but that it prevents them from being celebrants of that mystery in its "genuine and integral substance."

From such a historical survey of current research into conciliar statements on the minister of the eucharist the conclusion may be reached that the decisions of previous councils do not close the door to eventual recognition of the Lutheran ministry by the Roman Catholic church.

2. The compelling force of such historical doubts as to the exact meaning of magisterial pronouncements may be questioned. The magisterial pronouncements can then still be understood at their face value as denying the validity of Lutheran or other orders.

In this case, however, several positions remain possible:

a. One can admit this conclusion (i. e., the denial of the validity of Lutheran or other orders) both for the sixteenth century and for today.

b. One can admit this conclusion for the sixteenth century but reject it for today, on the ground, either (a) that Lutheran thought has evolved, thus becoming more Catholic, or (b) that Roman Catholic theology has evolved, thus being now able to see as valid what sixteenth century theologians could not so see.

c. One can suspend judgment as to the value of this conclusion for the sixteenth century, on the ground that the theological situation was then too confused to admit of clear solution to the sacramental problems raised by the Reformation; and deny this value for today, on the same grounds as in (b), plus the ecumenically-orientated consideration that our problem is not to judge the past, but to prepare the future by trying to open new theological avenues.

d. One can deny the value of this conclusion even for the sixteenth century, on the ground that the Catholic position was then based, (1) on inadequate theological conceptions (for example, about the matter and form of the sacrament of orders), (2) on insufficient evidence and on misunderstanding concerning Lutheran intentions and conceptions. Current sacramental reflection makes (1) a plausible line of thinking, while recent re-assessments of Luther go in the direction of (2).

Response No. 4: Relationship of Ministerial Orders to the Church (presented by Maurice C. Duchaine, Kilian McDonnell, and Anthony T. Padovano)

1. The broad frameworks in which ministry is discussed in the Lutheran and Roman Catholic traditions are quite different. Lutheran theology of ministry is presented more in terms of a "word" theology, which, of course, does not exclude sacramental realities (since its confessions do speak of *ministerium verbi et sacramenti*), while Roman Catholic theology of ministry is presented more in terms of a "sacrament" vocabulary, which does not exclude "word" realities. The point of departure of the "word" vocabulary or theology is gospel and *ministerium verbi*. The point of departure of the "sacrament" vocabulary or theology is the church. The "word" vocabulary tends to make the minister a servant of the church. The two vocabularies are manifestations of differing views of theological realities and are not mutually exclusive, but are complementary.

The "word" vocabulary would find ample justification for taking *ministerium verbi* as its point of departure in the New Testament witness and the life of the apostolic church. These witnesses seem to place the prophetic role of Jesus and his ministers in the forefront of the witnesses' religious consciousness.

2. The essence of apostolic ministry is, but need not be, expressed in the concrete forms that ministry has thus far realized. The more fundamental gift of Christ to his church is the gift of ministry by which the word is authentically proclaimed and sacraments legitimately celebrated. The church is free to structure this ministry in the way she sees fit so long as the essential meaning and function of apostolic ministry is retained. In the case of the Seven mentioned in Acts 6, the church restructured ministry in response to an emergency situation

and developed an authentic expression of ministerial office. There is no reason why this basic power of the church for structuring of ministry need be confined to the apostolic period. It is quite possible to recognize or initiate new forms of charismatic or sacramental ministry so long as these forms conform to apostolic criteria and are accepted by the universal church as signs through which the church is expressed and in which the power of the Spirit is present. Nevertheless, the history of the church attests that the apostolic ministry is expressed in a preeminent way in the episcopate, presbyterate, and diaconate (see The Dogmatic Constitution on the Church, 20).

3. From the point of view of some contemporary studies on the priesthood, there has been a shift from a too exclusive emphasis on the cultic and accompanying ontological description of the priesthood to a more pastoral description. This pastoral approach allows for a more sympathetic understanding of functional descriptions of the priesthood, such as *ministerium verbi,* which have been stressed by Lutherans.

IV. THE ST. GEORGE SESSIONS

The St. George meeting was an intensive drafting session on the three chapters of the forthcoming statement. The material came especially from the Baltimore meeting, and each chapter underwent repeated scrutiny both in sub-committee and in full session.

The first paper presented was "Reflections of the Catholic Scholars," a document which had been originally drafted by Raymond E. Brown, submitted to the other Catholic participants and then revised by Brown and Maurice C. Duchaine. It is this paper which formed the basis for what is now chapter three of the statement. Arthur Carl Piepkorn submitted "A Lutheran Reflection," which he later reworked together with Warren A. Quanbeck and George A. Lindbeck, and which supplied the basis of what is now chapter two. As regards the material for the joint statement of chapter one, which had been prepared by Warren A. Quanbeck and Jerome D. Quinn, the group decided that this chapter should concentrate on the areas of agreement and disagreement between Lutherans and Roman Catholics on the question of eucharist and ministry, without attempting to cover all the bases on the subject of ministry. John Reumann and Duchaine were added to the redaction committee. In the course of discussions, all three chapters were seen, in effect, to be a "common statement," since neither side disagreed with what the other was saying to its church or churches.

After the last of the plenary meetings, a committee consisting of Quinn, Quanbeck, Duchaine, Reumann, Brown, and Walter J. Burghardt edited the final text of the three chapters in keeping with the previous discussions, and circulated the document by mail until a common accord was reached by the participants.

MINISTRY IN THE NEW TESTAMENT

By Jerome D. Quinn

This paper offers an essay toward the history of Ministry [1] in the New Testament period and its documents.[2] The span of time stretches

---

[1] For the use of *"M*inistry" and *"m*inistry," cf. the Joint Statement, chapter one, no. 9.

[2] Two bodies of primary documentation are available for this study. The first is from Judaism and includes the materials from the library of Qumran, the so-called "Dead Sea Scrolls," and similar recent discoveries. With these materials we are able, as no one since 70 A. D., to document the interests and goals and ideals of a significant stratum of the Palestinian Jewish community in the lifetime of Jesus and in the critical generation from his death to the fall of Jerusalem. To these we must add the works of Josephus and Philo as well as the most ancient stratum of the rabbinic materials.

The second body of documentation originates from the preaching and teaching of a new religious community, the Christians who appeared within Palestinian Judaism after the resurrection of Jesus. These literary materials began to appear well on in the forties of the first century and continued until the end of that century. Later generations of the Christian church gleaned from this literature a collection or canon of books that came to be defined as the New Testament. However, the remainder of these materials represented by the *Didache,* the First Letter of Clement of Rome, and the Letters of Ignatius of Antioch, are indispensable for the historical inquiry as it seeks to recover the concerns to which the later documents of the New Testament spoke.

The secondary documentation is both massive and growing. The books and periodicals cited hereafter refer to still other studies that will enable the reader to deepen and broaden his grasp of the issues, historical and theological, that are rooted in the subject of the Ministry of the church. Whenever possible, French and German contributions have been cited in their English translations. The reader today is fortunate to have the great *Theologisches Wörterbuch zum Neuen Testament, (TWNT)* edited by G. Kittel and G. Friedrich, available through Volume VI *(rho)* in an English version, edited by G. W. Bromiley as *Theological Dictionary of the New Testament* (Grand Rapids: Eerdmans, 1964-1968). This translation (cited hereafter as *TDNT*) has, with one exception, not attempted to update the original articles. The reader should, of course, be aware that *TWNT,* I-III date from 1933-1938; IV from 1942; and V-VI from 1954-1959.

from the birth of Jesus of Nazareth to the death of the last apostolic witness, a period of roughly three generations. The central generation, from the crucifixion of Jesus in about 30 AD to the fall of Jerusalem in 70 AD, is the most critical for this study, though it cannot be understood in isolation from the work and words of Jesus that preceded it nor the developments between 70 AD and the end of the first century.

I

It is incontrovertible that Jesus of Nazareth had followers in the period before the crucifixion.[3] It is likewise beyond dispute that some of those persons (like Simon Peter) remained in the midst of the generation after the resurrection. Behind and prior to questions that must arise about the Twelve, the apostles, the prophets, and the teachers, about the *episkopoi, diakonoi,* and *presbyteroi* of the first century churches, one must try to expose and explain how Jesus associated men with his work and word. What were the relationships between Jesus and these associates? How did he link himself with them and they with him? Did these relationships specifically differ from person to person or from group to group? Were they intended to develop, and, if so, how? The generation that followed the resurrection of Jesus was already posing these questions, though not from a primarily historical concern. The answers differed and provoked controversy then. They still do.

The Gospels and Acts, from their earliest strata (Mark, Q) designate those associated with Jesus as "disciples" *(mathētai).*[4] The term is not employed by the rest of the New Testament and T. W. Manson has noted that "it is . . . curiously rare in the utterances of Jesus himself."[5] It is evident from the varied uses of the term in

---

[3] Robert P. Meye, *Jesus and the Twelve* (Grand Rapids: Eerdmans, 1968), pp. 88-90 has pointed out that "New Testament scholars are wholly agreed that Jesus, as other teachers in the contemporary Jewish and Greek cultures, had a group of disciples to whom he particularly directed his teaching . . . Even those who cannot accept the historicity of the Twelve believe that Jesus had a circle of disciples who were in some way closer to him than all the rest." This serious and stimulating study on "Discipleship and Revelation in Mark's Gospel" will be cited hereafter as Meye, *JT.*

[4] K. Rengstorf, *"mathētēs," TDNT,* IV, 415-460, especially 441-455. The *"mathētēs,"* i. e., one who is learning as a pupil, implies a teacher, *"didaskalos,"* and Meye, *JT,* 30-87, develops very persuasively the Markan portrait of Jesus the teacher.

[5] T. W. Manson, *The Teaching of Jesus* (New York: Cambridge University Press, 1935), p. 237 [cited hereafter as Manson, *TJ*]. Mark 14:14 and Luke

Mark, Luke-Acts, and Matthew that a generation of theological reflection had already occurred.[6] As the historico-critical inquiry has inched its way back from this documentation certain characteristic elements of discipleship appear to be traceable to the *Sitz im Leben Jesu* and to influence, if not control, the latter developments.

The first and in many respects the key historical memory concerning those most closely associated with Jesus' work was that he himself had initiated the relationship, that the invitation, indeed summons, into such an association was rooted in his expressed will.[7] His eye had searched them out[8] and his word surprised them at their everyday tasks. The Markan tradition expressed that word as *deute opisō mou* (Mark 1:17 = Matthew 4:19) and again as *akolouthei moi* (Mark 2:14).[9]

Simon and Andrew, according to the Markan tradition, heard Jesus state his purpose for the command to come after him: "and I will make you become fishers of men" (Mark 1:17 = Matthew 4:19,

---

6:40 = Matthew 10:24-25 (Q) belong to the earliest traditions, and Luke 14:26-27 = Matthew 10:37-38 (Q) may be a striking witness to the *ipsissima vox Jesu* if Manson's reconstruction of the Aramaic original is correct (237-240). The only remaining examples of the term *mathētēs* placed on the lips of Jesus are Luke 14:33 (L) and Matthew 10:42 (cf. Mark 9:41).

[6] Cf. the summary of Meye, *JT*, 228-230, and footnote 70 below. The lengthier treatment of Sean Freyne, *The Twelve: Disciples and Apostles* (London: Sheed and Ward, 1968), is a significant contribution to this subject, though the exposition of Matthew on discipleship would have profited from P. S. Minear, "The Apostolic Structure of the Church," *Andover Newton Quarterly* 6 (1966), 15-37.

[7] Cf. K. H. Schelkle, *Discipleship and Priesthood* (New York: Herder and Herder, 1965), pp. 9-32 (cited hereafter as Schelkle, *DP*).

[8] Cf. Mark 1:16, 19; 2:14 and Schelkle, *DP*, 10-11.

[9] The tradition records for the sons of Zebedee simply *ekalesen autous* (Mark 1:20 = Matthew 4:21). Their response is then described as *apēlthon opisō autou* (Mark 1:20), which in Matthew 4:22 becomes *ēkolouthēsan*, the term used to denote the response of Simon and Andrew as well as Levi (Mark 1:18 = Matthew 4:20 and Mark 2:14 parrs.). Thus the actions from the point of view of Jesus, the initiator, can be described as an imperative to come (cf. J. Schneider, *"erchomai,"* *TDNT*, II, 669) after (cf. H. Seesemann, *"opisō,"* *TDNT*, V, 289-292) or to follow (cf. G. Kittel, *"akoloutheō,"* *TDNT*, I, 210-215). These imperatives the tradition interprets as his *calling* them (cf. K. L. Schmidt, *"kaleō,"* *TDNT*, III, 487-491). No responding word appears from those so addressed. They are described as simply doing what they were asked, coming after or following Jesus himself, entering his company. The relationship with him is central and determinative, and there is no promise that it will ever be other than one of subordination.

except for *genesthai*).[10] Their following is to issue in Jesus' own appointment or designation [11] for the task described metaphorically as fishing for men. That metaphor, as Wuellner remarks,[12] is "properly understood as a symbol for mediumship or partnership in the revelation event," in what is taking place in the works and words of Jesus of Nazareth. These men are summoned to listen to his words and to see his works, "to be with him" (cf. Mark 3:14) so that through their acts and words in turn the "revelation event" reaches others.[13]

The appointment and the task imply, indeed demand, an authority, an "enablement." [14] Mark 3:15 and 6:7 witness to that author's belief that Jesus himself conferred an initial and limited authorization on certain associates in his historical ministry.[15] The text of Mark 6:12-13, 30 implies that the authorization extended not only to acts of exorcism but also to their preaching and teaching. Moreover, the mission charge of the Sayings Source appears to confirm the Markan narrative with its version of Jesus' word, "He who

---

[10] That the metaphor goes back to Jesus' own word has been disputed (cf. R. Bultmann, *History of the Synoptic Tradition,* second edition [New York: Harper and Row, 1968], pp. 28, 386-387, [hereafter *HST*], and E. Schweizer, *The Good News According to Mark* [Richmond: J. Knox, 1970], p. 48). The reasons for skepticism seem to melt before the study of Wilhelm Wuellner, *The Meaning of "Fishers of Men"* (Philadelphia: Westminster, 1967), cited hereafter as Wuellner, *MFM.* He notes, "A primarily linguistic orientation can only list this metaphor along with others and conclude that Jesus used it explicitly for some elsewhere yet to be defined task of his disciples, and implicitly for speaking of his own mission" (p. 135). Cf. Meye, *JT,* 100-110.

[11] Cf. H. Braun, *"poieō," TDNT,* VI, 473-474; Schelkle, *DP,* 12-13; Meye, *JT,* 105.

[12] Wuellner, *MFM,* 201.

[13] Cf. Meye, *JT,* 103.

[14] W. Foerster, *"exousia," TDNT,* II, 569.

[15] The *exousia* is explicitly ordered to exorcism and reminds the readers of Mark that the work of those "authorized" begins as did the work of Jesus, with an exorcism that manifested his own *exousia* (cf. Mark 1:27). The incident of Mark 9:17-18 indicates that the "enablement" was derived and limited. The contrary impressions of others, including the disciples (Mark 9:28), need not impugn the historicity of the authorization (*pace* V. Taylor, *The Gospel According to Mark* [London: Macmillan, 1957], p. 303 [cited hereafter as Taylor, *Mark*]). That a criminal eludes a policeman would not lead one to think that the officer had not been duly appointed. Cf. Meye, *JT,* 178-181.

hears you hears me and he who rejects you rejects me, and he who rejects me rejects him who sent me" (Luke 10:16, cf. Matthew 10:40).[16] This authorization to speak is, like that to act, held in subordination to and dependence on Jesus himself.[17]

That Jesus actually called individual men into association with himself and his work, authorizing them to act and speak in his behalf, has thus far occupied this inquiry. One cannot avoid any longer the question of whether these individuals were also members of a group or groups that as such had a special association with Jesus. The Markan tradition remembers that the first persons that Jesus joined to himself come as pairs of brothers (Simon and Andrew; John and James, Mark 1:16-20) and the "mission" of Mark 6:7 sees these men and others sent out "two by two." [18] A grouping of three (that

---

[16] As T. W. Manson, *The Sayings of Jesus* (London: SCM, 1949), p. 78, [hereafter, *SJ*] has remarked, "The disciple represents in the fullest sense Jesus, and Jesus represents in the fullest sense the Kingdom of God. What they offer is God's offer and what they claim is God's claim." Besides its synoptic parallels this saying is presented in yet another form in John 13:20 (cf. C. H. Dodd, *Historical Tradition in the Fourth Gospel* [New York: Cambridge University Press, 1963], pp. 343-347). That all of these lines of transmission go beyond the first generation Palestinian church (*pace* Bultmann, *HST*, 143, 147, 155, 163) into the teaching of the historical Jesus seems historically credible. If indeed a form of the rabbinic proverb, "The one sent by a man is as the man himself" (cf. K. Rengstorf, *"apostolos,"* *TDNT*, I, 415) was current in Jesus' day, it has been audaciously reworked and extended in this logion.

[17] Mark 9:39 and 10:14 make clear that this authority to speak for Jesus can be abused and stands under his judgment (cf. Meye, *JT*, 180).

[18] Why not singly but in teams? Mutual human support and security are surely involved, but that could be readily provided by a non-disciple, a member of the family or a friend. These men go out precisely as pairs of men who have been with Jesus and this simplest of groupings adds an element that has been best described by Schelkle, *DP*, 80: ". . . this 'two by two' is . . . destined to give security to the message. If personal genius were what mattered, an individual left to himself might be capable of delivering the proclamation. Yet precisely this is not required: what is required is faithfulness to the assigned message. The message is guaranteed by this, that two keep each other in mind of it and vouch for each other in its preaching . . . In proclaiming it [the word] he has only to do his service to it. He is not lord, but 'minister of the gospel' (Colossians 1:23; Ephesians 3:7) and 'minister of the word' (Luke 1:2; Acts 6:4)." These pairs of men are witnesses of the revelation-event and what has happened in the words and work of Jesus. Their task is performed according to the laws of evidence accepted by Israel (cf. Deuteronomy 19:15). Thus, according to Luke 7:19, the Bap-

partially coincides with the pairs of brothers first called) emerges at Jesus' explicit initiative,[19] and a group of four is once glimpsed.[20] There is the faintest trace of seven.[21]

Was there, finally, a group of twelve [22] that the historical Jesus associated with himself and his task? As a group, it is inherently no more improbable than the smaller groupings noted above and even the most astringent historical criticism is prepared to admit most of those. The evidence that the first and second generation churches believed that such a group existed is found in documentary strata as diverse as I Corinthians 15:5, the four gospels and Acts, and Revelation 21:14. The last decade of German criticism, however, has seen an influential minority arguing at length that the Twelve were the creation of the first generation church. Their thesis in turn has undergone a severe critique.[23] Ironically enough, the historicity

---

tist sends "two of his disciples" to hear Jesus cite his works and his preaching in answer to the inquiry that they have been authorized to make (cf. Jesus' own conduct in Mark 11:1 and 14:13).

[19] Mark 5:37; 9:2; 14:33. They witness the raising of Jairus' daughter, the transfiguration, and the Gethsemane prayer. Again the ancient Israelite laws of evidence seem to determine the number.

[20] Mark 13:3. This group of Peter, James, John, and Andrew coincides with the two pairs whom Jesus first called. The order of the names here, however, coincides with Mark 3:16-18. There seems to have been distinct pressure on the Markan tradition that dictated not only the names of "the three" but the order in which they were to appear. Andrew's blood relationship with Simon and the priority of his call before the sons of Zebedee do not suffice to bring his name next to Peter's when James and John are also to be listed. That the sons of Zebedee were quite conscious of the special character of their relationship with Jesus in his ministry is evident from Mark 10:35-41. Even Bultmann (*HST*, 345) admits that here as well as at 5:37 and 13:3 "the naming of the disciples is original."

[21] Mark 8:8 where the number of baskets apparently corresponds to the number of those commissioned to gather the left-overs. The possibility of such a grouping would scarcely be worth mentioning if it did not also inexplicably occur in such diverse later witnesses as John 21:2 and Papias (*ap.* Eusebius, *HE* 3.39.4). If Mark 2:15 does refer only to those five called up to this point in his narrative, the grouping seems to be simply *ad hoc* (though curiously the Talmud, *Sanhedrin* 43a, ascribes five disciples to Jesus). The same must certainly be said for "the ten" of Mark 10:41. The relation of the 70 (72) in Luke 10:1, 17 to the ministry of Jesus is too complex to be broached in this survey (cf. K. Rengstorf in *TDNT*, II, 634-635).

[22] Cf. K. Rengstorf, *"dodeka," TDNT*, II, 321-328.

[23] The studies of G. Klein, P. Vielhauer, *et al.* are cited in the bibliography of Meye, *JT*, 235-248. Meantime, the translation of W. Schmithals, *Das*

of the betrayal by Judas appears to be the ineradicable taproot that anchors "the Twelve" in the history of Jesus.[24]

The group of three noted above and several of the pairs certainly existed within the Twelve. It is possible that several of the other groupings partially overlapped.[25] One would infer from this inclusion that the Twelve also were conceived of as "learners," as recipients of an authority to do and to teach what Jesus was doing and teaching. But one must still ask what is it that specifies and distinguishes the

---

Kirchliche Apostelamt, has appeared as *The Office of Apostle in the Early Church* (New York: Abingdon, 1969). Meye's own critique of their position appears from pp. 192-209. See also Freyne, *op. cit.* in footnote 6, and J. Giblet, "The Twelve, History and Theology" in his *The Birth of the Church* (New York: Alba, 1968), pp. 66-81.

[24] Thus "the Twelve" of I Corinthians 15:5 cannot be understood apart from the "he was betrayed" of 11:23. One may, of course, join the harmonizers and historicizers of the Western tradition and substitute "the Eleven" (perhaps from Matthew 28:16) but of course that number stands in function of "the Twelve" and is historically inexplicable apart from the betrayal by Judas (cf. Rengstorf, *TDNT,* II, 326, and Meye, *JT,* 202-204). In like manner, the archaic tradition recorded in Mark 14:10 tears apart every hypothesis into which it is sewed. Finally, the origin of the saying of Jesus reported in Matthew 19:28 (cf. Luke 22:28-30 [Q?]) must ultimately be assessed against the ineluctable scandal of the betrayal; for, ". . . it is hard to see how the primitive Church could have invented a saying which promises a throne, amongst others, to Judas Iscariot" (T. W. Manson, *SJ,* 217). That Luke 22:30 has no "Twelve" before "thrones" (but has it before "tribes of Israel") is a parade example of the way this author has softened the edges of a logion that was acutely embarrassing (*pace* G. Krodel, "Forms and Functions of Ministries in the New Testament," *Dialog* 8 [1969], 195, fn. 27, for it is precisely because of "Luke's restriction of the apostles to the Twelve" that he feels compelled to edit a saying that implies a limitation in Jesus' knowledge).

A happy effect of this as yet unfinished debate has been to remind exegetes that one does not proceed from an *a priori* and perhaps irrelevant definition of a "group" or "body" of men whose existence is then verified (or denied) in first century Christian history. "The Twelve" are no more intelligible historically as an *ad hoc* committee convened by Cephas to prepare a report on the resurrection than they are as "a College of Cardinals, systematising the doctrine, and superintending the organisation, of the Primitive Church" (B. H. Streeter, *The Primitive Church* [New York: Macmillan, 1929], p. 42).

[25] Perhaps the variations in the lists of the names of those who constituted "the Twelve" must ultimately be traced to the *Sitz im Leben Jesu* and a fragmentary memory of which persons in such smaller groups were actually numbered among the Twelve.

Twelve from the other groupings? The archaic logion of Matthew 19:28 (cf. Luke 22:28-30) conceives them as the leaders of a new amphictyony [26] around something greater than the Temple (cf. Matthew 12:42 = Luke 11:31—Q). They are all indisputably sons of Israel and yet they are a new beginning of the people of God. They are defined over against the twelve tribes of Israel from whom they have been chosen and to whom they are being sent. That mission will have reverberations to the end of history and the final judgment. God will accordingly seat them on thrones beside the "throne of glory" of the Son of man. There is no mistaking here the rich oriental and Old Testament imagery for royal rule.[27] The central task of the ancient king and his court was judgment and this is precisely the issue of the work of the Twelve with Jesus. They are to rule [28] and judge [29] with him. If the Twelve are, in a famous phrase, "the eschatological regents," [30] their rule is defined and specified by the one who shared his rule with them. They are the ministers of one who is to be crucified as "King of the Jews" (Mark 15:26) and the scandal of the cross is measure of their rule (cf. Mark 10:42-45).

There is evidence that the historical Jesus conceived and spoke of his death in terms of the levitical priesthood and sacrifice.[31] There is no question that the first Christian generation employed the vocabulary of Old Testament sacrifice and priestly office to express what

---

[26] Cf. K. Rengstorf, *"dōdeka,"* TDNT, II, 321-322, 326.

[27] Cf. O. Schmitz, *"thronos,"* TDNT, III, 160-167, esp. 164-165. He calls attention to the plural "thrones" in Daniel 7:9 as the vision of "one like a son of man" begins. On the relation of the Qumran scrolls to these concepts, cf. fn. 52 below.

[28] Cf. K. Stendahl, "Matthew," in *Peake's Commentary on the Bible,* edited by M. Black and H. Rowley (New York: Nelson, 1963), 790 and the citations there as well as F. Büchsel, *art. cit.* in fn. 29, p. 923. Rengstorf (*art. cit.* in fn. 26) apparently has misgivings about applying the term "rulers" or "leaders" to the Twelve. If, of course, those terms mean simply "despots" or "tyrants," the case is prejudged. That Jesus conceived of leadership or rule in quite different terms is evident (cf. Mark 10:42-45), but it is still leadership. That even among the Twelve there were those who had difficulty in grasping and implementing Jesus' concept of leadership is indisputable (cf. above fn. 17 as well as Mark 10:35-41), but *abusus non tollit usum.*

[29] Cf. F. Büchsel and V. Herntrich, *"krinō,"* TDNT, III, 921-941.

[30] R. Bultmann, *Theology of the New Testament* (London: SCM, 1952), vol. I, p. 37.

[31] Cf J. D. Quinn, "Propitiation," in *Lutherans and Catholics in Dialogue III: The Eucharist as Sacrifice* (1967), pp. 43-44.

Jesus had done on the cross [32] and the Letter to the Hebrews contains a full theological orchestration of the notes already heard for a generation. It is not so often recalled that elements of this same levitical tradition are also used to denote the role of the Twelve. Indeed, their very number as corresponding to the twelve tribes implies that the role of the sons of Levi in Israel found some counterpart in the task shared with the Twelve. The affirmation of Mark 3:14 that Jesus "appointed *(epoiēsen)* twelve," with its peculiar use of *poiein*, is to be read not only in continuity with the *poiēsō* of Mark 1:17 [33] but also with an eye to the use of this term for the appointment of priests for Israel.[34] In this light, the command of the historical Jesus [35] at his last supper with the Twelve, "Do this *(touto poiēte)*," was an appointment to a ritual function that must be understood against the back-ground of Israel's priestly worship.[36] Jesus' task of bringing the kingdom and rule of God was completed by his priestly offering of his body on the cross. The Twelve whom he associated with himself in this task, he also designated to proclaim that death by repeating what he had said and done at his last supper with them. The cross again is the center and measure of the act which the word of Jesus empowered them to perform.

In summary, then, Jesus came to the cross after he himself had associated various individuals and groups with his work. He had authorized them to do and to teach what they had learned from him. One group, the Twelve, which included several of the smaller groups,

---

[32] Cf. on this point and what follows, H. Schlier, *"Grundelemente des priesterlichen Amtes im Neuen Testament,"* in *Theologie und Philosophie* 11 (1969), 161-180. An English summary is available in *Theology Digest* 18 (Spring, 1970), 11-18.

[33] Cf. fn. 11 above, as well as Schelkle, *DP,* 112-116.

[34] Taylor, *Mark,* 230, cites the LXX passages. The incident of the temple tax may be instructive for the way in which the Matthean church viewed the role of at least Peter (Matthew 17:24-27: cf. J. D. M. Derrett, "Peter's Penny: Fresh Light on Matthew 17:24-27," in *Novum Testamentum* 6 [1963], 1-15).

[35] The *poiēte* command is witnessed to by Paul (I Corinthians 11:24) and the longer text of Luke 22:20. According to J. Jeremias, *The Eucharistic Words of Jesus* (London: SCM, 1966), pp. 237-255 (hereafter *EWJ*), it is "very probable that the command goes back to Jesus himself." I find his arguments for the longer text of Luke (pp. 139-159) quite convincing.

[36] As Jeremias, *EWJ,* 249-250 notes: ". . . as can be seen from comparison with Exodus 29:35; Numbers 15:11-13; Deuteronomy 25:9 . . . ('Do this' is) an established expression for the repetition of a rite."

he summoned specifically to share in communicating the rule, the judgment, and the sacrifice that he was bringing to the people of God. To single out these particular groups and some of their functions is not to deny that other men and women were associated with and were followers of Jesus. It is to say that Jesus designated some followers, as individuals and as groups, for a particular share in his work. The influence and development of these groups belongs to the history of that first Christian generation which followed upon the resurrection of Jesus of Nazareth.

II

Within a few years after the resurrection, a distinction appeared among those who accepted Jesus as Lord. The first congregations of Christian believers had been believing Jews and remained recognizably such among their confreres. This study will designate these churches, found principally in Palestine and above all in Jerusalem, as Jewish Christian.[37] Other congregations soon appeared (usually outside of Palestine) that received not only Jews but pagans directly into the company of Christian believers.[38] These congregations will be treated below (section III).

The importance of the Jewish Christian church of Jerusalem is hard to overestimate. Every other Christian congregation, in the first

---

[37] The title has been chosen deliberately with an eye to the continuing dialogue on this phenomenon and its development. The stimulating and controversial work of H.-J. Schoeps, *Theologie und Geschichte des Judenchristentums* (Tübingen: Mohr, 1949), represents one position. A more popular presentation of his principal conclusions and ongoing revision is available in his *Jewish Christianity* (Philadelphia: Fortress, 1969), cited hereafter as Schoeps, *JC*. The theological scope of the author's studies can be seen in his *The Jewish Christian Argument* (London: Faber, 1963). His study, *Paul: the Theology of the Apostle in the Light of Jewish Religious History* (London: Lutterworth, 1961), is to be consulted on this topic. Another position is that represented by Jean Daniélou, *The Theology of Jewish Christianity* (Chicago: Regnery, 1964), cited hereafter as Daniélou, *TJC*. An excellent summary of the present state of the question is that of M. Simon and A. Benoit, *Le Judaisme et le Christianisme antique* (Paris: Presses Universitaires, 1968), pp. 258-274.

[38] There is no hard evidence for a congregation composed *only* of converts from paganism in the first Christian generation (*pace* W. Marxsen, *Introduction to the New Testament* [Philadelphia: Fortress, 1968], p. 32). At best one is dealing with churches in which the Jewish Christians are a minority. W. Marxsen, *ibid.*, pp. 97-100, would distinguish in the Roman church a third "stratum" of converts from paganism who had then more or less embraced Judaism. He calls them "proselyte Christians."

generation, perhaps as far removed as Gaul and Spain,[39] felt the formative influence not only of Jewish Christians but also of the Jerusalem church. The Christian gospel was carried out into the *orbis terrarum* from Jerusalem by those eyewitnesses and ministers of the word whose national, cultural, and religious background was nothing if not Jewish. Thus the Jerusalem church was the first *mater et caput omnium ecclesiarum*. Precisely because this enormously influential congregation was Jewish, it served as a bridge for the passage of Jewish elements into the life of the "mixed churches" outside of Palestine as well as a "brake" on the converts from paganism who brought no authoritative religious history into the Christian community.[40]

The oldest record of the Jerusalem kerygma (I Corinthians 15: 4-7) explicitly links the appearances of the risen Jesus to both individual persons and to groups, to Peter and James as well as to the Twelve, five hundred brethren, and "all the apostles." Women, of course, were unable to give legally acceptable evidence in the Jewish world at that time [41] and thus have been excluded *de iure* from this record of official witnesses, though the oldest accounts of the resurrection note that *de facto* they were the first to see the risen Jesus. The elements of the social structure of the most primitive Jerusalem church can be glimpsed behind this Pauline citation. The narrative of Acts 1:13-14 proposes [42] that the first gatherings of believers in

---

[39] Romans 15:24 and II Timothy 4:10 (a variant reading of Sinaiticus, C, and a few other mss. as well as Eusebius, *HE,* 3.4.8).

[40] Even Paul finally clinches his varied argument for women keeping their heads veiled in the Corinthian worship-assemblies by saying, (I Corinthians 11:16) "We recognize no other practice nor do *the churches of God."* The latter phrase apparently refers to the Palestinian Jewish Christian congregations (cf. I Thessalonians 2:14).

[41] J. Jeremias, *Jerusalem in the Time of Jesus* (London: SCM, 1969), pp. 374-375. Note how emphatic Acts 1:21 is that one of the *men (andrōn)* who have followed Jesus is to be chosen to fill out the Twelve.

[42] Luke-Acts is, of course, a primarily theological exposition. It is not scientific history, but does contain "material from the rich tradition concerning the time of the apostles" (J. Munck "Primitive Jewish Christianity" in M. Simon [ed.] *Aspects du judéo-christianisme* [Paris: Presses Universitaires de France, 1965], p. 83). As Munck points out, Haenchen has denied the existence of such a tradition (*Die Apostelgeschichte,* thirteenth edition [1961], pp. 87-99; cf. fn. 65 below) but J. Jervell, *"Zur Frage der Traditionsgrundlage . . ."* in *Studia Theologica* 16 (1962), 25-41 has demonstrated its existence (cf. *NTA* 8 [1963], No. 202). A valuable and not unsympathetic critique of Haenchen's stance is found in C. K. Barrett, *Luke the Historian in Recent Study* (London: Epworth, 1961). H. J. Cadbury, *The Book*

Jerusalem were for prayer and the author differentiates three groups within the assembly. He first lists by name eleven persons, beginning with Peter. He then notes "the women and Mary the mother of Jesus" and finally "his brothers." [43] Each of these groups had had some encounter with the risen Jesus, but this does not seem to be the principle of differentiation from the rest of the assembly, for at least two men outside these groups, Joseph Barabbas and Matthias, had also seen the Lord. On the other hand, even within the group of the brothers of Jesus, there is evidence only for James having seen him risen.

Luke, immediately after describing an already differentiated community at prayer, narrates another act of this Jerusalem congregation, undertaken at Peter's initiative and before the Pentecost experience of the Holy Spirit. This is the election of Matthias to bring the Twelve back to its full complement.[44] Luke envisions certain qualifications for the candidates (a number are presumed). They must be men; they must have accompanied not only Jesus but the original Twelve from the time of John's baptism. These conditions would exclude the group of women as well as the members of Jesus' family. Finally, the candidate must have seen the risen Jesus. The whole assembly then offered two candidates and after prayer, cast lots [45] to

_____

of Acts in History (London: Black, 1955) and the more recent studies of A. N. Sherwin-White would considerably qualify Haenchen's thesis. Thus the latter in his *Roman Society and Roman Law in the New Testament* (Oxford: Clarendon, 1963), p. 189, can say, "For Acts the confirmation of historicity is overwhelming. Yet Acts is, in simple terms and judged externally, no less of a propaganda narrative than the Gospels, liable to similar distortions. But any attempt to reject its basic historicity even in matters of detail must now appear absurd."

[43] Cf. Mark 6:3 = Matthew 13:55 — James, Joses, Simon, Judas. Luke-Acts never identifies any one person with the title "the brother of the Lord," and even here the term is used in another sense in the very next verses.

[44] The historicity of the incident and its significance in the Lukan plan is convincingly expounded by K. Rengstorf, "The Election of Matthias" in *Current Issues in New Testament Interpretation,* edited by W. Klassen and G. F. Snyder (London: SCM, 1962), pp. 178-192. Its parallels with Qumran are detailed by J. Fitzmyer, "Jewish Christianity in Acts in Light of the Qumran Scrolls" in L. Keck and J. Martyn (ed's) *Studies in Luke-Acts* (New York: Abingdon, 1966), pp. 250-251 (cited hereafter as Keck, *Studies*).

[45] Acts 1:15-26: it is significant that choice by lot *(klēros)* was a practice of the priestly tradition in Judaism in designating those who would exercise the priestly ministry (cf. J. Fitzmyer in Keck, *Studies,* 250, and Yohanan

determine who would succeed to Judas' place (*topon;* al. lect., *klēron*) among the Twelve. That "place" Luke designates as "this ministry" (Acts 1:17, 25: *diakonias tautēs*),[46] "his office" (1:20: *episkopēn autou*),[47] "apostleship" (1:25: *apostolēs*),[48] and becoming a "witness" (1:22: *martura*)[49] with the remaining eleven to the resurrection of Jesus. The terminology is that of Luke and it bears moreover the weight of a generation of Christian reflection on the phenomenon of the Twelve. The historian still must attempt to discern the functions of the original structure in the first years of the Jerusalem church and determine which of its germinal elements (if any) made it possible for the generation following to apply the terminology of Ministry, superintending office, witness, and apostleship to the Twelve. The group was evidently considered of decisive importance to those earliest days [50] and there is no question of the leadership of Peter among them,

---

Ahroni, "Arad: Its Inscriptions and Temple," *BA* 31 [Febr., 1968], 11). Luke begins his gospel with the note that "according to the custom of the priesthood it fell to him [Zecharia] by lot *(elache)* to enter the temple of the Lord and burn incense" (Luke 1:9). Cf. Jeremias, *JTJ*, 201-202, and W. Foerster, *"klēros,"* *TDNT*, III, 758-764, esp. 761, 763, as well as H. Hanse, "lagchanō," *TDNT*, IV, 1-2.

[46] Cf. H. Beyer, *"diakonia,"* *TDNT*, I, 87-88. The significance of the demonstrative, *tautēs,* should be noted in Luke's phrase. To be numbered among the Twelve is to have more than *diakonia* in general; it is to have *this* particular Ministry which he will further specify as *"apostolē"* (1:25).

[47] Citing LXX Psalm 108:8. The Old Testament served as a kind of theological dictionary for the terminology used to designate an essentially new phenomenon. Here the official prayerbook of Judaism is employed to provide a term that will describe the function of those who led and directed the prayer of the first Christian communities (cf. Acts 6:1-4 and the comments below). Cf. H. Beyer, *"episkopē,"* *TDNT*, II, 606-608.

[48] Cf. K. Rengstorf, *"apostolē,"* *TDNT*, I, 446-447, which should be read in conjunction with his *"apostolos,"* ibid., 407-445. The progress of critical study on this much vexed question has been summarized recently by R. Schnackenburg, *"L'Apostolicité: état de la recherche,"* in *Istina* 14 (1969), 5-32 (cited hereafter as Schnackenburg, *Apostolicité*), and R. Brown, "The Twelve and the Apostolate," JBC (*ut cit.* fn. 83), 795-799.

[49] Cf. H. Strathmann, *"martus,"* *TDNT*, IV, 474-504 and esp. 492-494 on the Lukan use of the term.

[50] In this respect the witness of Acts 1:13-14, placing this group first among the three noted and recording eleven names, is in agreement with Paul and the kerygma of the Jerusalem church (I Corinthians 15:5). The central fact that this notice presupposes is their having seen the risen Jesus. Paul also knows that the title *apostolos* and the term *apostolē* can be applied to at least one of their number (cf. Galatians 1:18-19; 2:8).

both within the community as well as when the Twelve addressed themselves to their primary task, the conversion of Israel.[51] Their original title was singularly modest, simply the number, *twelve*.[52] Moreover Luke remembers that on occasion two of their number, Peter and John, functioned as a pair in proclaiming the gospel (Acts 3:1, 11; 4:13, 19) to unbelieving Jews as well as in ministering to a new congregation of believers (Acts 8:14).[53]

An internal crisis overtook the expanding Jerusalem church within this period, a few years after Pentecost. With it came a profound clarification of how the Twelve functioned *vis à vis* the Jerusalem congregation (as distinguished from their function for unbelieving Israel). According to Acts 6:1 ff., inequities had occurred in the giving of relief to the poorest members of the church, the widowed

---

[51] Again the witness of Acts (cf. 1:13, 15; 2:14 etc.) is that of Paul (note the position of Cephas in I Corinthians 15:5 as well as Galatians 1:18; 2:8). Rengstorf (*art. cit.* fn. 44) has made a strong case for the Twelve having as their primary goal the task of the conversion of Israel. That this is not simply the theological construct of Acts can be inferred from Paul's notice that God "worked through Peter for the *apostolē* to the *circumcised*" (Galatians 2:8) as distinguished from the mission of Paul and Barnabas to the uncircumcised (Galatians 2:8-9). It has been noted above that this function is traceable to Jesus' ministry.

[52] The Qumran community of the "new covenant" has also a council of twelve (1 Q S 8.1) who represent the twelve tribes of Israel. They have, moreover, the function of judging and "reconciliation" and are described as a "foundation." A group of three priests is noted in the same text, but their relation to the "twelve men" is unclear. (Cf. C. S. Mann, "The Organization . . . of the Jerusalem Church in Acts," in J. Munck, *The Acts of the Apostles* [New York: Doubleday, 1967], pp. 279-280, though I should not subscribe to Mann's saying, "Only by a perversity of scholarship is it possible to deny that the Jerusalem church. . . . received its structure from Essene models.") There is no evidence for the direct influence of this Qumran structure upon the origin or development of the Twelve (cf. J. Fitzmyer in Keck, *Studies,* 246-247, and the negative verdict of P. Benoit, "Qumran and the New Testament" in J. Murphy-O'Connor [ed.], *Paul and Qumran* [Chicago: Priory, 1968], pp. 14-16). With the Essenes and the earliest Jewish Christians we are rather dealing with two basically Jewish communities drawing upon sources common to both.

[53] It may be more than coincidence, in the light of what is said below on the Twelve sharing their functions, that when Paul pays his first visit as a Christian to the Jerusalem church, he meets a pair, Cephas and James, each of whom exercises leadership in his own group (i. e., the Twelve or the family of Jesus) in the Jerusalem congregation.

women. In the face of the resultant grumbling, the Twelve [54] assembled the congregation [55] and proposed to turn over what had apparently been one of their responsibilities, the distribution of food to the poor. This, they proposed, should be entrusted to seven men chosen by the assembly and then commissioned by the Twelve to this service. The Twelve reserved to themselves "preaching the word of God" (Acts 6:2) and proposed to devote themselves "to prayer and to the ministry of the word" (Acts 6:5: i. e., to the preaching to the Jews, and a leadership in the Christian assemblies for worship and the study of the Old Testament scriptures).[56]

The author of Acts emphasized the function of the Twelve in the worship of the earliest Jewish Christian church.[57] In Acts 6:1-5 he presupposes that a certain leadership in "the prayer" of the Jerusalem church had been reserved to the Twelve. The first converts are said to have "devoted themselves to the apostles' teaching and fellowship, to the breaking of bread and (the) prayers" (Acts 2:42). The *klasis tou artou* for Luke certainly refers to the eucharistic meal.[58] One would infer that the Twelve are described as carrying out the command, "Do this . . ." that Luke had previously recorded in his narrative of the last supper.[59] Luke, of course, is not unaware that

---

[54] Acts 6:2; this is the only time that Luke employs *hoi dōdeka* technically in this volume of his work, though he uses it half a dozen times in his gospel.

[55] *to plēthos*, a term that is parallel to the use of *rabbim* at Qumran (cf. J. Fitzmyer in Keck, *Studies*, 245-246).

[56] For this interpretation of *hē diakonia tou logou*, cf. B. Gerhardsson, *Memory and Manuscript* (Lund: Gleerup, 1964), pp. 240-245, 331.

[57] It is worth pondering that both the earliest Jerusalem church (Acts 2:46) and a pair from the Twelve (Acts 3:1) participate in "the prayer (*hē proseuchē*)" of Judaism, the public worship of the temple. Thus Peter and John, in Acts 3:1, are about to assist at the evening oblation of the lamb (cf. Exodus 29:39 ff., and F. F. Bruce, *The Acts of the Apostles* [London: Tyndale, 1952], p. 103, cited hereafter as Bruce, *Acts*). Such *communicatio in sacris* is noted even for Paul (Acts 21:23-27).

[58] Cf. the materials assembled by J. Behm, *"klasis," TDNT*, III, 726-743. The interpretation followed here is that of J. Dupont, "The Meal at Emmaus," in J. Delorme *et. al., The Eucharist in the New Testament* (Baltimore: Helicon, 1964), pp. 105-121, and also of J. Jeremias, *EWJ*, 118-122. For the latter the four phrases of Acts 2:42 "describe the sequence of an early Christian service" (p. 119). Thus Luke would be describing the Twelve as initiating and presiding over a Jewish Christian worship-assembly that included the eucharistic *klasis*.

[59] Cf. above and fn. 35.

"the apostles" are a wider group than the Twelve.[60] He may well imply that a function given to the Twelve was capable of being shared with others. Indeed, the fact that Matthias was now numbered among the Twelve, sharing their Ministry, certainly means that he was to function with them not only in "preaching the word" but also in leading "the prayer" of the community.

The crisis that precipitated the creation of the Seven, witnesses to another form of sharing, precisely because these men are not to be counted among the Twelve but rather the Twelve are represented as turning over a function that had been theirs to another group. The new structure of the Seven [61] has again a modest appellation. The text does not call them *"diakonoi,"* though they are given a service to perform. The number is staffed from a minority group within the Jerusalem church, the Hellenist Jewish Christians.[62] Their names are all Greek. The qualification for their task is not that they had seen the risen Jesus but that they be "full of the Spirit and wisdom" (Acts 6:3). They receive their office in a setting of worship which apparently specifies the significance of the imposition of hands by "the apostles." [63] The Qumran documents have revealed no parallel thus far to this structure in the Jerusalem church.[64] Moreover, it is striking

---

[60] In this connection one must consider not only the Lukan usage in Acts 14:4, 14 (the Western variants do not affect *apostoloi*) but also his narrative of the institution of the eucharist, where in the context we meet "the Twelve" (Luke 22:3), "my disciples" (Luke 22:11), and "the apostles" (Luke 22:14). The evidence cited in fn. 54 must also be weighed, for Luke (like Mark) never employs the *phrase* "the twelve apostles." Matthew, of course, speaks several times of "the twelve disciples" and once of "the twelve apostles" (10:2).

It is significant that Luke places the dispute on precedence (and leadership) immediately after the command to repeat the supper action and the betrayal prophecy (22:24 ff.). To lead the eucharist is to lead the community, but that leadership always stands under the judgment of the cross.

[61] *hepta;* Acts 6:3; 21:8. For a quite different approach see E. Schweizer, *Church Order in the New Testament* (Naperville: Allenson, 1961), pp. 70-71 (cited hereafter as Schweizer, *CONT*).

[62] Cf. J. Fitzmyer in Keck, *Studies,* 237-239 (*pace* Schweizer, *CONT,* 30). A. Spiro has argued persuasively that the "Hellenists" are Samaritan Jewish Christians (cf. Munck, *ut cit.* fn. 52, pp. 285-300).

[63] Acts 6:6; again we may be dealing with a group wider than the Twelve (cf. fn. 60).

[64] Cf. P. Benoit, *"Les origines apostoliques de l'Episcopat selon le N. T."* in H. Bouëssé and A. Mandouze, *L'Evêque dans l'église du Christ* (Paris:

that the Seven are never depicted as exercising the function for which they were chosen.[65] Instead they exercise a form of ministry (Acts 6:4: *diakonia*) which the Twelve had reserved when they appointed the Seven. Stephen preaches Jesus as Lord in the Jerusalem synagogue worship-assemblies. Philip later preaches in Samaria and then along the Mediterranean coast until he settles in Caesarea. He is the only one of the Seven who receives a title indicating his function and that title is "the evangelist" (Acts 21:8), i. e., one who preaches the good news about Jesus as the Christ.[66]

The way in which the Seven understood and preached the gospel now precipitated an external crisis for the Jerusalem church. With the assassination of Stephen "a great persecution arose against the church in Jerusalem, and they were all scattered throughout the region of Judea and Samaria," and then Luke notes, "except the apostles" (Acts 8:1). The storm had broken over the Hellenist front of the Jerusalem congregation. The Seven were scattered (providentially as events proved) while the Twelve remained, apparently because the orthodoxy (or orthopraxy)[67] of the latter in the eyes of their fellow Jews was still intact.[68] The gospel was carried to Samaria and the Mediterranean coastal towns; Christian churches were formed in Galilee and Damascus (Acts 9:31) and then in Phoenicia, Cyprus, and Antioch (Acts 11:19). In all of this missionary work the gospel was addressed only to Jews. Peter alone had dared to admit gentiles directly into the church and even he had to answer for it at length

---

Desclée de Brouwer, 1963), pp. 34-35 (cited hereafter as Benoit, *Episcopat;* this full dress, critical article should not be confused with a considerably earlier, more popular exposition, now reprinted in this author's *Exégèse et Théologie* [Paris: Cerf, 1961], vol. II, pp. 232-246).

[65] Cf. E. Haenchen, "The Book of Acts as Source Material for the History of Early Christianity," in Keck, *Studies,* 264, and Schweizer, *CONT,* 49 with fn. 162.

[66] Luke does not say this preaching of the Seven was done without the approval or supervision of the Twelve. In fact, Peter and John are dispatched to Samaria to review Philip's work (Acts 8:14-17) and Peter later appeared in Caesarea also, to do what apparently Philip (then residing in that city, Acts 8:40; 21:8) did not feel free to do, i. e., admit a gentile family into the Christian community. It is not often noted that it is as the leader within a group of *seven* Jewish Christians that Peter preached to Cornelius (Acts 10:23, 45 and 11:12).

[67] W. D. Davies, "Torah and Dogma: A Comment," *HTR* 61 (April, 1968), 87-105, and cf. Schweizer, *CONT,* 40, fn. 116.

[68] Cf. Schweizer, *CONT,* 42, fn. 126 and Haenchen in Keck, *Studies,* 262-264.

before the Jerusalem church (Acts 11:1-18). At last, in Antioch, in the early forties, the gospel was addressed to gentiles as such (Acts 11:20) and the first mixed congregation outside of Palestine appeared and prospered. The Jerusalem church sent down Barnabas to inspect this new kind of Christian church and he was more than satisfied with it. For help in ministering to it he sent for a convert from Tarsus, a Jew named Saul, to whom the risen Jesus had once appeared (Acts 11:25-26).[69]

The appearance of Paul, entering a position of leadership in one of the newly founded churches, makes it imperative at this point to summarize the function of a group of men, numerically undefined, that were called, from the earliest days of the Jewish Christian church, *hoi apostoloi*, "the apostles." [70] From the first line of his earliest letters Paul will style himself *apostolos* and will spend no little time vindicating that title as truly his and his Ministry as an authentic *apostolē*. What constituted this group? What was their function antecedent to Paul? As noted above, "all the apostles" figured in the most archaic record of the Jerusalem kerygma as a group to whom the risen Jesus appeared (I Corinthians 15:7). Whereas Paul never even intimated that he should be considered one of the Twelve, he did insist tirelessly that he was truly to be counted, even though as least, among "the apostles" (I Corinthians 15:8-10). He did not begrudge members of the Twelve the title "apostle" or an "apostleship." [71] He was convinced that he too belonged to a wider circle that had received this title and task. The most recent studies indicate that the group which Paul entered were, from the very first days of the Jewish Christian church, believers who were witnesses to Jesus' resurrection and envoys commissioned by the risen Christ. They were "the qualified missionaries of primitive Christianity." [72] Up to the founding

---

[69] Again note the conscious effort to form a pair for their work of teaching and later for their preaching. Neither member of this pair belonged to the Twelve or the Lord's brothers (cf. fn. 53), though later Luke calls both *"apostoloi"* (Acts 14:4, 14).

[70] The further historical question, whether Jesus bestowed such a title on a group associated with him before the crucifixion will not be broached. The critical outcome of such an inquiry would resemble that for a term like *mathētēs;* Jesus may well have used such language but the terms received a quite new significance in their use after the resurrection.

[71] Cf. fn. 50 above.

[72] So Schnackenburg, *Apostolicité,* 9. They could have been associated with all or part or none of Jesus' earthly ministry. The encounter with the risen Jesus is the *sine qua non* and foundation of their office.

of the congregation in Syrian Antioch, Jesus had been proclaimed as Lord and Christ only to Israel, whether in Palestine [73] or abroad, whether by the Twelve or by the Seven or by the apostles. When Barnabas and Paul, witnesses of the risen Jesus, began to preach to the pagans, they extended the mission and concept of the *apostolē* as drastically as did the Seven when they began to proclaim Jesus to yet unbelieving Jews without themselves having seen the risen Lord. [74] The way in which Paul in particular developed the content of *apostolos* and *apostolē*, stamping it indelibly with his own style, [75] belongs to the history of Ministry in the mixed churches (section III below).

Toward the mid-forties of the first century, two events precipitated another crisis for the Jerusalem church. The first mentioned by Luke was a famine; [76] and the second was an outbreak of persecution that struck at the leading members of the Twelve. James, son of Zebedee, was beheaded and Peter was imprisoned to await the same fate. Both events brought new organizational developments within the Jerusalem church.

With the famine there appear for the first time Christian *presbyteroi* [77] (presbyters, elders) among the Jewish Christians of Jerusalem.

---

[73] Apart from the preaching to the centurion, Cornelius, which not only is difficult to anchor chronologically but also did not historically affect the orientation of the Twelve or other groups in the Jerusalem church. It remained an incident, not a precedent, for some years.

[74] In Luke's theology, their special and lasting endowment with the Spirit and wisdom may well be considered as equivalent to an encounter with the risen Jesus, for as D. W. Smith (*Wisdom Christology in the Synoptic Gospels* [Rome: Angelicum, 1970, unpublished dissertation], p. 260) has noted, ". . . several passages from Acts (cf. 10:14 with 10:19) parallel the Spirit with the glorified Jesus in such a way that Jesus seems to become present to his Church through the Spirit which is his gift . . ." The anarthrous "full of Spirit and wisdom" of 6:3 becomes in the description of Stephen (6:5) "full of faith and the Holy Spirit" which in its turn and with a slight variation becomes the description of Barnabas "full of Holy Spirit and faith" as he is dispatched by the Jerusalem church to the new congregation of Antioch (Acts 11:24). On the lasting character of this endowment with the Spirit, see J. Hull, *The Holy Spirit in the Acts of the Apostles* (London: Lutterworth, 1967), pp. 123-124.

[75] Cf. Schnackenburg, *Apostolicité*, 11.

[76] Acts 11:28: the event figures also in Josephus (*Ant.* 3.15.3 and 20.2.5 as well as 20.5.2) and Suetonius (*Claudius*, 18.2).

[77] Cf. G. Bornkamm, *"presbyteros,"* TDNT, VI, 651-680 (esp. 662-663), and Fitzmyer in Keck, *Studies*, 248-249.

The structure was certainly borrowed directly from the organization of contemporary orthodox Judaism. The evidence of Acts is persuasive. The term *presbyteroi* occurs eighteen times in that book. On its first occurrence it has the ordinary sense of "older men" (Acts 2:17 = Joel 3:1). After that a very significant distinction appears. The term is used first to describe an influential body of men within Judaism as such.[78] Then with Acts 11:30 it is used to denote an influential body within the Jerusalem Christian congregation itself. Thus there are Jewish *presbyteroi* and Jewish *Christian presbyteroi*. We first meet the latter as administrators [79] of the famine relief fund that the mixed congregation of Antioch sent up "by the hand of Barnabas and Saul." The reader of Acts is immediately struck by the fact that these *presbyteroi* received the gift and not the Twelve. Luke immediately explains by noting the second contemporary crisis. The central structure had been under attack: one of its members was already dead; Peter himself had narrowly escaped death. He fled the city and there is reason to believe that the others had already taken a similar course, for the last word of Peter to the Jerusalem church was, "Tell this to James and to the brothers" (Acts 12:17). This statement implies that the leadership of the Jerusalem church had been left in the hands of the family of Jesus, for this James seems to have been the oldest of the "brothers of the Lord." Again there is no indication that this action of sharing their function with another group dissolved or compromised the authority and primacy of the Twelve and Peter.[80] As noted above a distinct stratum within the Jerusalem congregation, present from its beginnings, was constituted by the members of Jesus' family who were, of course, like him, of Davidic descent.[81] James apparently enjoyed a certain primacy among them not only by primo-

---

[78] Acts 4:5, 8, 23: a group on a par with "rulers, scribes, and high priests" (cf. P. Benoit, *Episcopate*, 19-25 *et passim*).

[79] The Jewish Christian origin and Palestinian background for the Letter of James seem assured. If one is convinced by the case made for a very early dating of this document (around the mid-forties of the first century), then one must note the Ministry of healing exercised by the *presbyteroi* in the congregation(s) to which the letter is directed (James 5:14-15).

[80] The passing on of further leadership functions here is not basically different from the first sharing of their *diakonia* with the Seven.

[81] Cf. S. E. Johnson, "The Davidic Royal Motif in the Gospels," *JBL* 87 (June, 1968), 149.

geniture but also because the risen Jesus had appeared to him (I Corinthians 15:7).[82]

Within a few years of the famine,[83] at the time of the Jerusalem "council," Peter (as Acts 15 narrates events) took the initiative and proposed the case for the "apostles," Barnabas and Paul, before their fellow apostles and the Jerusalem *presbyteroi*. It was James, however, who spoke for the Jerusalem church and its *presbyteroi*. He proposed the compromise which made possible a *modus vivendi* between the Palestinian Jewish Christian churches and the mixed churches now being organized in the Roman world at large, especially by Paul of Tarsus.

During the next decade, James' leadership continued,[84] for on Paul's last trip to Jerusalem (again with a collection) in about 58 AD, he had an official audience with James "and the *presbyteroi* were present" (Acts 21:18). Paul reported on the success of the mission among the gentiles and demonstrated with the collection the real unity that those mixed congregations had with the Jewish Christian church of Jerusalem. James in his turn explained how successfully the compromise of the previous decade had worked for the mission to the Jews. "You see, brother, how many thousands there are among the

---

[82] H. von Campenhausen, *Jerusalem and Rome* (Philadelphia: Fortress, 1966), pp. 3-19, presents the arguments against there ever having been a "caliphate" or a hereditary succession in leadership in primitive Christianity. The use of later models, exotic or commonplace, from the history of religion, has perhaps impeded an assessment of the admittedly fragmentary evidence for one of the methods of providing leadership that was tried in the first and the beginning of the second century (cf. the past paragraph of fn. 24 above).

[83] Galatians 2:9 witnesses to a group of three, James, the brother of Jesus, as well as Cephas and John, surviving (?) members of the trio within the Twelve, who appear to be leading the Jerusalem church and are styled ironically by Paul as "pillars." That term may be an actual citation of the terminology already employed by the Jerusalem congregation (cf. their use of *pistis* in Galatians 1:23). The dating of Paul's visit in Galatians 2:1 is so vexed that the historian can scarcely affirm more than that such a trio functioned in Jerusalem before 50 AD and that it bears an obvious resemblance to the trio within the Twelve. Cf. J. Fitzmyer, "A Life of Paul" (p. 218) and "The Letter to the Galatians" (pp. 241-242) in R. Brown *et al.*, editors, *The Jerome Biblical Commentary* (Englewood Cliffs, N. J.: Prentice-Hall, 1968), cited hereafter as *JBC*.

[84] His prestige and that of his congregation certainly extended as far as Antioch, as Galatians 2:12-13 makes painfully clear.

Jews of those who have believed; they are all zealous for the law" (Acts 21:20).[85] The Twelve had been driven from Jerusalem, but apparently even the most suspicious had been unable to undermine or impugn the orthodoxy of James. Thus under his leadership the Jerusalem church had been able to win many more from Israel to belief in Jesus. James then cited the slanderous rumor that Paul despised the law and taught his *Jewish* converts to apostatize. In order to give it the lie, he suggested that Paul participate publicly in the worship of the temple and Paul agreed readily. The plan miscarried. Paul was imprisoned and eventually carried off to Rome for trial. By this time the days of the Jerusalem church were numbered. Palestine was in political chaos, and, in AD 62, James himself was murdered at the instigation of Ananus, the Sadducean high priest.[86] By AD 66 the great revolt had erupted. In the next four years it resulted in ". . . the destruction of Jewish and Christian communal life . . ." [87] in Palestine. The Jewish Christian churches, and above all the Jerusalem church, were caught between the millstone and the grinder. Their pagan contemporaries treated them as Jews and thus as traitors to and revolutionaries against Rome. Their orthodox Jewish confreres considered them not only heretics but now in addition "pacifists and defeatists."[88] Eusebius says that the Jerusalem church fled across the Jordan into Pella.[89] Meanwhile Palestine was sealed off from the *orbis terrarum*,

[85] Historically speaking the compromise of James is as unimpeachably apostolic in its motivation as the mission of Paul. The portrait of "this last Davidian and this first curialist . . . this fearsome ecclesiastical politician" (E. Stauffer, *New Testament Theology* [London: SCM, 1955], p. 34) is quite overdrawn. We "gentiles," the heirs and beneficiaries of Paul, have tended to forget that the conversion of Israel was a practical, pressing, and critical concern for that first generation church (as it had been the first concern of their Lord). I should submit that the delay in the conversion of Israel posed far deeper questions of theology and apologetics than the delay of the parousia. To take up a famous image, the latter is a secondary crater in the vast problem of the fate of Israel (cf. Wuellner, *MFM,* 206).

[86] Josephus, *Antiq.,* 20.9, 197-203.

[87] W. F. Albright, *History, Archaeology, and Christian Humanism* (New York: McGraw-Hill, 1964), p. 57.

[88] W. F. Albright, *The Archaeology of Palestine* (Baltimore: Penguin, 1960), pp. 240-242 (the quotation is on p. 241).

[89] *H. E.,* 3.5.3. The historicity of this notice has been the object of an ongoing critique by S. G. F. Brandon since the publication of his *The Fall of Jerusalem and the Christian Church,* second edition (London: SPCK,

until in 70 AD the Jewish nation had been annihilated and Jerusalem was in ruins. Jewish Christianity survived into the following generation, but as the *magni nominis umbra,* wilting and dying like a great tree whose roots have been slashed. As late as the reign of Domitian, we have some evidence that the Jerusalem church was still led by another surviving "brother of Jesus" (Simeon; Simon). This experiment with a hereditary form of leadership apparently atrophied and disappeared with Jewish Christianity itself.

III

The mixed churches that had begun to appear thirty years before the fall of Jerusalem as a happy side-effect of the mission to the Jews, were by 70 AD (and more by default than by their own design) the guardians and interpreters of the gospel of Jesus Christ.

It had been Paul's systematic and brilliant apostleship to the gentiles that had raised in acute, practical form the question of the identity of the church over against Judaism. But he was indeed a premature birth. In his activity and in his correspondence he presented the theological rationale for the radical independence of the Christian faith, but he was in no position (nor did he intend) to tear apart the chrysalis of Judaism within which the first generation churches were developing.

Powerful opponents were never persuaded by Paul's ideas or arguments, but they died, and Paul's new ideas conquered (as valid new ideas do) by surviving their opponents — not by convincing them.[90] It was not Paul's theology but the armies of Vespasian and Titus that ripped away the chrysalis of orthodox Judaism. It was Paul's theology that made it possible for those mixed congregations of the second generation to rescue that which was of intrinsic value from the shambles of Palestinian Christianity and to survive an age of transition.

1957). His arguments have, by and large, not been found demonstrative (cf. M. Simon [*ut cit.* fn. 37], p. 271).

Hopefully the excavations that have begun at Pella will shed some light on the earliest Christian history of a church that produced the apologist, Aristo (c. 140), and to which the Letter to the Hebrews may have been addressed (thus H. Cazelles, *Naissance de l'Eglise* [Paris: Cerf, 1968], pp. 108-109).

90 The language is that of a theoretical physicist discussing the evolution in modern mathematical studies, but I cannot now trace the source in which I read it.

The mixed churches of the first generation are to a great extent the result of the apostolic Ministry of Paul. The apostleship itself developed under the pressure of his experience and thought; yet precisely because of the Jewish-Christian background of Paul and other apostles as well as their own Jewish-Christian members, the social structuring of the mixed churches reflected that of the "churches of God" in Judea. New elements were introduced into the structure of mixed congregations and older ones were modified, because of the converts from paganism and the pressure that arose from their living cheek by jowl with converts from Judaism.

From the Pauline correspondence itself we discern the nature and character of Paul's apostolic Ministry — a powerful, personal, and detailed control over every aspect of the Christian life of his foundations. His churches were his children in Christ,[91] the chaste spouse that he was presenting to his Lord (II Corinthians 11:2). The imagery attests not only to the heroic charity that impelled him but also to the unique and exclusive bond of the churches with the apostle himself. He was not only founder but model and final arbiter for these foundations, and he reserved to himself judgment on other apostles who entered his domain (cf. II Corinthians 11:4-5). He did not conceive his apostleship as ending with the conversion of his hearers; he remained their apostle (I Corinthians 9:2) after they became believers and addressed them moreover as both prophet and teacher,[92] with "the authority *(exousia)* that the Lord had given him" for upbuilding the church (II Corinthians 13:10).

As the Twelve shared out functions of leadership with other groups in the Jerusalem church, so Paul associated others with the tasks of his apostleship. Again the working in pairs or trios is conspicuous not only in his own correspondence but in Acts. These men share not only in administrative functions [93] but in the properly apostolic task of proclaiming the gospel to unbelievers [94] and the

---

[91] Cf. I Corinthians 4:14-17; Galatians 4:19; I Thessalonians 2:7-12.

[92] Cf. the excellent study of M. Bourke, "Reflections on Church Order in the New Testament," *CBQ* 30 (October, 1968), 493-511, esp. 494-501 (cited hereafter as Bourke, *CBQ*).

[93] Acting as messengers (I Thessalonians 3:6 of Timothy), and supervising finances (II Corinthians 8:16-19, 22-23 of Titus and "the brother"). A glimpse of a functionary in the entourage is provided by Romans 16:22.

[94] II Corinthians 1:19 states this of Silvanus, Timothy, and Paul proclaiming *(kēruchtheis)* Jesus Christ, the Son of God, to the Corinthians upon their arrival among them. The use of the first person plural in II Corinthians

further teaching and direction of the congregations.[95] If the prophet, Silas, of the Jerusalem church (Acts 15:32), is indeed the Silvanus of I Thessalonians 1:1 and II Thessalonians 1:1, the way in which Paul linked the prophetic Ministry with his exercise of apostleship may be illuminated. Finally, these co-workers regularly did the baptizing (cf. I Corinthians 1:14-17).

The way in which Paul with his aides structured the communities that he founded is much less clear.[96] From the first of his extant letters (dating from about 51 AD) we read, "But we beseech you, brethren, to respect those who labor among you and *are over you in the Lord* [97] and admonish you, and to esteem them very highly in love because of their work." The Greek term for "those who are over you," literally "those who have been set over you," may advert to the Thessalonians having a part in the choice of their leaders. In any case it is a leadership that the apostle acknowledges and supports.

In correcting and instructing his Corinthian converts, Paul ap-

---

3—4 and 6 in describing the ministry Paul shared is in striking contrast to the first person singular of his defense of his personal apostleship (II Corinthians 11—12).

[95] Thus Timothy in I Thessalonians 3:2 is "our brother and *God's servant (synergon tou theou)* in the gospel of Christ, to establish you in your faith and to exhort you." Paul's co-workers in his apostolic task are God's co-workers (cf. I Corinthians 3:9 of Paul and Apollos, "We are God's fellow workers"). Cf. G. Bertram, *"synergos," TWNT,* VII, 869-875.

The written evidence of Paul's style in leadership and teaching is the epistolary itself, and it is striking that, excluding the pastorals, only three letters are dispatched under the name of Paul alone (Galatians, Romans, Ephesians). All of the remainder are sent as the communication from two or three together (thus Paul, Silvanus, and Timothy for I and II Thessalonians; Paul and Timothy for II Corinthians, Philippians, Colossians and Philemon; Paul and Sosthenes for I Corinthians). In the light of the evidence noted in the previous paragraphs, one simply cannot dismiss this as a superficial formality. It has its significance not only for the Pauline (and first generation) concept of the apostolate and the sharing of this Ministry but also for the exegesis of many a passage in which the first person plural occurs. Indeed, much critical analysis of the letters has not been critical enough in "the quest for the historical Paul."

[96] "Since the apostle is the pre-eminent figure, and since he, Paul, is the principal director of the community, offices of guidance other than his are of relatively slight importance," Bourke, *CBQ,* 503.

[97] *proïstamenous hymōn en kyriōi,* I Thessalonians 5:12-13. Cf. B. Reicke *"proïstēmi," TDNT,* VI, 700-703, who remarks, "the reference is to office-bearers though not to a technical title."

parently bypassed the local leadership [98] and addressed the congregation as a whole. In I Corinthians 12 (immediately after his treatment of the Lord's supper) he turned to the question of the unity of that church amid its varied gifts, services, and works.[99] In summarizing his argument (12:27-31) he remarked emphatically that "God has appointed in the church first apostles, second prophets, third teachers, then workers of miracles, etc."

The three-fold ministry of the word, which Paul here singled out as in some sense distinct from the following charismata and functions, belonged to the apostleship as well as to the local congregation.[100]

---

[98] Though one cannot ignore I Corinthians 16:15-16 with its reference to Stephanas' household, "first fruits (aparchē) of Achaia," who "have devoted themselves to the service (diakonia)" of the congregation. Paul there urges the Corinthian believer "to be subject to such men and to every fellow worker and laborer (synergounti kai kopiōnti)." The latter terms again are central to Paul's vocabulary for the apostleship and those who share its task (cf. F. Hauck, "kopos", TDNT, III, 827-830; Bertram, ut cit. fn. 95; and J. H. Elliott, ut cit. in fn. 113, pp. 381-382).

Since Stephanas was the leader of the trio that came to consult Paul in Ephesus (I Corinthians 16:17), it is possible that the local leadership was actually with Paul as he dictated the letter (I Corinthians 1:16 certainly sounds as if Stephanas was given the chance to look over the first draft). There would thus be no reason to counsel the leaders of the Corinthian church in writing. They had appealed the problems of their congregation directly to Paul and now Paul in turn directs his letter to the church, but not without saying, "Give recognition to such men" (I Corinthians 16:18).

In the next generation, in still another letter to the Corinthian congregation, it appears that I Clement 42:4 understood that Stephanas' household did lead the Corinthian church when he notes that the apostles "preached from district to district and from city to city, and they appointed their first fruits (aparchas), testing them by (or with regard to) the Spirit, to be bishops and deacons (episkopous kai diakonous) of future believers." The Pauline use of aparchē here is striking (cf. G. Delling, s. v., TDNT, I, 484-486). The passage of course should be read along with I Clement 45 and that author's concept of succeeding to the apostles.

[99] I Corinthians 12:4-6. Both Käsemann and Küng appear to assume that the Corinthians were Paul's ideal or model congregation or church. The evidence might well be read otherwise, with an appropriate modification of the Tübingen theologians' conclusions. If Paul ever favored a church as approaching his "ideal," that at Philippi would be among the strongest contenders for the honor. Curiously, that is the one Pauline congregation where we know that there were leaders called episkopoi and diakonoi (cf. Bourke, CBQ, 501, 502).

[100] Cf. for example, Jean Daniélou, The Theology of Jewish Christianity (Chicago: Regnery, 1964), p. 350, "In the opinion of the present writer . . .

This was not simply an umbrella, missionary structure. Prophets and teachers in the Corinthian congregation were certainly part of the local church.[101] The triad may well derive from a way of structuring leadership that was employed in the first mixed congregations in which Paul worked. Thus in Acts 13:1, the text explicitly notes "prophets and teachers" but the list of five includes Barnabas and Saul who are "apostles" as well.[102] A given leader, accordingly, may have had several charismata for the building up of the church. On the other hand, the charisms (even that of apostleship) functioned *through* as well as *for* the church. Thus Acts 13:2-3 portrays the Spirit giving his command to the leadership of the Antiochene church in an assembly for worship, and the assembly itself sends those already charismatically endowed on their mission. In any event, the apostles-prophets-teachers triad took a certain precedence over the other gifts and services with which the Corinthian congregation was familiar.[103]

Paul notes further gifts and ministries found in the Corinthian congregation, among them "helpers" and "administrators." [104] In Romans 12:8 the *proïstamenos* figures again, and now as one who has received a charism (gift) that he must use with zeal.[105] Finally, and

---

[there is here] a missionary priesthood (as distinguished from a stable one attached to one place), that of the *apostoloi*. The various roles assigned to these *apostoloi* are all related to this primary and distinct vocation. They are essentially preachers, and this aspect of their ministry is indicated by the terms prophet and didascalos. As prophets they announce the Kerygma to pagans; as didascaloi they prepare those pagans who have decided to receive baptism." Also Bourke as noted in fn. 92.

101 Cf. C. K. Barrett, *The First Epistle to the Corinthians* (London: Black, 1968), p. 295.

102 Cf. fn. 60 above and note that four out of the five leaders cited for the Antiochean church had Jewish names (X. Leon-Dufour, *The Gospels and the Jesus of History* [London: Collins, 1968], p. 174).

103 Somewhat later Ephesians 4:11 inserts "evangelists" and "pastors" into the archaic triad, between "prophets" and "teachers," witnessing to a further development in the structuring of the Ministry (cf. Bourke, *CBQ*, 506-507).

104 I Corinthians 12:28. C. K. Barrett *The First Epistle to the Corinthians* (*ut cit.* fn. 101), pp. 295-296, notes that the helpers "May foreshadow the work of deacons . . . , whose main task in the early church was that of ministering the church's aid to the needy," and administrators "that of bishops . . . , the name sometimes given to those who presided over the church's affairs (cf. Romans 12:8). There were local ministries (cf. Philippians 1:1), in contrast with the peripatetic ministry of apostles, and secondary to the ministry of the word exercised by prophets and teachers."

105 Cf. Reicke, *ut cit.* fn. 97.

perhaps not by accident, in a letter written half a dozen years later from his Roman prison, Paul greeted explicitly the *episkopoi* and *diakonoi* of the Philippian church.[106] The local and subordinate leadership that had been present from the beginning and that had been designated as it developed with several general titles now had the names linked to it that would remain constant while the development continued.

With this the evolution of the structures in the mixed churches has been traced up to the outbreak of the Palestinian revolt. The star of Jewish Christianity had begun to set. Furthermore, the leadership of the first generation was now being thinned at every level, in mixed as well as Jewish Christian congregations. The imprisonment of Paul was as sharp a setback to the mixed churches as the assassination of James was to the Jerusalem church and the Jewish Christians. The martyrdom of Peter, perhaps in AD 64, was grim news for both.

The last of Paul's letters, the Pastorals, appear to have been dispatched in 67 AD.[107] In their final form, the *episkopos* appears (only in the singular: I Timothy 3:2; Titus 1:7) and *diakonoi* (I Timothy 3:8, 12), but a term now appears for the first time in the Pauline corpus. These letters speak of *presbyteroi* (I Timothy 5:1, 17, 19; Titus 5:2). The structure and the name have been seen in the Jerusalem church. Now the *presbyteroi* appear in the mixed congregations of the *orbis terrarum*. It is more than possible that not only the title and structure had come from the Jewish Christians but that some of the very persons who bore the title had belonged to the now fragmented Jerusalem church. The functions of these *presbyteroi* seem to have coincided for all practical purposes with those *proïstamenoi* that Paul put in charge of his churches from the beginning. Luke, of course, actually called the leaders of the Pauline foundations *presbyteroi* (Acts 14:23) but he probably applied the term to men whose function corresponded to what was current when he wrote this volume

---

[106] Philippians 1:1 (cf. E. Best, "Bishops and Deacons . . .", *Studia Evangelica* [Berlin: Akademie, 1968], vol. IV, pp. 371-376).

[107] The vexed questions on the dating and authorship of the Pastorals deserve a volume in themselves. The latest edition of C. Spicq's *Les Epîtres Pastorales* (Paris: Gabalda, 1969) in two volumes (cited as Spicq, *EP*) is the most detailed of recent commentaries. The hypothesis within which I submit my observations is that Luke drafted a first form of these letters under Paul's direction c. AD 67. He then re-edited them after completing Luke-Acts and attached them as the third "volume" to that work, c. AD 80-85.

(after 70 AD). Indeed at one point he says that the *presbyteroi* of Ephesus came to hear Paul's farewell speech (Acts 20:17). He then cites what may be an earlier source and there these same hearers are called *episkopoi* (Acts 20:28).[108] Thus the members of a structure known in the Jerusalem church as *presbyteroi* corresponded with the leaders in the mixed congregations known as *episkopoi*. The coincidence was, however, not total. For all the ambiguities of the data, we still can say that all *episkopoi* were *presbyteroi* but all *presbyteroi* were not *episkopoi*, somewhat as all the Twelve were apostles but not all apostles belonged to the Twelve. The Pastorals demand practically the same qualifications for an *episkopos* as for the *presbyteroi*, and the latter appear to share in the functions of an *episkopos*. By the time of the Pastorals, however, an *episkopos* can be conceived of as functioning alone in his authority over a congregation (as does the father of a family, to use the comparison of 1 Timothy 3:4-5, 15). The *presbyteroi* on the other hand are once noted explicitly functioning as a body, a *presbyterion*.[109]

The closest parallel to the Christian *episkopos* in the structure of a Jewish community is the *mebaqqer* ("overseer" — the literal sense of the Greek term also) among the devout Jews gathered at Qumran. There "the *mebaqqer* is an interpreter of the law, a preacher and pastor and the officer most closely concerned with the initiation of novices." [110] The parallel to the Christian *episkopos* is striking but unfortunately no direct link with Qumran can be adduced.[111] If ever the Qumran "overseer" were associated with aides that corresponded to the "deacons" of the Pastorals, the case for direct borrowing would be more than a hypothetical possibility.

The developments of the deacons and their functions constitutes

---

108 Cf. Bruce, *Acts,* 377. J. Dupont, *Le Discours de Milet* (Paris: Cerf, 1962), pp. 28-29 would admit *"l'essentiel de la pensée de l'Apôtre."* He is impressed by the resemblances to the language of the Pastorals.

109 I Timothy 4:14. I Clement never speaks of a *presbyterion;* Ignatius a few years later (and in Asia Minor) does so frequently. On the other hand Ignatius speaks only of the *episkopos* whereas I Clement never uses the term in the singular, except for God, though apparently considering *episkopoi* as largely synonymous with *presbyteroi* (I Clement 44.1, 4, and 5). Like the Pastorals, I Clement associates *diakonoi* immediately and only with *episkopoi*, whereas in Ignatius they are separated from the *episkopos* by the *presbyteroi* and are apparently subject to the latter (*ad Magn.* 2.1).

110 C. K. Barrett, *The Pastoral Epistles* (Oxford: Clarendon, 1963), p. 58.

111 Cf. Fitzmyer in Keck, *Studies,* 247-248, and Benoit (*ut cit.* fn. 52), p. 16.

still another study. To keep this disquisition within reasonable limits, it suffices to observe that in the first century they appear as assistants to the *episkopoi* (never to the *presbyteroi*).[112] The deacons stand to the *episkopos* as the Seven did to the Twelve.

The generation after the fall of Jerusalem saw a continuing development of Ministry in the mixed churches.[113] It is notable that even in this period the New Testament documents do not explicitly name those who conducted the eucharist.[114] Even in the previous generation, as noted above, one can only reasonably infer that the Twelve and the apostles carried out the supper command of Jesus as they presided over the Christian assemblies for worship. Similarly one can only infer that they shared this function with others as they certainly shared their apostolic Ministry of preaching and teaching. It is distinctly possible that in the oldest Jewish Christian churches the Ministry of prophets and teachers included leading the eucharist[115] whereas in the mixed congregations the *presbyteroi-episkopoi* eventually emerged with this function.[116]

The laying on of hands to designate men for a share in apostolic Ministry was certainly employed on occasion in the first generation (Acts 6:6 of the Seven; 13:3 of Barnabas and Paul). The Pastorals

---

[112] Cf. the references in fn. 109, adding *Didache*, 15.1. On the diaconate in the Pastorals, see Spicq, *EP*, I, 74-77, 456-463.

[113] Many useful as well as controversial observations on this period are found in Schweizer, *CONT*, as he discusses various forms of ecclesial Order that can be glimpsed in the later documents of the New Testament and the apostolic fathers. J. H. Elliott, "Ministry and Church Order in the New Testament: A Traditio-Historical Analysis (I Peter 5:1-5 & parallels)," *CBQ* 32 (July, 1970), 367-391, is a provocative recent contribution on the *presbyteroi* and the *neōteroi* in this period.

[114] The only individual ever named as presiding is Jesus himself at the original supper, though, of course, Paul scarcely intended to exclude himself when he made his appeal to "the cup of blessing which *we* bless" (I Corinthians 10:16; the observation is Bourke's, CBQ, 507) and Luke thought of Paul as leading the "breaking of the bread" in Acts 20:7, 11.

[115] Thus *Didache*, 15.1 and perhaps 10.7 (cf. Bourke, *CBQ*, 508).

[116] *Didache*, 15.1 seems to witness to a church (or churches) where the older Jewish Christian structure was being phased out in favor of the *episkopoi-diakonoi* (*Didache* never speaks of *presbyteroi*). By the time of I Clement 44.4 there are *presbyteroi-episkopoi* in the Corinthian church "who have blamelessly and holily offered the sacrifices" (of the episcopate). A few years later, in the churches of Asia Minor, the *episkopos* or one whom he has appointed (*epitrepsēi*) is to preside at a "valid" (*bebaia*) eucharist (Ignatius, *Smyrn.*, 8.1 and Bourke, *CBQ*, 508-509).

alone remember that Paul as well as the *presbyterion* had so designated Timothy (I Timothy 4:14; II Timothy 1:6).[117] The more generic *katastēseis* of Titus 1:5 leaves room for other means of appointing the *presbyteroi* of Crete,[118] and of course there is no indication of the way in which Titus himself was appointed by Paul to his function.

Finally, the Pastorals depict not only Timothy and Titus but also the persons whom they in turn associated with their Ministry as teaching, witnessing to and guarding the faith, and directing the churches.[119] With this stage in the sharing of the apostolic ministry, the phenomenon designated by "apostolic succession" is present in all but name.[120]

IV

In summary, from this brief survey of the development of Christian Ministry in the first century, the following points are noted.

1. The Ministry of the church is ultimately rooted in the way in which the historical Jesus called disciples, and particularly the Twelve, to share his task.

2. The elements of both appointment by the risen Jesus and sharing of functions with others are characteristic of the Ministry of the Twelve and of the apostles from the earliest days of both the Jewish Christian and mixed churches. The functions for which those who had not seen the risen Lord are designated include proclamation of the gospel to unbelievers as well as teaching and directing communities of believers.

3. The means of appointment, the *how* of designation, apparently admitted of considerable variety, and it is quite possible

---

[117] Cf. Bourke, *CBQ*, 504-505, with its discerning critique of E. Käsemann on the theological implications of such a practice.

[118] As does the *cheirotonēsantes* of Acts 14:23. I Timothy 5:22 also mentions a laying on of hands in the context of *presbyteroi*, but it is not altogether clear that the author is referring to a designation for this Ministry (cf. Spicq, *EP*, I, 546-549).

[119] Cf. Bourke, *CBQ*, 505-506.

[120] And within a few years of the final edition of the Pastorals, I Clement 44.2 employs the critical verb when he says ". . . they [our apostles — Peter and Paul?] appointed *(katestēsan)* those who have already been mentioned [the *episkopoi* and *diakonoi* of 42.4], and afterwards added the codicil that if they should fall asleep, other approved men should succeed *(diadexontai)* to their ministry *(leitourgian).*"

that several different means of appointment flourished simultaneously in different apostolic churches.

4. The sharing of apostolic Ministry is the historical matrix from which succession to the apostolic Ministry emerged. It is important to note that just as the original apostles' sharing in the Ministry of the Twelve did not make them one of the Twelve, so the sharing of a Silvanus and a Timothy in the apostolic Ministry of Paul did not make them apostles. In like manner, the successors of the apostles are *successors,* not apostles. There was an untransmittable, personal qualification for the apostle as there was for being numbered among the Twelve.

5. The structures of first century Ministry involved leadership both by groups (of two, three, seven, twelve; *apostoloi;* prophets; teachers; *episkopoi; diakonoi; presbyteroi*) and by single individuals even within the groups (Peter; Paul; James; Titus in Crete; Timothy in Ephesus; the *episkopos*).

6. Though there was development in Ministry in the first century, it was not unilinear. It is historically more exact and eventually more instructive theologically to respect the differences in structuring the Ministry that existed simultaneously in different churches (Jerusalem; Corinth; Ephesus; Rome, etc.).

7. The appointment to the specifically eucharistic Ministry is governed by the observations in no. 2-3 above. There is no evidence in the New Testament that every baptized person was *ipso facto* enabled to preside at the eucharist.[121] This is not to say, however, that this Ministry could be bestowed only on certain believers. The New Testament does not envision any priestly caste or clan from which those who are to undertake specific Ministries must be chosen.

8. Ministry in its various forms is a gift (charism) of the *Spirit,* and exists, as do other *charismata,* for the upbuilding of the church.

---

[121] Cf. J. H. Elliott, *The Elect and the Holy: An Exegetical Examination of I Peter 2:4-10 and the Phrase Basileon Hierateuma* (Leiden: Brill, 1966), and particularly the summary on pp. 219-226.

THE SACRED MINISTRY AND HOLY ORDINATION IN THE SYMBOLICAL BOOKS OF THE LUTHERAN CHURCH

By Arthur Carl Piepkorn

1. *General.* In the course of the confessional revival in the Church of the Augsburg Confession during the nineteenth and twentieth centuries, Lutheran theologians interpreted the statements of the symbolical books about the sacred ministry in three typical ways.

Stated in an extreme form, the first view holds that the sacred ministry is only the activity of the universal royal priesthood of believers, the public exercise of which the Christian community has solemnly committed to certain persons merely for the sake of good order and efficiency. At the opposite extreme is the position which sees the sacred ministry as the contemporary form of the primitive apostolate and as the personal representation of Christ. A third view occupies the middle ground between these two positions and incorporates elements of both. It sees the sacred ministry as a divine institution that is essential to the church's existence. It regards the responsible public proclamation and application of the gospel and the administration of the sacraments as the primary content of the sacred ministry. It looks upon ordination as the indispensable act of admission to the sacred ministry.

The modifications of these views are many. Each theologian believes that he has the authority of the symbolical books for his view. Almost all of the positions that Lutheran theologians currently take reflect to a greater or lesser degree the traditions of their own past which they are espousing or against which they are reacting.

2. *Sources.* The primary sources in the symbolical books for a doctrine of the sacred ministry are Articles 5, 14, and 28 of the Augs-

burg Confession (1530), Articles 13, 14, and 28 of the Apology (1531), Articles 4 in Part Two and 9 and 10 in Part Three of the Smalcald Articles (1536—1538), and the Treatise on the Authority and Primacy of the Pope (1537).[1] Except for the Smalcald Articles, which are by Luther, these are all from Philip Melanchthon's pen.

It is essential that one keep in mind the historical antithesis or at least the historical situation that conditioned a particular affirmation of the symbolical books.

3. *Lay people and clergymen.* The church consists of preachers and Christians (LC Decalog 262), rectors *(Pfarrherr)* and parishioners (LC Introduction 2-3); rectors and people (SC Introduction 6), bishops, rectors, and preachers on the one hand and Christians on the other (SC Table of Duties 2-3); laymen (FC Ep Summary Concept 5; SD Summary Concept 8) and the ministers of the word who preside over the community of God (FC SD 10, 10). The presbyters are a part of the total church (Ap 22, 1.2.4). The church is beyond *(supra)* the ministers; no minister has superiority or domination over the church at large (Tr 11).

4. *The divinely ordained purpose of the sacred ministry.* God instituted the sacred ministry *(ministerium ecclesiasticum; Predigtamt)* of teaching the gospel and of administering the sacraments. His purpose in so doing is that men might obtain the faith that God forgives them by grace for Christ's sake through faith. The divine word and the sacraments are, as it were, means by which God gives the Holy Spirit that works faith when and where God wills in those who hear the word of God and receive the sacraments. The Lutherans reject the position that the Holy Spirit is received by purely interior preparation, meditation, and activity without the external word of God personally communicated through the sacred ministry (AC 5). The antithesis here is the asserted position of the Enthusiasts, who depreciated the sacred ministry.

The content of the sacred ministry is the responsible public proclamation of the gospel and the administration of the sacraments (AC 14; Ap 13, 7-9). It is not the offering up of an expiatory sacrifice

---

[1] This paper uses the following abbreviations: AC, Augsburg Confession; Ap, Apology of the Augsburg Confession; SA, Smalcald Articles; Tr, Treatise on the Authority and Primacy of the Pope; SC, Small Catechism; LC, Large Catechism; FC, Formula of Concord; Ep, Epitome; SD, Solid Declaration; WA, *Weimarer Ausgabe,* the critical edition of Martin Luther's works; CR, *Corpus Reformatorum* (for the works of Philip Melanchthon).

which earns forgiveness of sins for the living and the dead. The sacred ministry *(Kirchendienst)* is "the Word preached and heard" (FC Ep 12, 22; SD 12, 30).

The obligation of the incumbents of the sacred ministry to proclaim and apply the gospel of divine grace in Christ does not exclude the proclamation of the word of God as judgment. On the contrary, it implies the latter as a necessary corollary of the sacred minister's primary task.

5. *The sacred ministry and the world.* The sacred ministry is part of the equipment of the church for an outreach into the world. God's gift of pastor-teachers to the church and their proclamation of the gospel have in view the "edification" of the church (Tr 67). This is so not only in the metaphorical sense of the interior fortification of the church through an increase of devotion. It also looks to the literal building up of the church by the incorporation into it of those who are not as yet a part of it.[2]

6. *Functional and personal elements in the sacred ministry.* The symbolical books see the sacred ministry chiefly but not exclusively in dynamic and functional terms. Nevertheless, the symbolical books are conscious of the fact that apart from its incumbents the sacred ministry is an abstraction. "The authority of the *bishops* according to the Gospel is the authority or commandment to preach the Gospel, to retain sins, and to administer the sacraments" (AC 28, 5).[3] The ministry of the divine word and sacraments is committed to *bishops as bishops* (AC 28, 21). *"Priests . . .* are called to teach the Gospel and administer the sacraments to the people" (Ap 13, 9). "The Gos-

---

[2] LC Our Father 52-54: "So that we who have accepted [the divine Word] may remain with it and daily increase in it and that it may find a response and acceptance among others and go mightily throughout the world, so that the Holy Spirit may lead many to come to the kingdom of grace and become partakers of salvation"; "that [the kingdom of God] may come to those who are not yet in it"; "that the Gospel may be purely proclaimed throughout the world." Of interest is the stress in the Wittenberg ordination formularies of the late 1530s (WA 38, 423—33) on ordination as the fulfillment of the petition that Christ commanded his disciples to offer, imploring the Lord of the harvest to send out laborers into the plentiful harvest (Matthew 9:37-38; see John 4:35). The prayer of the rite invokes the Holy Spirit to the end that God's ministers may be his evangelists with great masses of people *(scharen/hauffen)* *(ibid.,* 429, 6—430, 13).

[3] "According to the Gospel" is in the symbolical books as a synonym for "by divine right *(jure divino)*" (AC 28,21 Latin; see also Tr 60-61 and SA II, 4,1).

pel gives *those who rule over the churches* the command to teach the Gospel, to remit sins, and to administer sacraments. . . . This authority by divine right is common to *all who rule over churches,* whether they are called pastors, presbyters, or bishops" (Tr 60-61).

The church has the divinely imposed responsibility not merely of proclaiming the gospel and administering the sacraments but also of choosing, calling, and ordaining fit persons to carry out these functions (Tr 67.72; Ap 13, 12 German). God gave to the church the concrete persons who discharge these functions, the "pastors and doctors" *(pastores et doctores)* that is, those who are engaged in the public and responsible "teaching of the Gospel" *(docendi evangelium)* (Tr 60-67).[4] We may have here a recognition that Ephesians 4:11 by a kind of hendiadys is describing a single office with the words "pastors and teachers."

God wills to preach and to work through the human beings that the church has chosen and ordained to the sacred ministry (Ap 13, 11-12 German). Thus the incumbents of the sacred ministry are the human instruments through whom the Holy Spirit sanctifies and governs the church.

A minor problem arises on occasion when one tries to ascertain if "ministry" *(ministerium)* in a given passage means generally and abstractly the function of preaching the gospel and administering the sacraments — as it does frequently — or if it means concretely the incumbents of the sacred ministry as they engage in these functions. Sometimes, as in AC 5, 1 Latin and 28, 9, this is a matter of exegetical decision. Of interest is the fact that *Predigtamt* (literally, "the office of preaching") occasionally (for instance, AC 5, 1 German and Ap 7, 20 German) has "the Gospel" or "the Gospel and the sacraments" as an explanatory apposition. To be effective, the gospel must actually be preached and the sacraments must be administered. But these are precisely the functions the symbolical books attribute to the incumbents of the sacred ministry.

7. *The sacred ministry as service.* The sacred ministry is a form of service *(ministerium: diakonia),* not a source of privilege, prestige,

---

[4] At another place, however, outside the symbolical books, Melanchthon would differentiate the authority to teach the gospel *(potestas docendi evangelium)* from the authority to govern the church *(potestas gubernationis ecclesiae).* The former is common to the clergy and to the *doctores* (like himself); the latter — the administration of the church *(administratio ecclesiae),* which includes the administration of the sacraments *(administratio sacramentorum)* — belongs to the clergy alone (CR 24, 313).

and power. The linkage of *ministerium* with *diakonia* goes back to the Vulgate version of Ephesians 4:12. Although the cognate vocable *diakonos* ("servant") comes in the later New Testament documents to have the technical meaning of "deacon," it would probably be less misleading to translate *diakonia* as "service" rather than "ministry" in twentieth century English.

8. *The sacred ministry as an order in the church.* To give the sacred ministry an exclusively functional character and to eliminate distinctions between "lay people" and "ordained persons," some theologians argue that the Lutheran view of the sacred ministry sees it only as a function or office that exists only in its actual discharge, but never as an order in the church. But the symbolical books see the sacred ministry both as an office *(ministerium; Amt)* and as an order or estate *(ordo; Stand)* within the church (Ap 13, 11-12; 22, 13; 28, 13; SA III, 11, 1; compare SC Table of Duties 1, *heilige Orden und Stände,* "holy orders and estates"). This differentiation does not, of course, carry with it any narrowly clerical or hierarchical implications.

9. *The clergyman as the representation of God and of Christ.* In his proclamation and application of the gospel and his administration of the sacraments, the officiant or celebrant acts in the place of God and in the stead of Christ *(vice Christi),* not in his own person (Ap 7, 28.47; 13, 12).

God preaches through the chosen clergy of the churches (Ap 13, 12 German).

It is God himself who baptizes (LC Baptism 10).

The absolution is to be believed as nothing less than a voice sounding from heaven (Ap 12, 40), that is, from God himself. The confessor who administers absolution is ordinarily an ordained clergyman (Ap 12, 109, "the confession which is to be made to *priests,"* and 176, "the *ministers of the Gospel* should absolve those who are converted"; Tr 60).

The symbolical books imply that the celebrant of the sacrament of the altar will be an ordained clergyman (AC 24, 34 German, "the *priest* and others"; FC SD 7, 32, quoting Luther approvingly, "the *priests* who administer it.")[5] Christ binds his promise and activity in

---

[5] The case (1531) of John Sutel in Göttingen makes it clear that in the mind of the early Lutheran community the mere possession of a call without a public ordination through the laying on of hands did not authorize the recipient to preside over the eucharistic assembly and pronounce the formula of consecration. Luther counsels Sutel to refrain from celebrating the

the sacrament of the altar to the speaking of the celebrant who consecrates the elements. "The words are spoken by the mouth of the *priest*, but by God's power and grace through the words that he speaks, 'This is my body,' the elements set before us in the supper are consecrated" *(gesegnet, consecrantur)* (FC SD 7, 76; see also 77-81).[6]

The immorality or unbelief of an unworthy clergyman does not invalidate the gospel that he preaches or the sacraments that he administers (AC 8, 1-3; Ap 7, 3.19. 28.47; LC Sacrament of the Altar 5.16; FC Ep 12, 27; SD 7, 32.89).

The symbolical books make frequent use of Luke 10:16 (AC 28, 22; Ap 7, 28.47; 12, 40; 28, 18-19): "He who hears you, hears me." They see this passage as imposing on the clergy the obligation of teaching according to Christ's word and not according to human traditions (Ap 28, 19).

10. *Authority (potestas)*. The authority of bishops *(potestas episcoporum)*, the "power" of the keys *(potestas clavium)*, or ecclesiastical authority *(potestas ecclesiastica)* is primarily the responsible public proclamation and application of the gospel and the administration of the sacraments. These are described as the specific tasks and missions not only of an office in the church but of bishops and priests as public persons (Ap 13, 9.12; 28, 12).

The symbolical books accept the distinction between the authority of the clerical order *(potestas ordinis)* and the authority of jurisdiction *(potestas jurisdictionis)*. The former is the competence of the pastor/bishop to do everything that he needs to do in order to proclaim and apply the gospel and to administer the sacraments. The latter is his competence — to be exercised in accordance with the instructions contained in the word of God — to excommunicate notorious evil livers and to reconcile them to the church again when they come to

---

sacrament of the altar until he "publicly before the altar with prayer and the laying on of hands receives from the other clergymen the evidence [of the legitimacy of his status] and authority to celebrate the sacrament of the altar" *(tum publice coram altari a reliquis ministris cum oratione et impositione manuum testimonium accipies et autoritatem coenae tractandae* [WA Br 6, 43—44]).

[6] The word in the Greek original of St. John Chrysostom (347?-407) that the Formula of Concord here renders with *gesegnet* is *metarrhythmizei*, one of the technical terms that the Greek fathers used to describe the sacramental change.

a better mind (Ap 28, 13).[7] The jurisdiction of the pastor/bishop in another place is seen as embracing reconciling sinners, rejecting doctrine that contradicts the gospel, and excluding from the communion of the church by means of the divine word alone, without human coercion, those whose impiety is a matter of public knowledge. Herein the churches must obey them (AC 28, 20-21; SA III, 9; Tr 74).[8]

Minor episcopal functions, such as the administration of confirmation and the consecration of bells, do not, in the view of the symbolical books, require consideration (Tr 73).

11. *The sacred ministry as the identifying "mark" of the church (nota ecclesiae).* Ap 7, 3 identifies the "signs" *(signa)* of the church as the word of God, the response of the church to the divine gift in the form of its "profession" of confidence in him, and the sacraments. Paragraph 20 of the same article calls the "pure teaching of the Gospel and the sacraments" the characteristic marks or "notes" *(notae)* of the church. To be "signs" or "marks" of the church the word of God must obviously be proclaimed and applied and the sacraments administered at concrete times and in concrete places. Since this proclamation and application of the gospel and this administration of the sacraments is precisely the task of the sacred ministry, the sacred ministry itself becomes a "mark" or characteristic of the church.[9]

12. *The sacred ministry and the universal priesthood of the faithful.* The symbolical books nowhere attempt to derive the sacred ministry from the universal priesthood of the faithful.[10] The doctrine of the universal priesthood of believers had receded into minor importance — even for Luther himself — by the time the symbolical books were being framed. The classical prooftext for this teaching, I Peter

---

[7] These *potestates* correspond to the authority to sanctify and the authority to rule.

[8] The authority to proclaim the gospel and to administer sacraments implies the authority to ordain. In the *Loci communes* of 1538 and 1541 Melanchthon includes in the authority of the clerical order *(potestas ordinis)* the command to call — in the broad sense that includes ordaining — ministers *(mandatum vocandi ministros)* (CR 21, 501). So does the *Confessio Saxonica* of 1551 (CR 28, 413, *ordinare ministros rite vocatos,* "to ordain rightly called ministers").

[9] See also Luther, *Von den Conciliis und Kirchen,* WA 50, 632, 35—633, 11.

[10] The Wittenberg ordination formula H of the late 1530s stresses that the sanctification represented by the vocation into the holy and divine ministry is a second sanctification, the first being through the divine word and the sacrament of baptism (WA 38, 424, 23—425, 5.28-34).

2:9, is cited only once in the symbolical books (Tr 69): "Since the church exclusively possesses the priesthood, it certainly has the right to choose and ordain its ministers." [11] It may be that the term "royal priesthood" is here best taken as another designation for the people (that is, the new Israel) of God: "Since only the church is the new Israel of God, it certainly has the right to choose and ordain its ministers." ("Church" here is obviously not to be equated with a local congregation.)

The attitude of the symbolical books toward the Levitical ministry of the Old Testament is superficially ambivalent. They reject the late medieval suggestion that the Christian priesthood perpetuates the Levitical ministry as a function that earns the forgiveness of sins (AC 28, 39.61; Ap 13, 7; 24, 26.53-55), particularly when the obligation of sacerdotal celibacy is inferred from this thesis (Ap 23, 27. 41-42). At the same time the symbolical books identify the sacrifice of the Levites forecast in Malachi 3:3 with the sacrificial activity of those who preach the gospel in the New Covenant and with the good works that this proclamation produces (Romans 15:16) (Ap 24, 34).[12] The rejection of the Levitical ministry would seem to involve only the rejection of the misunderstanding and distortion of the function of the Levitical ministry as a service that earned forgiveness of sins. Again, the sacred ministry of the New Covenant is not bound to members of a single tribe functioning exclusively in one temple in a single Holy City; nor do they function by the leave of a single person, the bishop of Rome (Tr 25-26).

13. *The spiritual paternity of the clergy.* The clergy are spiritual fathers (LC Decalog 158-59). The use of *Pfarrkinder* (literally, "parish children") to describe the parishioners in the symbolical books has the fatherhood of the clergy as its correlative.

14. *The unitary character of the sacred ministry.* The symbolical

---

[11] The only other passage in Melanchthon's works known to this writer in which the church's authority to choose and ordain clergymen is related to I Peter 2:9 is in his *Loci communes* of 1535. Here he argues not only from the cited passage, but also from Ephesians 4:8. The priesthood *(sacerdotium)* in this passage is the authority to administer the gospel *(jus administrandi evangelii);* thus it includes the church's right and obligation to administer the gospel by calling fit persons into the service of the gospel (CR 21, 505).

[12] This is, of course, wholly consistent with the transfer in I Peter 2:9 of the title "a kingdom of priests and a holy nation" of Exodus 19:6 from the Israel of the Old Covenant with its Levitical priesthood to the Israel of the New Covenant.

books see the sacred ministry as unitary. There is basically only one holy order. That is the presbyterate-episcopate of the New Testament.

The symbolical books never call into question the existence of the sacred ministry itself by divine right *(jure divino)*. What they do call into question is the postapostolic differentiation of grades within it by the separation of the presbyterate from the episcopate and, by implication, the subsequent introduction of the initially lay office of deacon into the major orders of the sacred ministry. These developments, they insist, exist only by human right *(jure humano)*.

Regardless of their title, all ordained clergymen have the same basic authority to discharge the duties of their office (AC 28, 8.21; Tr 60-61.74). The terminology of the symbolical books reflects a recognition of an inevitable hierarchical structuring of any social institution like the church, but this does not have to do with inherent spiritual authority. They use the term "bishop" both for the head of a medieval diocese [13] and — on the analogy of the episcopal "parish-sees" *(paroikiai)* of the first three centuries — for the chief pastor of a town. They also use "rector" *(Pfarrherr);* "presbyter"; "pastor" (Tr 65); "preacher" (*Prediger,* especially to designate assistant clergymen); "priest" *(sacerdos/Priester);* and "minister" *([Kirchen]/diener).*

15. *The diaconate and minor orders.* By the sixteenth century the diaconate had become a purely vestigial stage in the "course of honors" *(cursus honorum)* without any real function in the church in the Holy Roman Empire. The term *diaconus/Diakon* in the Lutheran documents of the sixteenth century (for example, Ap 13, 11 German) must be understood as referring to ordained priests serving as curates or assistants to the rector of a parish.

The symbolical books were even less under constraint to discuss the lower orders of the clergy. These too had by the sixteenth century become only nominal stages in the process of becoming a priest. The tonsure was frequently received in order to secure the valuable legal and canonical immunities that attached to clerical status, with no intention of taking higher orders.

16. *The adiaphoristic nature of church polity.* As long as the divinely ordained necessity of the sacred ministry is recognized and

---

[13] Not all sixteenth century bishops were in episcopal orders, however. For example, both Archbishop Gebhard II von Waldburg (1547-1601) of Cologne and his successor in the archsee, Archbishop Ernest of Bavaria (1554-1612), were only in priest's orders.

provided for, polity is an adiaphoron as far as the symbolical books are concerned.

Although the hierarchical structuring of the church is of human right only, the symbolical books affirm their preference for episcopal polity (Ap 14, 1.5). The ideal is a universal episcopalism in which all bishops are equal in office, united in doctrine, belief, sacraments, prayer, and works of love (SA II, 4, 9).

17. *The authority of bishops.* Bishops have the right to establish regulations for the government of the church and for worship in the interest of good order, and the congregations and subordinate clergy are bound in charity to obey such canons, but the bishops have no authority to make the salvation of the faithful dependent on obedience to such regulations nor may they properly institute any regulation and declare that observance of it earns forgiveness of sins (AC 28, 30-64). Change is of the nature of humanly established canons, and even the ceremonial injunctions of the Council of Jerusalem and the liturgical directives of the apostles were temporary in character (AC 28, 53-54.65-66; Ap 28, 16). The Apology sees the issue precisely as the question if the bishops have by divine right the authority to make laws the observance of which is useful for the attainment of everlasting life (Ap 28, 6). This it denies.

The authority of the bishops dare never conflict with the gospel, and if the bishops teach or enjoin something that does contradict the gospel (AC 28, 34), God has commanded the faithful not to obey (*ibid.*, 23-28, quoting the sacred scriptures, canon law, and St. Augustine; see also Tr 60-82).

18. *The secular power of hierarchs.* The symbolical books urge ecclesiastical authorities in the Holy Roman Empire — especially prince-bishops and prince-abbots — who also possess temporal power not to confuse the two (AC 28, 1-2). Both types of authority derive from God, but their ends are different (*ibid.*, 10-17). Pastors and bishops have no right to arrogate authority in temporal matters to themselves. Specifically, they have no divinely given authority in matters affecting matrimony and taxation (AC 28, 29; Tr 77-78.80-81; SC Marriage Booklet 1).

19. *Apostolic succession.* Without discussing the necessity of a succession of ministers, the symbolical books operate explicitly with the concept of a *de facto* succession of ordained ministers (SA III, 10; Tr 72, *adhibitis suis pastoribus*, "using their own pastors for this pur-

pose").[14] It is noteworthy in this connection that St. Jerome regards all presbyters as well as all bishops as "successors of the apostles" *(apostolorum successores).*[15] The bishops — that is, the pastors of town-dioceses — are the successors of the apostles in the government of the church (SA II, 4, 9).

The political situation in the sixteenth century throughout northern Europe — the domains of the King of Sweden excepted — made it a practical impossibility for the adherents of the Augsburg Confession to perpetuate the historic episcopate with apostolic succession.

20. *The papacy.* The papacy, in the sense of the Roman bishop's claim to universal primacy of jurisdiction, is a historical phenomenon that exists by human right only, not by divine right (Tr 1-21).

The bishop of Rome is by divine right the bishop and pastor only of the church of Rome. In addition he is the pastor of those who of their own will or through a political arrangement — that is, in both cases, by human right — have attached themselves to him (SA II, 4, 1). The papacy is not a universal institution; the Eastern churches have never been under the pope. In the patriarchate of the West, the medieval papacy did not exist for at least the first 500 years (*ibid.*, 4-5). The Smalcald Articles are dubious about the value of the papacy even as a humanly instituted symbol of Christian unity (*ibid.*, 7-8). As long as the pope insists on the last seventeen words of *Unam Sanctam,*[16] he is the antichrist of II Thessalonians 2:4 (*ibid.*, 4.10-13).

There is no consensus of the fathers that would refer the rock of St. Matthew 16:18 to St. Peter, according to the Treatise on the Authority and Primacy of the Pope. But the Treatise agrees that St. Peter is the rock on whom the church is built, although he has this foundation-status because he is a "minister." Since the other apostles (and all clergy) received the same authority that Christ conferred on

---

14 The sentence containing the words *adhibitis suis pastoribus* regrettably disappeared in the process of printing and it is missing in the Latin Book of Concord of 1584. The words in question are missing in the German translation by Guy Dietrich (1506-1549) and in Theodore G. Tappert, editor, *The Book of Concord* (Philadelphia: Fortress Press, 1959), p. 332.

15 *Letter 146 (85) to Evangelus,* 1 (Migne, *Patrologia latina,* 22, 1194).

16 "Further, we declare, state [and] define that for every human being it is absolutely necessary for salvation to be under the bishop of Rome *(Porro subesse Romano pontifici omni humanae creaturae declaramus, dicimus, diffinimus omnino esse de necessitate salutis)*" (Denzinger-Schönmetzer, *Enchiridion Symbolorum,* 33rd ed. (Hereafter cited as DS) (Freiburg: Herder, 1965), 875.

the prince of the apostles, "upon this rock" really means "upon this ministry" (Tr 22-29).

While Christ commanded St. Peter to shepherd and rule the church by means of the divine word, this conferred on him no special superiority, since St. Peter had the word of God only in common with the other apostles (Tr 30).

21. *The sacramental nature of order.* The term "sacrament" is applicable both to the sacred ministry itself and to ordination by the laying on of hands (Ap 13, 9-13).

22. *Ordination jure divino.* Ordination is effective *(rata)* by divine right (Tr 65). Obviously this implies as a lesser included principle that ordination itself is by divine right. Ordination can be called an adiaphoron only in a most narrow and technical sense.

The church institutes clergymen by divine command (Ap 13, 12). Because the authority to minister the gospel exists wherever the church is, the church necessarily possesses the authority to choose, call, and ordain ministers (Tr 67). The churches are compelled *(coguntur)* to exercise this authority (Tr 72).[17]

The need for ordination that the adherents of the Augsburg Confession felt increasingly from the 1530s onward is reflected in the Ordination Register of Saint Mary's Church, Wittenberg, which provides data on 1,979 clergymen ordained between 1537 and 1560. Of these at least 1,025 (possibly as many as 1,069) are known to have been recruited from other professions and crafts, because the former profession or craft of the person ordained is listed; ninety-two were former manual laborers.[18] It is possible that many more of the 900-plus other ordinands had been recruited from other professions and crafts, since it is unlikely that all of them were university graduates.

The necessity of ordination was the issue in the famed "Freder ordination controversy" (1550—1556), which involved primarily John Freder (1510—1562) and the Pomeranian reformer John Knipstro (1497—1556). A general synod of the clergy of Pomerania decided the controversy in 1556 by ruling that "the calling or election of a per-

---

[17] Preaching on Acts 13:1 ff., Luther had declared in 1524: "One must not act on God's behalf unless one is called and ordained by God. . . . I preach in that name, because I have been ordained thereto *(Nemo in causa Dei agere debet, nisi sit vocatus et ordinatus a Deo. . . . Ego praedico in eo nomine, quia ordinatus ad hoc)"* (WA 17, 1, 508, 10-11; 509, 16-17).

[18] See *Die Bekenntnisschriften der evangelisch-lutherischen Kirche* (Göttingen: Vandenhoeck & Ruprecht, 6th ed., 1967), p. 501, n. 1.

son *(vocatio vel electio personae)* must be distinguished from the ordination" and by committing itself to "the general rule of Luther" that "there must be a rightful vocation and ordination to the sacred ministry wherever the church of Christ is." The Wittenberg faculty, with Melanchthon concurring, rejected the position that ordination was an adiaphoron and held that Freder's vocation did not constitute an ordination.[19]

23. *The essentiality of ordination.* Only persons who are duly chosen, called, and ordained *(rite vocatus, ordentlicher Beruf)* are competent publicly and responsibly to proclaim the gospel and to administer the sacraments (AC 14).

The verbs in AC 14 *(debeat/soll)* allow no option; they are the same verbs which describe the indispensable relation of good works to faith in AC 6. They have the force of the modern English "must" rather than "should." [20]

The *docent* ("they teach") with which the article begins, along with the location of the article among the doctrinal articles rather than among the reform (or "abuse") articles, indicates that the thesis of the article is a dogmatic statement.

That AC 14 implies ordination is clear from a number of facts:

First, it is the response of the Lutheran theologians to the charge that John Eck (1486—1543) made in his *404 Propositions* that the Lutherans denied the existence of the sacrament of orders, called it a figment of human invention, and asserted that any layman at all can consecrate churches, confirm children, and so on.[21] The Lutheran response is that laymen are not admitted to the really crucial tasks of publicly and responsibly proclaiming the gospel and of administering the sacraments.

---

[19] James Henry Balthasar, *Erste Sammlung einiger zur Pommerischen Kirchen-Historie gehörigen Schriften* (Greifswald: Andreas Buss, 1723), p. 114. See the comprehensive excursus on the controversy in Hellmut Lieberg, *Amt und Ordination bei Luther und Melanchthon* (Göttingen: Vandenhoeck & Ruprecht, 1962), pp. 360—71.

[20] See, for example, the letter *Ejus exemplo* of Innocent III to the archbishop of Tarragona (the profession of faith of Durandus of Huesca) (1208): *"Non potest nec debet eucharistiam consecrare . . . nisi sit presbyter . . . regulariter ordinatus* (No one can or may consecrate the eucharist . . . unless he is a priest . . . regularly ordained)" (DS 794).

[21] Wilhelm Gussmann, *D. Johann Ecks Vierhundertvier Artikel zum Reichstag von Augsburg 1530* (Kassel: Edmund Pillardy, 1930), nos. 267 to 268, pp. 134 and 177—78.

Second, the word *rite* in *rite vocatus* implies in the normal terminology of the sixteenth century a formal ordination as something over and above a mere calling.[22] Both *vocatio* ("calling") and *ordinatio* ("ordination") are extensively used in this period to describe the whole process of election and ordination.[23]

Third, the "canonical form of church government" *(politia canonica)* which Ap 28, 12 "does not reprehend," includes ordination.

Fourth, in 1530 there was still a ray of hope that the growing schism might be healed and that the bishops might consent to permit the proclamation of the gospel. Under these circumstances the Augsburg Confession would not have proposed pretermitting ordination.

Fifth, the *Confutatio pontificia* accepted Article 14 in principle. It would not have done so if it had understood the article as suggesting that ordination was not necessary. The particular point on which the *Confutatio* insisted was that a bishop perform the ordination. This is clear from the Apology on Article 14. The first draft formulates the proviso in these words: "that ordination be performed by bishops *(ut ordinatio fiat ab episcopis)."* In its final form the Apology restates the proviso: "as long as we use canonical ordination *(si tamen utamur ordinatione canonica)."* The Apology makes it clear that it has no quarrel with ordination or even with episcopacy, but that episcopal ordination is not available to the proponents of the Augsburg Confession. The implication is that they may have no alternative but to avail themselves of ordination by clergymen in presbyter's orders.

---

[22] See Hans Asmussen, *Warum noch lutherische Kirche? Ein Gespräch mit dem Augsburgischen Bekenntnis* (Stuttgart: Evangelisches Verlagswerk, 1949), pp. 182—86; Ernst Sommerlath, *"Amt und allgemeines Priestertum," Schriften des Theologischen Konvents Augsburgischen Bekenntnisses,* 5 (Berlin: Lutherisches Verlagshaus, 1953), 57-58.64; and Martin Dörne, *Lutherisches Pfarramt: Rechenschaft und Wegweisung* (Leipzig: A. Deichert, 1937), pp. 14—15. For a medieval example of the use of *rite* see chapter 1, *De fide catholica,* of Lateran IV (1215): "[*Hoc*] *sacramentum nemo potest conficere nisi sacerdos qui* rite *fuerit ordinatus* (No one can confect [this] sacrament except a priest who has been duly ordained)" (DS 802).

[23] A not untypical statement is one that Luther makes in a sermon of 1524: *"Sed nos qui jam habemus ministeria commendabimus in nostrum ministerium. . . . Si . . . scimus pium hominem, extrahimus eum et damus in virtute verbi quod habemus auctoritatem praedicandi verbum et dandi sacramenta. Hoc est ordinare.* (But we who already have ministries will recommend [others] into our ministry. . . . If . . . we know a devout man, we take him out and by virtue of the Word that we possess we give him the authority to proclaim the Word and to administer the sacraments. This is what it means to ordain)" (WA 15, 721, 1-5).

114

The number of such ordinations prior to 1530 was very small; indeed, regular ordinations in the Church of the Augsburg Confession did not begin until 1535 and on a large scale not until 1537.

Sixth, Ap 13, 11-12 relates the sacred ministry to ordination by using the term *ordo* for both.

Seventh, the edition of 1540 explicates Melanchthon's intention by adding after *vocatus:* "as St. Paul commends St. Titus to appoint presbyters city by city *(sicut et Paulus praecipit Tito, ut in civitatibus presbyteros constituat)*" (CR 26, 360).[24]

Eighth, when the Greek translation of the Augsburg Confession was drawn up in 1559, it added to *rite vocatus* in Article 14 the words *pros ten hyperesian* ("to the ministry"). In 1584 the Lutheran theologians of the University of Tübingen published their correspondence with His All-Holiness Jeremiah II, the ecumenical patriarch. In 1576 Jeremiah had indicated his understanding of the Augsburg Confession by paraphrasing the Greek translation at this point: *ei mē hypo tōn tachthentōn enthesmōs pros tautēn tēn hypēresian* ("except by those who have lawfully been instituted for this service"). In this sense he approved the article. Martin Crusius (1526—1607) significantly translated this phrase into Latin in these words: *nisi rite vocatus et ordinatus ad hanc functionem* ("unless he has been duly called and ordained to this function"). In 1577 Luke Osiander the Elder (1534—1604) and Crusius included in their summary of the areas where Jeremiah and the Lutherans agreed, the thesis "that it must not be granted to anyone to take to himself the office of teaching or administering the holy sacraments in the church unless he be lawfully called *(me nomikos klēthenta)*, but that in a case of necessity even a layman can rightfully baptize." How they understood this is apparent from their de-

---

[24] The bearing of this becomes clearer from another statement of Melanchthon in his disputation *De politia ecclesiae seu ministerio et ordinationibus* (date uncertain): *"Jus vocandi et eligendi ministros pertinent non tantum ad populum, sed Paulus jubet Titum constituere presbyteros, et Timotheo scribit: Nemo cito manum impone. Necesse est igitur, pastores a pastoribus ordinari. . . . Pugnat cum jure divino et cum veteri ecclesia dēmokratia in qua populus ad se rapit electionem, sine judicio et approbatione pastorum.* (The right of calling and choosing ministers [of the church] belongs not only to the people, but St. Paul directs St. Titus to appoint presbyters, and he writes to St. Timothy, 'Do not lay hands on anybody rashly.' It is accordingly necessary that pastors be ordained by pastors. . . . The kind of democracy in which the people snatch the election [of clergymen] to themselves without the judgment and the approbation of the pastors is in conflict both with the divine law and with the ancient church)" (CR 12, 490).

scription of a Lutheran ordination: "In a well-attended assembly of the people, after a sermon has been preached and a number of prayers said pertaining to this matter, the candidates are ordained *(cheirotonountai)* by the bishop of the place, with one or more sacred ministers assisting, and then [the newly ordained clergyman] assumes the care of the church committed to him." [25]

24. *The ordination rite and the imposition of hands.* Ordination need not be an elaborate ceremony. Originally ordination was a simple rite in which a bishop laid hands on the candidate (Tr 70).[26] Ap 13, 12 sees the imposition of hands in ordination as an integral part of what it is ready to call "the sacrament of orders." [27]

25. *The minister of ordination.* The differentiation of grade between bishop and presbyters is not by divine right (Ap 14, 1; Tr 65), and therefore by divine right presbyters have the authority to ordain. An ordination that a pastor performs in his own church upon qualified candidates is valid by divine right (Tr 65).

When canonical bishops have become heretics or refuse to ordain,

---

[25] *Acta et scripta theologorum Wirtembergensium et Patriarchae Constantinopolitani D. Hieremiae, quae utrique ab anno MDLXXVI usque ad annum MDLXXXI de Augustana Confessione inter se miserunt, graece et latine ab iisdem theologis edita* (Wittenberg: Haeredes Johannis Cratonis, 1584), pp. 104—105.148.176.

[26] The "custom" referred to in this passage was not ordination but the mode of electing and ordaining/consecrating the pastor/bishop. The first antithesis is between the election of the pastor by the people of the parish/diocese and the arbitrary selection of the pastor by higher authority. The second antithesis is between the simple primitive rite and the elaborate ceremonies into which ordinations and consecrations had developed in the late Middle Ages. The Wittenberg ordination rite of the late 1530s (WA 38, 423—33) called for the ordination to take place within a celebration of the holy eucharist and consisted of seven elements: (a) corporate prayer for laborers in the Lord's harvest; (b) *Veni Sancte Spiritus* with versicle, response, and the Whitsunday collect; (c) lessons; (d) obligation of the ordinands to the sacred ministry; (e) imposition of hands by the ordinator and the assistant ministers with the Our Father and an invocation of the Holy Spirit upon the ordinands; (f) "Go then and tend the flock" (I Peter 5:2-4) as a votum; (g) blessing of the newly ordained clergymen with the sign of the holy cross. There is some variation in parts and sequence among the four surviving rites.

[27] Compare Luther's statement in his *Commentary on Genesis* (on 28:17): *"Impositio manuum non est traditio humana; sed Deus facit et ordinat ministros* (The laying on of hands is not a human tradition; on the contrary, God makes and ordains ministers [of the church])" (WA 43, 600, 25-26).

"the churches are compelled by divine right to ordain pastors and ministers, using their own pastors for this purpose *(adhibitis suis pastoribus).*" Significant is the bracketing of "calling, choosing, and ordaining" under the singular noun *jus* in Tr 67 and of "choosing and ordaining" again under the same singular noun in paragraphs 67, 69, and 72.

Ordination by the existing bishops is permissible for the sake of love and good order, but it is not necessary (SA III, 10, 1). Under the circumstances, the adherents of the Augsburg Confession ought and propose to ordain fit persons to the sacred ministry. This procedure conforms to the primitive practice of the church at Alexandria, as St. Jerome reports, while canon law affirms that the validity even of a heretical ordination must be conceded *(ibid., 3).*

26. *The "ineradicable mark" (character indelebilis) of ordination.* The symbolical books do not address themselves to the somewhat metaphysical question of the "ineradicable mark" *(character indelebilis)* of ordination. In actual practice, the ecclesiastical authorities in the churches of the Augsburg Confession did not reordain those who had received holy orders in the medieval church. The present writer knows of no instance in the sixteenth century of the reordination of a clergyman who had received holy orders in the Church of the Augsburg Confession, had laicized or apostatized, and then sought readmission to the exercise of the sacred ministry.

27. *The competence of laymen as sacramental ministers.* While the ordinary minister of baptism and reconciliation/absolution is an ordained clergyman, the symbolical books, following a pseudo-Augustinian tradition of medieval canon law, allow a layman to be the extraordinary minister of these sacraments in a life-and-death emergency (Tr 67).

It is noteworthy that this passage does not accord a layman the authority to consecrate the eucharistic elements even in a life-and-death emergency. That a layman may not presume to do so is not in the premises wholly an argument from silence. The eucharist is not as indispensably necessary as baptism or reconciliation with the church (absolution).[28]

---

[28] For that reason the opinion of the Church of the Augsburg Confession of this period holds that a layman may not celebrate the eucharist even in an emergency (WA Br 7, 338—39, 365—66; WA TR 5,621, no. 6361). The assertion has repeatedly been made (for example, by Robert E. McNally, *The Unreformed Church* [New York: Sheed and Ward, 1965], p. 134, and by Clyde Leonard Manschreck, *Melanchthon, the Quiet Reformer* [New York: Abingdon Press, 1958], p. 72) that Melanchthon, the lay author of

The symbolical books concede to matrimony the status of a lesser sacrament (Ap 13, 14). While they do not discuss the question of the minister of marriage, Lutheran theology has always held that the contracting partners are the ministers of matrimony. The clergyman who presides at the liturgical exchange of their expressions functions (1) as a witness and (2) as the public representative of the church competent to impart the "priestly blessing" *(benedictio sacerdotalis)*, as it came to be called.

BIBLIOGRAPHY

Asheim, Ivar, and Victor R. Gold, eds. *Episcopacy in the Lutheran Church? Studies in the Development and Definition of the Office of Church Leadership.* Philadelphia: Fortress Press, 1970. Especially pp. 1—71, 155—174.

Blum, Georg Günter. *Tradition und Sukzession: Studien zum Normbegriff des Apostolischen von Paulus bis Irenäus.* Berlin: Lutherisches Verlagshaus, 1963.

Bouman, Herbert J. A. "The Ministry in the Lutheran Confessions." In: Erwin L. Lueker, ed., *Studies in Church and Ministry,* Vol. 4. St. Louis, Mo.: Concordia Seminary, 1968, pp. 257—77. (A copy of this unpublished manuscript is in the Fuerbringer Memorial Library of Concordia Seminary, St. Louis.)

Brunner, Peter. *"Vom Amt des Bischofs."* Schriften des Theologischen Konvents Augsburgischen Bekenntnisses, Vol. 9. Berlin: Lutherisches Verlagshaus, 1955, pp. 5—77.

Brunotte, Wilhelm. *Das geistliche Amt bei Luther.* Berlin: Lutherisches Verlagshaus, 1959.

Brunstäd, Friedrich. *Theologie der lutherischen Bekenntnisschriften.* Edited by Karl Janssen. Gütersloh: C. Bertelsmann Verlag, 1951, pp. 114—34, 198—221.

Fagerberg, Holsten. *Die Theologie der lutherischen Bekenntnisschriften von 1529 bis 1537.* Translated by Gerhard Klose. Göttingen: Vandenhoeck & Ruprecht, 1965, pp. 238—63.

Fraenkel, Peter. *Testimonia Patrum: The Function of the Patristic Argument in the Theology of Philip Melanchthon.* Geneva: Librairie E. Droz, 1961. Especially pp. 110—61.

the Augsburg Confession, the Apology, and the Tractate, presumed to celebrate the eucharist in Wittenberg in 1521. This assertion is based on a misunderstanding of a Latin account of Melanchthon's attendance with his students at a celebration of the eucharist in which both kinds were distributed to the communicants. Melanchthon says explicitly of himself: "I do not possess the authority to administer the sacraments *(Non habeo administrationem sacramentorum)"* (CR 24, 313).

Heubach, Joachim. *Die Ordination zum Amt der Kirche.* Berlin: Lutherisches Verlagshaus, 1956.

Heyl, Kornelius Freiherr von. *Ordination zum heiligen Predigtamt und apostolische Sukzession: Ein Prolegomenon zu einer Neubestimmung auf die Lehre vom geistlichen Amt.* Bleckmar-über-Soltau: Verlag "Lutherische Blätter," 1962.

Josefson, Ruben. "The Ministry as an Office in the Church." In: Anders Nygren, ed., *This Is the Church.* Translated by Carl C. Rasmussen. Philadelphia: Muhlenberg Press, 1952.

Kimme, August. *"Doctrina und ordo ecclesiasticus nach lutherischem Verständnis."* In: *Schriften des Theologischen Konvents Augsburgischen Bekenntnisses,* Vol. 8: *Konfession — Union — Oekumene.* Berlin: Lutherisches Verlagshaus, 1955, pp. 54—78.

Kramm, Hans-Herbert. *Bischof, Pastor und Gemeinde: Die lutherische Lehre vom Amt, gesehen vom Standpunkt eines deutschen Lutheraners in England.* Berlin: Lutherisches Verlagshaus, 1954.

Lerche, Johann Heinrich. *"Das Bischofsamt in der evangelisch-lutherischen Kirche."* In: Wilhelm Stählin and others, *Das Amt der Einheit: Grundlegendes zur Theologie des Bischofsamtes.* Stuttgart: Schwaben-Verlag, 1964, pp. 35—76.

Lieberg, Hellmut. *Amt und Ordination bei Luther und Melanchthon.* Göttingen: Vandenhoeck & Ruprecht, 1962.

Lieberg, Hellmut. *"Die Vollmacht des Amtes und der Ämter, Differenzierung und Zuordnung."* *Sanct Athanasius,* 17 (1966), 1—7.

Lindbeck, George. "The Sacramentality of the Ministry: Karl Rahner and a Protestant View." In: Friedrich Wilhelm Kantzenbach and Vilmos Vajta, eds., *Oecumenica: An Annual Symposium of Ecumenical Research — 1967.* Minneapolis: Augsburg Publishing House, 1967, pp. 282—301.

Persson, Per Erik. *Kyrkans ämbete som Kristus-representation: En kritisk analys av nyare ämbetsteologi.* Lund: C. W. K. Gleerup, 1961. Especially pp. 267—327.

Roloff, Jürgen. *Apostolat — Verkündigung — Kirche.* Gütersloh: Gütersloher Verlagshaus Gerd Mohn, 1965.

Schlink, Edmund. *The Coming Christ and the Coming Church.* Philadelphia: Muhlenberg Press, 1961, pp. 241—69.

Siegwalt, Gérard. *"Sacerdoce ministériel et ministère pastorale d'après les livres symboliques luthériens."* *Verbum Caro,* 22 (1968), 16—35.

THE ROMAN CATHOLIC DOCTRINE OF THE COMPETENT MINISTER OF THE EUCHARIST IN ECUMENICAL PERSPECTIVE

BY HARRY J. McSORLEY

I

We have chosen the rather restricted theme suggested by our title for two reasons. First, an adequate treatment of the Catholic church's doctrine on priestly ministry in general would have to be far more extensive than the present study (it is a ministry of the word and *seven* sacraments!) and would have to include a much fuller statement on the sacrament of ordination than we offer in this paper. Secondly, this more modest theme comes to grips indirectly — but quite definitely — with one of the most neuralgic problems of ecumenical theology: the Roman Catholic attitude toward the celebration of the Lord's supper by separated Christian communities.

Encouraging progress has been made toward unity in the expression of the Christian faith concerning the eucharist as sacrament and as sacrifice in the World Council of Churches, in the Consultation on Church Union and in the Lutheran-Roman Catholic theological consultation in the United States. Nevertheless, for Orthodox, Roman Catholic and many Anglican Christians a serious problem remains: that of the competence of a person to lead the eucharist who has not been ordained by a bishop who is himself rightly consecrated.

As the *Decree on Ecumenism* of Vatican II puts it: ". . . [We] believe that especially because of the lack [*defectus*] of the sacrament of orders . . . [the separated Churches and ecclesial communities in the West] have not preserved the genuine and total reality of the eucharistic mystery." [1]

II

From the earliest years of the sub-apostolic church concern was shown for the minister of the eucharist: "Let no man do aught pertaining to the church apart from the bishop. Let that eucharist be considered valid [*bebaia*] which is under the bishop or him to whom he commits it . . . It is not lawful [*exon*] apart from the bishop either to baptize, or to hold a love-feast [*agapen*]. But whatsoever he approves, that also is well-pleasing to God, that everything which you do may be secure and valid [*bebaion*]." [2]

Excursus: "Valid" and "Invalid," "Licit" and "Illicit"

In contemporary Catholic usage (canon law and theology) these terms have relatively clear meanings. A valid sacrament is one in which the minimum conditions are met on the part of the minister (in the case of matrimony, ministers), the recipient(s) and the rite itself (water, not corn syrup; bread, not cornflakes; words recognized by the church as expressive of Christ's intention). If any one of these minimum conditions is lacking, the sacrament is invalid, i. e., it is not a sacrament officially recognized by the church.

Because something is regarded by the church as a condition for validity, we need not suppose that this is a condition imposed *iure divino* and therefore unchangeable. The church has set human, canonical conditions for validity, such as restriction of holy orders to the male sex, the requirement that Catholics are to be married before a priest, etc.

A further distinction: a sacrament can be validly administered and received, yet, due to continuing hardness of heart toward a neigh-

---

1 *The Documents of Vatican II,* ed. W. Abbott (New York, 1966), p. 364, n. 22. Cf. our essay "Protestant Eucharistic Reality and Lack of Orders," *The Ecumenist* (July-August 1967), 68-75.

2 Ignatius of Antioch, *Letter to the Smyrneans,* ch. 8, 1 f. in *A New Eusebius,* ed. J. Stevenson (London, 1960), p. 48; cf. Rouet de Journel [=RJ], *Enchiridion Patristicum,* 18th ed. (Freiburg, 1953), p. 22 n. 65. The *Epistle of Clement to the Corinthians,* ch. 44, 4, likewise indicates episcopal leadership of the eucharist. In the *Didache,* however, prophets seem not only to share the role of leading the eucharist with bishops, but also to have a certain precedence: ch. 15, 1; cf. Küng, *The Church* (New York, 1967), pp. 382 and 409.

bor, lack of religious intent, or some other obstacle in an adult recipient, the healing and forgiving grace of the sacrament is not received. In this case we speak of a valid, but unfruitful reception of the sacrament. Cf. Schillebeeckx, *Christ: The Sacrament of the Encounter with God* (New York, 1963), pp. 147-52; Luther, *Large Catechism*, V, 9 f., 14.

It is well known that in the Bull *Apostolicae Curae* Pope Leo XIII declared Anglican *orders* invalid (DS 3319: *"actas irritas prorsus fuisse et esse omninoque nullas"*). This clearly says something about the status of Anglican ministers of the eucharist who have not otherwise received valid orders. Yet it is highly significant that, in the passage cited above from Vatican II, the council did *not declare* that the *Lord's supper* celebrated by Anglicans or by other Christian communities in the West *is invalid,* which was the view commonly held by Catholics prior to the council. Cf. our essay mentioned in note 1.

A sacrament is administered or received illicitly when some other condition established by the human law of the church is not met. The eucharistic fast is an example of a condition of liceity (cf. canon 858, par. 1), as is the requirement that catechumens be properly instructed prior to baptism (canon 752, par. 1). Disregard of these meaningful church laws could be sinful and the sacrament would be illicitly, though validly — but possibly unfruitfully — received.

In Ignatius of Antioch we do not find the terminological precision between valid and licit that is available today. Striving to manifest the New Testament teaching on unity among Christ's followers in the church and seeking to avoid the divisions and disorder that have no place in the Christian community, Ignatius insists on participation in one eucharist presided over by one bishop with his presbyterium and deacons — or by someone else with his permission: *Letter to the Smyrneans,* ch. 8, 1 f. Cf. also his *Letter to the Philadelphians,* ch. 3, 2 and ch. 4; M. Jourjon, *"La présidence de l'eucharistie chez Ignace d'Antioche,"* Lumière et Vie 16 (1967), 26-32; J. McCue, "Bishops, Priests, and Presbyters in Ignatius," *Theological Studies* 28 (1967), 828-34. In the latter essay McCue asks whether the apparent contradiction between Ignatius and Trent can be overcome by modifying the traditional interpretation of Trent. As will be seen, we answer that question affirmatively.

Ignatius is not interested in pronouncing on the validity or invalidity of the eucharist according to our understanding of those categories. He teaches that the quality of legal validity (*bebaia;* Schlier, *Kittel,* I, 603; Lampe, *Patristic Greek Lexicon,* pp. 294 f.) belongs to that eucharist led by a bishop or his appointee. Only this eucharist serves the unity of the church. The same is true of baptism. Only that baptism (or *agape* = eucharist?) is lawful or permitted (*exon;* Behm, *Kittel,* II, 557 — as distinct from physically possible; Arndt-Gingrich, *Greek-English Lexicon of the New Testament,* pp. 274 f.) in the church which is done with the approval of the bishop. For Ignatius, only such approved or "legal" acts of worship and liturgical fellowship foster unity and ward off schisms.

Unquestionably we find here the highest regard for lawful eucharistic celebration, i. e., one conducted in harmony with and approved by the bishop. But we do not find in Ignatius the answer to the questions: what about other unauthorized or illegal liturgies? Are they "invalid" in the contemporary sense, in the sense that they are simply not sacraments?

The question: can any layman administer baptism or can any Christian lead the eucharist in cases of need is one that does not occur to Ignatius. His concern is that *whoever* leads the eucharist should do so with the approval of the bishop. Not to do so would be unauthorized or illegal, since the unity of the church would suffer. Ignatius thus seems to use the terms *bebaia* and *exon* approximately in the way that "licit" is used today. He *may* have meant by these terms that nothing at all happens sacramentally if an unauthorized person baptizes or that the bread and wine do not become the body and blood of Jesus if someone other than the bishop or his appointee tries to lead the eucharist. On the basis of his writings, however, one cannot verify such a hypothesis.

The inner-Catholic debate over re-baptism and re-ordination of heretics and schismatics that began in the third century led to some terminological clarification. One theological — if not terminological — clarification that emerged was Augustine's distinction between the sacrament itself — which depends neither on the minister's holiness nor his faith — and the effect or use of the sacrament. *De baptismo,* VI, 1, 1; IV, 17, 24; I, 1, 2. This seems to correspond to the contemporary distinction between the validity and the fruitfulness of a sacrament.

According to Augustine, both baptism and ordination are sacraments and both involve a consecration. Once received neither is lost and neither is repeated. *Contra ep. Parmeniani,* II, 13, 28 and 30; RJ 1617 and 1620.

Augustine did not always speak so analytically. He could thus say of sinful bishops and priests: they are "not bishops," "not priests," or they are not "true priests." Cf. Y. Congar, *"Quelques expressions traditionelles du service chrétien,"* in *L'Episcopat et L'Eglise Univer-selle* (Paris, 1964), pp. 101 f., and K. Mörsdorf, *Die Entwicklung der Zweigliedrigkeit der kirchlichen Hierarchie, Münch. Theol. Zeits.* (1952), 1-16.

We find Augustine speaking of an "illicit" administration of baptism when a layman baptizes apart from necessity. This is a *"delictum,"* since it involves usurping the office [*munus*] of another. But what was administered cannot be said not to have been administered. *Contra ep. Parm.,* II, 13, 29; RJ 1618.

Mörsdorf, *art. cit.,* points out that there were many cases where canon law prescriptions pertaining to ordination — even that which emanated from the Council of Nicaea (canon 2, forbidding the ordination of neophytes on the basis of I Timothy 3:6 f.) were ignored (Ambrose!) without resulting in a declaration of nullity that would necessitate re-ordination.

Much more forceful than Nicaea was the sixth canon of the Council of Chalcedon, which declared that absolute ordination of priests and deacons (i. e., without attachment to a particular church, city, etc.) was *akyron.* One cannot conclude from this, says Mörsdorf, that Chalcedon regarded such ordinations as invalid in the sense that they are non-ordinations. He argues that the intent of the council is that they are *practically* invalid in that the one so ordained is assigned to no one and therefore, as the canon says, can work nowhere *(meda-mou).* The ordination is therefore *"vacua"* as one Latin version (the Hispana) of Chalcedon puts it.

Highly important is Mörsdorf's observation: "The use of the words *akyros, irritus, vacuus, invalidus, nullus,* was, neither before nor for a long time after Chalcedon, sufficiently precise or uniform." If this is true of these words that to some extent have a legal or canonical meaning how much more ambiguous are the terms *"posse"* and *"non posse"* when used by theologians, canonists and church documents in connection with the question: who is the minister of the sacrament of the eucharist?

The same is true of the term *"potestas,"* a word with several senses: physical, spiritual (virtue; grace), moral (influence), social, political, ecclesial. When St. Basil (RJ 919) says that those who have left the church do not have the *exousian* to baptize or to ordain, does he mean they are not *authorized* to do so, or that it is *absolutely* impossible for a schismatic bishop to truly baptize a dying infant? When it is said that only a bishop has the power to ordain, or only one with the power of the priesthood can consecrate, does this mean physical power? A spiritual power possessed by no one else in the church in any way? Does it mean authorization? Or does it mean the ability to ordain or consecrate lawfully and with ecclesial approval in order to serve and to manifest the unity of the church?

During the ordination of a priest the ordinand receives "the power to offer sacrifice to God and to celebrate Mass . . ." (*The Rites of Ordination* . . . [Washington, D. C., 1967], p. 42). Is this power analogous to that of the power he received as a deacon, "the power to read the gospel in the Church of God" (*ibid.*, p. 31), or, as a subdeacon, "the power to read the epistles" (*ibid.*, p. 24)? The latter "power" is one he has probably already exercised as a lector in the seminary or in his parish church.

A monograph is still needed on this question. This incomplete excursus is placed at the beginning simply to remind us of the extraordinarily complicated language problem that confronts us when we are reflecting on the church's doctrine on the minister of the eucharist.

III

Decisions of the Church's Teaching Office Concerning the Minister of the Eucharist

(1) *The profession of faith prescribed for Durandus of Osca and his Waldensian companions: 1208* [3]

"We firmly believe and confess that however good, religious, holy and prudent a man may be, he cannot and ought not *(non potest nec debet)* consecrate the eucharist nor perform the sacrifice of the altar unless he be a priest *(presbyter)* ordained by a visible and tangible bishop . . . And therefore we firmly believe and declare that whoever, without the previous episcopal ordination mentioned above, believes and contends that he is able *(se posse)* to perform the sacrifice of the eucharist, is a heretic . . . and he must be separated from the entire holy Roman Church." [4]

This teaching is directed against the action of Peter Waldes, a layman, who ordained bishops, priests and deacons, claiming that

---

[3] From the letter of Innocent III, *"Eius Exemplo,"* to the Archbishop of Terraco, 18 December 1208; DS 790-797.

[4] DS 794. The term "heresy" at this stage of the church's development did not necessarily refer to a denial of revealed truth as it does today. As P. Fransen and A. Lang have shown, it was also applied to those who defied the church's discipline.

he himself was invisibly ordained by God,[5] thus explaining the reference in the profession of faith to "visible" bishops.

To understand this document we must ask some of the questions we raised in the excursus. Does the *"non potest"* mean: not authorized? The *"nec debet"* used in conjunction with it suggests that it is an unauthorized act that one "should not" do.

Is this document teaching that ordination by a bishop is the *ordinary* way in which one is able to offer the eucharist? Or does it absolutely rule out any person as a legitimate minister of the Lord's supper unless he is episcopally ordained? If one takes this profession of faith as an unequivocal definition that it is absolutely impossible to offer the eucharist unless one is ordained by a bishop, one finds it impossible to explain the documented cases where simple priests have ordained other priests.[6]

As we read it, this document: (1) intends to express the church's traditional faith that the eucharist should be led by the bishop or someone appointed by him. It rejects as heretical those persons who think they can take it upon themselves to offer the holy sacrifice with no concern for church unity. Such a view would obviously divide the church by dividing and dis-ordering the sign of unity which is the eucharist. It is therefore a genuinely *heretical* view. (2) The document tells us nothing directly about the church's attitude toward the Waldensian eucharists other than that they are unauthorized and ought not be carried out. It in no way seeks to evaluate the religious or sacramental meaning of such eucharists even though it is clear that the church does not recognize them as her own.[7]

---

[5] A. Mens, *"Waldenser,"* Lexikon für Theologie und Kirche (Freiburg: Herder), 10, 934; L. Christiani, *"Vaudois,"* Dictionnaire de théologie Catholique, 15, 2594.

[6] Cf. C. Journet, *Church of the Word Incarnate* (London/New York, 1955), pp. 113-19; P. Fransen, *"Ordo,"* LThK, 7, 1215 f.

[7] The idea of church recognition was not foreign to Innocent III. Earlier in the profession of faith he affirmed that the church does not reprove sacraments administered by a sinful priest — *"dum Ecclesia eum recipit,"* DS 793. In the twelfth century Gratian, speaking of the sacraments of *ordained priests* and *bishops* who had fallen into heresy or schism, says they can be called *"irrita," "damnanda," "falsa"* and *"inania"* not according to what they are in themselves *(non quantum ad se)* — since they are holy and true even when celebrated by heretics — but because they are administered perfidiously and illicitly and because they do not confer the Holy Spirit on those who illicitly receive them. *Decreti secunda pars,* causa I, quest. 1, ch. 97, in *Corpus Iuris Canonici* (Leipzig, 1879), col. 396. Neither Gratian

Concerning the sacrament of the altar this council teaches: "Surely no one can perform this sacrament *(nemo potest conficere)* except a priest *(sacerdos)* who has been properly *(rite)* ordained according to the keys of the church which Jesus Christ conceded to the apostles and their successors." [8]

(2) *The Fourth Lateran Council: 1215*

The observations we made about the Waldensian profession of faith can also be made here since Lateran IV also had the Waldensians in mind. In what sense are we to take *"nemo potest conficere?"* Does it mean that the church does not recognize the eucharist celebrated by un-ordained ministers and that they therefore cannot perform the sacrament in a fully meaningful, ecclesial manner which would signify and enhance the church's unity? Or does this council intend to teach that anyone other than a priest who leads the eucharist is simply going through the motions as far as the making present of the body and blood of Christ is concerned? It would be difficult to prove that Lateran IV intended to define either of these things. The likelihood is that the council wished to express its strong opposition to such unauthorized eucharists and recalled the age-old order of the church without offering an explicit teaching concerning the intrinsic value or non-value of such liturgies.

(3) *The investigation of the integrity of the faith of the Armenians seeking reunion: 1351* [9]

Here we find the simple statement: "No one, not even a *sanctus,* can consecrate *(potest conficere)* the body of Christ except a priest." [10]

Again we ask, in what sense is *"potest"* to be taken? In the sense of "ecclesially empowered or authorized," or in the sense of: "the physical power of orders without which neither the sacrament nor the sacrifice of the eucharist would be perpetuated in the world?" [11]

---

nor the church documents — prior to Vatican II — speak of the sacraments of separated Christians whose ministers have not been "rightly ordained by a bishop" but who are clearly not perfidious or pertinacious in their separation from the Roman church. Would Gratian deny that they are "holy and true" in themselves?

[8] DS 802.

[9] In the letter, *"Super quibusdam,"* of Clement VI to Consolator Catholicos of the Armenians, 20 September 1351.

[10] DS 1084.

[11] C. Journet, *Church of the Word Incarnate,* pp. 23, 88 f.

None of the documents we have examined compel us to interpret *"posse"* in the latter sense.

It should be noted that this same teaching document asks the Armenians to believe that "no man outside the faith of this church and outside the obedience of the pope of Rome, can *(poterit)* finally be saved." [12] Church language about who *can* administer the eucharist is surely as ambiguous as the church's language about who *can* be saved. In the latter case the ambiguity was not cleared up for some Catholics until quite recently.[13]

In the same document to the Armenian Catholicos we find a clarification of the way *"potest"* is used in church documents that deal with the question: who *can* administer the sacrament of confirmation. It was explicitly said in earlier official teaching documents that *only bishops can* administer confirmation (not only as church *custom* demonstrates, but because only the apostles imparted the Holy Spirit by imposition of hands!).[14] But here we find the clarification that bishops are simply the *ordinary* ministers of that sacrament.[15]

(4) *The Council of Florence and the Decree for the Armenians: 1439*

In treating of the eucharist the Decree for the Armenians speaks of the matter, form and effect of the sacrament, but, in contradistinction to its affirmations about baptism and confirmation, the Decree says nothing about the minister of the eucharist. In its teaching about the minister of the sacrament of orders, however, the Decree advances beyond Thomas Aquinas, from whom much of the contents of the Decree were appropriated, by speaking of the bishop as the *ordinary* minister of ordination.[16]

Whereas the Decree explicitly recognizes extraordinary ministers

---

12 DS 1051.

13 Cf. DS 3866-3873.

14 DS 215 and 831.

15 DS 1069: *"si credis quod sacramentum confirmationis per alium quam per episcopum non potest ex officio ordinarie ministrari."* We ought to recall here that the practice of the church indicates that the sacrament of the priesthood *cannot* be administered *ex officio ordinarie* except by bishops. Cf. fn. 6 above for that practice. The Council of Florence explicitly stated this, DS 1326. Canon 951 of the CIC ought to be read in this light, namely, as a contemporary limitation of the extraordinary ministry of the sacrament of orders. Cf. W. Lohff, *"Ordo II. Im geltenden Kirchenrecht,"* LThK, 7, 1220.

16 DS 1326. Cf. Aquinas, *De fidei articulis et septem sacramentis* in *Opuscula,* ed. P. Mandonnet, vol. III (Paris, 1927), pp. 17 f.

of baptism and confirmation, it only implies that there are extra-ordinary ministers of the sacrament of orders. There is no hint here that the council would restrict this extraordinary ministry, as does Thomas Aquinas, to the conferral of the so-called minor orders.[17]

In the light of the development of the doctrine and practice relating to the competent minister of the sacraments of orders, confirmation, baptism, penance and the anointing of the sick,[18] it seems to us to be genuinely possible that the Roman Catholic church in the future could officially recognize someone other than a "rightly," that is, episcopally ordained priest as minister of the sacrament of the eucharist. Especially in view of the fact that priests have historically ordained other priests, this recognition might well extend to those ministers of separated Christian churches who have been ordained in a priestly — if not episcopal — "succession." Again, without violating any of her relatively few firm dogmatic commitments concerning the competent minister of the eucharist, as distinct from her purely ecclesiastical legislation and order, and recalling the apparently broader notion of the competent minister of the eucharist in the ancient church, there seems to be no intrinsic obstacle preventing the Roman Catholic church from *recognizing* (after the manner of Ignatius of Antioch) as legitimate and valid ministers of the eucharist those persons whose actual prophetic leadership in a separated Christian community is analogous to that of the prophets who seem to have led the eucharist in the church at the time of the *Didache*.

(5) *The Council of Trent*

(a) The canons on the Sacraments in General of Session VII (3 March 1547), promulgated without any explanatory "chapters," say nothing directly or specifically about the minister of the eucharist.

Canon 9 teaches that the sacraments of baptism, confirmation and orders "imprint a character on the soul, that is a certain spiritual and indelible sign because of which they cannot be repeated." [19]

---

[17] *Summa Theologiae*, III, q. 72, a. 11, ad 1. Cf. note 6 above for references to the fact that ordinary priests have legitimately conferred major orders.

[18] On the extraordinary ministers of the sacraments see J. van Beeck, "Towards an Ecumenical Understanding of the Sacraments," *Journal of Ecumenical Studies* 3 (1966), 79-84.

[19] DS 1609. This is a repetition of what was taught at the Council of Florence, DS 1313. On the meaning of this "character" see K. Rahner, *The Church and the Sacraments* (New York, 1963), pp. 87 ff.; P. Fransen,

Canon 10 rejects the view that "all Christians have the power *(potestatem)* of administering the word and all the sacraments." [20] This canon is directed against a view that was attributed to Luther [21] by the theological faculty of Paris in its *Determinatio super doctrina Lutheri hactenus revisa* of 15 April 1521.

The original statement of the error said that: "all Christians . . . have equal *(parem)* power in the ministry of word and sacrament." At the insistence of the Bishop of Bitondo *"parem"* was dropped, so as not to give the impression that all Christians have a real power of administering the sacraments, even though not equal to that of ordained priests.[22] The question still remains: does this canon teach that not all Christians have the authorization or power of administering all the sacraments? Such a teaching indisputably belongs to the permanent tradition of the church. The canon seems to us to teach clearly no more than this. To see it as saying something clearly — even by implication — about the competent minister of the eucharist is eisegesis.

(b) The Decree on the Most Holy Eucharist of Session III (11 October 1551) says nothing about the minister of the eucharist.

(c) The doctrine on the Most Holy Sacrifice of the Mass of Session XXII (17 September 1562) likewise says nothing which

---

"Ordo," LThK, 7, 1219; J. Mulders, *"Charakter,"* LThK, 2, 1020-1024; G. Lindbeck, "Karl Rahner and a Protestant View of the Sacramentality of the Ministry," in *Proceedings of the Twenty-First Annual Convention of the Catholic Theological Society of America,* vol. 21 (New York, 1967), pp. 267-288.

[20] DS 1610.

[21] Cf. *De captivitate babylonica ecclesiae . . .,* WA VI, 536 f., 564, 566; *Conc. Trid.* ed. Ehses, V, 835 f.

[22] *Conc. Trid.* V, 925, 971 f., 986. It is well known that Trent, unlike Vatican II, had nothing to say positively about the priesthood of all believers. The most it had to say was that not all Christians are priests of the New Testament without distinction *(promiscue),* DS 1767. In the discussions among the theologians at Trent on the sacrament of orders, the main reason used to oppose the view that all Christians are equally priests or that all have equal spiritual power is a biblical one: I Corinthians 12. The theologians rightly sought to uphold the distinction of roles, functions and offices in the church. Cf. *Conc. Trid.* IX, 18, 12 ff.; 19, 12 ff. This biblical basis was used in chapter 4 of the doctrine on holy orders and the "par" which had been suppressed at Bitondo's request in the canon on the sacraments re-emerged, DS 1767.

would definitively exclude the possibility of other competent ministers or ministerial offerers of the sacrifice.[23]

(d) The doctrine on the Sacrament of Orders of Session XXIII (15 July 1563) Canon 7 is the one most relevant to our question. After teaching that the power that bishops have of confirming and ordaining is not one that they have in common with priests,[24] the canon anathematizes those who say that persons "who have neither been rightly ordained nor commissioned by ecclesiastical and canonical power, but come from elsewhere, are legitimate *(legitimos)* ministers of the word and of the sacraments." [25]

The bishops at Trent paid very little attention to the latter part of the canon. Nearly all their attention was given to the protracted — but eventually unresolved — debate on the question: is the order of episcopacy *de jure divino* distinct from and superior to the priesthood? [26] After forty-five pages of recorded discussion on this question we finally find one bishop offering a statement of clarification pertaining to the ministry of those who had been separated from the church: "It is the mind of the council that it is anathema to say: they are legitimate ministers of word and sacraments who come from elsewhere than from the holy church and canonical powers." [27] To say that certain ministers are *illegitimate* is not nearly as strong as saying they *cannot* lead the eucharist.

Of importance, too, is the fact that during the discussion of the erroneous articles by the theologians, the following statement of the Spanish Dominican, Peter de Soto, went unchallenged: "Although all Christians can do everything which the ministers of the church do, they would not, however, be doing them legitimately. That they may be done legitimately, a supernatural power is necessary even for the

---

[23] DS 1752 simply mentions that there are priests in the church by the will of Christ to offer the holy sacrifice.

[24] This is incomprehensible unless we assume that the canon is teaching that only bishops — not priests — are the *ordinary* and *ex officio* ministers of holy orders. Cf. nn. 14 and 15 above and Trent's own teaching on the *ordinary* minister of confirmation, DS 1630.

[25] DS 1777. The studies of Fransen and Lang referred to in n. 4 demonstrate that one could also be *anathematized* by Trent for challenging the church's discipline as well as her doctrine. Cf. Fransen, "The Authority of the Councils," in *Problems of Authority,* ed. J. Todd (London/Baltimore, 1962), esp. pp. 72-78.

[26] *Conc. Trid.* IX, 43-88.

[27] *Ibid.,* IX, 88, 22 ff.; line 28 speaks of the *legitimate* minister.

lowest ranks of the ministry [for de Soto this included deacons, sub-deacons, acolytes, lectors, etc.], which power is granted by those having leadership in the Church." [28]

De Soto sees such a supernatural power as being necessary even for the "right" and "legitimate" exercise of the *minor* orders in the church. Thus, if someone were to read the lessons during the liturgy without having the supernatural power given to the lector (= ecclesial authorization or empowerment, accompanied by prayer for the grace of the Spirit), he would be doing so illicitly.[29]

The burden of Trent's teaching, then, is that those who are not ordained according to the canonical authority of the church — note that ordination by a *bishop* is not mentioned here — are not *legitimate* ministers of word and sacrament. Trent does not say that the word preached by illegitimately constituted ministers is a non-preaching of the word, nor that the eucharist celebrated by such ministers is not the sacrament of the eucharist. And from what we may infer from one

---

[28] *Ibid.*, IX, 16, 20-25: *"Nam licet omnes Christiani possent facere omnia, quae ministri ecclesiae faciunt, id tamen non legitime facerent. Nam quod legitime fiant, necesse est potestate supernaturali, etiam in infimis ministris, quae potestas ab habente principatum ecclesiae datur. Quare etsi infimi ordines hodie pertractentur a mere laicis, id tamen non recte fit, neque id legitime faciunt; sed unicuique, etiam minimo, tribui deberet suum ministerium, ut in primitiva ecclesia fiebat."* It has been suggested to me that de Soto is speaking only of the *sub-presbyteral* ministries when he says all Christians can do everything which the ministers of the church do, but not legitimately. De Soto does in fact use "ministers" in this restricted sense (*ibid.*, lines 9-10), but elsewhere (*Tractatus de Institutione Sacerdotum,* Dillingen, 1558) he applies the term to *all* ministers of word and sacrament. Trent itself uses "minister" both broadly (DS 1768, 1769, 1777) and restrictedly (DS 1768). It seems to us that when de Soto speaks of "ministers *of the Church*" in the present passage (lines 20-21), he means *all* the ministerial orders. In order to emphasize his point, he says on line 22 that a supernatural power of ministry is necessary for doing legitimately *even* what the lowest ministers do. De Soto knew that the German reformers were not concerned about laymen exercising the so-called minor orders. They claimed that any baptized Christian could absolve, offer mass, etc. De Soto concedes this point, but insists that they cannot do so *legitimately* unless they have received the power that comes with ordination. If our interpretation is correct, it means that de Soto has gone beyond the theory of orders he advanced in his treatise of 1558. In that work we find no counterpart of the broad principle he enunciated at Trent.

[29] It was noted at Trent that at the Seventh Ecumenical Council (Nicaea II) a reader was ejected from the council because he had exercised that office without having had the imposition of hands! *Conc. Trid.* IX; 26, 14 f.

of the few Tridentine theologians who spoke to the question, Peter de Soto, such a eucharist would be a eucharist, but one neither "rightly nor legitimately" celebrated.

Significant, too, is what Trent did *not* reject. While rightly excluding an exaggerated concept of the priesthood of all believers that would destroy any distinction of roles, functions and offices in the church — a concept that was never approved by the Lutheran confessional writings — Trent neither discussed nor rejected the argument of the Lutheran *Book of Concord* that, when bishops negligently fail to ordain priests for a given Christian community, the pastor of that congregation — himself an ordained priest — can validly ordain priests for that church.[30] This argument is based on the premise that the difference between bishops and priests is one of human, not divine, law, a premise that goes back at least as far as St. Jerome, whose opinion was not censured by Trent.[31]

(6) *The Encyclical, Mediator Dei, of Pius XII (20 November 1947)*

Although it far surpasses Trent in its positive appreciation of the priesthood of the faithful, this teaching document follows the lines laid down by Trent as far as our question is concerned: not all members of the church enjoy the same powers nor are they all qualified to perform the same acts.[32] The visible priesthood is not given indiscriminately to all members of the church, but only to designated men in the sacrament of holy orders. This sacrament "not only imparts the grace necessary to the clerical function and state of life, but imparts an indelible character besides . . ., qualifying them to perform those official acts of religion by which men are sanctified." [33]

---

[30] *The Book of Concord,* ed. Theodore G. Tappert (Philadelphia, 1959), "Treatise on the Power and Primacy of the Pope," 63-67.

[31] Nor by Vatican II. See K. Rahner's commentary to Article 20 of the Constitution on the Church in *Commentary on the Documents of Vatican II,* vol. I (New York, 1967), pp. 191 f. It is no refutation of the Lutheran argument to say, as Peter de Soto says elsewhere, that Jerome nevertheless attributes ordination to the bishop alone, *Tractatus de Institutione Sacerdotum* (Dillingen, 1558), p. 341. The question remains: is ordination restricted to the bishop by divine law, or by a purely human determination of the church? If the latter is the case — and the Roman Catholic church's own recognition of non-episcopal ordination of priests is one clear indication that it is — then the position defended in Melanchthon's "Treatise" should be given a fresh hearing by ecumenical theologians grappling with the problem of ministry.

[32] *On the Sacred Liturgy* (New York, 1948), n. 39.

[33] *Ibid.,* nn. 41 f.

It is further taught that, although the faithful participate in the eucharistic sacrifice, this "does not mean they also are endowed with priestly power" ("non idcirco sacerdotali etiam potestate fruuntur").[34] Further, the people, "since they in no sense represent the divine Redeemer and are not mediators between themselves and God, can in no way possess the sacerdotal power" ("nullo modo iure [sic] sacerdotali frui posse").[35]

This encyclical does not speak of the Lord's supper of the separated brethren, where the minister surely can be understood to be representing the Redeemer. Nor does it consider the possibility of exceptional situations where a group of Catholics, isolated from an ordained priest, might select one of their brethren who has been initiated into Christ's priesthood through faith, baptism, confirmation and the eucharist, to represent Christ as the leader of a eucharistic celebration. To construe the "powers" of the ordained priest in some physical way that would render impossible the suggestions just made would be to employ a concept of "power" that we have not seen in our study of the church's teaching documents.

(7) The Second Vatican Council

(a) The Constitution on the Church:

(1) N. 10 offers the most positive teaching to date of any official church document on the "common priesthood of the faithful," which is distinguished from the "priesthood of the hierarchical ministry." These "priesthoods" differ from one another "in essence, not just in degree." [36] It seems reasonable to us that at least one of the bases for this difference in essence is simply that the task (munus) of the ministerial priest (representation of Christ and leadership of the worshipping community) differs essentially from the task of the broader community of priests, which is that of active participation in the eucharistic prayer.

(2) The "sacra potestas" of the ministerial priest mentioned in n. 10 is never formally defined in the Constitution on the Church, not even in Chapter III which is an elaboration of the powers of the hierarchical priesthood.[37] One is justified in understanding this sacra

---

[34] Ibid., n. 82; DS 3849.

[35] Ibid., n. 84; DS 3850.

[36] Cf. the highly informative commentary of A. Grillmeier in Commentary on the Documents of Vatican II, vol. I, pp. 156-159.

[37] Cf. K. Rahner's commentary, ibid., p. 188 f.

potestas in terms of the documents we have already studied. It is an ecclesial authorization or empowerment to lead the worshipping community in such a way that the order and unity of the church are manifested. This task or role is of such importance in the church that the church prays sacramentally for the one ordained that the Holy Spirit be given him for fidelity to his priestly task and, the church's call of the man ordained being a permanent call to service, the priest is said to be marked with a spiritual but indelible character.

(3) Nowhere in the Constitution on the Church are we told anything about the Lord's supper that is celebrated by ministers of separated Christian communities who have not been "rightly ordained by the ecclesiastical and canonical power" [38] of the Catholic church.

(b) The Decree on Ecumenism:

Here for the first time the Catholic church speaks officially on the Lord's supper celebrated by the separated Christian communities in the West. As we have noted at the beginning of our paper, n. 22 of this Decree did not say these liturgies are simply invalid or non-sacraments because they are not led by "legitimate" ministers.[39]

On the contrary, the drafters of the decree of the Secretariat for Promoting Christian Unity explicitly turned back the proposal of 152 council fathers who wished to have the decree say: "especially because of a defect of the sacrament of orders [these separated Christian communities of the West] do not have the reality of the eucharist." Thirteen of these bishops gave as their reason that, in the absence of orders, there is neither the full nor partial reality of the eucharist but only a non-efficacious sign. This view, widely held by Catholics prior to Vatican II, but lacking foundation in the doctrinal statements of the church, was repudiated by the drafters of the decree.

The final version of the decree concerning the Lord's supper celebrated by the separated churches reads: "Although we believe [the Western ecclesial communities separated from us] have not preserved the genuine and integral reality of the eucharistic mystery in its fullness, especially because of a defect of the sacrament of orders, nevertheless when they commemorate the Lord's death and resurrection in the Holy Supper, they profess that it signifies life in communion with Christ and await his coming in glory."

---

[38] DS 1777.

[39] Cf. our essay mentioned in note 1.

Conclusions

1. It is official Catholic doctrine that Jesus Christ intended a diversity of ministries in his church and that the prayer of the church, by which she invokes the grace of the Holy Spirit on a baptized person who is thereby empowered or authorized to serve God's people as a leader of the eucharist, is a sacrament.

2. This sacrament is ordinarily administered by a bishop.

3. Those who have been rightly ordained but who have been separated from Catholic communion are ministers of true and holy sacraments, but these are ineffective and work only to the perdition of the minister and/or recipient if they are administered and/or received in pertinacious defiance of the church's order and unity.

4. There is some indication that other members of the church, such as prophets, who have not been sacramentally ordained, were once recognized as rightful leaders of the eucharist.

5. Ministers of the eucharist who have not been rightly ordained by "ecclesiastical and canonical power" are regarded as illegitimate ministers of the sacrament. In our view this is so mainly because the eucharist they lead does not manifest the unity of the whole church in which all Christians ought to be united in a bond of peace and fellowship with each other that is symbolized not only by a common eating and drinking, but also by the minister's unity with the local bishop who in turn is in union with the bishop of Rome.

6. The Roman Catholic church has made no definitive pronouncement on the sacramentality of the Lord's supper celebrated in churches whose ministry is regarded as illegitimate. The most it has said is that, mainly because of a defect of holy orders, these churches do not have the genuine and integral reality of the eucharistic mystery. The genuine and integral reality of the sacrament of unity requires that it be celebrated "under the bishop or him to whom he commits it."

7. On the level of ecumenical practice, when Catholics are forbidden to receive sacraments from any but "validly ordained" ministers (*Directory* of the Secretariat for Promoting Christian Unity, 14 May 1967, n. 55) this is not to be understood as an implication that the sacraments conferred by those ministers lack objective sacramental reality. It is rather a disciplinary measure taken by the church at this time, a measure which could be altered in the future.

8. In the light of the history of the practice and doctrine of the church concerning the minister of the eucharist and other sacraments, it is within the church's power of the keys to declare valid and legitimate ministries she has formerly called invalid or illegitimate.

APOSTLES AND APOSTOLIC
SUCCESSION
IN THE PATRISTIC ERA

By James F. McCue

In what one might call classical modern Roman Catholicism, one regularly meets with the view that apostolicity is the *nota ecclesiae par excellence,* the decisive mark by which to identify the true church of Jesus Christ. Jean Bainvel, writing early in the present century in the *Dictionnaire de théologie catholique,* calls it the *"marque distinctive de la véritable Eglise du Christ."* [1] And half a century later one finds substantially the same position in the second edition of the *Lexikon für Theologie und Kirche* and the *Handbuch theologischer Grundbegriffe: Für den, der die wahre Kirche Jesu Christi sucht, kann aus dem vierfachen Kennmal (nota), mit dem die diversen sich christlich nennenden Religionsgemeinschaften herausgefunden werden können* (Pius IX; D 1686), *nur die (in der Petrus-Nachfolge zusammengefasste) Apostolizität das ausschlaggebende Moment sein.* [2]

Nor is this all important characteristic simply or even primarily a matter of qualitative similarity to or identity with the church or the faith of the apostles. It is more centrally a matter of the historical continuity of the church in the present, through the apostolic succession in the hierarchy, with the apostles. Bainvel has put matters perhaps a bit bluntly, but his position is hardly eccentric:

> *Il s'agit ici de la succession des pasteurs ou de l'identité de gouvernement . . . Mais de ce que la doctrine serait ou semblerait être vraiment apostolique on ne peut rien conclure. Il en est*

---

[1] *"Apostolicité,"* in *Dictionnaire de théologie catholique* (1903 ff.) vol. I, 1625.

[2] A. Kolping, *"Notae Ecclesiae,"* in *Lexikon für Theologie und Kirche* (Freiburg: Herder), vol. VII (1962); *"Apostel,"* in *Handbuch theologischer Grundbegriffe* (Munich, 1962) I, 72.

autrement pour la succession légitime des pasteurs. Avec elle il y a continuité, sans elle, non; avec elle, d'ailleurs, on est sûr, sans autre examen, de la véritable doctrine, car c'est au corps des pasteurs qu'a été confié le dépot et qu'a été promis le Saint-Esprit pour le garder et le transmettre.[3]

While it is true that not a little recent Catholic literature on the subject has begun to move away from Bainvel and Kolping, these earlier views are still widely held within Roman Catholicism and are of considerable importance for Roman and non-Roman ecumenical relations. Because these views make some rather definite presuppositions about the early history of the church, it will be of some value to consider the early development of both the institutions and the theories of apostleship and apostolic succession. I shall attempt to trace these matters from their origins through the patristic era, though, as will be evident, my treatment will be even sketchier for the later period than for the earlier.

I.

Since there is simply no way of making a detour around the New Testament questions, I have had to evaluate complex materials and to form judgments about them, even though there is very little scholarly consensus on which one might rest. Practically every judgment made in the present action would be objected to by some scholars, and it is difficult to believe that at every point they shall turn out to have been wrong and I right.

It is generally acknowledged that it was in J. B. Lightfoot's 1865 commentary on *Galatians* that the traditional conception of the New Testament apostles (the Twelve plus Paul) came apart.[4] And if the most recent literature is to be taken seriously, we are farther from a solution to the problem of the apostles in early Christianity than we were immediately after Lightfoot.

We may begin by noting the kinds of problems that have arisen. 1) It has been observed that Paul speaks of others besides himself

---

3 *Dictionnaire de théologie catholique,* I, 1625.

4 As a matter of fact, one finds a similar "discovery" in Jerome, *In Gal.* 1.19 (PL, 26, 330, B—C). For a survey of the literature from the early nineteenth century down to the early 1950's, see E. M. Kredel, *"Der Apostelbegriff in der neueren Exegese,"* in *Zeitschrift für Katholische Theologie* 78 (1956), 169-193, 257-305. For a review of some of the more recent literature, see E. Güttgemanns, *"Literatur zur neutestamentlichen Theologie,"* IV; *"Mission, Verkündigung und Apostolat,"* in *Verkündigung und Forschung* 12 (1967)/2, 61-79.

and the Twelve as apostles, and 2) that Paul never does identify the Twelve as apostles. 3) Luke-Acts defines apostleship in such a way as to make the apostles and the Twelve identical, thereby apparently excluding Paul; only once does Acts expressly label Paul an apostle (14:14; but see also 14:4) and there he takes second place to Barnabas. 4) Apart from Paul and Luke-Acts, *apostolos* is used but rarely in the New Testament. Especially striking is the fact that it is used but once in Mark and once in Matthew.[5]

The tendency of recent scholarship has thus been to locate the origin of the use of *apostolos* as a Christian technical term in Pauline and Lukan circles and further to define the Pauline and the Lukan apostles antithetically. We cannot sift through all this literature at this point, and instead I shall try to set out the most important New Testament materials, indicate the direction which my own interpretation takes, and give a few of the reasons why.

II.

The *Pauline* literature is central to any discussion of *apostolos* in the New Testament, and though there would seem to have been a pre-Pauline *Apostelbegriff*, Paul is our earliest literature.

Whom does Paul call *apostolos?* Himself most clearly and frequently; also quite clearly Peter-Cephas (Galatians 2:8; cf. 1:18f.) and the otherwise unknown Andronicus and Junias (Romans 16:7); then less clearly Barnabas (I Corinthians 9:6; Galatians 2:9), perhaps James, the brother of the Lord (Galatians 1:19), and John (Galatians 2:9). It is not to our purposes to argue the details of these disputed identifications.

Of special importance is I Corinthians 15:4-9:

καὶ ὅτι ἐγήγερται τῇ ἡμέρᾳ τῇ τρίτῃ κατὰ τὰς γραφάς, καὶ ὅτι ὤφθη Κηφᾷ, εἶτα τοῖς δώδεκα. ἔπειτα ὤφθη ἐπάνω πεντακοσίοις ἀδελφοῖς ἐφάπαξ, ἐξ ὧν οἱ πλείονες μένουσιν ἕως ἄρτι, τινὲς δὲ [καὶ] ἐκοιμήθησαν. ἔπειτα ὤφθη Ἰακώβῳ, εἶτα τοῖς ἀποστόλοις πᾶσιν. ἔσχατον δὲ πάντων ὡσπερεὶ τῷ ἐκτρώματι ὤφθη κἀμοί. Ἐγὼ γάρ εἰμι ὁ ἐλάχιστος τῶν ἀποστόλων, ὃς οὐκ εἰμὶ ἱκανὸς καλεῖσθαι ἀπόστολος. διότι ἐδίωξα τὴν ἐκκλησίαν τοῦ θεοῦ.

We might first observe that this passage is a difficult one to systematize. Language is not used with technical rigor, and it is not always clear how various individuals and groups are to be related.

---

[5] I take the most commonly received readings of Mark 3:14 and Matthew 10:2 as the right ones.

If it were not quite clear from other sources that Cephas is both one of the Twelve and an apostle, one might be inclined to interpret this passage to suggest that he was not. Similarly, were it not that Paul here calls himself an apostle, one might suppose that the phrase "all the apostles" of v. 7 excluded the possibility of the addition of any more apostles.

However certain observations can be sustained. Clearly there are apostles other than Paul and the Twelve and the use of "all" suggests that they were probably rather numerous. In addition, whether or not Paul *thought* of the Twelve as apostles, he here clearly does not call them such. This passage does not tell against the thesis that the Twelve came to be called apostles only later, with Luke; of course the passage does not establish the thesis either, but is compatible with more than one view of the matter.

The chief point of the passage is not precisely Paul's claim to be an apostle, but rather his claim to be a witness to the resurrection. This claim, however, is made in the vocabulary of apostleship. Paul supposes that the claim to be an apostle includes the claim to have seen the risen Lord, though presumably not (cf. the more than 500 brothers) vice versa.

In two contexts apostleship emerges as an important focus of debate in Paul: vis-á-vis his rivals in Corinth, and vis-á-vis Peter and the others in Jerusalem.

For the situation in Corinth, I Corinthians 9:1-18 and II Corinthians 11 and 12 are crucial. What kind of "definition" of an apostle can we work out of these passages? An apostle is one (apparently an itinerant) who preaches the true gospel. There is a near equivalence between the *apostoloi* of I Corinthians 9:5 and τοῖς τὸ εὐαγγέλιον καταγγέλλουσιν of v. 14. I Corinthians 9:1 is usually and I think rightly read as though the third question — have I not seen Jesus our Lord? — functioned to define the sense of the second — am I not an apostle? But in expanding his claim to be an apostle in v. 2, Paul points to the results of his preaching among the Corinthians rather than to his visions. Again, in II Corinthians 11 and 12 the marks of the true apostle are to be found in what he does.

Similarly the false apostle is not one whose credentials are not in order; he is one who preaches a gospel other than the one preached by Paul (II Corinthians 11). Pseudo-apostles are not men who claim to be of the original twelve but are not, nor are they those who falsely claim to have had visions of the risen Lord; or at least this is not the line of attack which Paul takes or even suggests.

But if one would insist that Paul's conception of the apostle is primarily if not exclusively functional, then one must come up with a description of the apostolic function. In I Corinthians 12:28 Paul lists apostles together with other ministers which God has established in the church:

Καὶ οὓς μὲν ἔθετο ὁ θεὸς ἐν τῇ ἐκκλησίᾳ πρῶτον ἀποστόλους, δεύτερον προφήτας, τρίτον διδασκάλους, ἔπειτα δυνάμεις, ἔπειτα χαρίσματα ἰαμάτων, ἀντιλήμψεις, κυβερνήσεις, γένη γλωσσῶν.[6]

It is difficult to say exactly what kind of priority is referred to by the *prōton*. The simplest interpretation, one consonant with the material which we have already considered, is that the apostle is a missionary, one who comes (is sent) to new places to begin the work of proclaiming the gospel and gathering a community, and who as witness to what is at the heart of the gospel has a special foundational role.[7]

The second focus of discussion of apostles in Paul is his encounter with the Jerusalem church. When Paul first uses *apostolos* in Galatians the immediate context suggests a missionary understanding: Paul is called and sent directly by God to proclaim his Son to the Gentiles, and he begins his work without first checking with those at Jerusalem who were apostles before him.[8] These pre-Pauline Jerusalem apostles were, presumably, those first missionaries who had preached the gospel at Jerusalem and then going out (to some extent, at least) from Jerusalem had preached to the Jews elsewhere. These apostles are identified with Jerusalem in a way in which it would be difficult to identify Paul with any single place, yet Paul would appear to be thinking of his own task as paralleling theirs. Thus if there was a difference between Pauline and pre-Pauline conceptions of apostleship, this difference is perhaps best thought of as a difference of degree rather than as an abrupt difference in kind. That Paul calls atten-

---

[6] Ephesians 4:11 sheds no additional light here, even if one assumes it to be authentically Pauline.

[7] This may be the place to note that Paul's understanding of apostleship is inextricably bound up with more central themes, and not least with his eschatology. See Güttgemanns, *"Literatur zur neutestamentlichen Theologie,"* 62-64, and the literature there referred to. For a variety of reasons it has been impossible here to develop the topic within the larger context of Paul's theology as a whole. And to admit this short-coming is not to escape its consequences.

[8] Galatians 1:17 οὐδὲ ἀνῆλθον εἰς Ἰεροσόλυμα πρὸς τοὺς πρὸ ἐμοῦ ἀποστόλους.

tion to the fact that he did not first confer with those who were apostles before him before going forth to preach the gospel at least strongly suggests activity of a similar sort was the work and responsibility of these same apostles.

And though Paul insists that his mission and his gospel are not derived from the Jerusalem church, it is apparent that he regarded the Jerusalem church and its leading figures as having a special place in the church. Presumably (but only that) Paul considered the Jerusalem church important both because of the importance of Jerusalem within the Jewish world and also because here were concentrated many of the earliest witnesses of the risen Lord and many of the earliest followers of Jesus. Though there are obviously many important differences between Paul and Acts, one might at least note here that the two are in agreement in according to Jerusalem a central place in the early life of the church and in according to the leadership of the Jerusalem church a broader leadership role in the church at large.

To summarize: In Paul *apostolos* is most commonly used to designate a productive missionary preacher of the gospel, who is sent out to bring the gospel to new listeners, who has seen and been commissioned by the risen Lord, but this is not altogether clear and does not seem to have been very important polemically. Jerusalem is seen as the original community, the one from which apostles first come forth. Presumably these first apostles were largely drawn from those who had been the closest followers of Jesus. Hence Paul's own status — a late comer and former persecutor of the church who does not work under the direction of the original community at Jerusalem — requires some defense and explanation. Thus there appears as the background and context of Paul's discussion of apostleship a view of apostleship that shows significant similarities to the later view of Acts.

III.

Aside from the Pauline corpus it is in *Luke-Acts* that *apostolos* is most often used in the New Testament, and this double work is the principal New Testament source of the subsequent main-stream understanding of the term. The principal features of the Lukan apostle are as follows:

1. Whereas except for Matthew 10:2 and Mark 6:30, the other synoptics never speak of the Twelve as apostles, Luke adds to the account of the calling of the Twelve the detail that Jesus expressly

called them apostles; and throughout the third gospel they are referred to as the twelve apostles.

2. It would *seem* that for Luke-Acts the Twelve *alone* are apostles. The definition of an apostle implicit in Acts 1:21-22 would limit apostleship to those who, *inter alia*, had been with Jesus since the beginning of his public career. This would apparently rule out Paul's claim to be an apostle; and though Paul plays a very important role in Acts he is only once or twice (14:4 and perhaps 14:14) called an apostle, and there he is listed after Barnabas.

3. The emphasis is on witness to *both* the earthly career of Jesus and his resurrection.

4. The emphasis is on their authority in the Jerusalem church.

5. The problem of succession and unification in authority is important.[9] A sustained effort seems to be made in Acts to present all missionary and expansive efforts as being subordinated to the twelve apostles. (Cf. 9:26-30; 8:14-17; 6:1-6.)

It would seem that the Lukan emphasis upon the Twelve as *the* apostles is part of a general effort in Luke to bolster confidence in the resurrection by stressing that its witnesses were Jesus' earliest followers and the subsequent leaders of the church. This would appear to be a fairly common theme in late first century Christian writing (cf. the Johannine writings), and would seem to be the decisive factor here. (This point I shall develop more fully in subsequent publications.)

IV.

Apostolos is used but infrequently in the rest of the New Testament. At only one point does *Matthew* use the word and there it is

---

[9] This is complicated by the sudden emergence in Acts 15 (cf. 11:30 as well) of the *presbyteroi* alongside the *apostoloi* as the leaders of the Jerusalem church. Six times in this chapter *hoi apostoloi kai hoi presbyteroi* is used as a formula. Simultaneously James emerges as the principal leader of the Jerusalem church. Günter Klein, *Die Zwölf Apostel: Ursprung und Gehalt einer Idee* (Göttingen, 1961), pp. 173-174, interprets the replacement of the apostles by presbyters (completed in Klein's view by 21:18, where James is surrounded by the elders at the head of the Jerusalem community and there is no mention of apostles) in apostolic succession terms. Somewhat subtly perhaps, Acts would be insinuating that the elders in the post-apostolic generation accede to the authority originally exercised by the apostles. This is part of Klein's general thesis that the author of Acts is trying to "save" Paul by integrating him into the apostles-apostolic succession chain.

used with reference to the Twelve: Τῶν δὲ δώδεκα ἀποστόλων τὰ ὀνόωατά ἐστιν ταῦτα.[10]

Similarly *Mark* uses *apostolos* but once. Mark 6:7 reads: Καὶ προσκαλεῖται τοὺς δώδεκα, καὶ ἤρξατο αὐτοὺς ἀποστέλλειν and 6:30, which clearly looks back to 6:7 ff. reads: Καὶ συνάγονται οἱ ἀπόστολοι πρὸς τὸν Ἰησοῦν. Both Klein and Schmitals argue that this passage was inserted into Mark at a time when the Lukan usage had made the identification of the Twelve and the apostles a truism. However, there seems little besides a general theory about New Testament apostleship to lead one to this assumption, and it thus seems more economical to suppose that Mark and Matthew each on one occasion use *apostolos* and identify the *apostoloi* with the Twelve.

This would not altogether eliminate a uniquely important role for Luke-Acts, but would make the Luke-Acts contribution less a *creatio ex nihilo* than Klein and Schmitals would have it. The identification of the Twelve as *apostoloi* in Matthew and Mark is quite casual and nonfunctional and in Mark at least would seem to be part of the redactional material. Presumably then the earliest synoptic materials did not (or at least did not regularly or insistently) identify the Twelve as apostles; and Luke's *apostolous ōnomasen* (6:13), while not absolutely original with Luke, is probably a retrojection of later usage into the preresurrection career of Jesus.[11]

Before continuing with the other New Testament materials we might briefly consider the question of whether "the Twelve" was also derived rather from the post-resurrection community than from the pre-resurrection career of Jesus. Without pretending to settle the matter decisively I would note that 1) the Twelve are a part, and already an archaic part, of some of the earliest New Testament traditions; and 2) that the simplest explanation of this is the one actually given in the synoptics and John — *viz.* that Jesus had an inner-circle of twelve followers.

---

[10] Matthew 10:2. Sys. has *māthātōn* rather than *apostolōn*, a reading which Klein prefers. While this suits his thesis that Luke marks an absolute beginning in identifying the Twelve as apostles, there is little else to be said for it. It is not even clear (given *tous dōdeka mathātas* of 10:1) that *mathāton* is the *lectio difficilior*, and it is further to be noted that the tendency which Klein must conjure up to corrupt the entire Greek mss. tradition at 10:2 has left 10:1 entirely intact.

[11] Cf. Jacques Dupont, *"Le Nom d'apôtres a-t-il-été donné aux Douze par Jesus?"* *Orient Syrien,* I (1956), 266-290, 425-444.

1) Paul, in what is clearly traditional material (I Corinthians 15:3-5) speaks of the Twelve as a group needing no further identification, though nowhere in his writing are we told who the Twelve are, nor do they *qua* the Twelve play any significant role in Paul's theology or in his career as he describes it.[12]

The Twelve are brought sharply into focus and named in the synoptics and in Acts, and are referred to in John.[13] Yet the variations in the listing of names is such as to suggest that the twelveness of the group was more firmly fixed in the tradition than the actual names of at least several members of the group.

2) The simplest, though (alas!) not the only, assumption in this instance is that the Twelve do derive from the pre-resurrection career of Jesus. To assume otherwise is to suppose that a group which was formed only after the resurrection, and which was by the 50's already a badly faded memory, yet managed to impress itself on a widely diversified body of New Testament materials. Until the Lukan reconstruction, the Twelve do not seem to have performed a theologically significant function; and though doubtless the connection of the Twelve with the idea of the church as the New Israel must have been

---

[12] P. Vielhauer has argued, and Klein and Schmitals consider his argument decisive, that I Corinthians 15:3-5 presents the Twelve as a group constituted only by the resurrection appearance, and thus as coming into existence only subsequent to Jesus' earthly career. See *"Gottesreich und Menschensohn in der Verkündigung Jesu,"* in *Festschrift für Gunther Dehn,* ed. W. Schneemelcher (Neukirchen, 1957), pp. 62-64. Vielhauer argues that since Paul refers to the Twelve rather than to the Eleven he could not be referring to the group described in Luke-Acts, and thus must be referring to a group constituted by the post-resurrection appearance. But this is to suppose, quite arbitrarily, that if there was a pre-resurrection group of twelve that it must have been precisely that described by Luke-Acts. It is at least possible, and this possibility Vielhauer does not even bother with, that the Judas and Matthias materials are legendary in a way in which the Twelve are not. I must admit, however, that to refute Vielhauer is not equivalent to proving that the Twelve do derive from the pre-resurrection period. It is only to argue that I Corinthians 15:3-5 does not tell *against* this hypothesis.

[13] Note however that Vincent Taylor, who apparently harbors no doubts about the pre-resurrection historicity of the Twelve, points out that most of the references to the Twelve are found in Markan constructions rather than in self-contained pieces of traditional materials. See *The Gospel According to St. Mark* (London, 1952), p. 620. Taylor has there also compiled statistics on the use of "the Twelve" in the entire New Testament.

apparent during these formative decades, it is actually very little stressed in the materials that we actually have.[14]

We may now briefly conclude our survey of *apostolos* in the New Testament. *John* uses *apostolos* but once (13:16), and there in the non-technical sense of one who is sent. Still, I would suggest that in John we have virtually all the components of the Luke-Acts concept of apostleship. This is most evident in the farewell discourses. These are delivered to the inner circle of disciples, who on two occasions (6:70 and 20:24) are identified as the Twelve. A theme running through these discourses is that as the Father has sent the Son into the world, so the Son sends his closest followers (17:18-19). It is through them (17:20) that others are to be brought to faith. These are the ones with whom Jesus has dwelt for a considerable time (14:9), to whom he has revealed all that could be revealed at the time and to whom the Paraclete will come to perfect this initial revelation (14:25-15:15). Though John does not use *apostolos* in these farewell discourses, he uses *apostellein* six times and the synonymous *pempein* nine times. Finally, this sending would seem to involve pastoral responsibility (21:15-17).

Revelation uses *apostolos* more technically than does John, in ways now suggestive of Paul, now of Luke-Acts. In 2:2 we have καὶ ἐπείρασας τοὺς λέγοντας ἑαυτοὺς ἀποστόλους καί οὐκ ἐισίν. Unless we are to assume that people were going around claiming to be Bartholomew or Thomas we must suppose that Revelation is using *apostolos* rather as Paul would. In 18:20 οἱ ἅγιοι καὶ οἱ ἀπόστολοι καὶ οἱ προφῆται are urged to rejoice over the destruction of Babylon. The *apostoloi-prophātai* juxtaposition is characteristic of the more open-ended Pauline concept.[15]

In 21:14 however, we have the twelve apostles of the lamb, who are the foundation on which the new Jerusalem is to be built. It is difficult not to see in this a conception rather closely related to that of Luke-Acts. Since no one would claim that apostleship is a central

---

[14] It is clearest in Revelation 21:14. While the motif is recognizable in Matthew 19:28 and Luke 22:30, it is being used for quite alien purposes in both of these passages.

[15] Note that the change in order in II Peter 3:2 to *prophātai-apostoloi* presupposes a significantly different understanding of apostle. It is impossible to determine if II Peter knows of *twelve* apostles, but the apostles in that work are clearly a bounded group, belonging to the past, which is now normative for the church. Prophets and apostles are here roughly equivalent to Old and New Testament.

concept in Revelation, it seems quite possible that this lack of systematization (or even this incoherence) caused the original audience of Revelation less discomfort than it does Klein or Schmitals.

The apostle functions quite differently in the *Pastorals* than he did in the Pauline letters; and the principal difference arises from the fact that the Pastorals are concerned with the question of how the church is to function after the age of the apostle, the heroic age of beginnings. As the answer is worked out in the Pastorals the Pauline conception is not repudiated, but only that feature remains which can survive into and be imitated by the post-apostolic age: Paul's fidelity to and transmission of the gospel revealed to him.

V.

There is a pre-history question which is so often asked that it can scarcely be avoided, though I am inclined to think that it contributes little to our understanding of the subject: What are the extra New Testament sources of the New Testament concept of apostle?

K. H. Rengstorf can still serve as the classical illustration of the attempt to derive the New Testament *apostolos* from Jewish roots.[16]

The Jewish *shaliach* is, according to Rengstorf, the antecedent of the New Testament apostle, and we can learn what Luke and ultimately what Jesus meant by considering this Jewish prototype. But the evidence for any direct derivation is so weak (some might wish to say weaker than weak) that it would be very foolish to try to derive any features of the New Testament apostle from the Jewish *shaliach* unless these features are already evident in the New Testament itself.[17]

More recently and in vigorous opposition to the "conservative consensus" (Klein's phrase), Schmitals has attempted to derive the New Testament apostleship from gnostic circles in Syria. The theory

---

[16] *Theological Dictionary of the New Testament,* ed. G. Kittel (London, 1964) I, 407-445.

[17] With the following comment of Jürgen Roloff I am in complete agreement: *"Gerade weil die religionsgeschichtliche Untersuchung des Saliah-Institutes ergeben hat, dass es sich dabei allenfalls um einen formalen äusseren Anknüpfungspunkt für den christlichen Apostolat, keinesfalls um mehr, handeln kann, müssen wir damit rechnen, dass das Wort ἀπόστολος bereits in den ältesten uns zugänglichen neutestamentlichen Schichten Träger einer ganz bestimmten kerygmatischen Interpretation ist, die diese formale Analogie weit hinter sich zurückgelassen hat."* *Apostolat-Verkündigung-Kirche* (Gütersloh, 1965), p. 36.

has not been generally accepted.[18] Indeed, it seems legitimate to ask whether it is especially helpful to seek the extra-Christian sources of the concept of apostleship, given the centrality of the concept of mission or sending in primitive Christianity. It is not really particularly surprising that the principal New Testament ministers are called by a substantive formed from the commonest New Testament verb for "to send." One could, of course, ask why this mission thrust was so characteristic of early Christianity; but that is not the question which Rengstorf and Schmitals ask. Rather they take this larger *apostellein* structure for granted, and then ask why within it there were *apostoloi*.

VI.

The problem of the relationship between main-stream and non-main-stream Christianity in the second century is a difficult one. We are still without a serviceable map of the period. In what follows I shall first consider that literature which subsequently would be taken up as its own by main-stream Christianity. Secondly I shall briefly consider some of the literature that was not so taken up.

I Clement takes us, if at all, only slightly beyond Paul. In 5:3 we are told: λάβωμεν πρὸ ὀφθαλμῶν ἡμῶν τοὺς ἀγαθοὺς ἀποστόλους, and then Peter and Paul are presented to us. In 42:1 we read Οἱ ἀπόστολοι ἡμῖν εὐηγγελίσθησαν ἀπὸ τοῦ κυρίου Ἰησοῦ Χριστοῦ, and one might be inclined to interpret this as a reference to the Twelve; but in light of 5:3, of 44:1 (οἱ ἀπόστολοι ἡμῶν), and of 47:4, the reference is seen to be to Peter and Paul.

I Clement distinguishes more clearly (at 47:4) between apostles and non-apostles than had Paul. There is some dispute as to whether or not Paul considered Apollo to be an apostle,[19] but I Clement distinguishes quite clearly between Peter and Paul, apostles, and Apollo is simply one approved by the apostles. His authority would thus appear to be derivative from the apostles, a theme to which we shall return when we consider more precisely the matter of apostolic succession.

In addition, I Clement introduces an expression that will eventually become almost a synonym for Paul: τοῦ μακαρίου Παύλου τοῦ ἀποστόλου (47:1). In later Christian usage *hoi apostoloi* eventually comes to mean the Twelve and *ho apostolos* comes to mean Paul.

Ignatius of Antioch also falls somewhere in between the Pauline

---

18 For a brief, incisive critique, see Güttgemanns, *op. cit.*, pp. 68-70.
19 See Klein, *op. cit.*, p. 90 n. 427, for literature.

and later uses of *apostolos*. He does not identify the Twelve as apostles or as *the* apostles; in fact, he nowhere speaks of the Twelve.[20] Yet much of what he says about the apostles suggests that he thinks of them as a limited group acting in unison, and at least in this respect his views suggest those of Acts. The following two passages are illustrative:

Mag. 6:1:

προκαθημένου τοῦ ἐπισκόπου εἰς τόπον θεοῦ καὶ τῶν πρεσβυτέρων εἰς τόπον συνεδρίου τῶν ἀποστόλων.

Trall. 3:1:

ὡς καὶ τὸν ἐπίσκοπου ὄντα τόπον τοῦ πατρός, τοὺς δὲ πρεσβυτέρους ὡς συνέδριον θεοῦ καὶ ὡς σύνδεσμον ἀποστόλων.[21]

The expressions σύνδεσμον and συνέδριον suggest activity as a group. One is inclined here to see Jesus surrounded by the Twelve as the archetype of the bishop surrounded by his presbyters, but it should be noted that Ignatius never puts this fine a point on it.[22]

It should also be noted that Ignatius, like I Clement, expressly identifies Peter and Paul as apostles (Rom. 4:3).

Polycarp refers to the apostles but twice, *Phil.* 6:3 and 9:1. In 6:3 we have καθὼς αὐτὸς ἐνετείλατο καὶ οἱ εὐαγγελισάμενοι ἡμᾶς ἀπόστολοι καὶ οἱ προφῆται, οἱ προκηρύξαντες τὴν ἔλευσιν τοῦ κυρίου ἡμῶν. Here, despite the order *apostoloi-prophātai*, the reference is clearly to Old Testament prophets and to the apostles as *the* bearers of the message of the new covenant.[23] 9.1 speaks of αὐτῷ Παύλῳ καὶ τοῖς λοιποῖς ἀποστόλοις. This could be interpreted in either a Pauline or a Luke-Acts way and does not enable us to assign Polycarp to either tradition.

The date and place of origin of the *Didache* are obscure, and the relation of this work to main-stream Christianity undefined. The

---

[20] Curiously there are only two references to the Twelve in the apostolic fathers (Barnabas and Hermas), compared with about twenty-five in the New Testament. There are eight or nine references each to Peter, Paul and James. Cf. E. Goodspeed, *Index Patristicus, sive Clavis Patrum Apostolicorum Operum* (Chicago, 1907).

[21] See also *Trall.* 2.2, *Phil.* 5.1, *Smyr.* 8.1.

[22] Klein, *op. cit.*, pp. 93-94, argues against the suggestion made here.

[23] M. Hornschuh, in *New Testament Apocrypha*, ed. E. Hennecke and W. Schneemelcher, tr. R. McL. Wilson (Philadelphia, 1965), II, 75, assumes that this refers to the Twelve. This may well be, but if one agrees that the Twelve only gradually came to be identified as apostles and as *the* apostles other interpretations are possible.

Didache shows no trace of the Luke-Acts conception of apostleship.[24] The apostle is practically identified with the itinerant prophet in 11:3-5:

Περὶ δὲ τῶν ἀποστόλων καὶ προφητῶν, κατὰ τὸ δόγμα τοῦ εὐαγγελίου οὕτω ποιήσατε. πᾶς δὲ ἀπόστολος, ἐρχόμενος πρὸς ὑμᾶς δεχθήτω ὡς κύριος· οὐ μενεῖ δὲ εἰ μὴ ἡμέραν μίαν· ἐὰν δὲ ᾖ χρεία, καὶ τὴν ἄλλην· τρεῖς δὲ ἐὰν μείνῃ, ψευδοπροφήτης ἐστίν.

This would seem to differ from Paul if Paul is understood to have required an appearance of the risen Lord as the basis for apostleship, but it should be remembered that in contexts in which Paul discusses false apostles he never refers to the matter of a special appearance of the risen Lord.

Barnabas was probably written in Alexandrian circles ca. 130, and clearly identifies the Twelve as apostles. Jesus, we are told, chose apostles during his life-time to preach his gospel (5.9). In a subsequent passage we are told, in explanation of Numbers 19 (?), that, "The boys who sprinkle are (= represent) they who preached to us the forgiveness of sins, and the purification of the heart, to whom he gave the power of the Gospel to preach, and there are twelve as a testimony to the tribes, because there are twelve tribes of Israel" (8.3). Unfortunately, the next verse goes on: "But why are there three boys who sprinkle? As a testimony to Abraham, Isaac, and Jacob, for these are great before God." It would at least seem that one of these verses is a later interpolation, and v. 3 would seem the better candidate. Accordingly there is some reason to suppose that this identification of the Twelve as apostles is secondary and later.[25]

The Shepherd, whatever its date, refers once to the twelve apostles (Sim. 9.17.1), but does this so casually that one is inclined to suppose that this was a familiar motif. Unfortunately, however, the work twice (Sim. 9.15.4; 9.16.5) speaks of the "forty apostles and teachers" with the same casualness though I have been able to find no other trace of this conception in the early literature.

Of the apologists it is *Justin* who most frequently uses *apostolos*. Whenever he uses the word in the singular he is referring to Christ, the apostle (or apostle and angel) of the Father. For the rest, in no fewer than twenty-seven places Justin speaks of the apostles (plural)

---

24 The title by which the work is commonly known goes: Διδαχὴ τῶν Δώδεκα 'Αποστόλων. However, the title would seem to be secondary. See J. P. Audet, *La Didaché. Instructions des Apôtres* (Paris, 1958), 94-100.
25 Cf. Klein, *op. cit.,* pp. 96-97.

151

in a way that might be described as a development of the Luke-Acts pattern.[26] It was the twelve apostles, the inner circle of Jesus' companions during his public ministry, who were terrified at his death, reassured and instructed after his resurrection, and through whom the gospel was preached to all the world. Going out from Jerusalem, they brought the gospel to the Gentiles. Justin goes beyond the Luke-Acts pattern (though not counter to it) by virtually identifying, for the church in his time, the apostles with the τὰ ἀπομνημονεύματα τῶν ἀποστόλων.[27] The apostles appear as *the* link between the *Logos* and the church. They were the principal recipients of the teaching of Jesus while he was on earth. What the prophets had foretold obscurely, Jesus interpreted to the apostles ,and persuaded them was true.[28] It was they whom he reassembled after his resurrection, they whom he persuaded of the necessity of his death (Dial. 106.1) It was they who then went out and preached Jesus as the Christ; and finally, it was they who through their memoirs now provide the church with Jesus' understanding of the scriptures (the Old Testament), of Israel and of himself.

We have here obviously come a long way toward what might be called the classical view of the apostles, the view which we find fully in Irenaeus a generation later. On two principal points does Justin differ. 1) Paul is nowhere mentioned by Justin, nor is there any reference in his work to Paul's writings; and 2) there is no suggestion of a doctrine of apostolic-episcopal succession.

1) It seems altogether inconceivable that Justin could have written, as he tells us, a σύνταγμα κατὰ πασῶν τῶν γεγενημένων αἱρέσεων (1 Apol. 26.8), Marcion's included, without being aware of the existence of the Pauline writings and of the claim that Paul far surpassed all others as an interpreter of Jesus. It is difficult, consequently, to avoid the inference that Paul's total absence from Justin is not fortuitous.[29]

---

[26] I have no wish to suggest (or to deny) that Justin knew Luke-Acts.

[27] E. g. *1 Apol.* 67.3; *Dial.* 100.4.

[28] *Dial.* 76.6.

[29] For a discussion of those passages in Justin sometimes adduced as evidence of his knowledge of the Pauline corpus, see Klein, *op. cit.*, pp. 192-201. See also W. Schneemelcher, *"Paulus in der griechischen Kirche des zweiten Jahrhunderts,"* in *Zeitschrift für Kirchengeschichte* LXXV (1964), 8. Paul's absence from the two apologies is perhaps less puzzling if we note that in Tertullian's *Apology* there is but one likely reference to Pauline literature

2) It is not surprising that we find no hint of a normative episcopal ministry in succession to the apostles. This idea functions (and in its fully developed form is found) only in the intra-Christian polemic against gnosticism. At least to my knowledge it is not to be found, during the second century at any rate, in apologies directed against Greeks or Jews. We can only wonder whether Justin's lost work against heresies was similarly without reference to episcopal-apostolic succession, or whether it anticipated the views of Irenaeus and Tertullian.

VII.

When we turn to materials that lie outside the main-stream between the New Testament and Irenaeus we find that the tendencies observable in the orthodox literature are present, though often in more extreme form.

The *Kerygma Petrou,* for example, presents the Twelve in much the same way as does Luke-Acts.

> "I have chosen you twelve because I judged you worthy to be my disciples (whom the Lord wished). And I sent them, of whom I was persuaded that they would be true apostles, into the world to proclaim to men in all the world the joyous message that they may know that there is (only) one God, and to reveal what future happenings there would be through belief on me (Christ), to the end that those who hear and believe may be saved; and that those who believe not may testify that they have heard it and not be able to excuse themselves saying, 'We have not heard.' " [30]

If we agree with the editors of *Kerygma Petrou* and include Clem. Alex. *Strom* VI. 5. 43 among its fragments, it would appear that the apostles' mission to the Gentiles was to take place only after twelve years spent preaching to Israel. There is no trace of Paul in the extant fragments of *Kerygma Petrou* but these are so few as to make an argument from silence rather valueless.

The *Epistola Apostolorum* would appear to have been written at

(c. 31), where the reference is perhaps to I Timothy 2:2. There is also very little evidence of a knowledge of Paul in Tertullian's *Adversus Judaeos,* which we might take to be a rough parallel to Justin's *Dialogue.* If we knew only these works of Tertullian we would perhaps have a number of interesting theories about what Tertullian had against Paul.

30 *N. T. Apocrypha,* II, 101. The *Kerygma Petrou* can be dated with some confidence before the middle of the second century. *Ibid.,* 95.

about the same time as *Kerygma Petrou*.[31] Its apostolic authorship is put forth in the following terms:

> "(We), John and Thomas and Peter and Andrew and James and Philip and Bartholomew and Matthew and Nathanael and Judas Zelotes and Cephas, we have written (or, write) to the churches of the East and West, towards North and South, recounting and proclaiming to you concerning our Lord Jesus Christ, how we have †written† and *heard* and *felt* him after he had risen from the dead, and how he has revealed to us things great, astonishing, real." (*N. T. Apocrypha*, I, 192)

The apostolic name-list differs somewhat from those which we find in the canonical materials. It includes Nathanael (which is but one of many features which it has in common with John). Simon the Zealot and James of Alphaeus disappear and are replaced by Jude the Zealot and perhaps Cephas.[32] Whereas the canonical writings list two Simons, one of whom is renamed Peter-Cephas, *Epistola Apostolorum* lists no Simons, only a Peter and a Cephas who are clearly meant to be distinct.[33]

The letter deals with a post-resurrection appearance, and only eleven apostles are named. This suggests familiarity with the Judas tradition and probably a lack of familiarity with the Matthias tradition. Yet elsewhere the authors refer to themselves as "we twelve." [34] This suggests what we have already seen in the canonical materials: the number is more firmly fixed than the actual composition of the group.

The apostles in *Epistola Apostolorum* are sent out in much the same way as they are in the canonical materials.

> "He answered and said to us, 'Go and preach to the twelve tribes of Israel and to the Gentiles and Israel and to the land

---

[31] Cf. *N. T. Apocrypha*, I, 190-191, for the evidence.

[32] For a closer analysis of the various name lists, see T. Schermann, *Propheten und Apostellegenden* (TU, 31, 3) (Leipzig, 1907), pp. 198-231. For Jude the Zealot cf. *app. crit. ad Mt.* 10: 3, and Schermann, 198, 202, 217. In a number of old Latin mss., Jude the Zealot replaces Thaddaeus.

[33] According to Schermann, *op. cit.*, p. 206, Clement of Alexandria also distinguishes Cephas from Peter. Unfortunately, Schermann does not say where Clem. Alex. does this, and I so far have been unable to locate the passage.

[34] *N. T. Apocrypha*, I, 203. This is in the Ethiopic version; the Coptic version simply has "we." One could argue with about equal plausibility for either reading.

of Israel towards East and West, North and South; and many will believe in me, the son of God.' And we said to him, 'O Lord, who will believe us and who will listen to us and how can we do and teach and tell the wonders and signs and mighty deeds, as you have done?' And he answered and said to us, 'Go and preach (and teach) concerning (the coming and) the mercy of my Father. As my Father has done through me, I will also do through you in that I am with you, and I will give you my peace and my spirit and my power, (that it may happen to you) that they believe.'" (*Ibid.*, p. 212)

Of special interest is the way in which Paul is integrated with and subordinated to the twelve. What Klein would claim to find in Acts is carried through here in great detail.

" 'And look; you will meet a man whose name is Saul, which being interpreted means Paul. He is a Jew, circumcised according to the command of the law; and he will hear my voice from heaven with terror, fear, and trembling; and his eyes will be darkened and *by your hand* be crossed with spittle. And *do all to him as I have done to you.* Deliver (?) (him?) to others. And this man — immediately his eyes will be opened, and he will praise God, my heavenly Father. And he will become strong among the nations and will preach and teach, and many will be delighted when they hear and will be saved. Then will he be hated and delivered into the hand of his enemy, and he will testify before mortal (mss. AU: and perishable) kinds, and upon him will come the completion of the testimony to me; because he had persecuted and hated me, he will be converted to me and preach and teach, and he will be among my elect, a chosen vessel and a wall that does not fall. The last of the last will become a preacher to the Gentiles, perfect in (or, through) the will of my Father. As you have learned from the Scriptures that your fathers the prophets spoke concerning me, and it is fulfilled in me' — this certain thing he said — 'so you must become a leader to them. And *every word which I have spoken to you and which you have written concerning me,* that I am the word of the Father and the Father is in me, *so you must become also to that man, as it befits you. Teach and remind (him)* what has been said in the Scriptures and fulfilled concerning me, *and then he will be for the salvation* of the Gentiles.'

"And we said again to him, 'When, Lord will we meet that man, and when will you go to your Father and to our God and Lord?' And he answered and said to us, 'That man will set out from the land of Cilicia to Damascus in Syria to tear asunder the Church which you must create. It is I who will speak (to him) *through you,* and he will come quickly.' " (*Ibid.,* pp. 213-214)

Some groups, of course, went further than this and rejected Paul altogether. (Cf. Irenaeus, Adv. Haer. I.26.2; III.15.1) The somewhat later Pseudo-Clementines continue this.

One also finds groups in the second century who minimize the importance of the Twelve, subordinate them to Paul, or simply reject the version of Christianity associated with them. Marcion is the best known, but there were others as well. Some, finally, set themselves above all apostles.[35]

In contrast, orthodox or main-stream Christianity more and more clearly put itself under the authority of the Twelve plus Paul, did not try to hierarchize these two quantities and did this principally through the formation of the New Testament canon.[36]

VIII.

In Irenaeus and Tertullian, the understanding of apostleship is closely and explicitly connected with the idea of apostolic succession. Before turning to them, therefore, we shall attempt to bring into sharper focus the status of succession ideas prior to Irenaeus.

We have noted in Acts a tendency to ascribe to the Twelve a unique leadership role. In the Pastorals and in I Clement one can further observe efforts to transfer the authority of the apostles (though in these works not identified as the Twelve) to the church leadership of subsequent generations. If those coming after Paul, or after the apostles more generally, are not themselves empowered with an authority equal to that of the apostles, they at least participate in the authority given to the apostles by Christ, and in their own day they represent that authority. How widespread views of this sort were at the end of the first century it is difficult to say.

At about mid-second century we find evidence for the episcopal succession lists that would play so important a role in the theory of Irenaeus. We have in Eusebius succession lists for Rome, Jeru-

---

[35] For references see *N. T. Apocrypha* II, p. 41.

[36] The formation of a New Testament canon in the second century is an important part of the history of the understanding of the apostles and of apostolicity. Space and time prohibit a treatment of that topic here. For literature cf. *Die Religion in Geschichte und Gegenwart,* 3rd ed. (Tübingen, 1957 ff.) I, 1138.

salem, Antioch, and Alexandria, and via Eusebius we are led back to Hegesippus in the middle of the second century, searching out the successions at Rome and Corinth.[37] These early succession lists have generated a good bit of scepticism.[38] The Roman list has been most closely studied. E. Caspar has argued, convincingly I think, that the early Roman list was originally an apostolic rather than an episcopal succession list; that is, it is a list of leaders in succession to the apostles rather than a list of bishops going back to Peter as the first. This interpretation, since it does not require a monarchical episcopacy at Rome in the first century, fits in better with what we know of Rome through I Clement.[39]

It is worth noting that, so far as can be determined, it was the conflict with gnosticism that produced Hegesippus' interest in "the successions" at Rome and elsewhere.[40] The same kind of conflict would seem to have been responsible for the interest in authority and succession in the Pastorals;[41] and while the argument that gnosticism lay behind the controversy reflected in I Clement seems to me unconvincing it is nonetheless the case that here too it is intra-Christian dissension that precipitates apostolic succession ideas.

To judge from the roughly contemporary procedures of Hegesippus and the gnostic Ptolemy,[42] at least some orthodox and some gnostics appealed to a succession by means of which the authentic apostolic tradition is transmitted and safeguarded.

---

[37] To speak of Hegesippus as a mid-century figure is to push the chronology a bit. His *Hypomnemata* was not written before 174. This work, however, would *seem* to reflect his activities over the several preceding decades, and for this reason he is usually taken to be a generation earlier than Irenaeus even though there is some chronological overlap. See C. H. Turner, "Note on the Chronology of Hegesippus," in *Essays on the Early History of the Church and the Ministry*, H. B. Swete, ed. (London, 1918), p. 207.

[38] For literature, see J. Quasten, *Patrology* (Westminster, 1950), I, 286.

[39] *Die älteste römische Bischofsliste* (Berlin, 1926), p. 253.

[40] See Eusebius, *H. E.*, IV. 22; H. J. Lawlor, *Eusebiana*, Oxford.

[41] *Introduction to the New Testament*, P. Feine, J. Behm, completely reedited by W. Kümmel, 14th ed., tr. by A. J. Mattil Jr. (Nashville, 1966), pp. 266-268.

[42] *Letter to Flora*, in Epiphanius, *Panarion*, XXXIII, 3-7. The relevant passage is as follows: Μαθήση γὰρ, θεοῦ διδόντος ἑξῆς καὶ τὴν τούτου ἀρχήν τε καὶ γέννησιν, ἀξιουμένη τῆς ἀποστολικῆς παραδόσεως, ἣνἐκ διαδοχῆς καὶ ἡμεῖς παρειλήφαμεν. (PG 41, 568B.) The καὶ ἡμεῖς could be interpreted as presupposing an antecedent claim on the part of Ptolemy's orthodox opponents, but this is at least questionable.

It is only when we turn to *Irenaeus* that we see how the succession lists functioned polemically and theologically. Here, as in much of the earlier literature concerned with succession, we are in the middle of the dispute with gnosticism. It is interesting to note that in his presentation of the gnostics Irenaeus is concerned to show not only what they have said but their solidarity through succession with one another and ultimately with their common source, Simon Magus:

> *"Agressi sumus autem nos, arguentes eos a Simone patre omnium haereticorum, et doctrinas et successiones manifestare . . ." (Adv. haer.* III, *praef.)*

But of more consequence is his view of the role of *successiones* (διαδοχαί) among the orthodox. For Irenaeus it is the apostolic testimony and the apostolic authority that are crucial in the life of the church.

> "We have learned from none others the plan of our salvation, than from those through whom the Gospel has come down to us, which they did at one time proclaim in public, and, at a later period, by the will of God, handed down to us in the Scriptures, to be the ground and pillar of our faith. For it is unlawful to assert that they preached before they possessed 'perfect knowledge,' as some do even venture to say, boasting themselves as improvers of the apostles. For, after our Lord rose from the dead, (the apostles) were invested with power from on high when the Holy Spirit came down (upon them), were filled from all (His gifts), and had perfect knowledge: they departed to the ends of the earth, preaching the glad tidings of the good things (sent) from God to us, and proclaiming the peace of heaven to men, who indeed do all equally and individually possess the Gospel of God." (*Adv. haer.* III.1.1 [ANF trans.])

From this one might suppose that for Irenaeus the scriptures would have been sufficient for the definition of the Christian faith and the Christian community had it not been for the gnostic challenge. But the gnostics denied a) the infallibility of the apostles, b) the apostolicity, or at least the exclusive apostolicity, of the church's scriptures, and/or c) the rectitude of the church's interpretation of those scriptures.

Irenaeus devotes little attention to the first of these matters. He simply assumes that the apostles were fully enlightened with the coming of the Holy Spirit; and on this assumption he argues that the apostles would not have held back the more important parts of the gospel from those to whom they publicly entrusted the guidance of the churches. Hence one can look about today and see who those are who have been the recipients, *per successiones*, of the apostolic tradition. These apostolic bishops and the apostolic churches can serve as norms in determining which are the genuinely apostolic books and what is the truly apostolic faith.

Irenaeus does not seem to require an apostolic pedigree for the existence of a church; at least he nowhere says that this is necessary. That is, a church not established by an apostle is validated according to the Irenaean scheme of things not (or at least not primarily) through a succession of ordinations going back to an apostle. It is validated by being in agreement and harmony with the norm churches, those of apostolic foundation and public episcopal succession.

In Irenaeus' conception the apostolic church or apostolic *cathedra* is more central than the idea of conferral of power from one bishop to another through episcopal consecration or ordination.[43] Eleutherius holds the inheritance of the episcopate in the twelfth place from the apostles (III.3.3) not because one or several Western bishops have come to Rome to bestow apostolic power upon him, but because the church for which he has been consecrated is an apostolic church.

This is not to say that Irenaeus denies that bishops should be consecrated by other bishops. If one supposes that the liturgy for episcopal consecration in use at Rome in Eleutherius' time was substantially that preserved in Hippolytus' *Apostolic Tradition*, then presumably Eleutherius was consecrated in a rite that included the laying on of hands by other bishops. But it is more difficult to ascertain precisely how the various parts of the consecration liturgy were understood. Though we may be inclined, because of later developments, to see the laying on of hands as a conferral of (apostolic) power, the very essence of the right, one might just as plausibly interpret this as an expression of the unity of the churches represented by their bishops. My point is not that this was in fact the unique understanding of the rite prevalent in the second century. I would argue only that the fact

---

43 A. Ehrhardt, *The Apostolic Ministry* (Scottish Journal of Theology Occasional Papers, no. 7), 1958, p. 82, maintains that in the Pseudo-Clementines it is enthronement rather than the laying on of hands that is given greater emphasis. I have not had time to check this suggestion. Eusebius, *H. E.*, VII, 19, also reflects a strong early emphasis on the apostolic chair. Cf. also G. Dix, "Ministry in the Early Church," in *The Apostolic Ministry*, ed. K. E. Kirk (London, 1946), p. 206.

of ordination by *(inter alia)* other bishops does not necessarily mean that the other bishops' actions were understood as the communication of apostolic power, already possessed by the consecrating bishops, to the bishop elect. Election by the people and their presence along with the presbyterate are also part of this liturgy, and there is no reason to suppose that these were just the trimmings, the episcopal laying on of hands the essence. If it is not putting too fine a point on the matter, we might say that one becomes a successor to the apostles through ordination for an apostolic church rather than simply through ordination by any bishop whatsoever; and thus the "bearer" of apostolicity in the ordination rite is the church — i. e., the people and the presbyterate — rather than the participating bishops.[44]

One of the crucial disputes over the episcopacy in the later patristic era had to do with the question of the unworthy minister: Did a bishop who was seriously delinquent as a Christian cease thereby to be a bishop? It is difficult to be certain just how Irenaeus would have answered this question, though I am inclined to interpret him in a Donatist rather than Augustinian fashion. The following passage is crucial:

> *"Quapropter eis qui in Ecclesia sunt presbyteris obaudire oportet, his qui successionem habent ab Apostolis, sicut ostendimus; qui cum episcopatus successione charisma veritatis certum secundum placitum Patris acceperunt: reliquos vero qui absistunt a principali successione, et quocunque loco colliguntur, suspectos habere, vel quasi haereticos et malae sententiae, vel quasi scindentes et elatos et sibi placentes, aut rursus ut hypocritas, quaestus gratia et vanae gloriae hoc operantes. Omnes autem hi deciderunt a veritate. Et haeretici quidem alienum ignem afferentes ad altare Dei, id est alienas doctrinas, a coelesti igne comburentur, quemadmodum Nadab et Abiud. Qui vero exsurgunt contra veritatem, et alteros adhortantur adversus Ecclesiam Dei, remanent apud inferos, voragine terrae absorpti, quemadmodum qui circa Chore Dathan et Abiron. Qui autem scindunt et separant unitatem Ecclesiae, eandem quam Hieroboam poenam percipiunt a Deo.*

> *"Qui vero crediti quidem sunt a multis esse presbyteri, surviunt autem suis voluptatibus, et non praeponunt timorem*

---

44 Caution is necessary here. Obviously Irenaeus and the second century church did not pull rites apart the way we might be inclined to. The above analysis may at least serve to suggest that Irenaeus did not automatically take for granted the view that apostolic succession was simply a matter of physical continuity of episcopal consecrations.

Dei in cordibus suis sed contemeliis agunt reliquos, et principalis consessionis tumore elati sunt, et in absconsis agunt mala, et dicunt, Nemo nos videt, redarguentur a Verbo; qui non secundum gloriam judicat, neque faciem attendit, sed in cor: . . . Ab omnibus igitur talibus absistere oportet; adhaerere vero his qui et Apostolorum, sicut praediximus, doctrinam custodiunt, et cum presbyterii ordine sermonem sanum et conversationem sine offensa praestant, ad conformationem et correptionem reliquorum." (*Adv. Haer.* 4.26.2-4)

The simpler (though not the only) interpretation of this passage is that one who has been ordained (how else account for the *"crediti sunt a multis esse presbyteri"?*) may indeed fall short of the demands of the office, and thereby cease to be a part of the apostolic succession and tradition. Thus factors other than the once-for-all and publicly ascertainable ordination would seem to be required to make a bishop a bishop. To classify Irenaeus according to later categories, he would seem to be developing here a Donatist rather than an Augustinian conception of the episcopacy. Indeed, it may be appropriate to note here that none of the early witnesses to a "high" conception of authority — I Clement, Irenaeus, Cyprian — actually absolutizes church authority. I Clement criticizes the Corinthians because they have ousted from the ministry those who served worthily and blamelessly; and Irenaeus and Cyprian both seem to envisage situations in which properly ordained bishops would have to be put aside (presumably from below) for failure to minister worthily. Thus, though certain expressions may seem to lend support to later absolutizing tendencies, for these earlier writers apostolic succession "guarantees" nothing.

Tertullian's views coincide in a general way with those of Irenaeus, though an ambiguity surfaces here that was not apparent in Irenaeus.[45] Certain churches are apostolic because they were founded by apostles and are united under bishops in succession to these apostles. But churches which are not of apostolic foundation are said to be apostolic for a variety of reasons. Sometimes he considers a church which was founded as an offshoot from a church that is apostolic in its foundation as being *eo ipso* apostolic. At other times apostolicity is defined, in the Irenaean fashion, in terms of doctrinal agreement and peace with the principal churches.

---

45 The ecclesiology here described is that of the Catholic Tertullian. I have not attempted here to trace the development of the ideas of the Montanist Tertullian.

In the former sense he writes:

". . . Having, on the authority of a prophecy, which occurs in a psalm of David, chosen Matthias by lot as the twelfth, in the place of Judas, they obtained the promised power of the Holy Ghost for the gift of miracles and of utterance; and after first bearing witness to the faith in Jesus Christ throughout Judaea, and founding churches (there), they next went forth into the world and preached the same doctrine of the same faith to the nations. They then in like manner founded churches in every city, from which all the other churches, one after another, derived the tradition of the faith, and the seeds of doctrine, and are every day deriving them, that they may become churches. Indeed, it is on this account only that they will be able to deem themselves apostolic, as being the offspring of apostolic churches. Every sort of thing must necessarily revert to its original for its classification. Therefore the churches, although they are so many and so great, comprise but the one primitive church, (founded) by the apostles, from which they all (spring). In this way all are primitive, and all are apostolic whilst they are all proved to be one, in unbroken unity, by their peaceful communion, and title of brotherhood, and bond of hospitality – privileges which no other rule directs than the one tradition of the selfsame mystery." (*De praescriptione haereticorum,* c. 20 [ANF trans.])

But then further on in the same work he writes:

". . . To this test, therefore, will they be submitted for proof by those churches who, although they derive not their founder from apostles or apostolic men (as being of much later date, for they are in fact being founded daily), yet since they agree in the same faith, they are accounted as not less apostolic because they are akin in doctrine." (*Ibid.,* c. 32)

The difference between the two should not, however, be exaggerated. While according to the former view the very existence of a church would depend upon its derivation from a church of apostolic foundation, even here the emphasis does not fall on a quasi-physical transmission *via* ordination of apostolic-episcopal power and authority. It is the handing-on of the orthodox faith that is crucial: "from which all the other churches, one after another, derived the tradition of the faith and the seeds of doctrine . . . that they may become churches." It is the reception of the orthodox faith that makes a community a church. It may very well be that the practice with which Tertullian was familiar required that the bishop of a new church be consecrated *(inter alia)* by the laying on of hands by other bishops; but his understanding of apostolic succession does not bring this to the fore or even, strictly speaking, require it. Secondary apostolic churches would be derived from the preaching and missionary efforts coming from the original apostolic churches, the handing on of their *regula fidei* and of their scriptures.

There is another aspect of Tertullian's thought which is relevant to some of the later uses to which the understanding of succession would be put. In *De exhortatione castitatis* (c. 7) Tertullian bases his argument against the remarriage of a widower on the supposition that in cases of necessity the layman has the prerogatives of the priesthood, not only to baptize but to "offer" as well:

> ". . . Therefore, if you have the right of a priest in your own
> person, in cases of necessity, it behooves you to have likewise
> the discipline of a priest whenever it may be necessary to have
> the right of a priest. If you are a bigamist, do you offer?"
> (ANF, vol. 4, p. 54)

It should be noted first that this work is generally ascribed to Tertullian's Catholic period, and so ought not simply be put aside as one aspect of his heresy. Moreover, even if one were to consider some of the views expressed in the work as already Montanist, one would still have to grant that the point under scrutiny here is put forward by Tertullian as being non-controversial, indeed as being sufficiently agreed upon that it can serve as a basis for settling a dispute between Tertullian and his more lenient opponents.

Thus we must ask whether Tertullian is here presupposing a eucharist celebrated by unordained laymen, or whether something less or other than the eucharist is intended here. Since the offering is spoken of exactly in parallel to baptizing, and since the whole point of the passage is the possibility, in case of necessity, of the layman acting precisely as an ordained minister would, to suppose that Tertullian is here merely saying that in the absence of a priest the layman may offer thanksgiving in his heart (or some such) is to make nonsense of the argument.

We are therefore led to suppose, at the very least, that Tertullian took it for granted that a quite proper eucharist could take place, in case of necessity, without ordination of the celebrant by a bishop standing in the apostolic succession. In addition, in the absence of contrary evidence we may assume that Tertullian knew whereof he spoke, and that this was the tradition at least at Carthage and presumably in the area dominated by Carthage. Whether ca. 200 this view extended beyond that area I do not know.

One might wish to contrast this with Tertullian's own earlier criticisms of the heretics (gnostics):

> "Their ordinations, are carelessly administered, capricious, changeable. At one time they put novices in office; at another time, men who are bound to some secular employment; at another, persons who have apostatized from us, to bind them by vainglory, since they cannot by the truth. Nowhere is promotion easier than in the camp of rebels, where the mere fact of being there is a foremost service. And so it comes to pass that to-day one man is their bishop, to-morrow another; to-day he is a deacon who to-morrow is a reader; to-day he is a presbyter who to-morrow is a layman. For even on laymen do they impose the functions of priesthood." (*De praesc. haer.,* c. 41)

But the point of this criticism is the undisciplined character of the heretical communities. There need be no contradiction between a view that it is possible in case of necessity for a layman to officiate at the eucharist, and that it is wrong or undesirable to mix up the orders as was allegedly done in the gnostic communities. In *De baptismo,* c. 17, Tertullian makes a similar point: the layman may baptize in cases of necessity, but this must be done with considerable circumspection lest the layman be guilty of usurpation.

The importance of *Hippolytus* in all this is variously assessed. C. H. Turner, while supposing that there is no very important difference between Hippolytus and Tertullian or Irenaeus, does find hints in Hippolytus' vocabulary that point toward a conception of succession as the personal possession of the bishop.[46] But in his evidence he is simply mistaken: Irenaeus has already (III.3.1) spoken of bishops as "successors" and not simply as "in the succession to," and Tertullian (*Adv. Marc.* IV.5) has spoken of a bishop as *"summus sacerdos."* The fact that it is in Hippolytus that we first have the Greek equivalents — διαδοχος and ἀρχιερτσια — is of no substantial importance.

More recently, G. Blum has tried to differentiate Tertullian and Hippolytus, while recognizing a basic similarity of outlook between the latter and Irenaeus. This differentiation is achieved at the expense of Tertullian who, Blum alleges, makes of the bishops *"in keinem noch so modifizierten Sinne Nachfolger der Apostel."*

"Die Bischöfe [for Tertullian] *sind in keinem noch so modifizier-*

---

46 "Apostolic Succession," p. 129.

ten Sinne Nachfolger der Apostel. Als apostolici seminis traduces (pr. 32; 40, 13) haben sie vielmehr nur eine funktionale Bedeutung bei der Übermittlung der reinen apostolischen Lehre. Ihre Vermittlerrolle entbehrt einer dogmatischen Begründung, und über eine besondere Vollmacht und Geistbegabung, ein charisma veritatis wie bei Irenäus, finden wir keine Andeutung. . . . so hat der Episkopat für ihn doch nur rein menschliche Autorität." [47]

True it is that Tertullian does not speak of a *charisma veritatis* and that the bishop is described in functional terms. But one ought not overlook the principally functional analysis in Irenaeus. A *dogmatische Begründung* is no more to be found in Irenaeus than in Tertullian. Moreover since Tertullian quite clearly sees the episcopacy as instituted by the apostles (*De praesc. Laer.* c. 32), and considers it the work of the Holy Spirit to secure the unity and truth of the churches' faith (*ibid.* c. 28), it is difficult to take the differences between Tertullian and Irenaeus (and Hippolytus) as more than differences in emphasis.

The seventh book of *Clement of Alexandria's Stromata* provides a very interesting contrast to the writings of Irenaeus and Tertullian. In the fifteenth chapter of that book Clement takes up the objection raised against Christianity by the existence of so many competing sects. As is clear from chapter seventeen, the sects or heresies are the same ones being *fought* against by the Western writers. But whereas for them it is scripture taken in conjunction with the historic episcopacy that constitutes and makes present the apostolic tradition, in Clement it is the scriptures plus the Christian gnostic that constitute and make present that tradition. In the entire *apologia* for othodoxy against what we would call gnosticism Clement nowhere refers to the bishops. The scriptural canon would seem to be sufficiently firm for Clement that the circumscription of the written basis for Christian thought and life does not seem to have been an urgent problem; and given "the prophets, the Gospel, and the blessed apostles," [48] those who devote their lives to understanding this material are the surest guides. "This Gnostic [= perfect Christian], to speak compendiously,

---

[47] G. G. Blum, *"Der Begriff des Apostolischen im theologischen Denken Tertullians,"* Kerygma und Dogma 8 (1963), 102-121. Cf. also G. G. Blum *"Apostolische Tradition und Sukzession bei Hippolyt,"* in *Zeitschrift für die neutestamentliche Wissenschaft und die Kunde der älteren Kirche 55* (1964), 95-109.

[48] *Strom,* VII, 16.

makes up for the absence of the apostles, by the rectitude of his life, the accuracy of his knowledge . . . [49] And further,

> "On account of the heresies, therefore, the toil of discovery must be undertaken; but we must not at all abandon [the truth]. For, on fruit being set before us, some real and ripe, and some made of wax, as like the real as possible, we are not to abstain from both on account of the resemblance. But by the exercise of the apprehension of contemplation, and by reasoning of the most decisive character, we must distinguish the true from the seeming." [50]

The ecclesiastical tradition (VIII, 16), the ecclesiastical canon (VII, 15), these function normatively for the theologian-gnostic, but he it is who brings these to bear effectively in the present.

Clement introduces as well the argument from greater antiquity into his refutation of the heresies (VII, 17), but here again there is no reference to the bishops as spanning the time between the foundation of the church and the present.

Thus if we would talk about "apostolic succession" in Clement, we should ascribe it to those teachers who make up for the absence of the apostles by their study and their teaching — a *successio doctorum* rather than a *successio episcoporum*.

> "Those, then, also now, who have exercised themselves in the Lord's commandments, and lived perfectly and gnostically according to the Gospel, may be enrolled in the chosen body of the apostles. Such an one is in reality a presbyter of the Church, and true minister (deacon) of the will of God, if he do and teach what is the Lord's; not as being ordained by men, nor regarded righteous because a presbyter, but enrolled in the presbyterate because righteous. And although here upon earth he be not honoured with the chief seat, he will sit down on the four-and-twenty thrones, judging the people, as John says in the Apocalypse." [51]

This is not to deny that there were bishops in Alexandria in Clement's day; there were.[52] But he does not seem to have thought of them as successors to the apostles or as the prime guarantors of apostolicity.

---

[49] VII, 12.

[50] VII, 15.

[51] VI, 13.

[52] Though it is open to question whether the bishop was thought of at this time in Alexandria as a *primus inter pares* within the presbyterate, or in a more primatial way. Cf. G. Bardy, *La théologie de l'église de saint Irénée au concile de Nicée* (Paris, 1947), pp. 119-120.

G. Bardy, who can scarcely be accused of exaggerating differences between the early fathers and the full blown Catholic understanding of things, states in his summary of *Origen's* ecclesiology: *"il n'y a pas, comme saint Irénée une théorie de l'épiscopat et de la succession apostolique."* [53] It would be difficult not to agree. Origen writes at some length about priests and bishops, but the focus is primarily on their pastoral responsibilities and on the holiness requisite thereunto.

J. Daniélou has, I think, quite rightly described the context in which Origen's thinking on the specific problems of hierarchy and ministry is developed:

> "It will thus be seen that Origen was faced with two problems, both of them created by the circumstances of the time. The first one turned on the relationship between the visible hierarchy of presbyters and the visible hierarchy of doctors. There were two distinct types of authority in the early Church. Both could be traced back to the charismata of the early days, but they were each derived from different ones. The two hierarchies took up different attitudes on certain points. The presbyters turned more towards the worship of God, the didaskaloi rather to the ministry of the word and to Scripture. The presbyters regarded martyrdom as a redemptive sacrifice; the didaskaloi saw it as the perfection of the gnosis. Clearly, Origen represents the viewpoint of the *didaskaloi.* But his writings belong to a period when the two hierarchies were showing signs of coalescing. The teaching office was in process of becoming a function of the priestly hierarchy. However, in Origen a certain dualism is still perceptible." [54]

Where Origen does speak of something approaching apostolic succession it is to connect the *doctores ecclesiarum* with the *apostoli:*

> *"Haec etenim, quae prius in litteris erat et secundum litteram intelligebatur, modo in ecclesiis Christi, revelante Domino, loquela effecta est, loquentibus de ea et disserentibus primo sanctis Apostolis et removentibus superficiem litterae, proferentibus vero de ea spiritalem loquelam. Sed et singuli quique doctores ecclesiarum litteram legis loquelam et disputationem evangelicam faciunt."* [55]

In connection with Clement and Origen we might note that the church in Alexandria (and Egypt) apparently did not use the same episcopal ordination practices that we find in other places. At least

[53] *Op. cit.,* p. 164.
[54] Jean Daniélou, *Origène* (Paris, 1948), p. 62.
[55] *Hom. in Jos.* 20.5.

down through the time of Origen, the bishop of Alexandria seems to have been chosen and consecrated by the presbyters of that city.[56] From this one could not directly conclude that in Alexandria there could have been no notion of episcopal apostolic succession. Apostolic succession as succession to an apostolic chair would be reconcilable with Alexandrian practice; but apostolic succession as the transmission of authority and/or power through consecration by bishops would not be reconcilable.

We might also note that the Alexandrian practice was used by certain later Western writers — Jerome and Ambrosiaster — to support the view that basically a bishop was nothing other than a presbyter, a kind of *primus inter pares*.[57] This view, to my present knowledge not wide-spread during the patristic era, seems to have been eliminated almost entirely subsequent to Augustine.

Cyprian combines the principal elements of the ecclesiologies of Ignatius of Antioch and Irenaeus/Tertullian, though owing to the passing of the gnostic crisis he emphasizes succession less than some earlier writers. The church was founded upon the apostles; and as a sign of the solidarity of the apostolic office, Jesus first endowed Peter with the apostolic power and authority. Indeed it is from the *cathedra Petri* that the *unitas sacerdotalis exorta est;* and the church that is or possesses the *cathedra Petri* is the *ecclesia principalis*.[58]

Through the unity of the apostles (a unity manifested in the priority of Peter) the church was one; through the unity of the bishops the church is and has always been one.[59]

Cyprian is quite at ease in calling the apostles bishops (Ep. 3. 3 and 67, 4) and in calling the bishops successors of the apostles (Ep. 66, 4; 65, 16, 65, 3). The older idea of apostolic churches, however, does not seem to have functioned significantly in Cyprian, and in general he seems to hold for a radical equality among all bishops and all churches.

We should also note in Cyprian the non-permanent, non-automatic character of inclusion in the apostolic succession. A bishop whose life is not worthy of his position is, for that reason, no bishop

---

[56] For details and documentation, see W. Telfer, "Episcopal Succession in Egypt," in *Journal of Ecclesiastical History* III (1952), 1-13.

[57] Again, see Telfer for details and documentation.

[58] *Ep.* 59, 14.

[59] According to the Pseudo-Cyprianic *De aleatoribus,* 1 (CSEL, III/3, 93) each individual bishop is installed in the chair of Peter.

at all, and should be repudiated by his people; and a bishop who goes into schism likewise ceases thereby to be a bishop.

In both cases Cyprian's views are controlled by his larger views on the relationship between church and sacraments. A bishop is a bishop only insofar as he is at the head of his church; and if either through gross terpitude or heresy he should break the bond between himself and his church he simply ceases to be a bishop. Episcopacy (and thus apostolic succession) is still rooted firmly in the local church and is intelligible only if that relationship is kept in mind. To be a bishop at all is to be a bishop of a specific church (just as to be baptized at all is to be baptized into a specific church). An episcopacy, or apostolic succession, that would be created solely through episcopal consecration and which could exist apart from or independent of a specific Christian community is nowhere in sight.

On this point C. H. Turner claims to see evidence already in Cyprian of a shift from an emphasis on bishops of the churches to an emphasis on bishops of the church:

> ". . . the common relation of the episcopal order to the Church Catholic tends to assume bigger proportions, while the individual relation of each as representing and expressing the tradition of a particular group of Christian people tends by comparison to retire into the background."

However exact this may be as a description of Cyprian, and I am inclined to think that the picture is over-drawn, one can scarcely take issue with Turner's subsequent remark:

> "There is of course no necessary antagonism between these two conceptions, which when held in equipoise complement and correct one another. But a shifting of the emphasis on to one side of the truth can be felt at work from the beginning of the third century; and it marks the first stage of a long and far-reaching development, in the course of which an integral element of the doctrine in its original form, namely the relation of the bishop to his own people, and consequently their indirect share in the Apostolic Succession, dwindled and disappeared." [60]

As on so many other matters so here *Augustine* is difficult to put into a single neat package. In his anti-Manichaean writings he frequently introduces apostolic succession ideas that in content and function are very much like the views of Irenaeus and Tertullian. The

---

[60] "Apostolic Succession," in H. B. Swete, *Essays on the Early History of the Church* (London, 1918), pp. 131-132.

public and unbroken succession of bishops going back to the apostolic foundations of certain churches is the surest guarantee of the apostolicity of the church's scriptures and of its faith.[61]

This idea carries over into his anti-Donatist writings, though what is now more important is the idea — also common to Irenaeus and Tertullian — that to be part of the Catholic church one must be in communion with the apostolic churches.[62]

In all of this the matter of episcopal consecration need be no more central in Augustine than it had been in Irenaeus or Tertullian. The important thing is the almost tangible continuity between the apostles and the present provided by the unbroken succession of bishops in the apostolic *cathedrae*.

But though Augustine's understanding and use of the idea of apostolic succession is not to my present knowledge much affected by his general understanding of sacrament, it is in that understanding of sacrament that one finds the key to the subsequent transformation of this idea.[63] For in contrast to most of the earlier writers whom we have considered, Augustine develops a general concept of sacrament — baptism, eucharist, and orders — that is significantly more independent of the church-community than had earlier been the case. In opposing the Donatists Augustine develops a more individualistic conception of sacrament than that which had prevailed previously. One receives orders as one receives baptism, if a valid minister performs the rite. The reality of one's baptism or one's orders depends on God and God's instrument, the minister of the sacrament. In recognizing Donatist orders (including their episcopal consecrations) Augustine severs the earlier connection between bishop and church, and thus provides the conceptual framework for an understanding of episcopacy (and thus of apostolic succession) as something conferred once for all upon an individual through ordination by another bishop. Succession is thus basically a succession of ordinations, and one stands more logically in succession to him who ordained than to one's predecessor in a particular see.

I would note again that Augustine does not himself draw these

---

[61] C. Faustum, 33.6; 11.5; 13.5; 28.2; 32.19; C. ep. Manichaei, 4. For further references see F. Hofmann, *Der Kirchenbegriff des hl. Augustinus, in seinen Grundlagen und in seiner Entwicklung* (Munich, 1933), pp. 94-99.

[62] *C. litteras Petiliani*, 2.16.37; *C. Cresconium*, 2.37.46.

[63] This is at present only hypothetical, and my indicatives ought perhaps be made subjunctives.

conclusions for the doctrine of apostolic succession. His treatment of this latter is quite conservative. But his general understanding of sacrament points toward a new and significantly different view.

APOSTOLIC SUCCESSION: NOTES ON THE EARLY PATRISTIC ERA

By Walter J. Burghardt

The following observations do not constitute a scholarly article in their own right. They simply record the conclusions of research I did for the 1969 Lutheran-Catholic international conversations at Nemi, outside Rome. Nor is it my purpose to challenge the interpretations drawn from the evidence by James F. McCue elsewhere in this volume. I appear here in print because the dialogue group feels it important for our discussions and convictions on ministry to give quasi-permanent form to certain affirmations of mine on the early understanding of apostolic succession which paint a picture with broader strokes than Professor McCue was asked to use.

I find different aspects of "succession to the apostles" suggested or stressed by different writers, in different periods, at different places. Call these, if you will, different "moments" in the development, though the moments are not always chronologically distinct.

There is, first, the *principle* of succession, presumably going back to the mind of the apostles, and through the apostles to an ordered plan of God. The principle emerges from Clement of Rome about the year 96.[1] Clement's thesis, as I read him, is this. The apostles personally ordained some men to the ministry, to the presbyteral office in the local churches. They stipulated that, upon the death of these men whom they themselves had appointed, other approved men should succeed to the ministry of these local officials. They provided or stipulated — in a manner not disclosed by Clement — that these local officials would be appointed "by other reputable men with the consent of the whole church." These "appointers" exercise in this respect the function the apostles had exercised in the first Christian generation.

---

[1] Cf. *Epistola ad Corinthios* 44, 1-3.

This is not a succession to apostleship (for Clement, the apostolate as a distinct office apparently passed away with the original apostles); it is a succession to the *episkopē* which the apostles had exercised, specifically the *leitourgia*.[2]

There is, second, succession in episcopal *office*. Here the significant segment of testimony is a set of writers (Hegesippus, *ca.* 175; Irenaeus, *ca.* 180; Tertullian, *ca.* 200) who used the so-called episcopal lists, the uninterrupted series of *episkopoi* of an apostolic see, as a theological argument for the authenticity of the doctrinal tradition. There is an important interplay here. On the one hand, the argument is from legitimate office to authentic doctrine; apostolic succession here is not simply doctrinal succession; legitimate appointment or election is an indispensable aspect of apostolic succession. Here Tertullian is eloquent, in an argument which was part of his regular equipment against the Gnostics: "Let them show the origin of their churches, let them unfold the series of their bishops succeeding one another from the beginning, so that the first bishop had as warrant and predecessor one of the apostles or one of the apostolic men who remained to the end in communion with the apostles." [3] On the other hand, without orthodox doctrine succession ceases or never really begins; bishops are in the true succession in so far as they teach the true doctrine. Irenaeus expresses these twin facets of succession constantly: "All who wish to see the truth can look in every church at the tradition of the apostles made manifest in all the world. And we can enumerate those who were appointed *(instituti sunt)* bishops by the apostles in the churches, as well as their successions *(successiones)* down to our own time — men who have neither taught nor known anything like the ravings of these [Gnostics]." [4] In the pithy summation of Molland, "A bishop is found in the succession if he is the legitimate successor of his predecessors and if he remains faithful to the doctrine of the church." [5]

---

[2] Hans von Campenhausen sees here Clement's "theory of the apostolic origin of the presbyteral system, and of the lifelong tenure of the office, once it has been bestowed" (*Ecclesiastical Authority and Spiritual Power in the Church of the First Three Centuries* [tr. J. A. Baker; Stanford, 1969], p. 91).

[3] *De praescriptione haereticorum* 32, 1.

[4] *Adversus haereses* 3, 3, 1.

[5] Einar Molland, *"Le développement de l'idée de succession apostolique,"* in *Revue d'histoire et de philosophie religieuses* 34 (1954), 22. I have profited much from Molland's study, but he is perhaps precocious when

There is, third, specifically *doctrinal* succession. Here we confront a succession from the apostles not so much in episcopal office as in a line of teachers who have received and transmitted apostolic doctrine with Christian fidelity. In this area, as you might expect, it is Clement of Alexandria and Origen who come on strong. Although their approach has at times been exaggerated, it remains a fact that the succession of their predilection is the succession of Christian teachers, whether on the episcopal level or not. It can refer, for example, to the Christian gnostic who even "supplies by substitution for the absence of the apostles"; [6] it can refer to those spiritual teachers who know how to interpret scripture as it ought to be interpreted.

A fourth moment in the evolution comes early in the third century. Here three developments are crucial. In the first place, authority, power, *jurisdiction* is claimed in connection with apostolic succession. The crucial evidence is the Montanist Tertullian's attack on an elusive bishop (Zephyrinus? Callistus? Agrippinus?) who apparently was convinced that the power to forgive certain sins was not a personal prerogative of Peter but has come to every church which has a spiritual relationship to him engendered by the seed of doctrine and possessed in consequence of its having received its faith from him or (as some interpret the text) simply because a chain of predecessors links it to Peter. [7] In the second place, whereas for Irenaeus, Hegesippus, and Tertullian, "bishops have their place in the apostolic succession only in connection with the churches over which they preside," with Hippolytus, perhaps for the first time, "succession from the apostles seems to be a personal possession of the bishop. . . . For the first time, apparently, the bishops are not merely in the succession from the apostles, but they are themselves 'successors of' the apostles." [8] In the third place, the Hippolytean idea in the evolution of apostolic

---

he finds in Irenaeus the precursor of both the Protestant idea (doctrinal succession) and the Catholic idea (use of episcopal lists as theological argument).

[6] Clement of Alexandria, *Stromata* 7, 77, 4.

[7] See Tertullian, *De pudicitia* 21, 1 ff.; William P. Le Saint, in *Ancient Christian Writers* 28 (Westminster, Md., 1959), 284-86; Molland, *art. cit.,* p. 24.

[8] C. H. Turner, "Apostolic Succession," in H. B. Swete (ed.), *Essays on the Early History of the Church and the Ministry*, 2nd ed. (London, 1921), p. 129. Cf., e. g., Hippolytus, *Refutatio omnium haereseum* 1, prol. 6; also the Prayer for the Consecration of a Bishop in Hippolytus' *Traditio apostolica* (in the edition of Gregory Dix [London, 1937], pp. 4-6).

succession comes to full flower in Cyprian, with whom, as Molland has noted, the distance, the important difference, between the apostles and the bishops disappears, and the apostolate *is* the episcopate.[9]

There is, fifth, the approach to apostolic succession not from a doctrinal or sacramental but from an almost exclusively *historical* perspective. This involves a heavily juridical view of succession: an office is ultimately justified because it can be traced back to the apostles. Of course, communion with other bishops, with the catholic and apostolic church, is necessary, but the stress is dominantly on the historico-juridical.[10]

There is, sixth, the agonizing conflict (from Cyprian to Augustine) on the validity of orders conferred *outside the unity* of the church, and the relation of the proffered solutions to apostolic succession. In the third and fourth centuries it was common ground that the gift of the Holy Spirit could not be conferred outside the church. Reordination, therefore, was demanded in the Cyprianic view. Not so Augustine: for the continuance, within the church, of the ministry of a schismatical or heretical clergy, nothing more was necessary than their reconciliation to the Catholic body and the sanction of Catholic authority. It is noteworthy, however, that Augustine apparently did not see such orders, conferred outside unity, as technically in the apostolic succession.[11]

There is, seventh, the fact that after Cyprian, surely with the fourth century, the idea of bishop (in distinction from presbyter) as successor to the apostles in *leitourgia* (the Christian ministry) is quite

---

[9] Cf. Molland, *art. cit.,* p. 25; see Cyprian, *Epistolae* 3; 66, 4; 75, 16. This view of things is visible in those lists (from the middle of the fourth century) of bishops of Rome where Peter is always counted as the first bishop. Contrast this with Irenaeus and Eusebius, neither of whom counts the apostles as units in the episcopal list.

[10] In this connection Eusebius is central. I do not see that Molland is justified (cf. *art. cit.,* p. 19) in ranking Eusebius among those whose primary conception of apostolic succession is Protestant because doctrinal. This is not to deny Eusebius' concern for orthodoxy as a vital element in authentic succession. But I find at least implicit in Eusebius a juridical view of succession; the episcopal lists of the four principal churches, as he gives them, seem to involve an office which is ultimately justified because it can be traced back to "the apostles."

[11] Cf. Turner, *op. cit.,* pp. 145 ff., and his observation (p. 170) that the Augustinian solution "was so enormous a revolution in the ideas and practice heretofore prevalent, that it took nearly a thousand years before the older conceptions were finally ousted even in the West."

the common thing. Not that he inherits apostleship; he is not simply identifiable with the apostles. Rather that, in the minds of the fathers at least, the bishop, like the apostle, represents within his community the unity of the church, is the primary guardian of the tradition of the apostles, and exercises jurisdiction (authoritative teaching, juridical action) after the fashion of the apostles.

From the above, what is "normative" here? What is binding on later ages? This is as difficult to answer as the question, what is "normative" for Christian ministry in light of the New Testament evidence? Perhaps a restatement of the essential *fact* as I see it will be sufficient for our purposes in the present dialogue. In the first two centuries of patristic thought, great emphasis is laid on the need of being in the *doctrinal* succession of the apostles (fidelity to the gospel); for otherwise one is not really a Christian. But this is not *simply* guaranteed by looking at the doctrine. There is a mutual interplay: doctrinal *integrity* and an identifiable *chain* (most often of those in an official position). Put another way: doctrinal communion and legitimate appointment. The *manner* of appointment is often difficult to determine — more difficult the farther back you go. And, of course, still to be satisfactorily determined is the precise meaning of *episkopoi* and *presbyteroi* in the first two centuries — an issue of vital importance in the quest for the normative.

A CONTEMPORARY VIEW
OF APOSTOLIC SUCCESSION

By Warren A. Quanbeck

That conversation between Roman Catholics and Lutherans on the question of apostolic succession is possible today is itself a testimony to the continuing reality of the grace of God. Between 1520 and the present Lutherans and Catholics have on this topic addressed to each other language of such violence that humanly speaking it seems unforgivable. Noting only the more properly theological language, we hear Catholics designating Lutherans heretics and rebels, and Lutherans accusing Catholics of distorting the gospel, perverting the scriptures and in a crescendo of polemical eloquence, describing the papacy as anti-Christ. When one recalls the less descriptive and more uninhibited war of tracts and pamphlets which has accompanied the already sufficiently colorful theological discussion one is not surprised that in addition to theological difficulties there are emotional barriers to overcome.

I understand my task as that of presenting a contemporary view of the question of apostolic succession which can serve as a starting point for theological discussion. The first section of the paper is an attempt to communicate the religious and theological concerns of the Lutheran Reformation on this question, concerns which are not always obvious to Roman Catholics because of the sensitivity of the issue and the emotionally charged language in which it is discussed. The second section discusses briefly the factors which create a new situation in theological study and in relationship between the churches and thus offer a more promising atmosphere for our discussions. The third section attempts to assess the meaning of the apostolic office for the first Christian generations. The fourth section seeks to sum up what apostolic succession can mean for us today.

A. It is generally recognized today that the Reformation of the sixteenth century is a product of many complex factors. The rising sense of national identity, the economic and social revolution of the

178

time, the new understanding of history and human life generated by the new learning of the Renaissance, an accumulation of grievances against the authorities in Rome, objections to abuse of power, to laxity in religious and moral discipline and to confusion in doctrine — all of these elements were present among the reformers. That so many were present in combination helps us understand why the movements of the sixteenth century were more effective than earlier attempts at reform. But it is important to note that the Reformation was not just the product of a decline of religious fervor, rejection of traditional piety, or the general secularization of life in its time. It had a strong religious and theological motivation rooting in a renewal of one of the deepest and most persistent strains in the Christian religion, the prophetic and apostolic emphasis upon the sovereign freedom of God in his gracious activity toward his people. Most of the reformers were in fact men who valued the religious traditions of the Middle Ages highly, and could only be brought to stand against traditional religious authorities because they were conscious of protesting against the authorities in the name of the authority Jesus Christ.

The reformers in the Lutheran tradition did not find it easy or congenial to reject the authority of the pope and the bishops. They had been brought up in the conviction that to obey Christ is to obey the persons through whom Christ speaks, namely, the properly constituted authorities in the church. Luther is scathing in his denunciation of the heretics who wish to have Christ without having his church. He and his friends did not turn away from the traditional authorities because of historical amnesia or a radical distaste for everything from the past. When they stressed the importance of faith, of justification by grace alone, of the priesthood of the faithful, they thought of themselves not as innovators but as men who stood on scriptural and apostolic ground. So convinced were they of the biblical and apostolic character of the message they proclaimed that they could not renounce it even at the insistence of the religious authorities whom they respected so highly.

It is this crisis of faith and obedience that underlies the Lutheran objections to apostolic succession. When authorities whose duty it is to hand on the gospel, to safeguard sound doctrine, and to tend the flock of God refuse free course to the word of God, defend patent misunderstandings of doctrine, and excommunicate those who refuse to recant their defense of the gospel, it is understandable that earnest men should raise questions about the true authority of the bishops and the effectiveness of their relationship with the apostles. It is in this context that we must understand the strong, and shocking, language about the papacy as anti-Christ. It is not merely vehement abuse but is an attempt to register the dismay of earnest men who detect at the center and heart of the church a religious authority who denies the very thing he is appointed to support and defend. The reformers, unlike many humanists of the period, pay the papacy the high compliment of taking seriously its claim and acknowledging that the pope stands in the sanctuary of God. They then turn away in disappointment and sorrow and avail themselves of apocalyptic language to express their horror at the spectacle of a bishop who forbids the proclamation of the gospel of the glory of God. It is this acceptance of a common starting point and polarization of conclusions that helps explain the closeness and distance of Roman Catholic-Lutheran relationships. Ours is a quarrel within the family, and like many family quarrels a very bitter one which seems to defy the possibility of reconciliation.

B. Fortunately a new situation is being created for us today by developments in theological scholarship and in the relationships of the churches to each other. Several factors contribute to this new situation.

1. Historical-critical study of the Bible has made a major contribution by showing how complex and rich the theological world of the Bible is, indicating that many of the conflicting viewpoints have real roots in the scriptures. This enables us to see that the solution of the conflicts of the sixteenth century lies not in the triumph of one view and the elimination of the others. It is rather a case of recognizing what is valid in each of the viewpoints and working toward new syntheses which apprehend the apostolic message in more comprehensive and deeper ways. This of course does not mean that all have won and all shall have prizes, a theological positivism in which superficial good intentions or weariness with dialectics lead us to abandon study, reflection and discussion. But it should mean openness to the genuine insight in the position of others and willingness to learn even from traditional opponents. Above all it means that the theologian exert himself to do justice to the great wealth of contemporary biblical-theological studies. We now see that the Bible confronts us not with just one theology but with many theologies, not just an impressive solo aria but a complicated polyphonic anthem, whose appreciation demands careful study and repeated hearing, and where even rival music-critics can enrich our understanding.

2. Historical studies have also transformed the understanding of the growth and significance of the church's theological statements. Where earlier theologies often ignored the historical context of theological formulations and the historical relativity of the language in which they were couched, today only fits of absentmindedness can provide any excuse for the theologian who fails to deal with the linguistic, literary and historical contexts. Just as the Bible is now read against the background of its several environments, so creeds and dogmatic formulations are seen in the setting of their time. The more traditionalist theologians in all groups have viewed this approach with some suspicion, seeing in it a relativizing tendency which takes away the force and authority of dogmatic statements. This has unquestionably happened in some cases, but most scholars would recognize that the loss of immediate legal force has been more than compensated for by the great increase in intelligibility of the dogmatic texts and in their applicability to the understanding of our contemporary situation.

3. Historical studies have helped to transform the situation also through the vast amount of knowledge given to the illumination of traditional theological problems. To understand why the authors chose one method in preference to another, one term rather than another current at the time, enables us to appreciate their sublety and force and to grasp their intentions more adequately, even though we may also recognize clearly that their method and terminology may be inadequate or inappropriate to the context in which the question is being raised in our time. In this way a deeper comprehension of the past is combined with a more poignant awareness of the need for theological formulations which address contemporary man in his situation.

4. Improvements in the climate of relationships between the churches is another important factor in the changing situation. Some of this is simply cultural maturation, the ability to see strengths and weaknesses in one's self or one's heritage, and the poise to confront differing viewpoints without being defensive. Part of it is due to the tireless work of missionaries and churchmen frustrated by the disastrous effects of disunity upon the effectiveness of preaching or the evoking of love among the brethren. Some of these men such as Nathan Soderblom, John R. Mott, William Temple, Paul Couturier, Gustav Weigel, Pope John XXIII, added a personal charisma so winsome or so nettling, that they could not be ignored. Because of their work the problem of Christian unity has achieved priority and we

181

are confronted by an inescapable challenge to move toward greater understanding and accord even on the most controversial topics.

C. Almost all churches agree that the apostles, in union with Jesus Christ, are the foundation of the church, and that to be the church it is necessary to be apostolic. This conviction is the foundation of the ecumenical movement. It enables churches to combine their efforts toward the recovery of unity in spite of sharp and painful differences.

What does apostolicity consist of, and how is it mediated in the life of the churches? Traditional Lutheran answers to these questions most frequently reflect the polemics of the post-Reformation period and therefore do not address themselves helpfully to the present ecumenical encounter. A number of attempts have been made to give a contemporary Lutheran treatment of this question. The 1958 *Declaration* of the United Lutheran Church of Germany, for example, attempts to move beyond the polemics of the past and give a positive appraisal of apostolic succession. It succeeds in many respects but at the key point of our concern it remains too defensive and too wary, and denies the necessity or even the advisability of apostolic succession through episcopal consecration. In its apparent conviction that apostolic succession can mean only an empty formality which in no way guarantees the apostolic heritage, it in effect closes off the theological conversation before it begins.

A more effective consideration of the problem of apostolicity today is offered in the essay of Prof. Edmund Schlink delivered in 1957 before the ecumenical commission of the United Lutheran Church of Germany. The essay may be properly criticized for an insufficiently nuanced reading of the New Testament evidence, since it seems to assume uniformity of theological language among the writers of the New Testament, and does not do justice to the differences which exist among them in the interpretation of many theological issues, including that of the role and authority of the apostles in the church. Nevertheless for our purposes the essay is useful, for it combines earnest attention to the theological concerns of the Reformation and openness to the possibilities of a developing ecumenical discussion. What follows is essentially a précis of his argument.

1. The question of apostolicity is a question of the apostolicity of the church, and not only one of apostolicity of the ministry. If discussion of this question is narrowed to a concern for what is meant by the word, "apostle," or to the problem of succession of ministers,

an important perspective on the entire problem is lost. The whole church is an apostolic church, built upon the foundation of the apostles and prophets. We must deal with the apostolic succession of the church and of the ministry, for both belong together.

2. The apostle announces the apostolic gospel, and as he does so, Christ speaks in and through him. His message is not simply a new arrangement of human wisdom; it is the proclamation of the word of God, the speech of God by which the worlds are created and by which God in Christ performs ever new miracles of grace.

3. The apostle represents Christ to the church in the exercise of leadership. He presides over the worship of God's people, he instructs the people in the meaning of their life as God's children and shows them how to serve God in the service of their neighbor, he leads them out of gatherings for worship into the world, that they may be really in the world and yet not of it.

4. The apostle represents Christ in being the bond of unity in the church. The New Testament shows each congregation as being complete in itself, the body of Christ with members differentiated as to function but having in common the responsibility to build up the body. Yet though these congregations receive the gifts of the Spirit for their growth into maturity in Christ they are not independent or autonomous congregations but must live in fellowship and unity with all other Christians in the world. The apostle has special responsibility to maintain this bond of unity among the congregations and Christians of the world.

5. In the work of the apostle it is important not only that he be called by Jesus Christ, but that he respond to the call. His calling is not a kind of honorary degree to be hung on the wall or stuffed into a desk drawer. It is an invitation to an activity, the exercise of a function. In the same way it is not enough that he be entrusted with the apostolic gospel; he must in fact be a proclaimer of the gospel.

6. The apostle stands with Christ over against the church, but he also stands with the members of the church as a sinner who lives by forgiveness. Even the most eminent apostles were sinners: Peter betrayed his Lord, Paul persecuted him. With other members of the church the apostle knows repentance and restoration. His person is nothing, his witness is everything. He lives by his service of the people and by the intercession of the people for him. He is dependent upon the people of the congregations not only for financial support but even more for the spiritual gifts of strengthening and courage.

Paul pleads with the congregations for their support in intercessory prayer that he may be enabled to carry out his ministry in spite of obstacles.

7. The apostle is sent into the congregations for service. The terms of his mission are clear: As the Father has sent the Son, so the Son sends his disciples. As the Son empties himself in order that the will of the Father may be accomplished, so the disciple empties himself in order that the will of his Lord may be done. The preeminence of the apostle is like the preeminence of the crucified and risen One in that it takes the form of the servant. He who humbles himself shall be exalted, but he who exalts himself shall be humbled.

8. The apostle is sent into a church which is a fellowship of charismatic gifts of the Spirit. He is himself equipped for his task by the Spirit's gifts. He may be exceptionally endowed, as Paul was: apostle, prophet, the gift of healing, the gift of tongues. But he is surrounded by others who also have received the gifts of the Spirit. The apostle's authority is never isolated. It is situated in the community of the Spirit. It is the apostle's task to help the congregation exercise responsible stewardship of the Spirit's gifts, so that they do not become occasions for display or rivalry, but lead to the building up of the congregation. The apostle must help the congregation to test the spiritual phenomena so as to distinguish between the work of the spirits and that of the Spirit. The apostle must also be open to the guidance of the Spirit in the community, and accessible to the assistance which can be received from other ministries empowered by the same Spirit.

9. Thus the apostle has a complex function in the life of the church. He is a founder of the church through his calling by Christ and his witness to the resurrection. He is a herald of the apostolic gospel and a prophetic interpreter of the implications of the message for new situations in the life of the churches. He brings to the church the *diakonia* of leadership, reproducing in his own life the servant form of his Lord. He is the bond of unity among the congregations, a witness to the unity in love which is the true destiny of God's people and God's gift to the world through them. His work is a constant interplay of past and present acts of God. He is called to be an apostle, and is an apostle when he responds to his calling through the empowering activity of the Spirit. He is the herald of a traditioned message and an effective herald as he proclaims it constantly in a living way. It is not possible to separate the call from the activity of the

apostle, the possession of the message from its proclamation, the pre-eminence of leadership from the humble exercise of leadership, the bond of unity from the active persuasion of the churches to live in fellowship and unity.

D. What can now be said about the meaning of apostolic succession?

1. There is no continuation of the apostolic office in the narrow sense of the term. Apostolic office as the foundation of the church comes to an end with the death of the last apostle. The two decisive qualifications for apostolic office are no longer possible, namely, that he be a witness of the resurrection, and that he has been appointed immediately by Jesus Christ. What continues in the church is the mission or service of the apostle.

2. The leader in the church, like the apostle, stands over against the churches as representative of Jesus Christ. When he proclaims the apostolic gospel, it is Jesus Christ who speaks through him. The promise to the apostles, "He who hears you, hears me," applies also to the contemporary minister of the word of God. God speaks through his messengers, and thus the congregation is confronted by something more than another human being. It confronts a man called as a servant, an ambassador of God.

The church leader represents Christ to the church in the administration of the sacraments and leadership in worship. For it is Christ himself who acts in the sacraments through the person and action of his minister. Through the leaders of the church Christ speaks his enlivening word and strengthens and guides his people for their mission as his body. The preeminence of the leader is not only a matter of calling, but of constant new obedience to the calling. Being in the Spirit is not a human attribute, but an ever new work of the Spirit acting in the faithfulness of God who ever creates anew. Neither the apostle nor the church leader should presume on his calling. They are called to a special relationship and service to God and remain in this relationship as they respond to the calling. Authority resides not just in the fact of the call but in an ever new appropriation of the call through the stirring up of the gift of the Spirit given in the laying on of hands (II Timothy 1:6).

3. The leader of the church, like the apostle, stands with all church members under the grace and judgment of God. His preeminence as leader does not mean exaltation or dominance, but precisely the opposite. Nothing humbles as thoroughly as the call to the minis-

try. Ordination means the end of personal plans, ambitions and methods. It means that Christ intends to shepherd his flock through this called servant, who is unworthy and incapable in himself, but becomes worthy through the dignity bestowed in forgiveness and capable through the Spirit's working in him.

4. The leader of the church, like the apostle, is called to service in the fellowship of the congregation. His *koinonia* is not only with fellow leaders but with all members of the church. As the discussion of the ministry at Faith and Order in Montreal in 1963 stresses, the New Testament does not distinguish as we do between the magisterium or the ministry of the word and the other ministries of the church. The gift of leadership is given together with the other gifts of the Spirit. The leader receives not only physical sustenance but also the support of prayer and intercession, the gifts of strengthening and encouragement. He not only gives judgment in the congregation but receives it as well. Members have the right and authority to support their leaders and also to assist them with advice and criticism.

5. The leader of the church, like the apostle, works in the context of the charismatic gifts. They are a reminder to him that the Spirit is the Lord of the church, and that the leader is not the only one with whom the Spirit has dealings. The members of the congregation have also received the Spirit, are also equipped for ministry, and some of them may have received gifts not bestowed on the leader. It is in fellowship with others who know the Spirit that the leader is equipped to guide the congregation in the stewardship of the gifts so that the congregation is built up and equipped for its mission in the world.

6. The leader of the church, like the apostle, is called to be a bond of unity in the church. The individual congregation receives the charisms of the Spirit to be built up for mission, but part of its completeness and health is to be found in its experience of fellowship with other Christians. It suffers with them, prospers with them, rejoices with them. Because of this concern for unity, the leader has a certain preeminence among the gifts of the Spirit (I Corinthians 12). Hence Paul exhorts Christians to recognize those who labor in their midst and are preeminent and show them honor for the sake of their work (I Thessalonians 5:12).

7. The office of leadership in the church, like that of the apostle whose mission and service it continues, is a complex combination. The leader is entrusted with the apostolic gospel in order that he may

proclaim it effectively. He is appointed to leadership so that he may be preeminent in service to the congregations, in worship, in the administration of sacraments, in the stewardship of the spiritual gifts, in the equipment of the saints of the work of ministry. He is placed in the church as a bond of unity in order that he may work unceasingly for the unity of God's people in faith and love. His is never an isolated authority. He is sent to congregations who have received the Spirit and is surrounded by others who have experienced the Spirit's generosity. He can be faithful in his calling only as he empties himself in order that Christ may live in him. To grasp the full meaning of leadership in the church as apostolic succession one must grasp this rich dynamic complexity of calling and response of tradition and traditioning of leadership in service, of life in the Spirit, of keeping unity in the bond of peace.

8. Since apostleship in the narrower sense is limited to the first generation of Christians, apostolic succession means a following in the apostles' footsteps, in obedience to those who were called as eyewitnesses of the resurrection of Jesus Christ. This succession can be founded on a general call addressed to all baptized people, or on the special calling to the ministry of word and sacraments.

Apostolic succession in the narrower sense as succession through episcopal ordination is not a *sine qua non* of the apostolic succession of church and ministry. It does not produce an apostolic succession and authority which are missing from other types of ordination. But ordination by episcopal imposition of hands should be seen as a sign of the apostolic succession of the ministry and of the church, and therefore a sign of the unity and catholicity of the church. Lutherans should for this reason acknowledge the usefulness of ordination by bishops through the history of the church as a sign of apostolicity, and where the sign is absent, recognize that it is right to work for its introduction. But the sign must never be separated from the reality which it signifies, namely the apostolic tradition. The sign of apostolic succession cannot take away the necessity of a constantly renewed submission to the gospel as it is communicated in the apostolic tradition, nor can it devalue the pastoral ministry which exists without episcopal ordination.

In our day the contributions of history, psychology and sociology give us clearer perspectives than in the past on the problems of authority and power. Historians can show us how ecclesiastical structures have reflected the understanding of power and the techniques of administration of their time. Psychologists and sociologists can help us

187

to understand what effects the possession and use of power have on individuals and groups. We should therefore be better equipped to grapple with the problems of bringing ecclesiology and ecclesiastical structures into correspondence. We can see, for example, that the complex relationships of the church leader with other church leaders, with the entire range of other ministries, with new manifestations of the Spirit's gifts suggest the need of structures that we do not presently possess. None of the standard-brand churches has been able to respond adequately to certain charismatic phenomena, or to certain demands for contemporary involvement in the world. The history of religious socialism suggests that the churches have not always had their antennae tuned to the voice of the Spirit. As a result genuinely Christian impulses have been forced into secular channels. Faith healing and glossolalia have also frequently been beyond the competence of conventional church administration, and have been forced to create new ecclesiastical organizations. The fact that these organizations manifest in time a sense of churchly and ecumenical responsibility suggests that they could have been accommodated in existing church structures. Fortunately we live in a time when willingness to experiment and innovate is respectable. Structural changes brought about by or following the Second Vatican Council have shown both ecclesiological and administrative imagination. That many Lutheran bodies are now rethinking questions of church and ministry indicates that even highly traditionalist organizations are capable of some mobility.

I have regarded the question "Where is the apostolic tradition to be found?" to be beyond the lines of this assignment. It is of course a closely related question and offers similar possibilities of ecumenical openness and potential convergence.

THE CHRISTIAN PRIESTHOOD: EPISCOPATE, PRESBYTERATE AND PEOPLE IN THE LIGHT OF VATICAN II

By JOHN F. HOTCHKIN

From the results produced, it is clear that the fathers of Vatican II consciously aimed at extending the unfinished work of Vatican I. After the earlier council had taken up the office and prerogatives of the primacy in the Roman Catholic church, its work had been interrupted by the advancing armies of Victor Emmanuel. This interruption left undone the task of presenting more fully the role and office of the episcopacy in the church, a work that had yet to be accomplished in order to redress an imbalance of teaching left when Vatican I was truncated.

Out of this effort there developed a still further felt need to present the church in more than strictly hierarchical terms. This in turn led the council fathers of Vatican II to their broader teachings on the whole people of God with a particular emphasis on the role and dignity of the laity.

Within these unfolding perspectives the question of the presbyterate and the diaconate remained somewhat marginal interests — with the exception of considerable concern over whether or not married men would be allowed to serve as deacons.[1] Sensing a lacuna, various council fathers during the second session began to voice the

---

[1] This uneven distribution of emphasis, first on the episcopate and then on the laity while passing over the presbyterate, drew attention and comment from different sources. Nikos Nissiotis dryly remarked, "It is an attempt to complete but not correct the formula of Vatican I by extending the idea of divine right by analogy also to the bishops" ("The Main Ecclesiological Problems of Vatican II," in *Journal of Ecumenical Studies* 2 [1965], 35).

need for a fuller treatment of the presbyterate. By the end of that session the draft of a "special message" to priests was presented, but it was rejected as inadequate by the assembly. At the same session the fathers sought further revision and restructuring of the brief statement on the presbyterate and diaconate inserted into the Constitution on the Church.[2] In the third session a list of "propositions" concerning the presbyterate was presented, and this, too, was rejected as being too skeletal. In the time remaining to it, the council prepared and passed a somewhat fuller decree "On the Priestly Life and Ministry" as a separate document. While more welcome than the meager offerings on the subject previously proposed, this document understandably bears marks of haste and pressure in its development and composition.[3] It is notably pastoral in tone. Along with Chapter III "On the Hierarchical Structure of the Church and in Particular on the Episcopate" (especially 28 and 29) of the Constitution on the Church, plus scattered references in Chapter II on "Bishops and Their Particular Churches or Dioceses" (especially 28 to 32) in the Decree Concerning the Pastoral Office of Bishops in the Church (both decidedly episcopal in orientation) and a brief passage in the Constitution on the Sacred Liturgy (41 and 42), this constitutes for the most part the explicit sayings of Vatican II on the relationship between bishop and presbyter.

---

[2] "The first draft of the Constitution (1962) spoke only very briefly on the priesthood, in Chapter III, Article 12, under the general heading 'the episcopate as the supreme degree of Orders.' Only ten lines were devoted to the priesthood, and the main interest attached to its orientation toward the episcopal office, and dependence on the pope or the competent bishop in matters of jurisdiction. Only two sentences were directly positive statements about the priesthood itself, one affirming the reality of the priesthood, in spite of its being oriented to the episcopal office, the other affirming its relationship to Christ in the celebration of the Eucharistic sacrifice and the administration of other sacraments.

"The revision of the text for the second session of the Council follows the same order (Article 14, on the episcopate as sacrament) but now has somewhat more than a page on the priesthood and the diaconate (Article 15, 1963). This text was discussed by the assembly with reference to the Constitution as a whole, from 30 September to 31 October 1963. Many of the bishops thought that it was not in its proper place, and it was then put at the end of Chapter III and divided into two Articles (28 and 29), one on the priesthood and the other on the diaconate" (Aloys Grillmeier, in *Commentary on the Documents of Vatican II*, vol. I [New York: Herder and Herder, 1966], p. 218).

[3] For a fuller account, cf. John Cardinal Heenan, *Council and Clergy*, (London, 1966), pp. 29-57.

All together, these statements would not seem to offer a very promising frame of reference for broad and searching ecumenical dialogue on the ministry. In fact, upon first reading they may simply seem to reassert the ministerial forms familiar to Roman Catholics.

So we read that by divine institution bishops have succeeded *in locum Apostolorum* as pastors of the church.

"Among those various ministries which, according to tradition, were exercised in the Church from the earliest times, the chief place belongs to those who, appointed to the episcopate, by a succession running from the beginning are passers-on of the apostolic seed. Thus, as St. Irenaeus testifies, through those who were appointed bishops by the apostles, and through their successors down to our own time, the apostolic tradition is manifested and preserved. . . . Therefore, the Sacred Council teaches that bishops by divine institution have succeeded to the place of the Apostles, as shepherds of the Church, and he who hears them, hears Christ, and he who rejects them, rejects Christ and Him who sent Christ" (Constitution on the Church, 20).

The mission entrusted to bishops is one which they receive directly from Christ.

"Bishops, as successors of the apostles, receive from the Lord, to whom all power was given in heaven and on earth, the mission to teach all nations and to preach the Gospel to every creature, so that all men may attain to salvation by faith, baptism and the fulfillment of the commandments" (Constitution on the Church, 24).

Thus they are direct subjects of the apostolic mandate given by Christ and not merely "vicars of the Roman Pontiffs" (Constitution on the Church, 27), even though their canonical mission is regulated by the primatial office, laws and customs.

So it is that bishops act in the person of Christ, sustaining his role as teacher, pastor and high priest.

"Bishops, as vicars and ambassadors of Christ, govern the particular churches entrusted to them by their counsel, exhortations and example, and even by their authority and sacred power. . . This power which they personally exercise in Christ's name is proper, ordinary and immediate" (Constitution on the Church, 27).

This power the bishops receive and hold in its fullness.[4]

---

[4] This use of pleromatic language not with direct reference to the *eschaton* but with application to the sacramental actions, orders and other aspects

". . . the Sacred Council teaches that by episcopal consecration the fullness of the sacrament of Orders is conferred, that fullness of power, namely, which both in the Church's liturgical practice and in the language of the Fathers of the Church is called the high priesthood, the supreme power of the sacred ministry. But episcopal consecration, together with the office of sanctifying, also confers the office of teaching and governing, which, however, of its very nature can only be exercised in communion with the head and members of the college. For from the tradition, which is expressed especially in liturgical rites of the Church of the East and of the West, it is clear that by means of the imposition of hands and the words of consecration, the grace of the Holy Spirit is so conferred, and the sacred character so impressed that bishops in an eminent and visible way sustain the roles of Christ Himself as Teacher, Shepherd and High Priest, and that they act in His Person" (Constitution on the Church, 21).

"The pastoral office or the habitual and daily care of their sheep is entrusted to (the bishops) completely" (Constitution on the Church, 27), and "every legitimate celebration of the Eucharist is regulated by the bishop, to whom is committed the office of offering the worship of the Christian religion to the Divine Majesty" as "a bishop marked with the fullness of the sacrament of Orders, is 'the steward of the grace of the supreme priesthood,' especially in the Eucharist, which he offers or causes to be offered, and by which the Church continually lives and grows" (Constitution on the Church, 26).

From these selected texts one perspective on the episcopal office and ministry is presented whereby "the individual bishops . . . are the visible principle and foundation of unity in their particular churches" (Constitution on the Church, 23). Other texts may be selected to point up the contrast between the episcopate and the presbyterate.

Priest-presbyters, the council affirms, "do not possess the highest degree of the priesthood" (Constitution on the Church, 28). Rather, "their ministerial role has been handed down to priests (presbyters) in a limited degree" (On the Priestly Life and Ministry, 2). Thus priest-presbyters "are dependent on the bishops in the exercise of their power" (Constitution on the Church, 28; and On the Pastoral Office of Bishops, 15).

---

of the pilgrim church is one of the more disconcerting features of certain Vatican II statements. Though used at a number of critical junctures, the term "fullness" remains quite elusive of definition.

Priest-presbyters are seen as representatives of the priest-bishop, for "in a certain way they make him present in every gathering of the faithful" (On the Priestly Life, 5). They act under the authority of the bishop and exercise their office "to the degree of their authority and in the name of their bishop" (On the Priestly Life, 6).

> "Associated with their bishop in a spirit of trust and generosity, they (priest-presbyters) make him present in a certain sense in the individual local congregations, and take upon themselves, as far as they are able, his duties and the burden of his care, and discharge them with a daily interest. And as they sanctify and govern under the bishop's authority, that part of the flock entrusted to them, they make the universal Church visible in their own locality. . ." (Constitution on the Church, 28).

When exercising the presidency of the eucharistic community, priest-presbyters are seen as substitutes for the priest-bishops required by the constraint of circumstances.[5]

> ". . . because it is impossible for the bishop always and everywhere to preside over the whole flock in his Church, he cannot do other than establish lesser groupings of the faithful. Among these, parishes set up locally under a pastor who takes the place of the bishop are the most important: for in a certain way they represent the visible Church as it is established throughout the world" (Constitution on the Sacred Liturgy, 42).

A comparison of such selected texts suggests the conclusion that the office and power of the presbyterate is entirely limited by, dependent on, derivative from and representational of the office and power of the episcopate. At least a clear difference of degree is exhibited as distinguishing the two.

The diaconate is posited at a still lesser degree: "At a lower level of the hierarchy are deacons, upon whom hands are imposed 'not unto the priesthood, but unto a ministry of service'" (Constitution on the Church, 29). Though the council restored this office as a

---

[5] This "practical" explanation of why priest-presbyters preside over local eucharistic communities raises a more serious question than the one it answers. For if it is truly unfortunate that priest-bishops cannot always preside at every eucharistic synaxis because of the relatively low ratio of bishops to people in the church, then one might plausibly argue that many more bishops should be ordained so that every president of the eucharistic assembly might be a bishop and this situation of constraint be overcome.

permanent service in the church, it did not elaborate the theological character of this order.[6]

And an even greater difference is indicated between the priesthood of the graded hierarchy and the common priesthood of all the faithful, for "they differ from one another in essence and not only in degree" (Constitution on the Church, 10).

Reading conciliar texts with this selectivity creates the impression of a carefully ordered and decisively calibrated hierarchical structure whereby that which is lower or lesser derives from that which is higher or greater. So it would appear that the presbyterate extends from the priest-bishop who shares with it to a limited degree the priesthood which fully is his. From this point of view, it would seem that a community which has not received the highest degree of ministerial order in the episcopacy would also lack the lesser degrees of order which emanate from it and may not authentically or effectively be exercised independently of it. So if the question is raised: "Is the validity of the eucharist so essentially related to an episcopally ordained ministry that communities which do not require episcopal ordination cannot be said to have a valid ministry and a valid eucharist?" there are Roman Catholic commentators on the council who would certainly be inclined to answer: yes.[7] Other commentators

---

[6] And, as Grillmeier has pointed out, some serious questions remain: "The formula, that deacons receive the laying on of hands not for the priesthood but for the performance of service is ambiguous in spite of its venerable age. The words are clearly intended, in the mind of medieval theologians, to exclude the power to celebrate the Eucharist or ordain priests, a claim which no one ever made for the diaconate. Insofar as the priesthood (sacerdotium) is identical with the state of the sacramentally ordained, with the higher clergy, with Ordo (meaning the ranks of those sacramentally ordained) and hence forms a contrast to the general priesthood of all believers, the deacon belongs to the sacerdotium" (op. cit., p. 228). No doubt as men once again take up this office on a permanent basis in the Roman Catholic church a much more thorough theological appreciation of its character will have to be achieved.

[7] For instance, Bishop Carlo Colombo: "Episcopal consecration, with the real transformation it accomplishes, is the supernatural basis indispensable for the subject to become a sacramental sign of the action of Christ. The actions performed by the bishop are not purely human actions, but to a certain degree, theandric ones, since Christ himself acts through him. For this reason they require a new and real basis. Episcopal consecration is what radically distinguishes authority in the Church from any purely juridical authority and introduces it into the mysterious order of Christ's re-creating salvific action" ("The Hierarchical Structure of the Church," in Vatican II, an Interfaith Appraisal, [Notre Dame, 1966], p. 213).

would be more nuanced, urging an historical interpretation rather than a speculative extrapolation of these conciliar teachings on the grounds that the council was primarily speaking to a number of unresolved historical questions within the Catholic church and these shaped the council's thought and expression. However, these commentators vary noticeably in their reading of that earlier history.[8]

---

[8] Here only a few brief examples can be given which may exemplify the complexity of the matter:

a) *Gregory Baum:* "If the priesthood in the Church is defined with reference to the eucharistic sacrifice, what is the bishop? Is he just a priest (presbyter) with new powers granted to him, especially the power of jurisdiction? Or is there a sacramental difference between priests (presbyters) and bishops? The Council of Trent left this question quite open: 'The bishops, who have succeeded the apostles, belong in a special way to the hierarchical order: placed, as the Apostle says, by the Holy Spirit to rule the Church of God (cf. Acts 20:28), they are superior to priests — they can confer the sacrament of confirmation, can ordain ministers for the Church and they have the power to perform many other functions that those of an inferior grade cannot' (DS 960).

"The Council of Trent did not precisely define in what the superiority of the bishop consisted, whether in sacramental participation or in the fullness of jurisdiction. Yet, by defining priesthood in terms of offering sacrifice, the Council of Trent encouraged the general tendency in Catholic thought to regard this priesthood as being fully embodied in the presbyterate and hence to consider the bishop as a priest (presbyter) with additional powers. In ordinary Catholic parlance, the priesthood refers specifically to the presbyterate. Until now we have tended to look upon the priest (presbyter) as the priest *par excellence.*

"In the *Constitution on the Church* of Vatican Council II, we are taught that the fullness of the ministerial priesthood is granted to the bishop. According to present teaching, therefore, the bishop is the priest *par excellence.* The bishop is not a priest (presbyter) with special powers; he differs from the presbyter by the degree of sacramental participation. The bishop is fully priest" (*The Ecumenist* 4 [1965], 4 f.).

b) *Bernard Dupuy, O. P:* "The form of bishop-priest relationship we know today was preceded by other types of this same relationship. Today it is thought that the 'bishop' related to Greek communities and 'priest' to Jewish communities; but the pastoral epistles themselves already seem to bear witness to a bishop-priest ministry on the way toward unification. The monarchical episcopate soon asserted itself almost everywhere. At the end of the 2d century, in St. Irenaeus and the *Traditio apostolica,* we find that the monarchical bishop is regarded as the inheritor of the apostles' functions and as the guardian of Tradition; we still have priests, but they do not have this function of the apostles' successors.

"In the Africa of Tertullian and Cyprian, only the bishop is called *sacerdos* and celebrates the eucharist; priests, who now seem to have only

In order to respond more directly to the immediate question within the full context of conciliar teaching, it is necessary to widen

---

a pastoral function of governing, no longer preside over the eucharist. After the Council of Nicaea in the 4th century, however, the situation reverses itself once again. Priests are *sacerdotes* once again and celebrate the eucharist for the bishop in his territory. The bishop becomes head of a *presbyterium* and the pastor of an entire region; we already have the territorial bishop which we know today.

"The conclusion is that the process of differentiating between bishop and priest has been a varied and progressive one. Fixed at Antioch at the end of the 1st century, the specific nature of the episcopal ministry was definitively recognized only in the second century when Gnosticism posed a challenge; it was recognized everywhere later, as a result of the crisis caused by the priest Arius.

"With this changing history in the background, it is easy to see why Vatican II, desiring to respect this history and the present ecumenical situation, chose to avoid dogmatic definition of a particular structure. In the *Constitution on the Church,* it calls the episcopate 'the apex of the sacred ministry' (Art. 21), but it chose not to declare dogmatically that only bishops can call priests to become members of the episcopal college. The older formula of this principle was. 'Quare soli Episcopi per Sacramentum Ordinis novos electos in corpus episcopale assumere *possunt;*' Vatican II substitutes for this a simple statement of fact: 'Episcoporum *est* per Sacramentum Ordinis novos electos in corpus episcopale assumere.'

"Vatican II thus left open the possibility of personal judgment on the historical facts. (In the Church of Alexandria, for example, the college of priests seems to have chosen its own bishop for several decades.) It obviously wanted to avoid creating ecumenical difficulties at a time when various Churches were talking about reunion. It also wanted to leave room for the case, however hypothetical it may be, where priests are isolated for a long time because of Church persecution. Most importantly, it wanted to avoid making a dogmatic determination of a point of doctrine that is far from settled" ("The Function of Priests and Bishops," *Concilium,* Vol. 34, pp. 82-84).

c) *Tomas Garcia Barbena:* "The doctrinal tradition stems from St. Jerome and follows a line by now well known to scholars, being transmitted chiefly through St. Isidore to Peter Lombard and the Scholastics. The Canons of Hippolytus (end of the 5th century), which derive from the *Traditio apostolica* of St. Hippolytus of Rome, stand in this line; they establish the equality of ordination of the bishop and the presbyter, 'all is done with him in the same manner as with the bishop except that he does not occupy the throne.' There is a continued assertion that ordination does not consist in the receipt of personal powers but in assuming membership in the presbyterate (*Constitutiones apostolicae,* Ch. 16). Another doctrinal tradition, originating with St. Epiphanius, is emphasized particularly in the works of Pseudo-Dionysius, whose influence on scholastic thought was so important. In the concept of Jerome and Isidore, the presbyterate is of the focus created by the particular texts under review so far. It is insufficient simply to fasten on those passages which speak of the difference between priest-bishops and priest-presbyters in order to determine how critical this difference may or may not be. It is also necessary to take into consideration a number of conciliar statements on the unity of the two and the similarity which results from this unity.

The unity of the priest-bishops and the priest-presbyters is established in the fact that there is but one priesthood in which both participate. This the council repeatedly emphasizes:

> "Priests, prudent cooperators with the episcopal order, its aid and instrument, called to serve the people of God, constitute one priesthood with their bishop although bound by a diversity of duties" (Constitution on the Church, 28).

> "All presbyters, both diocesan and Religious, participate in and exercise with the bishop the one priesthood of Christ and are thereby constituted prudent cooperators of the episcopal order" (On the Pastoral Office of Bishops, 28).

---

divine origin and the root of all power of sacrament and government inherent in the priesthood; the episcopate is an ecclesiastical institution designed to preserve the unity of the Church. The work of Pseudo Dionysius reveals a diametrically opposed conception: for him all power resides in the bishop and flows from him to the presbyters, created to make up for the insufficient numbers of bishops. . .

"A close comparison of the sections of *De Ecclesia* dealing with the college of bishops (22) and with the priesthood (28) will reveal that, whereas the sentences formulating the collegiality of bishops are perfectly coherent and show a definite criterion, those relating to the presbyteral college suffer from a certain ambiguity, with some positive elements and other apparently contradictory ones. The same hesitation can be found in the writings of authorities on the subject. Batazole shows that the concept lacks validity in the constitutional apparatus of the Church, since the local Church can theoretically function without presbyters ('Theoretically, in extreme cases, the bishop would be able to do without priests — although he could not do without the laity — only his function being constitutive of the Church' — *L'Episcopat et l'Eglise universelle*, p. 342), while O. Rousseau holds that *in extremis* a local presbyter cut off from communications with neighboring Churches could consecrate a bishop on his own ('And for the rest, it is not impossible to conceive an ecclesiology following which, deprived of its head, a presbyteral college would consider itself as the depository of the full power of the Holy Spirit and would proceed to the imposition of hands on its bishop' (*"La doctrine du ministère épiscopal et ses vicissitudes dans l'Eglise d'Occident"* in *L'Episcopat et l'Eglise universelle*, p. 296)" ("Collegiality at the Diocesan Level: the Western Presbyterate," in *Concilium*, Vol. 8, pp. 24 f. and 29).

And in the same vein:

> "All priests together with bishops so share in one and the same priesthood and ministry of Christ that the very unity of their consecration and mission requires their hierarchical communion with the order of bishops" (On the Priestly Life, 7).

This unity in one and the same ministry flows from the common source of both the episcopate and presbyterate, for the ministry of priest-presbyters like that of priest-bishops "takes its start from the gospel message" (On the Priestly Life, 2), and in this way can be said to be "established" by the Lord. Like the priest-bishops, so also "in their own measure priests (presbyters) participate in the office of the Apostles" (On the Priestly Life, 2). As shepherds of the Lord's people, priest-presbyters stand in common with priest-bishops as subjects of the apostolic mandate and mission:

> "The task of proclaiming the Gospel everywhere on earth pertains to the body of pastors, to all of whom in common Christ gave his command, thereby imposing on them a common duty. . ."
> (Constitution on the Church, 23).

Just as priest-bishops are bound together in collegial union, similarly "in virtue of their common sacred ordination and mission, all priests are bound together in intimate brotherhood" (Constitution on the Church, 28) so that "each and every priest is joined to his brother priests by a bond of charity, prayer and every kind of cooperation" (On the Priestly Life, 8).

As priest-bishops are, so are priest-presbyters responsible for the whole mission of the church and not just for some specific of deputed task:

> "The spiritual gift which priests (presbyters) receive at their ordination prepares them not for any limited and narrow mission but for the widest scope of the universal mission of salvation "even to the very ends of the earth" (Acts 1:8). For every priestly ministry shares in the universality of the mission entrusted by Christ to his Apostles. The priesthood of Christ, in which all priests truly share, is necessarily intended for all peoples and all times" (On the Priestly Life, 10).

Priest-presbyters, like priest-bishops, exercise their special eucharistic ministry "in the name of the whole Church" (On the Priestly Life, 2). As has been said of the priest-bishops, so also it is said of the priest-presbyters that they "represent the person of Christ" (Constitution on the Church, 28; cf. also On the Priestly Life, 13). Both priest-bishops and priest-presbyters stand in the midst of their people as fathers and as brothers among brothers (cf. On the Pastoral Office of Bishops, 16, and On the Priestly Life, 9). Priest-presbyters as well as priest-bishops are ordained to the ministry of teaching, sanctifying and governing for the sake of the church (cf. On the Priestly Life, 13; On the Pastoral Office of Bishops, 12, 13 and 16; Constitution on the Church, 21 and 28).

So closely do the characteristics of the presbyterium and the episcopacy match each other that it has been said the council has presented them as "mirror images." If the inner character of the office of priest-bishop and priest-presbyter are nearly identical, it remains to be seen whether the council lays down any sharp or decisive difference in the exercise of office by the two.

Articles 25-27 of the Constitution on the Church give a resume of the sacred powers exercised by the priest-bishop in his ministry. First place is given to his power to preach the gospel and to teach, for "among the principal duties of bishops the preaching of the Gospel occupies an eminent place" (cf. also On the Pastoral Office of Bishops, 12). In this respect, however, priest-bishops do not differ in the exercise of their ministry from priest-presbyters who also hold as their primary function the ministry of the word of God (cf. Constitution on the Church, 28; On the Priestly Life, 4).

Next, the priest-bishop acts as "the steward of the grace of the supreme priesthood, especially in the Eucharist." In this regard, again they do not differ from the priest-presbyters, who "exercise their sacred function especially in the eucharistic worship or the celebration of the Mass by which, acting in the person of Christ and proclaiming his Mystery they unite the prayers of the faithful with the sacrifice of their Head. . ." (Constitution on the Church, 28). It is added that "every legitimate celebration of the Eucharist is regulated by the bishop."

Subsequently, priest-bishops are described as those who "regulate by their authority" the regular and fruitful administration of the sacraments; they "direct the conferring of baptism" and act as "moderators of the penitential discipline." In the light of present practice whereby priest-presbyters act as the ordinary ministers of these sacraments, it is difficult to detect any very specific meaning in this language of regulation, moderation and direction beyond a possible jurisdictional reference.[9]

---

[9] Cf. Karl Rahner, in *Commentary on the Documents of Vatican II,* Vol. I, p. 217.

Much more significant is the way the council describes the power of the priest-bishops with regard to the sacraments of confirmation and orders. It states simply that the bishops are "the original ministers of confirmation (and) dispensers of sacred orders." This careful, restrained wording stands in contrast to the earlier Tridentine formulation on the same point: "If anyone says that bishops are not superior to priests; or that they do not have the power to confirm and ordain, or that they have it in common with priests. . .A. S." [10]

Vatican II mutes this earlier canon considerably. Even though in the Latin church bishops are generally the ones who administer the sacrament of confirmation, they are not here described as the "ordinary" but more simply as the "original" ministers of this sacrament. The sacred power to confirm is not uniquely theirs nor altogether distinctive of them, and this statement by the council accords better with the longstanding practice of the church in the East as well as with the 1946 decision by Rome which extends the administration of confirmation to presbyters as well as to bishops.

As for the power to ordain, Vatican II's formulation is still more reserved. Priest-bishops are simply referred to as "dispensers of sacred orders" with no further emphasis or elaboration on the point. A variety of factors seem to account for the striking simplicity of this statement. The council was aware of more recent historical studies which more clearly reveal the complexity and variety of ministerial development in the primitive church.[11] Also certain historical instances in the Roman Catholic church in which priest-presbyters had ordained other presbyters were generally recognized.[12] At any rate, the theological commission of the council took the following position: "The Commission states that there is nothing to be laid down on the question of whether the bishop alone may ordain presbyters; therefore it deals neither with the *quaestio juris* or the *quaestio facti.*" [13] Thus at the critical juncture when the question might be posed whether the Roman Catholic church can recognize the transmission of valid and worthy orders through what some have called "presbyteral succession," the council remains silent and leaves the question open.

---

[10] Sess. XXIII *De Sacramento Ordinis,* can. 7.

[11] Especially, it seems, of P. Benoit's work, *Les origines apostoliques de l'Episcopat selon le Nouveau Testament: L'Evêque dans l'Eglise du Christ* (1963).

[12] Cf. DS 1145, 1290.

[13] Schema 87.

It resumes its description of the ministry of the priest-bishop's ministry, speaking of his power to govern, that is, to shepherd or pastor the Christian people. And it bases this function of the bishop not simply on his canonical jurisdiction but on his "sacred power" by reason of his sacramental order. It is on this same basis — the "spiritual power" of his sacramental order — that the council establishes the ministry of the priest-presbyter to pastor the Christian community (cf. On the Priestly Life, 6).

The overwhelming and sustained parallelism in presenting the ministry of the priest-bishop and that of the priest-presbyter has led some commentators to the conclusion that Vatican II sees the two as "radically identical." [14] The least that can be said is that when a broad review is given to the teaching of Vatican II on the relationship between the episcopate and the presbyterate, what they share in common is far more fundamental, far more extensive and far more decisive than the distinction between them. If one were to say in a word what it is that constitutes the "difference in degree = *in gradu*" between them, the best way to put the matter succinctly would be to use the language of the council itself: "a diversity of duties."

To sum up thus far: Vatican II sees the ministry of the Catholic church as engendered by the gospel of Christ and developed under the guidance of the Holy Spirit through its own historic traditions.[15] It reaffirms the commitment of the Roman Catholic church to the priestly ministry of the episcopal presbyterate [16] which continues the

---

[14] E. g. Bernard Dupuy again: "Finally, it seems impossible to establish theologically a radical difference between the functions of the bishop and those of the priest. To repeat, it is a difference established in law, but it is not absolute and immutable.

"We find proof for this in the power to confirm and ordain. Trent reserved the power to confirm to bishops. Yet ancient Tradition, Eastern Tradition to the present day, and the decisions of Rome in 1946 accord this power to priests. As for ordination, historians have found several cases where simple priests were called upon to perform ordinations habitually reserved to bishops.

"The only way to square these facts and these variations in Church discipline is to regard the functions of the priest as a toning down of the bishop's functions. Their power, of itself, is radically identical *(potestas ordinis)*, but ordinarily it is bound *(potestas legata)*" (*op. cit.,* p. 85 f.).

[15] In this way Vatican II presents a more sensitively nuanced view of the origins of present ministerial forms than did Trent. Cf. Hans Küng, *The Church,* (New York: Sheed and Ward, 1967), pp. 418 ff.

[16] As distinct from the corporate or presbyteral episcopate of churches holding the presbyterian order.

one priestly ministry of Christ in the service of and for the sake of the people of God, who are taught, sanctified and pastored by it. The episcopal character of this presbyterate is expressed in the episcopal principle of its organization [17] and insured through the exercise of the episcopal office by its priest-bishops. Thus the presbyterate collaborates with and coheres in its episcopate, neither corporately absorbing it nor acting autonomously from it.

This conciliar affirmation does not seek to preclude the possibility or the fact of other developments of the Christian ministry within the traditions of the church. Neither does it offer specific criteria for determining the authenticity and efficacy of the ministries of other Christian churches not holding the episcopal presbyterate.

But still this review of conciliar texts must be further widened for they stand within the fuller context of Vatican II's teaching on the common priesthood of all the Christian people, a teaching not without serious ecumenical significance. The basic, foundational statement of the council on the common priesthood is set forth in the Constitution on the Church, 10:

> "Christ the Lord, High Priest taken from among men, made the new people 'a kingdom and priests to God the Father.' The baptized, by regeneration and the anointing of the Holy Spirit, are consecrated as a spiritual house and holy priesthood, in order that through all those works which are those of the Christian man they may offer spiritual sacrifices and proclaim the power of Him who has called them out of darkness into His marvelous light. Therefore, all the disciples of Christ, persevering in prayer and praising God, should present themselves as a living sacrifice, holy and pleasing to God. Everywhere on earth they must bear witness to Christ and give an answer to those who seek an account of that hope of eternal life which is in them."

Then this Constitution immediately proceeds to describe the relation between this common priesthood and the ordained priesthood:

> "Though they differ from one another in essence and not only in degree, the common priesthood of the faithful and the ministerial or hierarchical priesthood are nonetheless interrelated: each of them in its own special way is a participation in the one priesthood of Christ. The ministerial priest, by the sacred power he enjoys, teaches and rules the priestly people; acting in the person of Christ, he makes present the eucharistic sacrifice, and offers

---

[17] As distinct from a monarchical principle on the one hand (*pace* Ignatius of Antioch) or a congregational principle on the other.

it to God in the name of all the people. But the faithful, in virtue of their royal priesthood, join in the offering of the Eucharist. They likewise exercise that priesthood in receiving the sacraments, in prayer and thanksgiving, in the witness of a holy life, and by self-denial and active charity."

The chief elements that stand out in this description are: First, the difference (as it is said, "of essence and not only of degree") between the two forms of the priesthood. In pointing out this difference in kind or in form, Vatican II seems to recall Trent's rejection of the position that everyone in the church "without distinction" *(promiscue)* can do everything.[18] Rather it upholds the need that everything in the church be done with due and decent order while resisting any reductionism whereby one form of the priesthood would be simply absorbed or "subsumed" in the other.[19] Secondly, the council affirms the unity of the common priesthood and the ordained priesthood as "a participation in the one priesthood of Christ." As it affirms the sacred power *(potestas)* of the ordained, it also speaks of the power *(virtus)* of the faithful by reason of their common priesthood.

As the council builds on this fundamental statement, a number of very striking similarities appear between the priesthood of the ordained and that of the laity (". . . here understood to mean all the faithful except those in holy orders and those in the state of religious life especially approved by the Church" — Constitution on the Church, 31).

The similarity of the two is so close that at the outset one can see the difficulty the council experienced in finding appropriately distinctive language.[20] Even the term "ministerial" is not perfectly distinctive of the priesthood of the ordained, for the council also stresses the duty "to recognize the ministries and charisms" (Constitution on the Church, 30) of the laity, and regards all ministries as priestly (Constitution on the Church, 24). It might also be added that since both those who are ordained and laypersons are called by special vocation to their particular ministries as individuals, all ministries in the church are charismatic.[21]

---

18 Cf. DS 960.

19 Cf. George Tavard, "Does the Protestant Ministry have Sacramental Significance?" in *Continuum,* Vol. 6, No. 2, esp. pp. 262 f.

20 Cf. Grillmeier, *op. cit.,* pp. 157 f; and F. Klosterman, *Commentary on the Documents of Vatican II,* pp. 313 f.

21 Thus Hans Küng: ". . . the charismata are not primarily extraordinary, but common; they are not of one kind, but manifold; they are not limited

Not only bishops and presbyters, but also the laity stand under the apostolic mandate and share in the apostolic mission (cf. Decree on the Apostolate of the Laity, 3 and 4). "Since Christ in his mission from the Father is the fountain and source of the whole apostolate of the Church," and since "the laity derive the right and duty with respect to the apostolate from their union with Christ their Head," some council commentators speak also of the laity as sharing in the apostolic succession.[22]

Just as "Christ conferred on the apostles and their successors the duty of teaching, sanctifying and ruling in His name," so "the laity, too, share in the priestly, prophetic, and royal office of Christ and therefore have their own role to play in the mission of the whole People of God in the Church and in the world" (On the Lay Apostolate, 2; cf. also 10).

---

to a special group of persons, but truly universal in the Church. All this implies also that they are not a thing of the past (possible and real only in the early Church), but eminently contemporary and actual; they do not hover on the periphery of the Church but are eminently central and essential to it. In this sense one should speak of *a charismatic structure of the Church* which embraces and goes beyond the structure of its government. . . .

". . . how can we give a brief theological description of this charisma? In the widest sense it is *God's call to the individual person in view of a specific service within the community, including the ability to perform this service*" ("The Charismatic Structure of the Church," in *Concilium*, Vol. 4, pp. 58 f.).

[22] Hans Küng: "Basic is the point that the *whole Church* and *every individual member* share in this apostolic succession: the Church as a whole is committed to obedience to the apostles as the original witnesses and the original messengers. In the *negative* sense this means that the concept suffers from a clerical narrowing down if this apostolic succession is seen exclusively as a succession of ecclesiastical functions. In the *positive* sense it means that the whole Church is involved. It is the Church as a whole that we believe in when we say: 'I believe in the apostolic Church.' The Church as a whole is successor to the Apostles. And insofar as the Church is not an institutional apparatus but the community of the faithful, this means that every individual member of the Church stands in this apostolic succession" ("What is the Essence of Apostolic Succession?" in *Concilium*, Vol. 34, p. 28. Cf. also: *The Church*, pp. 355 f., and Johannes Remmers, "Apostolic Succession: An Attribute of the Church," in *Concilium*, Vol. 34, pp. 38-51).

Vatican II's teaching on the lay apostolate shows it to be much more directly and integrally based in the mission of the church than did Pius XI's description of "Catholic Action" as the collaborative involvement of the laity in the apostolate of the hierarchy (*"Quae Nobis"* 1928).

As "fellow-workers for truth" the laity as well as the ordained share in "the ministry of the Word" and their exercise of this apostolic ministry "does not consist only in the witness of one's way of life" but also "looks for opportunities to announce Christ by words addressed either to non-believers with a view to leading them to faith, or to believers with a view to instructing and strengthening them, and motivating them toward a more fervent life" (On the Lay Apostolate, 6).

The laity exercise the power of their royal priesthood by offering spiritual sacrifices, especially in the eucharist (Constitution on the Church, 34) which they offer "not only through the hands of the (ordained) priest, but also with him" (Constitution on the Sacred Liturgy, 48). As their function in the eucharistic assembly as active participants and not mere witnesses or respondents makes clear, the laity along with the ordained share a true power to "eucharistize."

Though by appearances "what specifically characterizes the laity is their secular nature" (Constitution on the Church, 31), this is not, as the council fathers themselves recognized, a definitive description of their role and function [23] since "the laity . . . exercise their apostolate both in the Church and in the world" (On the Lay Apostolate, 5; also 9).

"As sharers in the role of Christ the Priest, the Prophet and the King, the laity have an active part to play in the life and activity of the Church;" and as the presbyterate collaborates with the bishop, so the laity "cooperate" and "collaborate" in "close union with their priests" and thus "supply what is lacking to their brethren, and refresh the spirit of pastors and the rest of the faithful."

Again, this sustained parallelism in the council's description of the common priesthood of the laity and the special priesthood of the ordained prompts the conclusion that what they share in common is far more fundamental, far more extensive and far more decisive than the distinction between them. If one were to say in a word what it is that constitutes the "difference in kind" between them, the best way to put the matter succinctly would be to use the language of the council itself: "a diversity of service" which exhibits an even deeper "unity of purpose" (On the Lay Apostolate, 2) for "this very diversity of graces, ministries and works gathers the children of God into one,

---

[23] Since "it is true that those in holy orders can at times be engaged in secular activities and even have a secular profession" (Constitution on the Church, loc. cit.). Cf. also Klostermann, op. cit., pp. 310 f.

because 'all these things are the work of one and the same Spirit'"
(Constitution on the Church, 32).

Against this background a still further question of ecumenical
import presents itself: What is the attitude of the Roman Catholic
church after Vatican II toward the ministries of those churches which
do not claim an unbroken ministerial succession in either the episcopal
or the presbyteral line? While the council did not speak to this question directly, it did address the issue embedded in it both *in obliquo*
and provocatively when it spoke of communities isolated by reasons
of persecution or geography. And it offered this counsel:

> "In exceedingly trying circumstances, *the laity do what they can
> to take the place of priests,* risking their freedom and sometimes
> their lives *to teach* Christian doctrine to those around them, *to
> train* them in a religious way of life and in a Catholic mentality,
> *to lead them to receive the sacraments frequently,* and to develop
> their piety, especially toward the Eucharist. This most Sacred
> Synod heartily thanks God for continuing to raise up in our times
> lay persons of heroic fortitude in the midst of persecutions, and
> it embraces them with fatherly affection and gratitude" (On the
> Lay Apostolate, 17, emphasis added).

This teaching may well seem astonishing in the Roman Catholic
framework. For the obvious question that leaps to mind is how are
laymen, in the absence of ordained priests, going to lead those around
them to receive the sacraments (penance and the eucharist) frequently? Upon closer examination this text becomes even more poignant for the three tasks here ascribed to the layman, namely to
teach, to train and to lead to the reception of the sacraments seem
nearly identical with the three aspects of the ordained ministry: to
teach, to pastor and to sanctify through sacramental administration.

In the succeeding paragraph of this same statement the council
offers some further elements of a response as it considers the problem posed "wherever Catholics are few in number and widely dis-
persed." Here it urges Catholics to gather into small groups for:

> "In this way an *indication of the community of the Church can
> always be apparent to others as a true witness* of love. More-
> over, by giving spiritual help to one another through friendship
> and the sharing of experiences, they gain the strength to over-
> come the disadvantages of an excessively isolated life and activity,
> and to make their apostolate more productive."

Now since their apostolate is to carry on the mission of the church
itself, and since "the liturgy is the summit toward which the activity

of the Church is directed; (and) at the same time the source from which all her power flows" (Constitution on the Sacred Liturgy, 10), the question arises as to how these laymen could carry on a productive apostolate over an extensive period of time without celebrating the liturgy, and especially the eucharist. By encouraging them to the first, does the council at least by implication suggest they do the second? Can such a Christian community in isolation, without bishops or presbyters, go so far as themselves to ordain one of their members who has the charism and call to the special ministry of "the community of the church"? No Catholic theologian would say they could, except under these "trying circumstances." [24]

It may well be that such a community, even in difficult circumstances, insofar as it remains "an indication of the community of the church" would in its own way correspond to and fulfill Vatican II's definition of the local church:

> "This Church of Christ is truly present in all legitimate local congregations of the faithful which, united with their pastors, are themselves called Churches in the New Testament. For in their locality these are the new people called by God, in the Holy Spirit and in much fullness. In them the faithful are gathered together by the preaching of the Gospel of Christ, and the mystery of the Lord's Supper is celebrated, 'that by the food and blood of the Lord's body the whole brotherhood may be joined together'" (Constitution on the Church, 26).

As this statement appears in the conciliar document it is bracketed by references to the office of bishops, which makes it seem out of place

---

[24] Joseph Duss-Von Werdt: "It has long been recognized that any Christian can *baptize* — and not only Christians (baptism by heretics!). In contrast to the proclamation of the Word, it requires no charism. In *penance* a distinction would have to be made between forgiveness of sin (in the internal forum) and reconciliation with the community after excommunication through sin. For the latter, the qualified representative of the community is authorized. In the former every Christian can actively cooperate: lay confession has behind it a centuries old tradition in the history of the Church. What is the situation with the *eucharist?* Must a community now consisting solely of lay people be content with Scripture readings and 'spiritual communion'? Or must it not be recognized that the charism of leading might dawn on one of them, that they can accept this — at least as an 'emergency ordination'? The important thing is to remain ready for the free operation of the Spirit, to whom conditions cannot be prescribed by men — not even by an appeal to 'divine law'." ("What can the Layman do without the Priest?" in *Concilium*, Vol. 34, pp. 113 f.).

and interjected, which it is.[25] It is a conciliar teaching with its own history of development within the council process, and its full significance for the future cannot be completely foretold as yet. However, it is safe to say that the isolated community mentioned above would from a Roman Catholic perspective be frustrated in its ability to be an indication of the community of the church and a true witness of love if there were no way in which it could be a community of the altar.

Perhaps it would be faithful to Vatican II to say that there is no unbridgeable gap between the ordained priesthood and the priesthood of all the faithful. And wherever the faithful are gathered, however difficult their situation may be, the Holy Spirit will not neglect to bestow efficaciously upon individuals in their midst the charisms and gifts of ministry necessary for the life of the Christian community.

Of course from a Catholic viewpoint, a Christian community unable to make contact with the episcopal presbyterate is a community living in a serious emergency. Some might say that this is a peculiarity of the Roman Catholic outlook since many Christian churches have lived under the grace of God for many generations without any clear relationship to that special form of ministry. Others might say that since the crises which brought about division among Christians, the church has not ceased to live "in exceedingly trying circumstances."

Vatican II did not endeavor to answer directly these questions urged by ecumenical considerations. But neither did it foreclose the possibilities to be explored in ecumenical dialogue which alone in the end may be able to provide the answer.

---

[25] Cf. Karl Rahner, *op. cit.*, pp. 216 f., and *The Church after the Council* (New York: Herder and Herder, 1966), pp. 44-51.

A LUTHERAN VIEW OF THE
VALIDITY OF LUTHERAN ORDERS

By Arthur Carl Piepkorn

1. *Introduction.* A Lutheran clergyman is in general not likely to be disturbed by questions about the validity of his ordination or of the eucharist that he confects by virtue of the power conferred in his ordination. He may have an intellectual awareness that not all Christian communities are prepared to regard Lutheran clergymen as authentic incumbents of the sacred ministry. He knows — intellectually — that his Pentecostal fellow-Christians look upon Lutheran clergymen as false ministers of the gospel because of a defect of the Holy Spirit, in that they have not received the baptism of the Holy Spirit and do not have as proof of that baptism the ability to speak in other tongues as the Spirit gives utterance. He knows — intellectually — that most of his Eastern Orthodox and Roman Catholic fellow-Christians look upon Lutheran clergymen as false priests, as do some of his Protestant Episcopal fellow-Christians, because of a defect of the Holy Spirit in that prelates in the historic succession of bishops have not laid hands on them. When your average Lutheran clergyman is made existentially aware of these convictions of his Pentecostal, Roman Catholic, Eastern Orthodox, and Protestant Episcopal fellow-Christians, he is likely to react, according to his temperament, with resentment or with amusement. But he does not lose sleep through nocturnal doubts that he may really not be an ordained minister of Christ's one holy catholic and apostolic church after all. The very small number of Lutheran seminarians and clergymen who transfer their membership to the Pentecostal, Roman Catholic, Eastern Orthodox, or Protestant Episcopal churches for any reason — including doubts about their possession of the Holy Spirit in a manner and degree necessary to carry on a valid ministry — illustrates how little the depreciation of their ministry touches them.

This paper is accordingly not a *pièce justificative* for the reassurance of uncertain Lutheran clergymen, but an effort at specifying the problem areas in a Roman Catholic/Lutheran consideration of the issue.

The validity of Lutheran orders and of Lutheran eucharists could be defended in a variety of ways.

2. *Possible arguments from the sacred scriptures.* For instance, one could argue that the sacred scriptures nowhere specify who the president of the eucharistic assembly and the person who pronounces the eucharistic consecration is to be. There is nothing in the sacred scriptures that explicitly forbids setting up a roster of members of the local eucharistic assembly and designating one after the other of them as the president of the assembly for each Lord's day and designating others for other functions in connection with the celebration for a week at a time.

One might also argue — as far as explicit evidence in the sacred scriptures is concerned — that it would be wholly proper for one person to be chosen by the rest at their pleasure to serve as president of the eucharistic assembly for life strictly as a matter of good order and convenience. In a Christian community, of course, this would probably take place soberly, advisedly, in the fear of God, with prayer, and within some kind of ceremonial framework, but it would be a prudential solution based upon a purely ecclesiastical-human decision.

One might conceivably argue, to suggest a third option, that there are hints in the sacred scriptures that certain persons have received a special pneumatic gift for this kind of service. In this case the assembly's task is merely to discover and to recognize formally the inherent gift and the intention of the Holy Spirit and of the Lord of the church in imparting it to the individual(s) concerned.

One might also argue that it is in the nature of the divine economy of grace that every assembly (or intercommunicating complex of assemblies) of believers develops a form of ministry adequate to the group's sacramental awareness and conviction. If it believes that God wills the celebration of the sacrament of the altar in such a way that the communicants veritably receive the body and blood of Christ under the distribution of the sacramental species, its eucharistic presidents will then have the requisite power to confect a eucharist that realizes this conviction of the assembly.

None of these proposals are particularly congenial to Lutherans who stand committed to the Lutheran symbolical books.

3. *The thesis of this paper.* It is the thesis of this paper that, given the understanding of the nature of the eucharistic sacrifice

which this joint panel has reached and given the understanding of the nature of the sacred ministry (and specifically of the presbyterate) that *Lumen Gentium* 28 affirms, namely, "to preach the gospel, shepherd the faithful, and celebrate divine worship as true priests of the New Testament," the substantive matter at issue is the question of the minister of the sacrament of ordination.

This paper is in a sense a sequel to the present writer's paper of September 1968, "The Sacred Ministry and Holy Ordination in the Symbolical Books of the Lutheran Church" (see pp. 101—119, above), the contents and bibliography of which it largely presupposes.

I

4. *The form and matter of the sacramental sign.* A Lutheran notes that for Roman Catholics the valid dispensing of a sacrament requires that the minister of the sacrament accomplish the sacramental sign in the proper manner. Historically Lutheran orders for the administration of ordination have from the sixteenth century on called for the laying of the hands of the ordinator (and of his ordained assistant ordinators) upon the candidate for ordination. They have also called for either a declarative or precative formula of words to indicate the impartation to the candidate of the Holy Spirit and of the authority to proclaim the word of God responsibly and to administer the sacraments according to our Lord's institution, together with all the grace and spiritual equipment that the discharge of these tasks might require. In the light of the history of the whole church this formula must in its context be regarded as adequate. Finally, the Lutheran practice has been to combine into a single simultaneous and unitary sign the laying on of hands with the pronouncement of the formula of ordination.

On the matter of the sacrament of order, the Lutheran also observes that there have been differences in theological opinion in the Western church at even the highest levels. The custom of symbolizing the office to which a person was being ordained by giving him appropriate "instruments" in the course of the rite is not documentable before about the tenth century. By the time of the Council of Ferrara-Florence in 1439, the bishop of Rome felt safe in the *Decretum pro Armenis* in affirming that the *porrectio* or *traditio instrumentorum* was the sole matter of order, a position that was commonly affirmed by theologians subsequently. In 1947, however, Pius XII in *Sacramentum ordinis* defined — but only for the future — the matter of order as the laying on of hands.

The Lutheran also observes with interest that according to *Sacramentum ordinis* it is the *gloved* hand of the bishop that is involved in the matter of order by being laid upon the head of the ordinand and that there is therefore no direct skin contact of episcopal palm with diaconic pate. The Lutheran is likewise reassured when he reads a Roman Catholic treatise that affirms "that the laying-on of hands simply serves to designate the precise persons upon whom the blessing of ordination is being called down, and to express the will of the [ordaining] bishop that they should receive it." [1]

A Lutheran would observe that the formula of words that in scholastic language constitute the form of the sacrament is not a matter of divine revelation and that the practice of the church has not been wholly consistent. This is true both of the total church and of individual parts of the church, including the patriarchate of the West, where the form of the sacrament of ordination has undergone a great many changes.

A Lutheran feels that the formulas in use in the Lutheran community are at least as specific with reference to the nature and purpose of the action of ordination as the prayer of the Church Order ascribed to St. Hippolytus at the beginning of the third century or the thirty-one words that Pius XII specified as the form of ordination to the priesthood in *Sacramentum ordinis: "Da quaesumus omnipotens Pater in hunc famulum tuum presbyterii dignitatem; innova in visceribus ejus spiritum sanctitatis, ut acceptum a te, Deus, secundi meriti munus obtineat, censuramque morum exemplo suae conversationis insinuet"* (Almighty Father, we ask you to give to this your servant the dignity of a presbyter. Renew within him the spirit of holiness that he may retain the second-rank office received from you, O God, and by the example of his own behavior may persuasively impart a moral standard). [2]

5. *The minister of the sacrament of order.* Turning to the question of the minister of the sacrament of order, a Lutheran cannot find in the sacred scriptures evidence that bishops (in any sense that this term came to acquire in the patristic church) were the only ordinators in the apostolic period. Certainly, he feels, this cannot be

---

[1] John Bligh, *Ordination to the Priesthood* (New York: Sheed and Ward, 1956), p. 91, citing Claude de Vert, *Explication simple, littérale et historique des cérémonies de l'église* (Paris, 1710), 2, 149, as authority.

[2] Denzinger-Schönmetzer, *Enchiridion Symbolorum*, 33rd ed. (Hereafter cited as DS) (Freiburg: Herder, 1965), 3860.

proved by the passages conventionally alleged — Acts 6:6; 14:22; I Timothy 5:22; II Timothy 1:6; Titus 1:5. He observes further that the liturgical evidence of a later period is not decisive for establishing the principle that only bishops can ordain. We do not have any descriptions of or extensive allusions to the rite of ordination prior to the period in which the monarchial episcopate had triumphed. The tendency of liturgical theology is to derive its principles *a posteriori* from the liturgical data.[3] From the fact that the bishop was in fact the ordinary ordinator it was almost inevitable that he should be regarded as the sole proper minister of ordination. The matter of exceptions to this rule will be treated below.

While Lutherans would find it impossible in the premises to describe the superiority of bishops over priests as *de fide* and *jure divino,* they have always been ready to concede the canonical and functional superiority of those who have the responsibility of oversight over many churches in relation to those who are canonically and functionally subordinated to them as pastors of parishes. The Lutherans stand committed to the desirability of the traditional episcopal polity by their symbolical books (Apology, 14, 1.5). Even where the title of bishop was not or has not been preserved, the function of oversight was and is acknowledged as necessary and in accord with the divine will, although the mode and the extent of such oversight varies according to the constitution of the given ecclesiastical unit.

In those Lutheran communities that have preserved or recovered the historic episcopate, the competence to ordain belongs to the bishop alone. This is generally true of those Lutheran communities likewise that have retained or recovered an episcopal structure, although they may not have an "apostolic succession" of bishops. It is likewise generally true of those Lutheran church bodies who do not have a formal episcopal structure but whose size requires an office of oversight and administration under some name other than "bishop," at least to the extent that a licit ordination requires the authorization of the appropriate administrative officer (synod president, district president, and so on).

6. *The orthodoxy of belief and state of grace of the minister of order.* A Lutheran notes that in Roman Catholic theology the validity and efficacy of the sacrament of order is independent of the orthodoxy

---

[3] A classic example is the theory of the double power of the priesthood that Duns Scotus developed from the rite of ordination in his day.

and state of grace of the ordinator. With this principle he would concur.

7. *The intention of the minister of order.* In the light of standard Lutheran theological discussions of ordination it may be presumed that ministers of ordination in the Lutheran community have had the intention at least of doing what the church does, even though this begins to become an explicit requirement in Western theological reflection only about the beginning of the thirteenth century. The Lutheran concedes, of course, that this opinion has a long implicit history behind it, and that we may see it as far back as the mid-third century, when, according to Eusebius, St. Cornelius, bishop of Rome, asserted that the consecration of his rigorist rival, Novatian, was a mere "seeming and ineffective laying on of hands." [4]

8. *The intention of the ordinand.* It can be presumed from the understanding that Lutherans have of the nature of the sacred ministry that the candidates for ordination in the Lutheran church have had the intention of receiving what the church gives, and have thus met the minimum requirement in the way of intention that the certain opinion of Roman Catholic theologians has regarded as necessary.

9. *The orthodoxy of belief and state of grace of the ordinand.* A Lutheran would note that it is a common opinion in the Roman Catholic church that neither orthodox belief nor moral worthiness in the recipient is necessary for the valid reception of ordination.

If a Lutheran candidate for ordination received it in a state of moral unworthiness it can also be presumed that, according to the common Roman Catholic opinion, the requisite measure of sacramental grace was conferred through the revival of ordination when the moral indisposition was removed.

10. *The effect of ordination.* In describing the effect of ordination, a Lutheran does not habitually talk about "sanctifying grace" and "actual graces," although he affirms what he understands these terms as implying when a Roman Catholic theologian uses them. Specifically, in the light of I Timothy 4:14 and II Timothy 2:6, a Lutheran would agree that ordination has as one of its purposes to enable the person ordained to proclaim the word of God responsibly, to administer the sacraments according to our Lord's institution, to lead a worthy life, and to possess those competences that his service as a clergyman requires in his case.

---

[4] Eusebius, *Church History,* 6, 43, 9 (Migne, *Patrologia graeca,* 20, 620).

11. *Ordination not to be repeated.* Like the Roman Catholic, the Lutheran too sees ordination as conferring a spiritual authority on the recipient in a once-for-all fashion — namely the power to sanctify through the proclamation and application of the word of God and the administration of the sacraments according to our Lord's institution, the power to teach, the power to absolve, the power to excommunicate public offenders and the power to reconcile them to the church when they repent, and, as authorized, the power to ordain. At the same time the Lutheran is not unaware of the historical problems presented in the middle ages by *de facto* reordinations in cases of deposition or in cases of ordinations administered by heretical, schismatic, or simoniacal prelates.

A Lutheran does not normally talk about impartation of an ineradicable mark *(character indelebilis).* He regards this term as at best a metaphor based upon a nonbiblical, scholastic anthropology and psychology with which he is uncomfortable. If the purpose of the metaphor is to declare that a validly ordained person ought not to be reordained, the thrust of Lutheran conviction and practice is to affirm this. An ordained person who temporarily (or even with the intention of doing so permanently) renounces his tasks as an ordained clergyman is not again ordained when he resumes them. Admittedly there is some uncertainty and inconsistency among Lutherans when a person ordained in another communion becomes a Lutheran clergyman. Since a commitment to the teaching of the Lutheran symbolical books has historically been and continues widely to be an important preliminary to ordination in the Lutheran church, a clear distinction between this formal commitment to the Lutheran symbolical books and actual ordination has not always been made. If the candidate for the ministerium of the Lutheran church has already been ordained "as a minister of the Church of Christ," the tendency seems to be to require him merely to affirm his acceptance of the Lutheran symbolical books and then to install (or institute) him in his new ministry but not formally to attempt to "reordain" him.

The terminology *signum configurativum* (as conforming the ordained person to Christ as the preeminent Worshiper of the Father), *signum distinctivum* (as distinguishing the ordained from the unordained person) and *signum dispositivum* (as enabling him to exercise the authority of the sacred ministry) in speaking of the ineradicable imprint is not natively Lutheran, but the Lutheran has no problem in integrating it into the reality that he sees the basic metaphor as designed to convey.

12. *The sacramentality of the sacred ministry and of ordination.* Lutherans are not unwilling to describe as a sacrament both the sacred ministry itself and ordination through the laying on of hands (Apology 13, 9-13). Any difficulty that may exist lies in the conventional definition of the term "sacrament." As a "church-word" rather than a "bible-word" it admits of varying definitions. In the heightening polemical atmosphere of the later sixteenth and seventeenth centuries, both the Roman Catholic and the Lutheran theological traditions almost deliberately committed themselves to mutually exclusive definitions of the term "sacrament." In spite of this, the continuing willingness of the Lutheran community to attribute sacramentality to the sacred ministry and to ordination is a datum of its continuing commitment to the Lutheran symbolical books.

II

13. *Statement of the historical issues involved.* The historical issues revolve around two considerations: (1) Is the episcopate a divinely instituted order different from and intrinsically superior to the presbyterate, or was the episcopate originally identical with the presbyterate and was the former differentiated from the latter only by ecclesiastical, that is — for a Lutheran — human, right? (2) Are there instances of presbyteral ordinations to the presbyterate that the Roman Catholic church regards as presumptively valid?

14. *The synonymity of presbyter and bishop in the first five centuries.* The biblical evidence alleged in favor of the original identity of the episcopate and the presbyterate has been often rehearsed: The reference to bishops and deacons, with no mention of presbyters, in Philippians 1:1; the reference to the same officials of the Ephesian church as presbyters and bishops within the space of twelve verses in Acts 20:17-28; the reference to the presbyters that Titus had instituted in Crete as bishops (Titus 1:5-7); the listing of canonical qualifications for bishops and deacons but not for presbyters in the Pastorals; the designation of the authors of II and III John and of I Peter as presbyter and copresbyter (II John 1; III John 1; I Peter 5:1);[5] and the reference to presbyters but not to bishops in James.

The situation is not much different in the period of the apostolic fathers. In I Clement (about 96) the leaders of the Christian communities are bishops and deacons (42, 4.5); presbyter seems to be

---

[5] The textually dubious *episkopountes* ("exercising oversight") in I Peter 5:2 would, if it were original, not be without significance in this connection.

the synonym of bishop at least in 44, 5 (see verses 1 and 4); 47, 6; 54, 2; and 57, 1. The community of the Didache (first half of the second century) also operates with bishops and deacons (15, 1). The presbyters are named as the ruling officers in the Shepherd of Hermas (about 150) (Vision 2,4,2.3 [see 2,2,6; 3,7,8; 3,9,7]; apostles, bishops, teachers, and deacons appear in 3,5,1; bishops and *philoxenoi* [literally, "stranger-lovers"] appear in Similitude 9,27,2). There are presbyters and deacons at Smyrna and at Philippi according to the *Letter* of St. Polycarp (69?—155?) 5,3; the address and 6,1 speak only of presbyters; the reference to Valens the presbyter in 11,1 does not help us; St. Polycarp himself is called bishop only in the subsequently added titles of the *Letter* and of the *Martyrdom*. Presbyters are the ruling officers in II Clement 17,3 (about A. D. 150). Presbyter is a synonym of bishop in St. Irenaeus of Lyons (130?—200?), *Against the Heresies* 3,2,2 (see 3,3,2) and 4,26,5;[6] in Eusebius, *Church History*, 5,24,[7] quoting St. Victor of Rome (died 198); and in St. Clement of Alexandria (150?—215?), *Quis dives salvetur?*, 42.[8] The *Letter* of St. Firmilian of Carthage (died 268), reproduced in St. Cyprian's correspondence as *Letter 75*, 4.7.[9] can also be cited.

St. John Chrysostom recognizes the synonymity of presbyter and bishop in the New Testament in his *Homilies on Philippians* (on 1:1).[10] So does Theodoret (393?—458?) in his comments on Philippians 1:1 and I Timothy 3:1,[11] as well as Oecumenius (sixth century) in his *Commentary on the Acts of the Apostles* (on 20:17)[12] and St. Maximus the Confessor (580?—662) in his *Scholia on "Concerning the Divine Names" of Dionysius the Areopagite*, 1,1.[13]

St. Jerome (342?—420) sets forth his position unambiguously in his *Letter 146 (85) to Evangelus:*

> "The apostle clearly [teaches] that presbyters are the same as
> bishops. . . . Listen to another bit of evidence in which it is
> most clearly proved that the bishop and the presbyter are the

---

[6] Migne, *Patrologia graeca*, 7, 847-848. 1055.

[7] *Ibid.*, 20, 505.

[8] *Ibid.*, 9, 648.

[9] Migne, *Patrologia latina*, 3, 1206. 1209.

[10] St. John Chrysostom, *Interpretatio omnium epistolarum Paulinarum per homilias facta*, ed. Frederick Field, 5 (Oxford: J. Wright, 1855), 8.

[11] Migne, *Patrologia graeca*, 82, 560, 804.

[12] *Ibid.*, 118, 255.

[13] *Ibid.*, 4, 185.

same. . . . But at a later date the choice of one who was placed ahead of the others was undertaken as a remedy against schism, lest some one person by attracting a following would rend the church of Christ. Thus at Alexandria from St. Mark the Evangelist down to the bishops SS. Heraclas [died 247] and Dionysius [died 265], the presbyters always chose one of their own number whom they would place on a higher level and call bishop, just as if an army were to make an emperor, or deacons would choose out of their midst one whose diligence they knew and call him archdeacon. For, apart from ordination, what does a bishop do that a presbyter does not do?" [14]

In his *Commentary on Titus* (on 1:5) he states:

"The presbyter accordingly is the same as a bishop, and before rivalries came about in our religion through diabolical impulse and they would say among the people, 'I am of Paul,' 'I am of Apollo,' 'I am of Cephas,' the churches were governed by a common council of presbyters. Later on some individual believed that those whom he baptized were his, not Christ's, and it was decreed in the whole world that one of the presbyters should be chosen and placed over the rest and have the care of a single church and the seeds of divisions be removed. If anyone should think that this opinion, that the bishop and the presbyter are one and that the one designation refers to his age and the other to his office, is our own and not that of the Scriptures, let him read again the words of the apostle when he speaks to the Philippians. . . . Philippi is one city of Macedonia, and certainly in a single city there could not have been a number of bishops, as they are called. But because at that time the same persons were called bishops and presbyters, he speaks on that account without distinction about bishops as he does about priests. . . . On that account these things [are so] as we demonstrated that among the ancients presbyters and bishops were the same but gradually, in order that the emerging shoots of dissension might be plucked out, the whole responsibility was transferred to a single person. Therefore as the presbyters know that they are subject to the one

---

[14] *"Apostolus perspicue [docet] eosdem esse presbyteros quos episcopos. . . . Quod autem postea unus electus est, qui caeteris praeponeretur, in schismatis remedium factum est, ne unusquisque ad se trahens Christi ecclesiam rumperet. Nam et Alexandriae a Marco evangelista usque ad Heraclam et Dionysium episcopos, presbyteri semper unum ex se electum, in excelsiori gradu collocatum, episcopum nominabant, quomodo si exercitus imperatorem faciat; aut diaconi eligant de se, quem industriam noverint, et archidiaconum vocent. Quid enim facit excepta ordinatione episcopus, quod presbyter non faciat?"* (Migne, *Patrologia latina*, 22, 1193—94)

who has been placed over them by an ecclesiastical custom, so the bishops should know that they are greater than presbyters more through custom than through the verity of an ordinance of the Lord and that they [all] ought to rule the church in common." [15]

"Among the ancients bishops and priests [were] the same," St. Jerome says in his *Letter 69 to Oceanus*, 3.[16]

15. *The survival of the tradition of the synonymity of presbyter and bishop.* A relic of the old tradition emerges as late as the turn of the fifth/sixth century when the fourth of the Egyptian canons pseudonymously attributed to St. Hippolytus directs: "When a presbyter is ordained, all things concerning him shall be done as concerning a bishop, except taking his seat on the throne. And the bishop's prayer shall be said over him entire, except the name of 'bishop.' The bishop is in all respects the equivalent of the presbyter except in regard to the throne and ordination, because he was not given authority to ordain." [17]

St. Isidore of Seville (560?—636) in chapter 7 *("De presbyteris")* of his *De ecclesiasticis officiis* sees the authority to ordain and consecrate reserved to the bishops to prevent "a challenge to the discipline

---

[15] *"Idem est ergo presbyter qui et episcopus, et antequam diaboli instinctu studia in religione fierent, et diceretur in populis, 'Ego sum Pauli, ego Apollo, ego autem Cephae,' communi presbyterorum concilio ecclesiae gubernabantur. Postquam vero unusquisque eos quos baptizaverat suos putabat esse, non Christi, in toto orbe decretum est, ut unus de presbyteris electus superponeretur caeteris ad quem omnis ecclesiae cura pertineret, et schismatum semina tollerentur. Putet aliquis non Scripturarum sed nostram esse sententiam, episcopum et presbyterum unum esse, et aliud aetatis, aliud esse nomen officii, relegat apostoli ad Philippenses verba dicentis. . . . Philippa una est urbs Macedoniae et certe in una civitate plures, ut nuncupantur, episcopi esse non poterant. Sed quia eosdem episcopos illo tempore quos et presbyteros appellabant, propterea indifferenter de episcopis quasi de presbyteris est locutus. . . . Haec propterea, ut ostenderemus apud veteres eosdem fuisse presbyteros quos et episcopos; paulatim vero ut dissensionum plantaria evellerentur ad unum omnem sollicitudinem esse delatam. Sicut ergo presbyteri sciunt se ex ecclesiae consuetudine ei qui sibi praepositos fuerit esse subjectos, ita episcopi noverint se magis consuetudine quam dispositionis dominicae veritate presbyteris esse majores, et in commune debere ecclesiam regere."* (Migne, *Patrologia latina*, 26, 597—98)

[16] *"Apud veteres iidem episcopi et presbyteri [fuerunt]."* (Migne, *Patrologia latina*, 22, 656)

[17] Quoted in the translation of Francis Crawford Burkitt in Walter Howard Frere, "Early Ordination Services," *Journal of Theological Studies* 16 (1914—1915), 345—47.

of the church by many to destroy its harmony and generate scandals," and he sees the New Testament addressing bishops under the designation presbyters and comprehending presbyters under the name of bishop.[18]

Amalarius of Metz (780—851?) in chapter 13 *("De presbyteris")* of the second book of his *De ecclesiasticis officiis* commits himself to the view of St. Ambrose in his treatise on the letters to St. Timothy, that in ancient times presbyters were called both bishops and presbyters and to the now familiar view of St. Jerome as expressed in his *Commentary on Titus* and in his *Letter 146 (85) to Evangelus*.[19]

The fourth part of the eleventh/twelfth century florilegium on the ecclesiastical grades in manuscript Clm 19414 of the Bayerische Staatsbibliothek in Munich recently edited by Roger E. Reynolds goes back to a ninth century model, the *Collectio duorum librorum*. This document combines and adapts *De septem ordinibus* of Pseudo-Jerome (fifth century) and *De ecclesiasticis officiis* of St. Isidore. The section on the presbyter rehearses the tradition of its sources on the synonymity of presbyter and bishop in the New Testament. It cites the evidence of the Pastorals and goes on: "Thus you understand that the sum total of the priesthood is settled in the presbyters. Thus moreover presbyters are called priests, [a word] put together out of a Greek and Latin noun, because they give the holy thing just as the bishop [does]." [20]

According to Ludwig Ott [21] even John Duns Scotus (1264? to 1308) allowed a certain probability to St. Jerome's view.

The question of the divine origin of the episcopate was extensively argued at Trent, and that council did not undertake to define the preeminence of bishops of presbyters with reference to the power of jurisdiction and the power of consecration in terms of either divine or human-ecclesiastical law.

16. *Pre-Reformation ordinations by presbyters.* The earliest de-

---

[18] *"Ne a multis ecclesiae disciplina vendicata concordiam solveret, scandala generaret."* For the whole passage see Migne, *Patrologia latina*, 83, 787—88.
[19] Migne, *Patrologia latina*, 105, 1088-1091.

[20] *"Intelligis ergo in presbyteris summam sacerdotii collocari. Ideo autem presbyteri sacerdotes vocantur ex greco nomine et latino compositum quia sacrum dant sicut episcopus"* (Roger E. Reynolds, "A Florilegium on the Ecclesiastical Grades in CLM 19414: Testimony to Ninth-Century Clerical Instruction," *Harvard Theological Review* 63 [1970], 255).
[21] Ludwig Ott, *Fundamentals of Catholic Dogma*, trans. Patrick Lynch, ed. James Bastible, 6th ed. (St. Louis: B. Herder Book Company, 1964), p. 453.

scription of an ordination that has survived from the early church is in the *Apostolic Tradition* ascribed to St. Hippolytus of Rome (died 235). By this time the monarchical episcopate had been introduced in the church of the city of Rome.

In the era prior to the introduction of the monarchical episcopate, ordination would have been imparted by members of the local college of presbyter-bishops. Rome prior to the middle of the second century would have been a case in point.

In the second century it appears that the local college of presbyters instituted the bishop at Alexandria and Lyons.

Canon 13 of the Council of Ancyra (314), approved by St. Leo IV, bishop of Rome from 847 to 855, provided that neither chorepiscopi nor city presbyters may ordain presbyters or deacons outside their own *parochia,* unless the bishop has granted permission in the form of a letter for them to do so.[22]

According to Blessed John Cassian (360 to 435), the Egyptian presbyter-abbot Paphnutius apparently ordained his successor, Daniel, to both the diaconate and the presbyterate.[23]

Even prior to their respective consecrations as bishops, SS. Willehad (730—789) and Liudger (774?—809) were administering ordination to the presbyterate in their missionary districts.

In his *Vita Sancti Willehadi,* 5, St. Ansgar writes: "In the year of the Lord's incarnation 781, and in the fourteenth year of the reign of the noted prince Charles . . . the servant of God Willehad began to build churches throughout Wigmodia [a district of Lower Saxony]

---

22 John Dominic Mansi, *Sacrorum conciliorum nova et amplissima collectio,* 2 (Florence: Antonius Zatta, 1759), 517. The occasion of this eighteen-bishop council is uncertain and the canons (including this one) appear in various forms (see *ibid.,* cols. 525 and 531). Whatever the text of the canon may originally have been, it is noteworthy that a later generation saw nothing inappropriate about the version here cited.

23 *"Merito puritatis ac mansuetudinus [Danihelis] a beato Pafnutio solitudinis eiusdem presbytero . . . ad diaconii est praelectus officium. In tantum enim idem beatus Pafnutius virtutibus ipsius adgaudebat, ut . . . coaequare sibi etiam sacerdotii ordine festinaret, siquidem . . . eum presbyterii honore provexit.* (In view of [Daniel's] purity and gentleness the blessed Paphnutius, the presbyter of the same desert monastery . . . preferred [Daniel] to the office of deacon. Indeed, the same blessed Paphnutius rejoiced in [Daniel's] virtues to such a degree, that . . . he hastened to put [Daniel] on a par with himself even in the order of the priesthood, inasmuch as . . . he advanced him to the honor of the presbyteral office.)" John Cassian, *Conférences,* IV, 1, ed. E. Pichery (Paris: Les Éditions du Cerf, 1955), p. 167.

and to ordain presbyters over them who would freely confer on the peoples [of the area] the counsels of salvation and the grace of Baptism."[24] Section 8 of the same biography recounts that in 785 St. Willehad "restored the churches that had been destroyed, and appointed approved individuals to exercise authority over the individual localities who would give to the peoples [of the area] the counsels of salvation."[25] St. Willehad was not consecrated a bishop until 787.

Altfrid (died 849), second bishop of Mimigernaford (Münster-in-Westfalen) and the successor of its founder, St. Liudger, writes in his *Vita Sancti Liudgeri*, 19: "He baptized one Landric, the son of a certain prince [of Helgoland], and ordained him a presbyter after he had instructed him in the Scriptures."[26] Section 20 of the same biography states that St. Liudger, "in his accustomed fashion, with all longing and concern strove to do good to the rude peoples among the Saxons by teaching them and, after the thornbushes of idolatry had been rooted out, to sow the Word of God diligently in place after place, to build churches, and to ordain presbyters whom he had educated to be co-workers with him [in proclaiming] the Word of God in each of these places." During this period St. Liudger declined episcopal rank humbly *(pontificalem gradum humiliter)* and tried to persuade disciples of his to receive episcopal orders in his stead; he yielded only later to the arguments of Bishop Hildebald of Cologne and allowed himself to be consecrated.[27]

Following the lead of Hugo of Pisa (Huguccio; died 1210), many medieval canonists took the position that a simple presbyter was com-

---

[24] *"Anno incarnationis Domini 781 regni vero memorati principis Karoli 14mo . . . servus Dei Willehadus per Wigmodiam ecclesias coepit construere ac presbyteros super eas ordinare, qui libere populis monita salutis ac baptismi conferrent gratiam"* (George Henry Pertz, ed., *Monumenta Germaniae historica: Scriptores,* 2 [Stuttgart: Anton Hiersemann, 1963], 381, 48-50).

[25] *"Ecclesias quoque destructas restauravit, probatasque personas qui populis monita salutis darent singulis quibus locis praeesse disposuit"* (*ibid.,* p. 383, 1-3).

[26] *"Cuiusdam etiam eorum principis filium, Landricum nomine, accepit a fonte; quem sacris literis imbutum ordinavit presbiterum"* (*ibid.,* p. 410, 35-36).

[27] *Ibid.,* p. 411, 11-22. The quoted passage reads in the original: *"More solito cum omni aviditate et sollicitudine rudibus Saxonum populis studebat in doctrina prodesse, erutisque ydolatrie spinis, verbum Dei diligenter per loca singula serere, ecclesias construere, et per eas singulos ordinare presbiteros, quos verbi Dei cooperatores sibi ipsi nutriverat."*

petent to ordain to the presbyterate if the pope empowered him to do so.

Concretely, the bull *Sacrae religionis* of Boniface IX, dated February 1, 1400, provides: "We . . . grant . . . [to] the same abbot [of the Monastery of SS. Peter and Paul the Apostles and of St. Osith the Virgin and Martyr, of the Order of Canons Regular of St. Augustine, in Essex in the diocese of London], and [to] the abbots of the same monastery who are his successors for the time being in perpetuity, to have the power freely and licitly to confer on all professed canons, present and future, all minor orders, as well as the subdiaconate, the diaconate, and the presbyterate, at the times established by the law, and that the said canons promoted in this way by the said abbots are able to serve freely and licitly in the orders so received, notwithstanding any conflicting constitutions, apostolic and others, whatsoever, put forth to the contrary and reinforced with any degree whatever of firmness." [28] Because of the objection of Bishop Robert of London, who had the right of patronage in the monastery named, the same pope on February 6, 1403, in the bull *Apostolicae sedis* withdrew the permission granted in *Sacrae religionis,* again specifying that the privilege had authorized the abbots of the monastery to confer orders through the presbyterate.[29]

In the bull *Gerentes ad vos,* Martin V on November 16, 1427, conferred on the abbot of the Cistercian monastery at Altzelle in Upper Saxony the license and faculty "of conferring on each of the monks of the same monastery and on persons subject to you, the abbot, all holy orders, without in the least requiring a license to do this from the diocesan of the place, notwithstanding any constitutions and ordinances, apostolic and otherwise, to the contrary." [30]

---

[28] *"Nos . . . ut idem abbas et successores sui in perpetuum abbates eiusdem monasterii pro tempore existentes omnibus et singulis canonicis praesentibus et futuris professis eiusdem monasterii omnes minores necnon subdiaconatus, diaconatus et presbyteratus ordines statutis a iure temporibus conferre libere et licite valeant et quod dicti canonici sic per dictos abbates promoti in sic susceptis ordinibus libere et licite ministrare possint, quibuscumque constitutionibus apostolicis et aliis contrariis in contrarium editis quibuscumque quacumque firmitate roboratis nequaquam obstantibus . . . indulgemus"* (DS 1145).

[29] DS 1146.

[30] *"Singulis monachis eiusdem monasterii ac personis tibi abbati subiectis omnes etiam sacros ordines conferendi, dioecesani loci licentia super hoc minime requisita, constitutionibus et ordinationibus apostolicis ceterisque contrariis nequaquam obstantibus"* (DS 1290).

On Aug. 29, 1489, Innocent VIII, in the bull *Exposcit tuae devotionis,* conferred on Abbot John of Cîteaux and on "the four other aforesaid abbots of [La Ferté, Pontigny, Clairvaux, and Morimond], and to their successors [authority] freely and licitly . . . to confer lawfully upon any monks so ever of the said order, as religious of the aforesaid monasteries whom you shall find qualified therefor, the orders of the subdiaconate and the diaconate." [31]

As conservative a Roman Catholic dogmatician as Ludwig Ott sees this authorization of presbyters to impart orders as posing a question that demands one of two answers: (1) Either the popes of the fifteenth century "were victims of the erroneous theological opinions of their times"; or (2) "a simple priest is an extraordinary dispenser of the orders of diaconate and presbyterate, just as he is an extraordinary dispenser of confirmation. In this latter view, the requisite power of consecration is contained in the priestly power of consecration as *potestas ligata.* For the valid exercise of it a special exercise of the papal power is, by divine or church ordinance, necessary." [32]

With reference to the first answer, at least one Roman Catholic scholar holds that if the popes in question had erred in giving these faculties, the erring pope "in his official capacity as pope [would have] imposed material idolatry on those of the faithful who sought the ministry of men ordained in virtue of these bulls." [33] The final clause of the second answer is for a Lutheran, of course, not a necessary conclusion.

While a Lutheran will not insist that "ordinary minister" necessarily implies an "extraordinary minister" in certain circumstances — although this might very well be a legitimate inference — he observes

---

[31] *"Quibuscumque dicti ordinis monachis, aliis vero quatuor abbatibus praefatis ac eorum successoribus, ut suorum monasteriorum praedictorum religiosis quos ad id idoneos repereritis, subdiaconatus et diaconatus ordines . . . rite conferre . . . libere et licite"* (DS 1435). The diaconate was conferred in Rome at least as late as 1662 with the apparent knowledge and approval of the pope (Corrado Baisi, *Il ministro straordinario degli ordini sacramentali* [Rome: Anonima Libreria Cattolica Italiana, 1935], pp. 16—24). Elsewhere Cistercians made use of the permission until it began to fall into desuetude in the eighteenth century, and an order for the ordination of a subdeacon and deacon is still a part of the most recent edition (1949) of the *Rituale Cisterciense* (DS, p. 352).

[32] Ott, p. 459.

[33] Alban Baer, art. "Abbot, Ordination by," in H. Francis Davis, Aidan Williams, Ivo Thomas, and Joseph Crehan, eds., *A Catholic Dictionary of Theology,* 1 (London: Thomas Nelson and Sons, 1962), 4.

that the bull of union of the Armenians (*Exsultate Deo* of November 22, 1439; Eugene IV and the Council of Florence) declares with reference to the sacrament of order: "The ordinary minister of this sacrament is a bishop *(ordinarius minister huius sacramenti est episcopus)."* [34]

Gabriel Vásquez (1549—1604) asserts that Benedictine presbyter-abbots and Franciscan presbyter-missionaries in India had received authority to administer the sacrament of orders, but this statement still lacks documentation.[35]

While the historical evidence inclines most Lutherans to deny that the diaconate was originally an integral part of the clerical office, the Roman Catholic inclusion of the diaconate among the authentically sacramental grades of the clerical estate is not wholly without significance for the present discussion. If the making of a deacon is part of the single sacrament of order, it would seem to be important that in the case of the diaconate the minister of the sacrament has had to be a person in episcopal orders.

Granted the unity of the sacrament of order that Roman Catholic theology asserts, a Lutheran sees a number of questions arising. For instance, if there is only one sacrament, why should a minister who is competent to administer part of the sacrament not be competent to administer the whole sacrament? Concretely, if a priest is competent to ordain to the diaconate, why is he not intrinsically competent to ordain to the presbyterate? If the episcopal order is competent to coopt additional members of the order and if in emergencies laymen can by baptism coopt, as it were, additional members of the one holy catholic and apostolic church, why cannot the presbyterate function similarly, at least in a case of necessity? Again if a presbyter is competent to administer one properly episcopal function, namely confirmation, why is he not competent to administer another properly episcopal function, namely ordination?

---

[34] DS 1326. Canon 951 of the 1917 Code of Canon Law makes the point that a consecrated bishop is the ordinary minister of holy ordination, but it contemplates an extraordinary minister who may lack the "mark" of a bishop *(charactere episcopali careat)* but who "may receive either from the law *(a jure)* or from the Apostolic See by a special indult the authority *(potestatem)* to impart certain orders" (*Codex juris canonici Pii x Pontificis Maximi* [Rome: Typi Polyglotti Vaticani, 1923], p. 264).

[35] *Disputationes in partem tertiam Summae theologicae S. Thomae,* disp. 243, c. 4, cited by Piet Fransen, art. *"Ordo,"* in *Lexikon für Theologie und Kirche* (Freiburg: Herder), vol. 7 (1962), 1216.

If it be argued that to concede the validity of presbyteral ordinations to the presbyterate is depriving the bishop of a privilege that is exclusively his, a possible answer is that the alienation of an exclusive privilege is not something unique in the experience of the episcopal order. Once the monarchical bishop had established his preeminent authority, he was for a long time normally the only person that administered baptism, a privilege that he ultimately came to share with the presbyters. Until the fifth century it was his exclusive prerogative to preach during the Sunday eucharist; this prerogative too he had to share with the presbyters. Until the tenth century he alone administered absolution to the penitents who were undergoing public discipline; thereafter this became a competence of the presbyters as well. The once exclusively episcopal privilege of administering chrismation was widely delegated to presbyters in the Eastern church at an early date. In more recent times the administration of the parallel Western ceremony of confirmation has ceased to be the exclusive province of the bishop in the Roman Catholic church.

The Lutheran church does not equate any ecclesial community — its own, the Roman Catholic (SA III, 12, 1) or any other large or small — with the one holy catholic and apostolic church. It respects the right of the Roman Catholic church to determine the canonical licitness of the ordinations performed within that communion and does not seek to impose Lutheran standards of canonical licitness upon the Roman Catholic community. By the same token it reserves to itself the right to establish its own standards of canonical licitness in the case of ordinations on those points where the divine law *(jus divinum)* makes no prescriptions and to reject those of other denominations as binding in matters that cannot be established as being of divine right.

ORDAINED MINISTER AND LAYMAN IN LUTHERANISM

By John Reumann

An answer to the question posed by the Catholics, "What differences does Lutheranism see between the ordained Lutheran minister and the Lutheran layman?" could be ventured simply by jotting down impressions one has. But such an answer might vary with the Lutheran making it.

Accordingly, in order to do justice to the complex evidence, noting the tendencies and tensions which have appeared in the Lutheran understanding of "ministry," it is necessary (1) to examine the topic in the Reformation, especially in the confessions; (2) to see something of the historical development since the sixteenth century, in Europe and more particularly in America, particularly the discussion in the nineteenth century; (3) to summarize what constitutions, commission reports, and other documents of Lutheran bodies in America say on ordained ministry and laity, and then to draw on what further evidence is available from sociological surveys, current periodical literature, and other sources on how Lutherans are thinking about what is a question in all Christendom, the relation of the ordained and the unordained in ministry.

This survey of theological, historical, constitutional, sociological, and other material will be presented generally along chronological lines, from past to present, and in a way which concentrates geographically more and more on the United States. No attempt is made to encompass many developments in other parts of the world, and backgrounds prior to the Reformation period, especially in discussion of the biblical sources, are only alluded to, not evaluated.

I. "MINISTRY" IN THE REFORMATION ERA

1. What the Reformers have to say about "ministry" must be seen *in light of* the theology and practices of the church of *the Middle Ages*. This means both that they were influenced by earlier and cur-

rent views of the ministry — in the case of conservative reformers like Luther, the tendency was to hold on to many existing structures — and were in reaction against certain existing understandings. (Then, and to this day, Lutheran views on ministry are often stated against the foil of medieval, or later, Catholic positions.) In particular, Reformation statements about the ministry are reacting to a clear and rigid *distinction between laity and clergy,* the latter structured in a graded hierarchy.[1]

2. Nonetheless, it is to be noted, the doctrine of the ministry *cannot be called a major item* in Reformation controversy with Rome. There is in the Lutheran confessions, for example, "surprisingly little about the office of the ministry," it is "incidental and secondary to the real controversy." [2] Accordingly the Lutheran Reformation did not devote major attention to the topic, and there is a tendency today to regard what was done as "makeshift" or "temporary," or to claim that what Luther envisioned was never carried through.[3]

3. Coupled with this is the fact that for Lutherans matters of church structure and ministerial organization were and are *adiaphoral.* No one theory of church organization was espoused by the Lutheran Reformers as essential to the nature of the church or as *the* "biblical" one. What mattered instead was the word or gospel. This freedom

---

[1] Cf. G. Wendt, *"Klerus und Laien,"* in *Die Religion in Geschichte und Gegenwart,* 3rd ed. (=RGG[3]), edited by Kurt Galling and others, 7 vols. (Tübingen: J. C. B. Mohr [Paul Siebeck], 1957-1965), III, 1663; William H. Lazareth, "Priest and Priesthood," in *The Encyclopedia of the Lutheran Church* (=Enc. Luth. Ch.), edited by Julius Bodensieck, 3 vols. (Philadelphia: Fortress, 1965), 1964-1966; e. g., *Evangelisches Laien-ABC,* edited by W. Natzschka (Hamburg: Furche-Verlag, 1952), s. v. *"Laie,"* p. 121: *"Der wesentliche Unterschied zwischen L[aien] und Priester ist in der kath. Kirche ein Glaubenssatz und beruht auf dem Sakrament der Priesterweihe . . . . Der Ausdruck L. hat sich auch in der ev. Kirche erhalten und bezeichnet ein nicht theologisch gebildetes und nicht mit dem Pfarramt betrautes Gemeindeglied. Zwischen dem L. und dem Pfarrer besteht zwar kein grundsätzlicher Unterschied wie in der kath. Kirche, aber ein sachlicher, der in der bes. Aufgabe des geistlichen Amtes begründet ist . . ."*

[2] Edgar M. Carlson, "The Doctrine of the Ministry in the Confessions," in *The Lutheran Quarterly* (=LQ) 15 (1963), pp. 118 f.

[3] E. g., "Symposium on Ordination," in *Dialog* 8 (1969), p. 172 (a seminary student): "It is possible that part of the problem is because the Reformation Church itself is that kind of provisional emergency structure which never really intended to perpetuate itself indefinitely, and therefore we have more or less found ourselves stuck with emergency orders and emergency offices which are not very well defined."

about ministerial structure led inevitably, in different situations, to a variety of practices regarding the ordained ministry.

4. In particular, as a general impression, it has been claimed that *two strands* of thinking appear in Luther and the Lutheran confessions about the ministry, and that these two factors are repeatedly affirmed in succeeding centuries by Lutherans: 1) the *universal priesthood of all the baptized believers,* on the basis of which Lutheranism rejected as unbiblical any "qualitative distinction of clergy and laity grounded *de jure divino* in a special power of ordination" and any "clerical rank set over the laity . . . in hierarchic steps"; [4] 2) the necessity of *the public office of the ministry of the word,* instituted by God, through the church.

Sometimes one pole in this tension is emphasized more than the other, but extremes whereby only one strand is present have regularly been repudiated within Lutheranism. To the extent that both elements were present in the sixteenth century, some of the uncertainty in present-day discussion over the doctrine of the ministry among Lutherans can in part be traced.

5. Finally, by way of general comment, it needs to be added that the emphatic point in the Reformation view of the ministry is an understanding of it as *ministry of the word of God,* i. e., the gospel, or, to put it in terms of the confessions, justification and the forgiveness of sins (shorthand expressions of what the gospel means). What is said about ministry in the "structure of Lutheranism" is bound firmly to "the impact of the gospel *(evangelischer Ansatz),*" to use Werner Elert's characteristic phrase.[5] A key to the thinking of the confessions is the realization that the controversy is not "ministry versus ministry" but "the word versus the ministry" — i. e., ministry, in the sense of the hierarchy, had come to occupy, in the medieval church's life, the central place which belonged to the word of God. Edgar M. Carlson puts it thus:

> ". . . in Rome the ministry (i. e., the hierarchy) presided over the Word; in the Reformation view the Word presided over the ministry. In Rome the Word was an instrument through which the ministry functioned; in Luther the ministry was instrumental to the Word. . . . Therefore, the counterpart in Reformation

---

[4] G. Wendt, *loc. cit.*

[5] Werner Elert, *The Structure of Lutheranism,* vol. 1, trans. W. A. Hansen (St. Louis: Concordia, 1962), p. 344.

theology to the hierarchy in Roman theology is not the ministry but the Word." [6]

This formulation is admittedly oversimplified, but it makes the necessary point that Lutheranism is accustomed to discuss the ministry in light of the word, not to defend a divine order of ministers, as central.

A. Luther on "Ministry"

6. In summarizing Luther's views it makes a considerable difference for the outcome whether one begins with and emphasizes statements from his voluminous writings about the *universal priesthood of all the baptized* — e. g.,

"We are all priests, as many of us as are Christians. But the priests, as we call them, are ministers chosen from among us, who do all that they do in our name" [7]

or statements about *the public office of minister or preacher,* e. g.,

"It is true that all Christians are priests, but they are not all pastors. Over and above that he is a Christian and priest, he must also have an office and a field of work *(Kirchspiel)* that has been committed to his charge." [8]

". . . a distinction is given between preacher and layman." [9]

7. One recent study concludes that these two lines of thought coexist in Luther in an irreducible *tension,* but that the *"more prominent* notion" is of ministry as a *divine institution,* while the idea of it as "derived from the common priesthood" is a "subordinate line in Luther's thinking." [10]

---

[6] Carlson, *op. cit.,* p. 120.

[7] WA 6, 564, 11-12 ("The Babylonian Captivity of the Church," 1520) = *Works of Martin Luther* (Philadelphia: A. J. Holman, hereafter cited as PE, "Philadelphia Edition"), vol. 2, p. 279; = *Luther's Works,* American Edition, (hereafter cited as LW-AE), vol. 36, *Word and Sacrament,* ed. A. R. Wentz, p. 113.

[8] WA 31, 1, p. 211, 17-19 ("Exposition of Ps. 82," 1530); = PE 4, 314; = LW-AE, 13, 65.

[9] WA 30, 3, p. 525, 24 (*"Von den Schleichern und Winkelpredigern,"* 1532); = LW-AE 40, 392. Cf. also lines 20 f. (= LW-AE, 40, 391), Paul "makes an even clearer distinction when he speaks of the congregation as the laity" at I Corinthians 14:16 f.

[10] Brian Gerrish, "Luther on Priesthood and Ministry," in *Church History* 34 (1965), pp. 416, 409. Something of the same tension is seen in the articles by Klaus Tuchel, *"Luthers Auffassung vom geistlichen Amt,"* in

8. Another study which appeared about the same time attempts to show *development* in Luther's thought on the ministry *in three stages:* (1) up through 1519 there is little evidence that his view differed from that of the medieval church; (2) a great change took place in 1520-25, so that Luther, in protest against the "clerical priesthood of the papal system," vigorously championed the universal priesthood and local congregation, arguing that it transfers from itself whatever functional authority the ordained ministry possesses; then (3) Luther, because the notion that the ministry derives from the universal priesthood "did not wear well" and the universal priesthood "failed in maintaining the preachers," began again to give greater authority to the ministry as an office, different from the spiritual priesthood of all believers.[11]

9. Real *question* can be raised, however, *as to* whether the pictures of *stages* (2) and (3) are accurate. Attractive as it may be to assume that outbursts in Wittenberg (1521-22), the Peasants' Revolt (1524-26), and the Saxon Visitation (1527-28) convinced the "older Luther" of the need for an order of ministry, the fact is that the Luther of 1520-25 seems to have had no intention of doing away with an ordained ministry or of putting clergy under laity or of allowing the local congregation to eclipse the larger fellowship of the church. What is more, what is called "new" after 1526 in this picture of development can be well established in Luther in the earlier period.[12]

10. If such a "development" in Luther is thus *unlikely,* so also is the notion of an irreducible *tension* between two theories, for the theories as foisted on Luther prove "spurious." While later Lutherans were to debate a "theory of transfer" *(Übertragungslehre)* of authority from the universal priesthood to its ordained ministers, there is con-

---

Luther-jahrbuch vol. 25 (Berlin: Lutherisches Verlaghaus, 1958), pp. 61-98, and Regin Prenter, *"Die göttliche Einsetzung des Predigtamtes und das allgemeine Priestertum bei Luther,"* in *Theologische Literaturzeitung* 86 (1961), 322-332. Tuchel holds that Luther sees the ministerial office as instituted in Christ and created for the sake of order, but no real "doctrine of the ministry" emerges. Prenter finds only one origin, namely, in the *"Heilsgeschichte,"* through Christ himself. Tuchel seeks to write as an objective historian, Prenter operates more as a systematician.

[11] Lowell Green, "Change in Luther's Doctrine of the Ministry," in LQ 18 (1966), pp. 174, 178 f.

[12] So Robert H. Fischer, "Another Look at Luther's Doctrine of the Ministry," in LQ 18 (1966), 260-271. "Green is wrong in thinking that Luther's solution was to switch from a 'transferal theory' of the ministry to a divine institution theory" (p. 267).

siderable agreement that for Luther the "universal priesthood"[13] did not mean resignation of priestly rights to the clergy or even a "delegation theory."[14] As for the greater prominence assumed in Luther for the "divine institution" idea, the few texts offered as proof seem not to "prove anything of the kind."[15]

11. Thus we are left in Luther not with a wavering course of development back and forth or a tension for interpreters to resolve in one way or another, but a commitment to the fact that God instituted both the church (a universal priesthood) and its public ministerial office,[16] but not an office independent of the church, and not a priesthood merely of the laity but of the church as a whole. Thus, *the church* is *a priesthood; it* has *an ordained ministry."* To ask whether the special ministry rests on the common priesthood of believers or on a direct divine institution, whether its authority comes

---

[13] Hans Storck, *Das allgemeine Priestertum bei Luther, Theologische Existenz Heute,* N. F. 37 (Munich: Chr. Kaiser, 1953), p. 53, sees three functions designated in Luther by this phrase which stems from Exodus 19:6 (= I Peter 2:5, 9; cf. Revelation 1:6, 5:10, 20:6): "the unmediated and unbroken relationship in which the Christian stands to his God"; "the sacrifice which the Christian in all offices, presents for his neighbor"; "the power of the Christian to fulfill every spiritual office and its activity, which serves the further transmission of God's love." Universal priesthood does not mean the same thing as the office of the word; the two supplement each other. Wilhelm Brunotte, *Das geistliche Amt bei Luther* (Berlin: Lutherisches Verlagshaus, 1959), pp. 142, 200, emphasizes four features in Luther's concept: the equal spiritual authority and dignity of every Christian; the Christian's unhindered access to God and his word; the priestly office of offering oneself to God; and the task of proclamation given the Christian in his specific, given area.

[14] So Fischer, *op. cit.,* p. 268, against Gerrish who accepts a "delegation theory" as Luther's intention.

[15] Fischer, *op. cit.,* p. 269. The "proof" passage Gerrish cites is WA 50, 632 f. ("On the Councils and the Church," 1539) = PE 5, 275 f. = LW-AE 41, 154.

[16] Fischer, *loc. cit.* The only passages cited directly in Luther on the institution of the church's public ministry are Matthew 28:19 f. (the Great Commission from the risen Lord Christ) and I Corinthians 14:40 ("all things should be done decently and in order"), though indirect institution is seen in Titus 1:5 f., Ephesians 4:8, 11, and in use of general terms like "servants of Christ" in the epistles (Brunotte, *op. cit.,* pp. 127-129). It is characteristic of Luther and Lutheranism that an office of the ministry is insisted upon, as instituted by God through Christ; this ministry is accepted as biblical, but no attempt is made to ground it very specifically in biblical texts, certainly not in the historical Jesus.

"from below" or "from above," is to ask the wrong question of Luther. The real tension is the "wonder of *God's* working in and through *men.*" The ambiguity often stems from two uses of "ministry of the word," as (1) "the church's (the priesthood's) task of proclaiming the gospel," (2) "the public office in the church; the clergy are the special ministers of the church, around whom the church's order is built." [17]

Historians will probably continue to debate precisely where Luther stood, when, on the ministry and priesthood, seizing on phrases here and there, even those in a summary such as that just noted by Robert H. Fischer. It is significant that Fischer himself concludes by referring to a summary on the Lutheran confessions.

12. A note on *Melanchthon:* though (because?) he was a layman, Melanchthon seems to have stressed the dignity of the ministerial office more than Luther did and was more emphatic about its divine institution, omitting connections with the universal priesthood. The point is worth noting in that Melanchthon was author of some of the confessional writings and because his formulations were often stressed in Lutheran Orthodoxy.[18]

B. In the Lutheran Confessions

13. The pertinent sections in the confessional writings (where the structure of the church and the relation of clergy to laity were generally not primary issues) include Augsburg Confession, Articles 5, 14, and 28; Apology of the Augsburg Confession, 14 and 28; Smalcald Articles, Part III, Articles 9 and 10; and the "Treatise on the Power and Primacy of the Pope." [19]

---

[17] Fischer, *op. cit.,* p. 270.

[18] On Melanchthon, cf. Green, *op. cit.,* p. 180, note 19; Elert, *op. cit.,* p. 353; and Helmut Lieberg, *Amt und Ordination bei Luther und Melanchthon* (Göttingen: Vandenhoeck und Ruprecht, 1962), pp. 245 ff. Lieberg (p. 384) concludes that the major difference between Luther and Melanchthon on this point is that, in the latter, derivation of the ministerial office from the universal priesthood is lacking, but Luther's emphasis on the divine institution of the office means there is no contradiction.

[19] Cf. the General Index in *The Book of Concord: The Confessions of the Evangelical Lutheran Church,* edited by Theodore G. Tappert *et al.* (Philadelphia: Fortress, 1959), s. v. "Laity," "Pastors," "Ordination," also "Church Servants," "Preachers," and "Bishops." In the older edition by H. E. Jacobs, *The Book of Concord, s. v.* "Ministers," "Ministry of Word and Sacraments," "Laymen," etc.

14. 1) The *starting point* in the Augsburg Confession for such references as do occur is striking: Article 5, "The Office of the Ministry" (Latin, "The Ministry of the Church"; it really concerns the means of grace), comes immediately after the central article on *justification:*

> "To obtain such faith God instituted the office of the ministry, that is, provided the Gospel and the sacraments . . ." (Latin, "In order that we may obtain this faith, the ministry of teaching the Gospel and administering the sacraments was instituted . . .")

and just before Article 6 on "The New Obedience" ("It is also taught among us that such faith should produce good fruits and good works. . ."). The ministry is thus thought of in light of the gospel ("justification") and of bringing men to faith which produces fruits; it is seen in relation to salvation and the means of grace.[20]

15. Coupled with this starting point is the fact that when the *church* is discussed in Article 7 (". . . the assembly of all believers among whom the Gospel is preached in its purity and the holy sacraments are administered according to the Gospel") *"no mention* is made of the office of the ministry" [21] as constitutive for the church. Ministry is spoken of only in light of *the gospel* (Article 5) and in connection with *good order* (Article 14, "nobody should publicly teach or preach or administer the sacraments in the church without a regular call") and the power of *bishops,* which turns out to be the power of the gospel (Article 28, the power of bishops or of the keys is to preach the gospel, forgive sins, administer the sacraments, by divine right, and is not to be confused with jurisdiction granted by virtue of human right; the functions of spiritual and of temporal power are not to be mingled or confused). This means that while a ministry is implied in the church, it is "not an independently existing institution but only a service to the Gospel." [22]

---

[20] Cf. Leonhard Goppelt, "The Ministry in the Lutheran Confessions and in the New Testament," in *Lutheran World* (= LW) 11 (1964), pp. 410 f.: Edmund Schlink, *Theology of the Lutheran Confessions,* trans. by Paul F. Koehneke and Herbert J. A. Bouman (Philadelphia: Fortress, 1961), p. 104; Elert, *op. cit.,* pp. 339 f.; Peter Brunner, *"Das Heil und das Amt,"* in *Pro Ecclesia: Gesammelte Aufsätze zur dogmatischen Theologie* (Berlin: Lutherisches Verlagshaus, 1962), pp. 293-309; English trans. by Paul D. Opsahl, "Salvation and the Office of the Ministry," LQ 15 (1963), 99-117.

[21] Schlink, *op. cit.,* p. 202.

[22] *Loc. cit.*

16. 2) The *royal priesthood of all the baptized* — the emphasis on which in Reformation writings is "due in some measure to the claims made for the Roman priesthood" [23] — is presupposed, even in Article 14. The gospel and its functions are given to the church as a whole.

17. But while all justified Christians have a right and duty to proclaim the word, *a special office of preaching* is also assumed. "Because the spiritual office has been entrusted to all believers, its administration is not left to the whim of every individual believer. The public administration depends, rather, on the authorization of the assembly of believers. Because the ministry is entrusted to the church, the church calls the particular believer into the office of public preaching and administration of the sacraments" ("Treatise on the Power and Primacy of the Pope," 60-72).

18. Involved here is a *distinction* between *"private"* and *"public" functioning* and also a distinction between *"priestly"* and *"ministerial."* As Edmund Schlink puts it, " 'Ministerial' . . . means that in the congregation the preacher of the Gospel serves the priestly commission which God has given the whole congregation." [24] The fact that there is a *public ministry* does not, however, abolish the right of all believers to, or excuse them from, their priestly functioning.

19. 3) Within the total priesthood of the church there is thus, under the word of God, a *functional office of the ministry* which is completely *necessary* in the life of the church for proclaiming God's word in its various forms. This "office of preaching the Gospel and administering the sacraments" in the church is viewed as "spiritual government" in parallel with "civil government," in terms of the "two realms," both of which derive their dignity from the word of God. However, the *ordo* in the spiritual office is not that of the civil government (cf. Augsburg Confession, 16); it is not merely "created and instituted" (*geschaffen und eingesetzt*, as 16, 1, says of civil government) for good order, but is instituted by God's command and promise, originally in the calling of the apostles and thereafter through God's call in the church — "wherever God gives his gifts, apostles, prophets, pastors, teachers" (Treatise, 26) — to set forth the gospel.[25]

[23] Ruben Josefson, "The Ministry as an Office in the Church," in *This Is the Church,* edited by Anders Nygren, trans. C. C. Rasmussen (Philadelphia: Muhlenberg, 1952), p. 272.

[24] Schlink, *op. cit.,* p. 243.

[25] For this emphasis, cf. Schlink, *op. cit.,* pp. 229 ff., especially p. 241.

"Wherever the church exists, the right to administer the Gospel also exists. Wherefore it is necessary for the church to retain the right of calling, electing, and ordaining ministers" (*ibid.* 67).

20. The *functions* especially noted for this ministry within the priesthood of the church include preaching, teaching, administration of the sacraments, prayer with parishioners, etc.[26] One recent examination of "ministry" in the confessions led to the answer, "unexpected" and perhaps different from "the way in which we who are ministers have conceived of our office," that the "official and essential function" of the office of minister is "to absolve from sin" (Augsburg Confession, 25, 28; Apology 11, 12). *Absolution* would thus be "the central core of the conception of ministry," and the minister is a "forgiveness-man." This understanding of the ministry is then related to the universal priesthood by seeing the "mutual conversation and consolation of brethren" (Smalcald Articles, Part Three, 4) as "a sort of lay equivalent of the office of the keys for the clergy." [27]

21. As one nineteenth-century theologian, Charles Porterfield Krauth,[28] summed up the import of Article 5 in the Augsburg Confession: "there is such a thing as the ministry," it is "an institution" which did not "expire with the apostleship," but is "founded by authority," "exists by necessity," and "is intended to be permanent"; this ministry is "instituted by God" with its functions "to teach the Gospel" and "impart the Sacraments"; this ministry, which no man enters without a call of God mediated through the church, is "the ordinary medium by which men, led by the Word and Sacraments to a living faith, obtain salvation."

22. 4) This special office of ministry, instituted by God, called through the church, is regularly regarded as *one office*, where all are equal, without ranks and grades (which arise only by human authority). Though this ministry represents Christ — not itself (Apology, 7 and 8, 28 and 47) — it is not above the church ("the church is above the ministers," Treatise, 4). It is, further, a ministry where all ministers are on an equality (*ibid.;* also Treatise, 63), whether they are termed "pastors, presbyters, or bishops" (Treatise, 61). The "dis-

---

[26] References in *The Book of Concord* (Tappert and Jacobs editions), Index, s. v. "Pastors."

[27] Carlson, *op. cit.,* pp. 121-126.

[28] Manuscript Lectures, as summarized in R. F. Weidner, *The Doctrine of the Ministry: Outline Notes Based on Luthardt and Krauth* (Chicago: Wartburg Publishing House, 1907), pp. 88-93.

tinction between the grades of bishop and presbyter (or pastor) is by human authority" (Treatise, 63, citing Jerome) and "not by divine right." Involved here is a view of New Testament ministry reflecting, for all its variety, one office, the "proclamation of the divine word," and not a fixed hierarchy; cf. Luther's "Prayer of a Pastor," in WA 43, p. 513, "Lord God, Thou hast made me a bishop and pastor in the church. . . ." Just as no distinction between all the universal priests ("laity") and the public ministry ("clergy") is envisioned, except functionally, so also no distinctions within the public office of ministry are assumed, except functionally by human authority.

23. If we ask *why* the Lutheran Reformation insists on *an office of the ministry,* even though it has so radically changed the structures of the medieval church by emphasizing universal priesthood and the equality within the one office of proclaimer *(Predigtamt),* the answer is twofold, not merely on pragmatic grounds but because of a divine institution.[29] (1) There is, admittedly, a purely *practical, utilitarian* side — aesthetically, for the sake of good order, lest there be "a confused bawling such as . . . among frogs" (WA, 10, I, 2, p. 239, 25), and ethically, for the sake of the brother, so that no one claim what is the right also of every brother, at his expense. (2) The office of preaching, as already noted, is regularly traced back to *divine institution* (Augsburg Confession, 5).

Schlink sums up, "The church does not *transfer* its office of preaching the Gospel and administering the sacraments to individuals in its membership, but it *fills* this office entrusted to it by God, it *calls* into this office instituted by God." [30]

24. This office, it should be noted, is not only conceived of in light of the gospel, but also in terms of *service.* No attempt is made to establish the ministry as a priesthood, differentiated from the laity, on the basis of the words of institution for holy communion; this, Luther repudiates as destroying the *fraternitas Christiana* which is an essential feature at the Lord's supper.[31] Thus, even though there is a special ministry which exists on more than pragmatic grounds and "proclaims the Lord's death" sacramentally as well as in other forms of the word, this office of the ministry is not differentiated even here from the laity in the priestly church, except functionally. "Priests are not called to make sacrifices that merit forgiveness of sins for the

---

29 For this paragraph, cf. Elert, *op. cit.,* pp. 340-344.

30 Schlink, *op. cit.,* p. 245.

31 Elert, *op. cit.,* pp. 342 f., references in note 5 to Luther.

people, as in the Old Testament, but they are called to preach the Gospel and administer the sacraments to the people" (Apology, 13, 9).

25. 5) Of *ordination,* the Apology goes so far as to say on one occasion, "we have no objection to calling [it] *a sacrament"* (Apology, 13, 10, cf. 12), *if* it is "interpreted in relation to the ministry of the Word."

Luther himself, however, while taking over the term from the medieval church, denied the rite has sacramental character. All Christians are "ordained" through baptism. In any further sense, "to ordain means to select an individual for the sake of order and to confer on him the right to preach and to administer the sacraments" publicly.[32]

The confessions elsewhere stress that ordination belongs to *the whole church* (Treatise, 24; 66-69), and while Jerome is quoted to the effect that "apart from ordination, what does a bishop do that a presbyter does not do?" (Treatise, 62), the position of the Treatise is that *pastors* (= presbyter-bishops, in the argument there) administer ordination validly "by divine right" (Treatise, 65).

26. *Nowhere else* in the confessions, however, in listing the sacraments, is ordination considered for inclusion, and the context in Apology 13 is contrasting an ordination to the ministry of the word with the positions of (1) "our opponents" who interpret the priesthood "in reference to sacrifice," and (2) the "fanatics" who do not favor such an office as ministry of the word (Apology, 13, 7-13). Schlink calls the term "sacrament" as a designation for ordination *"questionable* inasmuch as the *mandatum* by which God instituted the ministry does not comprise an external sign; the laying on of hands at ordination, for example, was not commanded by Christ like water, bread, and wine."[33] The thrust of the entire section in the Apology (13, 7-13) is to underscore the fact that "the church has the command to appoint ministers . . . , God approves this ministry and is present in it" (Apology 13, 12), but the sacramental type of ordination in the medieval church, which made "priests" in contradistinction to "lay people," is rejected, as is the rejection of a ministerial office by the *Schwärmer.*

27. 6) What do the confessions say about *the laity?* Very little, even in comparison with the little said about the ministry. The cup should not be withheld from them at celebration of the Lord's supper

---

[32] *Ibid.,* pp. 346-348.
[33] Schlink, *op. cit.,* p. 245.

(Augsburg Confession, 22) — this is one of the few places where an issue specifically mentioning laymen comes to the fore, and the Reformation position is not merely that "among us both kinds are given to laymen in the sacrament" but also that the words of institution ("Drink of it") do not "apply only to priests" as if there were thereby a distinction between clergy and laity (cf. also Formula of Concord, Epitome, 7, 24).

Further, "in an emergency" a layman can absolve and become "the minister and pastor of another" (Treatise, 67).[34] The whole church, the royal priesthood, has the power of the keys, and even though it elects and ordains ministers, there may be occasions when the priest-layman must function as minister in that office for the brother's sake.

28. 7) While there is thus comparatively little on the ministry in the confessions, less on the laity, and very little directly on the relationship of the two, a few references do point up *differences between ministers and laymen* assumed in these documents. For one thing, the layman is *not* expected to be *so well trained theologically as the minister;* he would not be expected to know the confessions themselves, for example, in detail, but only their more popularized forms, the Small (and Large) Catechism(s) — these are termed "the layman's Bible" and "contain everything which Holy Scripture discusses at greater length and which a Christian must know for his salvation" (Formula of Concord, Epitome, Rule and Norm, 5); the Catechisms serve "ordinary people and laymen," pastors and theologians have the other confessional writings (Solid Declaration, Rule and Norm, 8).[35]

---

34 Carlson, *op. cit.,* p. 125, notes the use of this specific example of what a layman can do, in arguing for absolution as the essential function of ministry.

35 "It is as norms for the proclamation of the church that the Confessions are taken seriously. Laymen usually employ the shortest and simplest creedal form, the Apostles' Creed, when they make a public confession of their faith . . . . Relatively few laymen have any real acquaintance with the Augsburg Confession . . . . Only very exceptional laymen have ever read the other sixteenth century documents in the Book of Concord, and they are neither required or expected to do so. But ministers of the church are. Because of their responsibilities of leadership, ministers are expected to have a fuller knowledge than laymen of the historical landmarks of the church's developing understanding of God's revelation of himself. They are also expected to embrace as their own the understanding of God's revelation to which these statements bear witness. This is so because ministers are called not to speak for themselves alone but to speak for the church . . . to

29. Also to be noted is the expectation that laymen will *honor and be obedient* to the ministry (Augsburg Confession, 28, 55). Even though "some louts and skinflints" may "declare that we can do without pastors and preachers" — "what one can expect of crazy Germans" (Large Catechism, Preface, 6) — the obligations to give "double honor" to ministers, care for them, pray for them, and have patience with them are repeatedly emphasized (Large Catechism, 10 Commandments, 161; Lord's Prayer, 28; Apology, 4, 234).

30. Particularly suggestive is the order of the Table of Duties in the Small Catechism. Sections are paired in terms of subordination and reciprocal relation, as in the New Testament *Haustafeln:*

Bishops, Pastors, and Preachers	Duties Christians Owe Their Teachers and Pastors
Governing Authorities	Duties Subjects Owe to Governing Authorities
Husbands	Wives
Parents	Children
(Masters and Mistresses)	(Laborers and Servants, Male and Female) [36]

The table was probably suggested to Luther by John Gerson, and not all of the material was prepared by Luther himself (Tappert, p. 354, notes 8 and 9); the material consists simply of a catena of New Testament verses ("those who proclaim the gospel should get their living by the gospel," I Corinthians 9:14; "respect those who . . . are over you in the Lord," I Thessalonians 5:12; "obey your leaders and submit to them," Hebrews 13:17). The net effect, however, from this "Bible of the Lutheran layman," on which generations of catechumens were trained, was to inculcate in laymen *a high regard for the office of the ministry.*

31. 8) This picture of ministry and laity which emerges in the

---

proclaim good news." Theodore G. Tappert, "The Significance of Confessional Subscription," in *Essays on the Lutheran Confessions Basic to Lutheran Cooperation* (New York: National Lutheran Council, and The Lutheran Church — Missouri Synod, 1961), p. 28.

[36] In the Catechism, the order of the last two is "laborers . . . ," then "masters," but that comes from a literal following of the order of Ephesians 6:5-9. Actually the table in the Catechism had previously reversed the order found in Ephesians 5:22 ff. and 6:1-4 and at I Peter 2:18 ff., 3:1-7 (wives-husbands, children-parents) into the sequence given above — probably a sequence suggested by the "pastors-laymen" arrangement.

confessions has *by no means* been *exempt from criticism,* even on the part of those most loyal to the confessional writings. We have already noted the obvious fact that the positions hammered out were wrought often in the heat of conflict, in opposition to positions of the medieval church, sometimes with awareness that it was an "emergency situation." Some have felt that Luther's daring reemphasis on the universal priesthood and the positions in writings of 1520-25 were stultified by later events, and the "real Reformation position" was never carried through with regard to ministry. Others have felt that the "true Lutheran emphasis" was on the divinely instituted office of ministry and that this aspect needed further development. For such reasons, the ministry in the Lutheran church — precisely because it never was an article on which the church stands or falls but is in so many aspects a matter of human ordinance — could be subject to trends and change in ensuing centuries, with a variety of forms which in the eyes of some were almost an embarrassment — the embarrassment of freedom.

32. In our own day, *questions* have been raised *on New Testament grounds,* e. g., by Schlink and Goppelt, whether the confessions "have a biblical basis for teaching only one ecclesiastical office and concentrating in it the multiplicity of New Testament offices" (cf. I Corinthians 12:28, Ephesians 4:11), or "take too little account of the factors which make necessary the special ministry of the apostles alongside the ministry of all." [37] Goppelt would lay more emphasis than the confessions have occasion to, on the church "as a complete organism," where every member participates in serving, and "a special ministry . . . is responsible for the church as a whole"; "only this definition of the special ministry," he goes on, "can clarify something which is basically given no motivation in the confessions — the restricting of the administration of the sacraments to the ministry." [38]

33. Finally, a word about the "chicken-and-egg" question which, in one form or another, was to plague much future discussion among Lutherans: *which came first,* the *ministry or* the *church (Gemeinde,* priesthood of all believers)? An either/or is out of order. The position presumed above is that the word or gospel precedes and creates both. Schlink sees a reciprocal relation, like that of the church and

---

37 Schlink, *op. cit.,* p. 307, cf. p. 313; Goppelt, *op. cit.,* pp. 421-424.

38 Goppelt, *op. cit.,* p. 422.

preaching, in Augsburg Confession 7.[39] Luther, in speaking positively of the institution of the office of ministry by Christ, just as he does with regard to the universal priesthood, ties it together with the gospel and the sacraments, all bound to the "impact of the Gospel." [40] Both congregation and pastor are governed by the Lord in royal sovereignty. Ordained ministry and general priesthood of the baptized are properly not contrasts but function together. The church must have a ministry, but the forms are open, except for the requirement that it be a serving ministry of the word.

34. *Summary:* In the context of the priesthood of all believers and in order to proclaim the gospel, the Lutheran Reformation regards a functional ministry, instituted by God, as necessary in the church, a ministry of the office of the word, ordained normally by pastor-presbyter-bishops. Like the laity, this special ministry serves the gospel. Ministry and laity work reciprocally, but the ministry has functions which differentiate it from the general priesthood of the baptized.

II. HISTORICAL DEVELOPMENT IN LUTHERANISM

35. For reasons noted above, the concept of ministry among Lutherans has been *subject to change*, and that in several possible directions, as time passed after the Reformation and conditions changed. This development is noticeable in the European countries where the Reformation took hold — each land disparate, with its own history and development — and even more so in the new world of America. Factors other than theological were often at work, and there is truth in Elert's statement that in the intervening years "Luther's theological doctrine of the spiritual office flows unnoticed into the domain of sociology." [41]

36. If many changes from the medieval church's positions ensued in Reformation lands through the Evangelical understanding of universal priesthood and ministry, nonetheless some of the *most radical proposals* by Luther, e. g., in the Preface to his *Deutsche Messe* (1526), for voluntary *ecclesiolœ in ecclesia*, a "truly Evangelical church order" — that "those who mean to be real Christians and profess the Gospel with hand and mouth, should record their names on a list and gather in a house by themselves in order to pray, read, baptize, re-

---

[39] Schlink, *op. cit.*, pp. 246 f.

[40] Elert, *op. cit.*, p. 344.

[41] Elert, *op. cit.*, p. 353.

ceive the sacrament, and to practice other Christian work" (a kind of gathering which Luther himself realized "I cannot and do not yet dare organize")[42] — *failed to materialize.*

37. Instead, there arose a *variety of patterns* for church structure and ministry, including the consistory in German territories, the involvement of bishops and king in Sweden, the "free church" developed in Amsterdam, etc. There arose also, in fidelity to the Reformation's emphasis on ministry as a serving proclaimer of the word, a *new concept of "clergyman,"* the *minister verbi divini,* the *Prediger, Praedikant,* or *Pfarrer* (older terms like "priest" lingered, but that usage for Evangelical clergy was "reintroduced or at least aimed at" only really "at the time of Rationalism";[43] "pastor" became popular in the eighteenth century under the influence of Pietism;[44] "clergy" itself as a term can be said to reflect Anglican preference, "minister," the Free Churches[45]). In the Lutheran minister a "new social and vocational class" arose, drawn neither from the nobility nor generally from the peasantry. In particular this special ministry in Lutheran lands was characterized by a high educational training. The Reformation's emphasis on allowing the clergy to marry led to the creative development of the Lutheran parsonage. In these ways a distinct concept of ministry developed, akin to all other lay priests in the church but set off by calling, function, and such factors as theological education, public position, etc.

We note for our purposes the trends which set in under Lutheran Orthodoxy, Pietism, and then during the nineteenth-century Confessional Revival in Europe before turning to see how American Lutheranism is heir of all these developments.

A. European Lutheranism Generally

38. 1) *Lutheran Orthodoxy* endeavored to *follow the Reformation* heritage in (1) viewing the office of ministry, instituted by God, as the property of the church as a whole, and in (2) seeing that "the call to the office carries with it no class distinction before God and

---

[42] WA 19, 75, 5 ff.; = PE 6, 173; = LW-AE, 53, 64.
[43] Elert, *op. cit.,* p. 354.
[44] Wilhelm Pauck, "The Ministry in the Time of the Continental Reformation," in *The Ministry in Historical Perspective,* edited by H. Richard Niebuhr and Daniel D. Williams (New York: Harper, 1956), p. 116.
[45] *Ibid.,* but cf. use of the Latin *minister* in the confessions.

affords no . . . *character indelebilis"* [46] — i. e., is not a special order apart from the universal priesthood (though Orthodoxy, while preserving Luther's concept of a priesthood of all the baptized, "never helped it make a breakthrough" in church life [47]). The basic relationship of office to gospel was preserved, and Luther's successors were aware of the flexibility required in transitional times, but there was often unclarity over where what is essential for the church ends and where freedom in form begins.

39. The Lutheran fathers, of course, *further emphasized scriptural proof to develop their view of ministry.*[48] Thus Hollaz availed himself of Matthew 18:16 to distinguish the "representative church" (an "assembly of Christian teachers") from the "collective church" (consisting of "teachers and hearers"). This "representative church" could then be identified with the ministry, in distinction from the whole number of church members. Hutter voiced the view that "the aristocratic form of government" is best in the church — i. e., under Christ, "one equal ministry of teachers or pastors, or bishops of the church," as in apostolic times (but not changed into a monarchy, as the Catholics do). Schmid's summary on these scholastic theologians speaks of "the Ministry" as the "instrumentality" through which the entire number of those in Christ (who "cannot equally participate in all the affairs of the church by giving counsel, direction, or decision") can be represented. On this view, the ministry not only makes public proclamation but also *leads* the church. However, the texts Schmid cites scarcely require so complete an identification of ministry with leadership, and he himself, quoting Hollaz and Baier, speaks of a governing council which includes *laymen,* "provided they be experienced and skillful in sacred affairs, godly and peace-loving."

40. These Orthodox theologians refer frequently to the *status ecclesiasticus* as one of the three estates or hierarchies of the church (along with the political or civil authority, and the domestic).[49] They

---

[46] Elert, *op. cit.,* p. 354.

[47] Bernhard Lohse, *"Priestertum,"* III. *In der christlichen Kirche, 3. Protestantismus,* in RGG³, V, 580.

[48] Cf. Heinrich Schmid, *The Doctrinal Theology of the Evangelical Lutheran Church Verified from the Original Sources,* trans. C. A. Hay and H. E. Jacobs (Philadelphia: Lutheran Publication Society, 1899), par. 57, pp. 599-604, with references to the theologians cited above: Hollaz, *Examen* (1707), 1277; Hutter, *Loci Communes Theologici* (1619), 568, 581; Hollaz, 1320, and Baier, *Compendium* (1685), 773.

[49] Schmid, paras. 58 and 59, pp. 604-616.

maintain, with fuller precision, Reformation definitions of the ministry of the church, ordination, etc.[50] There is, however, a more definite emphasis on *differing ranks and grades* assigned to individual ministers, for reasons of outward order. Elert sees *departure from Luther* "in the fact that later dogmaticians divide spiritual authority into 'power of office' *(potestas ordinis)* and 'power of jurisdiction' *(potestas jurisdictionis),*" and now the power of jurisdiction is seen to add something to the office of the ministry, a power in which "ordination of ministers" and "censorship of morals" appear as accessories in Melanchthon's *Loci* (XIII, 16).[51] In this period the officeholder therefore sometimes becomes also a custodian of morals, and there is a tendency (e. g., in Johann Benedikt Carpzov I) to see the preacher also as *judge* and one who *disciplines.*[52] There is also a revival in the seventeenth century of the medieval concept of *Seelsorge,* the care of souls, and with it a tendency to govern and judge, not just to preach, on the part of those who held the *Predigtamt.*[53]

One has the impression that Lutheran Orthodoxy generally *enhanced* the status and concept of the *ordained* ministry and *minimized* the universal *priesthood of the baptized.*

41. 2) *Pietism* redressed this imbalance and *stressed,* as might be expected, the *priesthood of all believers,* often at the expense of any special clerical office. Already in 1675 Spener advocated in his *Pia Desideria* the restoration of universal exercise of the "spiritual priesthood" of all Christians, a Reformation theme which had lain dormant. Laymen should be built up in the word of God and, further, share in the administration of the church. Under Pietism cell movements, *ecclesiolae, collegia pietatis,* conventicles arose in many places, in many forms, throughout Evangelical territory and beyond, sometimes within the organized (state) church, sometimes apart from it. On the whole, Pietism did not lead, in the Lutheran church, to a full development of "universal priesthood," nor did it result in the loss of the

---

[50] Examples are given in Weidner, *op. cit.,* pp. 101-104.

[51] Elert, *op. cit.,* pp. 354 f. Elert writes (p. 355), "To be sure, one can offer no valid objection to the actual custom of carrying out the act of ordination only through ordained clerics (Enders [*et al., Luthers Briefwechsel*], 11, 40, 18 ff.); but the derivation of this custom as a right from the clergy's 'power of jurisdiction' really gives to this power a content which no longer has anything to do with the Office of the Keys."

[52] *Ibid.,* pp. 355 f.

[53] *Ibid.,* p. 363; cf. Pauck, *op. cit.,* p. 138.

Reformation sense of office of the ministry.[54] But it had the effect, like the Reformation itself, of opening the structures and reemphasizing the layman's role. It was from Pietist circles that many of the early European Lutheran settlers in America were to come, e. g., already in 1683, separatists from Spener's Frankfort group who came to Pennsylvania.

42. While pietistic movements always carried with them the twin dangers of separatistic tendencies and opposition to clergy (because of the predominantly lay participation in conventicles and the emphasis on universal priesthood), it must be remembered that Pietists varied considerably and many stayed *within existing church structures,* even among the ranks of the *ministers.* Spener, for example, "broke with the separatists for love of his church and his pastoral office." [55] Often these leaders themselves within the church promoted a new and fuller religious expression of faith among the lay priests. In connection with efforts at securing greater lay participation in church government, the principle of *"collegialism"* may also be mentioned, a principle which many Pietists endorsed. It argued that neither state nor church are divine institutions but corporate unities founded by means of a social compact of men voluntarily (contrast the medieval idea of a unity of church and state as *unum corpus christianum*). In a society which is often pluralistic religiously, each church group has the right to govern itself. In the church there are two classes of members: teachers and hearers (not three estates: nobility, clergy, and people), "and these two classes stand side by side with equal rights, the teachers having no sovereign authority over the hearers." [56] Such a view encouraged greater importance for the laity than one where the clerical estate was emphasized.

43. The general picture of development traced out above for Germany also applies elsewhere, e. g., in *Sweden.*[57] Luther's emphasis

---

54 Lohse, *loc. cit.*

55 C. Mirbt, "Pietism," in *The New Schaff-Herzog Encyclopedia of Religious Knowledge,* edited by S. M. Jackson (New York: Funk & Wagnalls), IX (1911), p. 55. Cf. Philip Jacob Spener, *Pia Desideria,* trans. T. G. Tappert, Seminar Editions, (Philadelphia: Fortress, 1964), p. 94: "No damage will be done to the ministry by a proper use of this priesthood. In fact, one of the principal reasons why the ministry cannot accomplish all that it ought is that it is too weak without the help of the universal priesthood."

56 E. Sehling, "Collegialism," in *Schaff-Herzog,* III (1909), p. 160.

57 Ragnar Askmark, *Ämbetet i den Svenska Kyrkan* (Lund: Gleerup, 1949); summary in English by C. G. Carlfelt in LQ 3 (1951), pp. 318 f.; and

on "universal priesthood" was taken over in principle, but never effected, for theoretical and practical reasons. Accordingly, Lutheran *Orthodoxy* came to dominate, with its "orders" — family, government, and clergy (representing the church). The clergy were a separate class in society, the *ecclesia representativa*. They exercised a power of the keys, not only to "loose" (absolve), but also to "bind," in the sense of discipline, even in the general community down to 1686. The clergy were self-perpetuating in the sense that synods were made up only of clerics, and ordination (at times vested with a sacramental meaning) was at the hands of the bishop and chapter. *Pietism* challenged this with an emphasis on universal priesthood, new birth (rather than baptism), and sanctification (more than justification); only a regenerate minister could rightly proclaim the gospel, it was understood. Thus the Swedish church reflects *two strands* of thought: (1) the ministry is a divine institution, the officeholders, in direct line, followers of the apostles; 2) this ministry, however, does not depend on the *potestas ordinis* of the bishop but the activity of God who calls men, with the universal priesthood (church) a feature of some importance.

44. 3) A final factor in European developments to be noted here is the *Confessional Revival* in the *nineteenth century* and the *ensuing debate* involving "high church" and "low church" wings *on the ministry* in Lutheranism.

Justus Henning *Boehmer* (1674-1749), a jurist who sought to apply older principles of canon law to post-Reformation conditions, initiated, according to Schlink, the *"theory of transference,"* i. e., that the priesthood of believers transfers in the local congregation its authority to one of its members who then serves as its minister.[58] This theory, building on the Reformation theme of universal priesthood, revitalized and actualized in Pietism, was further developed during the next century, e. g., by J. W. F. *Hoefling* (1802-1853), of Erlangen. Hoefling, though he "regarded the office of the ministry as the sacramental office of dealing with men in the name of God," thought that this ministerial office rests solely on the universal priesthood, "the only office which exists by divine right." [59] Here the public ministry

---

Conrad Bergendoff, "Wanted: A Theory of the Laity in the Lutheran Church," in LQ 3 (1951), pp. 83 ff.

58 Schlink, *op. cit.,* p. 244, note 13; E. Friedberg, "Boehmer, Justus Henning," in *Schaff-Herzog,* II (1908), p. 211.

59 I. Ludolphy, "Hoefling, Johann Wilhelm Friedrich," in Enc. Luth. Ch., p. 1032.

becomes but an "organization" or "concentration" or even "emanation" of the priesthood of all believers, "a 'community office' based on the 'collective right' of the whole congregation"; the pastor functions for and on behalf of the community; as Ritschl put it, he "represents" it in the divine service.[60] Such views were *opposed* — rightly, Schlink feels,[61] in light of the confessions — by such nineteenth-century theologians as Loehe, Klieforth, Vilmar, Dieckhof, and Stahl.

45. However, in the face of this "transference theory," in light of the revival of interest in the confessions, and amid the often revolutionary events of the day (1848!), some of these theologians forged a view of the office of the ministry with a "priestly significance almost in the Catholic sense." [62] A. F. C. *Vilmar* (1800-1860), of Marburg, a champion of confessional orthodoxy and the *"Theologie der Tatsachen"* ("facts," — vs. "rhetoric"), maintained that the statements on congregations ordaining ministers in the "Treatise on the Power and Primacy of the Pope" are merely "superfluous remarks about the emergency rights of the congregation in the practically inconceivable emergency of the absence of all pastors called by pastors." [63] Hence Vilmar held to an "inviolate rule" that *only a pastor* can decide whether someone is fit to be a pastor and install him in the office. In an age, the post-Napoleonic, when many institutions were crashing to the ground and the Lutheran church in Germany was menaced by unionism, Vilmar clung to a personal certainty about the "presence of Christ in the Church on earth" [64] and the need for a ministry which is not dissolved into a quintessence of congregationalism. F. J. *Stahl* (1802-1861), the jurist, who criticized the Augsburg Confession for omitting in its definition of the church (Article 7) "the organic side," namely "office and government," regarded both state (conceived as "Christian") and church as resting on divine ordinance, favored episcopacy because "it alone can guarantee authority of administration and spiritual care" ("no majority but authority"), and deduced from the confessions that there is not merely a functional office of preaching but also a *class* of preachers, divinely instituted, "in the specific ecclesiastical sense of a special profession which determines also the

---

[60] Schlink, *op. cit.,* pp. 244 f.

[61] *Ibid.,* p. 244, note 13.

[62] Lohse, *loc. cit.*

[63] Schlink, *op. cit.,* p. 244, note 12.

[64] F. W. Hoft, "Vilmar, August Friedrich Christian," in Enc. Luth. Ch., p. 2442.

entire orientation of life." [65] Here we have emphasis on a ministerial office, over against the laity, as constitutive of the church, with the universal priesthood minimized.

46. It may be remarked that this discussion over church office in German Lutheranism of the nineteenth century has its *ramifications in study of the early church*. The outcome of the views of men like Boehmer and Hoefling was the position of Rudolf *Sohm* (the church was originally charismatic, with no "ministry" or *Kirchenrecht*). The alternative position (excluding the traditional view that later orders, the threefold ministry, etc., were there at the outset) is that expressed by Adolf *Harnack,* that "ministry and legal ordinances were present from the beginning; they do not contradict the nature of the church." This dispute epitomized by Harnack and Sohm "has governed down to the present time" work on the character of the primitive church.[66]

47. Schlink dismisses both the nineteenth-century positions sketched above as guilty of exaggeration, compared with the confessional position, and regards Adolph *von Harless* (1806-79), of Erlangen (opponent of Loehe on some issues) and Theodosius *Harnack* (1817-89, the father of Adolf Harnack), as the figures of the period who "came closest to avoiding the twin dangers of denying either the universal priesthood or the divine institution of the public ministry." [67] Needless to say, both extremes still find expression today, sometimes in the opinions of "high church" versus "kerygmatic" theologians.[68] Moreover both nineteenth-century views were carried by Lutheran emigrants to the United States.

48. While our arrangement here of material may suggest, by moving at this point to the American scene, that the Loehe-Vilmar "high" view of the ministry would be dominant, it has already been noted that the *immigrants* prior to the Confessional Revival of 1817 and following years were usually *pietistic* in outlook. Moreover, other events have served to give *impetus* in more recent times *to the "uni-*

---

[65] I. Ludolphy, "Stahl, Friedrich Julius," *ibid.,* p. 2256; Schlink, *op. cit.,* p. 235, note 6.

[66] Hans Conzelmann, *An Outline of the Theology of the New Testament* (New York: Harper & Row, 1969), pp. 41 f.

[67] Schlink, *op. cit.,* p. 246, note 16.

[68] So Lohse, *loc. cit.,* mentioning H. Asmussen and G. Merz as Lutherans advocating a "priestly" concept of office. For "high church" and "kerygmatic" views, cf. Jürgen Roloff, "The Question of the Church's Ministry in Our Generation," in LW 11 (1964), especially 398-402.

versal priesthood" side of the coin — e. g., the outburst of lay power (John R. Mott), the Pentecostal movement, the "lay apostolate" in Roman Catholicism, "theologies of the laity," and all emphases on worldly engagement and secular Christianity [69] — just as some aspects of liturgical revival, the search for meaning for the professional ministry, etc., have given support to the stress on *ministerial office.*

B. In American Lutheranism

49. All of the patterns of ministry and laity in church life and government, plus all of the disputes over universal priesthood and public ministry noted above, were brought to the New World by Lutheran settlers. In addition, the absence of a state church or *Landeskirche,* to which many of them had been accustomed, the religious pluralism now encountered, the influence of the American frontier and the spirit of democracy (at times, perhaps, also anti-intellectualism and anti-clericalism, so that an educated ministry concerned about theological issues of past centuries was scarcely regarded as a necessity), and the frequent paucity of trained, properly called and ordained pastors exacerbated the situation.[70] All these factors help explain Conrad Bergendoff's statements, "In no area of doctrine has the Lutheran church in America had greater difficulty than in the matter of ministry," [71] and again, ". . . there is no clear doctrine of the laity in the Lutheran Church." [72]

---

[69] Cf. H. H. Walz, *"Laienbewegung, christliche,"* in RGG[3], IV, 203-206.

[70] That Lutheranism in America is inevitably varied follows from its varigated background in Europe and the fact that there were often "varied emphases and trends" in the Reformation and "no absolute uniformity"; what Willard D. Allbeck speaks of as "A Binocular View of Lutheranism in America," in LQ 14 (1962), 206-216, especially p. 214, applies above all to the ministry. In listing complicating factors above, I include the fact that conditions often militated against an educated ministry, but that is not to agree with Sidney E. Mead's contention ("The Rise of the Evangelical Conception of the Ministry in America [1607-1850]" in *The Ministry in Historical Perspective* [New York: Harper, 1956], p. 237) that the clergy who had previously been intellectual leaders were estranged from intellectual currents after the American Revolution; his point is less true of Lutheran clergy because of their tradition of training, but estrangement from the general culture in America was heightened for them by language barriers.

[71] *The Doctrine of the Church in American Lutheranism.* The Knubel-Miller Lectures, 11 (Philadelphia: Board of Publication of the United Lutheran Church in America, 1956), p. 19.

[72] LQ 3 (1951), p. 82.

50. Needless to say, the Lutheran pastor in the American scene had certain *social and theological dynamics* going for him: a particular, committed understanding of the gospel and its centrality; an education often far in advance of most people in the neighborhood; a set role in the liturgy (though this varied with trends in worship) and in the proclamation of the word and administration of the sacraments; an accustomed place in confirmation and instruction leading up to it; and a pastoral relationship with his people. In spite of all this inheritance, however, the minister, transplanted across the sea, having to adapt to new conditions, often had *a difficult time* sustaining *any* proper notion of *office* in a society where many a person conceived "no other idea of a clergyman than that of a hired man." [73] Muhlenberg, who arrived in Pennsylvania in 1742 to gather together the Lutheran settlers and minister to them and who found all sorts of itinerant "ministers" preying upon them and great churchly laxity, wrote, "A preacher must fight his way through . . . if he wants to be a preacher and proclaim the truth [in America]." [74] In spite of widespread depreciation of a "European ministry" and frequent opposition (in the spirit of the free churches and democracy) to office, doctrine, and liturgy, Muhlenberg, it can be said, "held to a high standard of the ministerial office." [75]

51. *Typical* of the *difficulties* faced in new, almost emergency situations are the *ordination* of the first Lutheran clergy and the *efforts to provide pastors* under such conditions. Justus Falckner, the first Lutheran to be ordained in America, was ordained in 1703 by the Swedish clergy in Pennsylvania, for the Dutch churches in New York — not apparently on commission from the bishops in Sweden but according to the custom of the Amsterdam church. The one acted for the other, according to the customs of the latter church. As for providing pastors, because of the shortage of pastors, can-

---

[73] Mead, *op. cit.,* p. 217, citing J. H. St. J. Crevecoeur, *Letters from an American Farmer,* p. 64.

[74] *The Journals of Henry Melchior Muhlenberg,* trans. T. G. Tappert and J. W. Doberstein (Philadelphia: Muhlenberg, 1942), vol. 1, p. 67. The context is struggles against itinerant interlopers, a quacksalver hired to preach by a congregation without a pastor, and the Moravian Count Zinzendorf who was ordaining Lutheran ministers on the strength of appointment by a Reformed preacher (p. 77). Cf. also, from a sociologist's standpoint, J. J. Mol, *The Breaking of Traditions: Theological Convictions in Colonial America* (Berkeley: Glendessary Press, 1968).

[75] Bergendoff, *The Doctrine of the Church in American Lutheranism,* p. 27.

didates who were still studying (usually under some pastor in his home) were sometimes "licensed" to preach, administer sacraments, etc. — although some Lutherans (in North Carolina) questioned the practice, and some later immigrants "looked askance at a type of clergy who could administer sacraments before proper ordination." [76] Such were the irregularities caused by the conditions in America.

52. Almost inevitably, Lutherans in America took on *a coloring from their surroundings,* even though opposing it at points and seeking to remain true to the Reformation. An interesting case is S. S. *Schmucker's* "Plan for Catholic Union on Apostolic Principles," issued in 1838 from the then new seminary at Gettysburg, which sought for an "American Lutheranism" in ecumenical context. Schmucker drafted an "Apostolic, Protestant Confession," seeking to update the Augsburg Confession and at times to correct "errors" in it. His "Article on the Church" does refer to the ministry, and the "Fraternal Appeal" from his pen envisions "free sacramental, ecclesiastical, and ministerial communion among the confederated churches." [77] We may note that even in a time when much of Lutheranism in America looked to some observers like a kind of "Methodistic Presbyterianism," Schmucker's projections included an office of the ministry.

53. However, not all Lutherans — and in particular many of the immigrants from Europe during the period of the Confessional Revival — agreed with what Schmucker proposed or with the church life and ministry which had developed among the earlier Lutheran settlers in America. Here we must reckon with the *variety of views* coming from nineteenth century Europe, which blossomed and developed yet further mutations in the freedom of the American scene. At one extreme might be placed the followers from Finland of the theories of Lars Levi *Laestadius* (1800-61), who in the 1870's formed the "Apostolic Lutheran Congregation" in Michigan (today, the Finnish Apostolic Lutheran Church of America, numbering, with related

---

[76] *Ibid.,* pp. 20-23, with references in the notes. Falckner's ordination is interpreted differently by Theodore G. Tappert, in *Episcopacy in the Lutheran Church?,* edited by I. Asheim and V. R. Gold (Philadelphia: Fortress, 1970), p. 163.

[77] *Fraternal Appeal to the American Churches: With a Plan for Catholic Union on Apostolic Principles,* by Samuel Simon Schmucker, edited by F. K. Wentz, Seminar Editions (Philadelphia: Fortress, 1965), especially pp. 164-168.

groups, some 20,000 members).[78] Here *spiritual priesthood of all believers* was more important than any special group of pastors. Every Christian is held to have the power of the keys. There is little stress on training for professional ministry, leaders rise directly out of the congregation. The universal priesthood, emphasized by the Reformation, reawakened in Pietism, is in this group radically developed along congregational lines.

54. At the opposite extreme, emphasizing *the authority of the pastor* might be cited the position of the *Buffalo Synod,* organized under J. A. A. *Grabau* (1804-79), who left Prussia in 1839 with a thousand sympathizers after he was arrested for opposing Friedrich Wilhelm III's attempted union of Lutherans and Reformed. In this group, ministers were looked upon as a rank or class, constituted by the word of God, to rule over the congregation, by divine right. Only pastors can decide doctrine, they alone have the power of the keys. The laity obey. One of the groups later to make up the "American Lutheran Church" formed in 1930 (subsequently merged into a larger body, The American Lutheran Church, 1960), the Buffalo Synod found its views especially opposed by the Missouri Synod because it thus subordinated congregations (universal priesthood) to the ordained ministry.[79]

55. Within these extremes, many other positions appeared. The *bulk of Lutherans* probably reflected the *twin* Reformation *emphases* of *ministerial office* and *universal priesthood,* to one degree or another. Typical might be the Theses on the Ministry by the Joint Synod of Ohio (later, part of the American Lutheran Church), 1868-70:

1. In the Christian church there is a *universal priesthood.* . . .

2. In the Church there is also a *public office of the ministry* . . . instituted by God. . . .

3. There is a *distinction* to be made between the evangelical pastoral office and the universal priesthood . . . not . . . that the public office of the ministry possesses a word of God, a Baptism, an Absolution and a Eucharist different from those given to the entire Church, but . . . that it publicly administers this word,

78 T. A. Kantonen, "Laestadius, Lars Levi," pp. 1242 f., and A. K. E. Holmio, "Apostolic Lutheran Churches (in America)," p. 97, in Enc. Luth. Ch.; Bergendoff, *Church in American Lutheranism,* pp. 25 f.

79 Bergendoff, *ibid.;* G. H. Lenski, "Grabau, Johannes Andreas August," in Enc. Luth. Ch., pp. 946 f.; F. Meuser, "American Lutheran Church," *ibid.,* p. 45.

baptism, absolution and eucharist. But . . . all Christians have the right and duty to make use of God's Holy Word, and, in cases of necessity, also to baptize and to absolve.

4. The church, i. e., all Christians, have the keys . . . but it does not follow from this, that every Christian is a pastor.

5. The pastoral office is not a human arrangement, but a divine institution, although the external appointment . . . is a work of the spiritual priesthood.

6. The call to the pastoral office comes from God . . . but mediately, through men, i. e., through the Christian congregation.

7. Ordination . . . is not a divine command . . . there is no absolute necessity for it, and yet it is necessary from a churchly point of view . . . and, in the regularly organized condition of the church is only to be administered by those who are already in the ministerial office.[80]

56. Sometimes, where the church being planted was not yet in a "regularly organized condition" but in an emerging, missionary situation, the *results,* while yielding some irregularities, worked out in *unexpected* ways. Settlers from *Norway,* for example, included both those from the state church with its university-trained pastors (who formed the Norwegian Synod in 1853) and those touched by the lay revivals of Hans N. *Hauge* (1771-1824); the latter, under the lay preacher Elling *Eielsen* (1804-83) formed in 1846 an "Eielsen Synod" (later largely absorbed into Hauge's Norwegian Evangelical Lutheran Synod). (To abbreviate a long story, there also emerged a more middle-of-the-road Norwegian group in the U. S., in fact two of them; eventually most of these merged and are today part of The American Lutheran Church). The significant thing is, however, that Eielsen, the lay preacher, sought ordination in America and secured it from a neighboring pastor. Bergendoff comments that, even in this group where the "universal priesthood" was strongly emphasized and amid the religious freedom and pluralism of America, "the American Haugeans still preferred an ordained clergy for the administration of sacraments." [81]

---

[80] *Minutes . . . Joint Synod of Ohio . . . 1870,* pp. 25 f., reprinted in *Documents of Lutheran Unity in America,* edited by Richard C. Wolf (Philadelphia: Fortress, 1966), no. 85, pp. 184 f., italics mine.

[81] *Church in American Lutheranism,* p. 24. Cf. E. C. Nelson, "American Lutheran Church," in Enc. Luth. Ch., pp. 49 f., and "Eielsen Synod" and G. E. Lenski, "Eielsen, Elling," *ibid.,* p. 769.

57. Another example: Muhlenberg, trained at Halle, and many early settlers in Pennsylvania and New York, reflected a Pietist background, but their development of a *ministerium* as the pattern of church government on the synodical level has been called an influence from Lutheran Orthodoxy.[82] Thus, the first Lutheran synod formed in North America, under Muhlenberg, at Philadelphia in 1748, involved six pastors and twenty-four laymen representing ten congregations, but the laymen were simply visitors, with no vote. The organization was first called the "United Pastors," later the Evangelical Lutheran Ministerium of North America (still later, the Ministerium of Pennsylvania, a name which survived until 1962; cf. "New York Ministerium," etc.). Thus, how the ministry was understood, especially in relation to the laity, does not always follow predictable patterns, and takes a profuse variety of forms.

58. Two other understandings of ministry must be mentioned as significant for U. S. Lutheran development. Wilhelm *Loehe* [83] has already been mentioned as a proponent of a "high" view of the *office of ministry* in nineteenth century discussion in Germany. Loehe had great influence in the American scene through pastors, missionaries, deaconesses, and other leaders trained at the institutions he created at Neuendettelsau, Bavaria, and sent to the United States, where they were instrumental in forming the *Iowa Synod* (later, part of the American Lutheran Church). Loehe was shocked at the "Americanization" of the ministry, the trend toward "democracy" and "majority votes," etc., eroding away pastoral authority. He was, moreover, favorable to episcopacy (for him, the episcopacy found in scripture, i. e., an episcopacy "identical with the presbytery"; he wrote, "Nor can we see how a congregation can be rightly cared for where such an episcopate does not enter into its full rights"). "Universal priesthood" meant for Loehe simply the prerogative of direct access to God and the offering of intercession and thanksgiving by every Christian. However, for all these emphases, Loehe did not think that differing opinions on the ministry need disturb confessional unity; to be in doctrinal agreement, Lutherans need not agree on every detail about church order. Loehe's position on the ministry, nonetheless, helped bring about a break with C. F. W. Walther, and helped prevent agree-

---

[82] So Bergendoff in LQ 3 (1951), p. 86.

[83] On Loehe, in addition to encyclopedia articles and German literature listed there, cf. G. Ottersberg, "Wilhelm Loehe," LQ 4 (1952), 170-190; Bergendoff, *Church in American Lutheranism,* pp. 29 f.

ment of the Iowa Synod with yet another German immigrant group, the Missouri Synod.

59. Under the Dresden pastor, Martin Stephan, some eight hundred Saxon Lutherans, including six pastors, ten theological candidates, and four teachers, had come to St. Louis in 1839, in part because of their opposition to the rationalism then widespread in the German churches. Stephan, however, was soon deposed for hierarchical tendencies and charges of immorality, and C. F. W. *Walther* (1811-87) became leader of the group which eventually developed into *The Lutheran Church-Missouri Synod.*[84] In light of its experiences in the American scene, the Missouri immigrants developed a thoroughgoing *congregationalism*. Here conditions allowed — at last! — fuller implications to be drawn and practiced from the "universal priesthood" emphasis of the Reformation. The "transfer theory" was widely espoused. The public ministry was retained, termed a divine institution, and congregations were said to consist of pastors and laymen, but the public ordained ministry was not always conceived of as "absolutely necessary." In line with this congregational emphasis, a local congregation was deemed able to call a pastor of its own without the cooperation of some other pastor. Walther and Loehe were unable to agree on the office of the ministry, even after a personal meeting in Germany in 1851, and theologians of the Iowa and Missouri Synods differed, as a series of theses and treatises put forth over the rest of the century shows.

60. *Walther's position,* which became normative for the Missouri Synod, is well summed up in his Thesis VII in "On the Ministry" (1851-52): "The holy ministry is the authority conferred by God through the congregation, as holder of the priesthood and of all church power, to administer in public office the common rights of the spiritual priesthood in behalf of all." Walther went on to elaborate this definition: ". . . the spiritual priesthood which all truly believing Christians possess, and the holy ministry [*Predigtamt*] or the pastoral office [*Pfarramt*], are not identical." An "ordinary Christian" is not a pastor just because he is a priest, and a pastor is not a priest because he

---

[84] Bergendoff, *ibid.,* pp. 28-33; Arnold C. Mueller, *The Ministry of the Lutheran Teacher: A Study to Determine the Position of the Lutheran Parish School Teacher Within the Public Ministry of the Church.* Authorized by the Board of Parish Education of The Lutheran Church – Missouri Synod (St. Louis: Concordia, 1964), pp. 52 ff.; cf. also encyclopedia articles and church histories.

holds the *Predigtamt*. Spiritual priesthood is not a public office in the church; however, the public ministry is "not an order different from that of Christians, but it is a ministry of service." Ministers differ in that they do *publicly*, in behalf of all, what every Christian originally possessed.[85]

61. It would require too much retracing of history to outline here debates among Lutherans in America over how the ordained ministry was regarded in the various groups in contradistinction to the unordained church members or spiritual priesthood. Typical of the *reaction to Walther's position* is that enunciated by the *Synod of Iowa* in its "Davenport Theses" (1873): ". . . we cannot concede that, according to the confession of our Church, the ministry originates through the transfer of the rights of the spiritual priesthood possessed by the individual Christian. In opposition to this view, we maintain that the public office of the Ministry is transmitted by God through the congregation of believers in its entirety and essence by means of the regular call, because the 'mandatum de constituendis ministris' [i. e., the command to ordain preachers] is not given to the individual members, but to the Church as such."[86]

62. As Lutherans closed ranks in the late nineteenth and the present century, *statements* often had to be worked out which *safeguarded both* the emphasis on *public ministry* and that on *universal priesthood* cherished by one group or another. Thus among *Norwegians,* the doctrinal agreements written for the United Church included a statement on *"Lay Ministries* in the Church" (1907):

1. God has given the Church, also the individual congrega-

---

[85] As summarized in Mueller, *ibid.,* pp. 52 f. Full translation of the ten theses by D. H. Steffens, "The Doctrine of the Church and the Ministry," in *Ebenezer,* edited by W. H. T. Dau (St. Louis: Concordia, 1922), pp. 152 f., reprinted in Bergendoff, *The Doctrine of the Church in American Lutheranism,* pp. 31 f.: (1) "The holy office of preaching *(Predigtamt)* or the ministry *(Pfarramt)* is not identical with that of the priesthood of all believers." This office is "no human institution," but is "instituted by God himself" (2) and is "not optional" (3). It is "no separate holy estate" (4). It is "conferred by God [*übertragen*] through the congregation" (6). "The holy ministry, indeed, has the right to judge doctrine; however, the laity also has this right" and thus has "seat and voice with the ministers in church courts and councils" (10). Fuller discussion in W. Dallmann, W. H. T. Dau, and Th. Engelder, ed., *Walther and the Church* (St. Louis: Concordia, 1938), pp. 71-74 for the ten theses.

[86] Wolf, *Documents,* no. 93, p. 210; = *Synodal-Bericht,* 1873.

tion, the means of grace, the power of the keys, the office of the ministry and the gifts of grace. The congregation and the individual Christian in it therefore possess all things. . . .

2. For the purpose of administering the means of grace in the congregation God has instituted the public office of the ministry, which the congregation by its call commits to one or more persons, who are qualified for it according to the Word of God. . . .

3. When the congregation has committed the office of the ministry to one or more persons, no one, except in a case of emergency, should publicly teach, or administer the Sacraments, without the call of the congregation. . . .

4. This office of the ministry does not, however, do away with the universal priesthood of believers; but it is the right and duty of every Christian as a spiritual priest to work for mutual edification . . . in accordance with the . . . gifts which God has bestowed. . . .

5. God also wills that the special gifts which He has bestowed upon certain individuals in the congregation . . . shall be employed by the congregation . . . called to this service in the congregation at its request . . . and under the supervision of the congregation. . . . [Such] Christian lay activity . . . shall not be considered unchurchly practice or religious fanaticism. . . .[87]

63. It is impossible to state in detail any single view of the ministry on which *all* Lutherans in this period would have agreed, between the Scylla of extreme congregationalism and universal priesthood (Laestadius) and the Charybdis of a class or order of minister-priests, minimizing the place of the laity (Grabau). Perhaps much of the position which would have gained *general assent* from a large number of Lutherans is outlined in C. P. *Krauth's* "Theses on Ordination," relevant items in which include these:

1. No one should preach publicly and ordinarily, and administer the Sacraments, unless he be rightly and legitimately called with the ordinary calling. . . .

7. The perpetual practice of the Apostolic and Primitive Church was, that the call should be given by the Church through distinctive parts of its organism, by clergy and people, each estate virtually possessing the power of veto, and every act requiring the concurrence of both.

---

[87] *Ibid.,* No. 99, pp. 229 f.

8. They who commit the vocation to ministers alone or to the people alone, give to a part which belongs to a whole. . . .

9. [Ordination, like calling,] belongs to the whole church. In the Lutheran Church ordination ordinarily was performed by the Superintendent with the co-operation of his colleagues in the ministry, and in this country is performed by the officers of the Synod in connection with other presbyters. . . .

16. An orthodox candidate cannot seek ordination from a heterodox minister without scandal and just suspicion of collusion. It is absurd that those whose doctrine is impure should examine and testify to the purity of the doctrine of others. . . .

18. The person ordaining should himself be an ordained minister [10 reasons are given].[88]

64. It is perhaps worth adding that, as usual in churches, finely wrought distinctions and principles *did not always work out in practice,* and what a group advocated, through theses or statements, did not always fully obtain in actuality. Thus, for example, in spite of Walther's clearcut position, the Missouri Synod, in practice, often had congregations where great deference was given to "Herr Pastor" (just as in other Lutheran bodies). In the period between 1860 and 1900, when waves of immigrants were coming from Germany and there was great growth of membership in Missouri congregations, there frequently just was not time to teach and train the laity adequately and integrate them into the fuller role developed in America. The leadership of the pastor could then reach "exaggerated dimensions," for people were trained to honor him and respect him by the confessional writings and Orthodox fathers. Thus even in a group particularly committed to the primary place of the universal priesthood (congregation over ministry), the public office of the ministry was often of far greater significance than public statements suggest.[89]

65. One other matter within Missouri Synod circles, a further ramification of Walther's views, deserves note: the position of *the teacher in the parochial schools* of the church.[90] With the confessions,

---

[88] Weidner, *op. cit.,* pp. 107-110.

[89] Cf. R. R. Caemmerer, "The Universal Priesthood and the Pastor," *Concordia Theological Monthly* 19 (1948), pp. 573 f. Bergendoff, *Church in American Lutheranism,* p. 35, notes "the powerful influence of the ministers and especially of the theological faculty, in the life of the Missouri Synod."

[90] For the following section, cf. especially Mueller, *op. cit.,* though the book is arguing one particular view, on authorized lines, however.

the point was accepted that there is but "one divinely instituted ministry" in the New Testament, that of *minister verbi domini,* though forms of this can vary from time to time and place to place. The term *Predigtamt* had been used in the confessions, but Walther tended to equate *Predigtamt* with *Pfarramt* and to use *Predigtamt* for both the pastoral ministry and for the ministry of teachers. Hence, when he spoke of *das Predigtamt* as the highest office in the church, this was taken by some to mean that the pastorate is the highest office, and that any other functions, such as teaching, must derive from it as auxiliary to it, while others held that the teaching office was just as legitimate an expression of ministry as the pastoral office.

66. The settlers who came with Stephan included teachers of religion. Over the years the system of parochial schools grew in Missouri congregations, with teacher-training institutes created, etc. In Germany, at least in some places and under Orthodoxy, the teacher had been considered a member of the clergy. Hence *two positions* emerged in Missouri, voiced in debate during the nineteenth century and down to the present decade: (1) the *pastorate* is the *one* divinely instituted office (even if called through the universal priesthood in the local congregation), and any *teaching* ministry is *subordinate* to it; (2) God has instituted the *office* of the ministry, but not the forms, and if the *pastorate* is one form descended from the single all-embracing office, *teaching* is another — teachers are part of the ministry and should be ordained, even if they teach secular subjects, and might even preach or assist at holy communion. While the practice was usually to install the teacher, there has been agitation to ordain him also (though these two terms have been used synonymously by some in this discussion) — and, we must add, these proposals have been made regarding male teachers, women called to teaching would not be ordained "for scriptural reasons." The net result with regard to the position of teacher in Missouri Synod circles has been to create a *third category:* a ministerial office that is not of the laity and not — at least in the opinion of all, or in certain ways — of the clergy. It constitutes an exception to the usual division into ordained ministry and unordained laity. "Special ministries of the word" is the phrase sometimes used to cover this and other varieties of service.

67. We have therefore reflected in Lutheranism "three rather definite concepts of the ministry": the episcopal (Church of Sweden, the early Swedish colony on the Delaware — otherwise not found in North America); the congregational (pietist groups, Missouri theory);

and the *presbyterial* (most common in U. S. Lutheranism).[91] The source of ministerial power has been seen in three different places: (1) the local congregation (Hoefling, Walther); (2) the ministry as a class separate from the local congregation (Vilmar, Stahl, Loehe, Grabau); (3) *the church considered as a whole,* in which the congregation and the ministry both take their place ("Lutherans in general").[92] Bergendoff concludes that for Lutheranism in America the presbyterial system prevails, and that while Walther and Missouri "interpreted the presbytery to include lay elders elected by the congregation" with no place for a "ministerium," most Lutherans in the U. S. developed "a *college of ministers* which perpetuated itself by providing for the education and ordination of their successors," *ordination* being *by ministers alone.*[93] One can thus speak of "two theories of the ministry existing today side by side in the Lutheran church," as Bergendoff does, depending on whether the emphasis is put on universal priesthood or the office of the ministry, but the general practical agreement among Lutheranism is somewhat surprising, given the fact that the Lutheran confessions prescribe no rigid doctrine here.

68. Chapters on "the ministry" in *recent symposia* by Lutheran professors of theology [94] refer, in one case, to the "remarkable unanimity by the Lutheran churches of the world" at this point, but also admit, in the other essay, that the Reformation point of view of the ministry, not as "an authority, but a service," is an answer "the Church is still trying to give" but has not yet been fully articulated, especially in a period when "the Church . . . tends to shape and use 'ministries' which forget to be 'ministries of the Word.'"

69. Accordingly the topic continues to be one of *lively debate*

---

91 Bergendoff, *Church in American Lutheranism,* pp. 33 f.

92 Weidner, *op. cit.,* p. 120. Of theologians in the General Council taking the third position, Weidner lists H. E. Jacobs as closer to Missouri in emphasis on the local congregation, and himself and C. P. Krauth as reflecting a less congregational view.

93 Bergendoff, *Church in American Lutheranism,* p. 34. One Danish group elected a senior member of its ministerium for life as "Ordainer."

94 T. F. Gullixson, "The Ministry," in *What Lutherans Are Thinking: A Symposium on Lutheran Faith and Life,* edited by E. C. Fendt (Columbus: Wartburg Press, 1947), pp. 289-306; Richard R. Caemmerer, "The Ministry of the Word," in *Theology in the Life of the Church,* edited by R. W. Bertram (Philadelphia: Fortress, 1963), pp. 215-232. The phrases quoted are from pp. 289 and 225 respectively.

among American Lutherans — in the Missouri Synod, especially on the status of teachers; in The American Lutheran Church (in the ALC as recently as 1950 it was discussed whether a layman could be president of a church college; [95] The ALC has requested the Lutheran Council in the U. S. A. to undertake a full study of ordination and ministry); and in the Lutheran Church in America, where there has been a number of commissions studying the ministry, (1938, 1952, 1966 ff.).[96] We take the LCA as an example here of such official study.

70. Study of the ministry in the *Lutheran Church in America* and its predecessor bodies seems not to have been oriented to the question of the relation of ordained ministry to laymen, though more recent discussion has raised the question repeatedly, What is the ordained ministry within the context of the whole people of God? Rather, these reports usually dealt with *practical questions,* such as licensure (it should be discontinued, according to the 1938 Report); the proliferation of men in special ministries which were not, however, "valid" by past definitions for retaining ministerial status, and the increasing number of those engaged in entirely secular work and not under church jurisdiction who insisted on being carried on the ministerial roll because their concept of ministry was that of an "order" with "indelible character" (the 1952 Report urged a broader view of ministry but at the same time more precise discipline so as to exclude those not actually functioning in the ministry of the word — "There is no ministry where there is no ministering"); or the place of commissioned, part-time ministries (the 1966 Report distinguished within "the whole set-apart ministry of the church," of which "the ordained clergy are only a part," among [1] the commissioned, limited-time ministry — officers committees of the local congregation, representatives on boards; [2] the commissioned, full-time ministry — business managers, parish workers, lay associates in local congregations, synodical staff members, lay missionaries; [3] the ordained ministry —

---

95 Bergendoff, LQ 3 (1951), p. 86.

96 United Lutheran Church in America, Eleventh Biennial Convention, 1938, *Minutes,* pp. 65-73; the Statement on "The Call to the Ministry," approved at the Baltimore convention as a "guide to the church" has also been printed separately. ULCA, Eighteenth Biennial Convention, 1952, *Minutes,* pp. 543-556 (phrases quoted below from pp. 544 f., 554). Lutheran Church in America, Third Biennial Convention, 1966, *Minutes,* pp. 434-447 and *passim* (pp. 440-443 cited below; the work of George Lindbeck on this commission is especially singled out in the *Minutes,* p. 447).

clergy, in ministry of the word, in administration, supervision, etc.). Generally these LCA statements reflect the Lutheran position consistently noted above through the centuries, with repudiation of a strictly congregational view where the office is derived from the universal priesthood ("The whole church is priestly because it is the body of Christ, the true and only priest," but the ordained ministry "cannot be derived from the priesthood of all believers; the individual is not everything the church is," 1952). Perhaps the clearest reference to ordained minister and layman comes in the 1952 Report:

> "The minister is not a priest with an indelible character upon whose ministrations in the sacraments the layman is dependent. Neither is he just another member of the congregation. But he stands before the congregation as the bearer of the office of Word and Sacraments upon which the congregation is dependent. It is, however, the living Word upon which the congregation is dependent, . . . the living Christ who must be brought to men in the 'mediated immediacy' of Word and Sacrament."

The 1966 Report, while speaking of ministries (commissioned, of limited term) where laymen and ministers have equal authority, and proposing expansion of the practice of commissioning for certain tasks, had "no intention to suggest any major changes in the ordained ministry, either in the direction of an elimination of the clergy or a greater separation of the ordained from the laity." Thus it speaks in a manner similar to the 1952 Report: clergy "do not stand over the people as lords, neither do they stand under the people as mere functionaries"; the clergyman receives "no indelible character that distinguishes him from the laity," but "remains, even after ordination, one of the people of God." The 1966 Report and its recommendations, however, were not as a whole adopted by the LCA convention, and the matter has been referred to a new "Commission on the Comprehensive Study of the Doctrine of the Ministry," to report in 1970.

III. IN CONTEMPORARY THINKING

71. While the doctrine of the ministry continued to be under study among Lutherans as part of the church's task "to rethink, renew, and reform the ministry entrusted to her," [97] there is meanwhile

---

[97] Lutheran Church in America, 1966 Report, *Minutes,* p. 435. For part III, section A, below, one unpublished study has been basic: Dagny Ohlekopf, "The Church's Concept of the Place and Role of the Ministry," part of a study on the church and the office of the ministry in The American

further evidence from constitutions and other documents, surveys, books, and periodical literature about how Lutheranism regards the ordained ministry and the layman. It needs to be said that much in this current picture reflects the variety of positions already noted in light of the *two prime emphases* which we have traced since the Reformation (universal priesthood and public ministry), and that contemporary Lutheran thinking is at many points *one with ecumenical wrestlings today,* especially Roman Catholic discussion, on ministry. We shall proceed in this survey generally from official documents to private and individual expressions of opinion.

A. Church Constitutions

72. The *Constitutions and By-Laws* of the three major Lutheran bodies in the United States do not offer much direct evidence on how the ordained Lutheran minister differs from the Lutheran layman. It might be claimed that these documents, like every Lutheran, assume the minister does differ — just as it is also known that there are other ways in which the minister does not differ from lay believers — but these differentiations are not spelled out. Indeed, no *definition* of the terms appears to be offered except in the ALC Handbook; here "clergy" denotes "the body of men set apart, by ordination, to the service of God, in the Christian Church, in distinction from the laity" ("pastor" is used for a clergyman "in charge of a congregation . . . ," "clergyman" for any ordained man), and "laity" denotes

---

Lutheran Church, the Lutheran Church in America, and The Lutheran Church — Missouri Synod, carried out by the research assistant in the Division of Theological Studies of the Lutheran Council in the U. S. A. The material was made available to me in manuscript form before it went to the Lutheran Council, or was available generally, by the kindness of Dr. Paul D. Opsahl. I cite by the pages of the typed manuscript of this significant study: for The ALC, pp. 63-76; for the LCA, pp. 92-128; for the LC-MS, pp. 164-196. (Cited as Ohlekopf, "Ministry," and the initials of the church body for the section.) While the LCA may appear to be most in flux and most to reflect current change (so Miss Ohlekopf concludes, "Ministry," LCA, p. 92), other Lutheran bodies are likewise examining the ministry. The 1959 convention of The Lutheran Church — Missouri Synod called for a study with special attention to the public ministry as over against the universal priesthood. In 1962 there was a "Special Study Commission on the Theological Foundations of the Ministry," which later turned its task over to a research committee at the St. Louis Seminary School for Graduate Studies. A "Church and Ministry" project was listed in 1965 convention reports but not for 1967 (Ohlekopf, "Ministry," LC-MS, p. 197, note 1).

"the people, as distinguished from the clergy" or "members of the church who are not ordained." [98]

73. A few *generalizations* can be made (see below for details). All three bodies assume a *public office* of the ministry, with clergymen *ordained by clergymen,* regardless of the emphasis on the universal priesthood. All three churches understand the ministry in explicit statements or implicitly from scripture and the confessions, which form the basis of the church's witness and life, to be rooted in *the gospel,* as a functional instrument for its proclamation. In the LCA the *pastor* may constitutionally enjoy *more power* in the local congregation. In all three churches, to varying degree, on the synodical level (both nationally and in adjudicatories between the local and national levels) *clergy* generally can *outvote* the *laity* and play a *greater role* in carrying out the church's work and decisions.

74. More specifically, *The Lutheran Church-Missouri Synod* reflects not only the sixteenth century confessions and the Orthodox fathers, but also more particularly *Walther's exposition* in his ten theses on the ministry (and nine on the church) as a basis for presenting the ministry; cf. the "Brief Statement" of 1932 and the "Common Confession" of 1950, as well as in the 1959 Convention's discussion of the ministry, though these recent statements seem to put more emphasis on the office of ministry as a "divine ordinance" than as something merely derived from the general priesthood.[99] In line with Walther's views, the local congregation is emphasized as the group which, through the voters' assembly, calls a pastor. Indeed, there is some uncertainty constitutionally over the precise role of the district president, whether he acts on his own in ordination or is simply an extension of "the Synod itself" (By-laws 3.07e; the Synod presumably having received the authority transferred from the general priesthood), and his signature is not required on a call (the 1967 convention turned down a request to put more power into the hands of the dis-

---

[98] Ohlekopf, "Ministry," ALC, pp. 63, 70. The "Definitions of Terms" in the *Handbook of The American Lutheran Church* (1965 ed.), p. 7, are not part of the Constitution and Bylaws, but have been approved by that body's Joint Council and General Convention.

[99] Ohlekopf, "Ministry," LC-MS, pp. 164-167, "Brief Statement," Articles 31-33; in Wolf, *Documents* no. 158, pp. 388 f. "Common Confession," Part I, in *Doctrinal Declarations* (St. Louis: Concordia, 1957), p. 76. *Reports and Memorials, Forty-Fourth Regular Convention,* LC-MS, 1959, p. 102.

trict president at this point).[100]   Important as the congregation is, however, care is taken to carry out Walther's thesis that "the congregation is not permitted, and dare not abrogate to itself the right, arbitrarily, to depose its minister." [101]   (In most Lutheran churches, a congregation calls a pastor for life, theoretically, but has a right of recall — almost never exercised.) In the guidelines for congregational constitutions, the parish pastor is not expected to be president of the congregation and may not even be required to be at the meetings of the voters' assembly. The role of the *laity* is in this and other ways stressed. A pastor, we may note, is permitted to fill temporarily the pulpit of a non-Lutheran congregation, but "will not publicly celebrate the Lord's Supper in that congregation." [102]

75. At times the phrase "pastors, *teachers,* and laymen" occurs in Synodical documents, reflecting the particular position of the "God-given ministry and office of the teacher" in the schools of the Missouri · Synod, noted above (see sections 65-66). Thus, teachers are advisory members of both Synod and district (while laymen are only when elected as delegates) and may not serve as lay delegates.[103] Their present status, similar to that of the pastor — a development which seems a departure from Walther's own ideas — has come in part of necessity in connection with government classifications for the draft and income tax regulations.[104]

76. *Other ministries* may be seen in such emerging groups as "full-time Church Staff Workers" (trained at the "Lutheran Lay Training Institute" for two years at Concordia College, Milwaukee), "full-time Lutheran Parish Workers" (two years at St. John's College, Winfield, Kansas), deaconesses (Valparaiso University), and the "lay

---

[100] Ohlekopf, "Ministry," LC-MS, pp. 167-169. Ordination and installation are held not essentially to differ.

[101] *Ibid.,* p. 178. Thesis 31 in Walther's essay, "The Proper Form of an Evangelical Lutheran Congregation . . ." in *Walther and the Church* (cited above, note 85), pp. 104 f.

[102] Bylaw 4.07. The Bylaws are sometimes more liberal than the Constitution, which renounces "serving congregations of mixed confession" or "taking part in . . . sacramental rites of heterodox congregations" (VI.2).

[103] Ohlekopf, "Ministry," LC-MS, pp. 185 ff., on "Distinctions within the Concept of the 'Laity'" (more accurately: a "class" between pastors and laity?).

[104] *Ibid.,* p. 187. Cf. Mueller, *op. cit.,* pp. 143, 145 f. (Lutheran teachers were generally given draft exemption, as "ministers of religion," and certain tax deductions).

apostolate" (emphasis at Concordia Teachers' College, River Forest, Illinois). On policy-making levels, laymen are said to have considerable numerical representation, but are less noticeable in administration.[105] Hence, there are frequent overtures to use the laity more, and some suggestions that a gap exists between proclaimed principles and actual clergy-lay relationships, so that charges of "clericalism" and "laicism" can arise.[106]

77. *The American Lutheran Church,* as noted above, provides definitions of "clergy" and "laity" in its Handbook, and in a 1964 "Statement on Ordination and Clergy Roster" speaks with great clarity on the gospel as the basis for ordination (Augsburg Confession, 5, 7, and 14 cited) and of ordination as consisting of three elements, "calling, sending, and blessing").[107] The Constitution states, "The pastor and laity constitute the membership of the congregation, the pastor's status differing only as to function." [108] The district president has a role not noted in the Missouri Synod: he must countersign all letters of call. This provision led some congregations of the Lutheran Free Church (a Norwegian group, the result of the spiritual awakening movement, stressing universal priesthood) to split off in 1962 (when the LFC joined The ALC, itself the result of a three-way merger in 1960) and create an "Association of Free Lutheran Congregations"; they regarded involvement of a district president as "a restriction on congregational freedom." [109]

78. The ALC Constitution holds that to *the clergy* "is committed the public administration of the Means of Grace" (Paragraph 701), a point stressed in fellowship talks between The ALC and the Mis-

---

105 Ohlekopf, "Ministry," LC-MS, pp. 191 ff.

106 *Ibid.,* pp. 193 ff. Note the symposium in the *American Lutheran,* cited below, note 136.

107 Ohlekopf, "Ministry," ALC, p. 63. The "Statement on Ordination and Clergy Roster," (which draws on Luther and the Confessions, plus Joachim Heubach, *Die Ordination zum Amt der Kirche* [Berlin: Lutherisches Verlagshaus, 1956], and the work of the ULCA commission of 1952) appears in the *Reports and Actions of the Second General Convention,* The ALC, 1964, pp. 137-142. On "blessing" in ordination, cf. Schlink, *op. cit.,* pp. 245 f., note 15. The book by Heubach, which sees ordination primarily as a theological matter, and only secondarily one of order, seeks to correct the older views of Georg Rietschel, said by Ewing (LQ 16 [1964], p. 213) to have influenced the 1938 ULCA statement on ministry.

108 Paragraph 701.

109 Ohlekopf, "Ministry," ALC, pp. 64 f.

souri Synod (1966).[110] The 1964 "Statement on Ordination and Clergy Roster" elaborates this, but also is open to "specialized ministries" of all sorts, "based on the ministry of the divine Word":

> "As Luther pointed out to the Bohemian Christians, the office of the ministry is based upon the need of the church as understood under the enlightenment of the Holy Spirit rather than upon the fact that all believers are priests.
>
> "Since the ministerial office is not precisely defined in the New Testament and the duties . . . and needs . . . are subject to variation, we are led to Luther's conclusion: namely, that God has left the details of the ministerial office to the discretion of the church, to be developed according to its needs and according to the leading of the Holy Spirit." [111]

79. In ALC congregations *the pastor* is an advisory member of boards of trustees and deacons, but without vote. In district conventions, where clergy usually outnumber lay delegates, it has been proposed to restrict the vote to clergy who are parish pastors, thus insuring a lay majority. In The ALC's "United Testimony on Faith and Life," the royal priesthood of all "members of the church" is noted and defined (as "full access to the throne of grace with no mediator save Jesus Christ"), and laymen are said to "exercise their royal priesthood and in no sense surrender it" when they call a pastor.[112] The list of *"lay activities* in the church" cited at another point in the same document states specifically:

> "(6) The Means of Grace have been given to the congregation, and, for the purpose of administering Word and Sacraments, God has instituted the public office of the ministry, which, by the official call of the congregation, is committed to one or more qualified persons. . . .
>
> "(7) The doctrine of the priesthood of all believers gives the individual member no right to assume any of the functions which belong to the public ministries of the congregation. . . ." [113]

---

[110] *Ibid.*, p. 67. See the essay, "The Doctrine of the Church in the Lutheran Confessions," from the ALC/LC-MS talks.

[111] *Ibid.*, pp. 67 f. *Reports and Actions*, 1964, pp. 139-140. The Luther reference is to WA 12, 191, 22; cf. 193, 35 ff. = LW-AE, 40, p. 37, cf. pp. 40 f.

[112] Ohlekopf, "Ministry," ALC, pp. 69 f.; The ALC *Handbook*, 1965, pp. 133 f., from the "United Testimony." A paper by D. N. Granskou is referred to on restricting the vote of non-parish clergy; this already holds true in some LCA synods on the district (not "synod") level.

[113] *Ibid.*, p. 71; *Handbook*, pp. 136-139.

80. References in documents of the *Lutheran Church in America* set the public ministry in the context of the church's *total ministry and the world:* the primary objective of the church is "to proclaim the Gospel through Word and Sacraments, to relate that Gospel to man's need in every situation, and to extend the ministry of the Gospel to all the world" (Constitution, Article V, Section 1, a); "there is a sense in which the ministry is one of all believers . . . there is also a special ministry . . . a 'ministry within a ministry,' which through Word and sacraments directs the general ministry of all the laity in all relationships of life" (1964 Report, Board of Theological Education, based on a composite response from seminary faculties).[114] The Commission report in 1966 on the ministry can be said to have stressed a broadening scope of the ministry of all believers, while stressing less the significance of the ordained ministry. If so, then the rejection of that report by the 1966 convention can be said to reflect the mood of a church "wanting to safeguard and recognize the status of the ordained ministry" and prevent further "loss of identity" on the part of the clergy.[115] Hence Franklin Clark Fry's comment that ". . . with the tide flowing so strongly toward lay vocations and the accent falling so heavily on the universal priesthood," he felt "the next declaration of the church needed to be on the Ministry, with a capital 'M,' to redress the balance." [116] In convention debate, some saw too much emphasis already on universal priesthood, the current trends being "not accurate to the normative Lutheran understanding of the minister, proclaiming the Word of God. You cannot be the laity to the world, unless you have first received the word of absolution. And it is this that constitutes the integrity of the holy office of the ministry" (William Lazareth).[117]

---

[114] LCA *Minutes,* 1964, pp. 582 f.

[115] So Ohlekopf, "Ministry," LCA, pp. 93 f.

[116] *Ibid.,* p. 93; LCA *Minutes,* 1966, p. 40. ". . . it might almost sound as if the ordained ministry were merely supplementary to all the rest. I regret the failure to call it distinctly the Ministry of Word and Sacraments, thus describing the inner substance of what ordination is and the holy authority it confers" (p. 41). There is also a fear expressed that a host of commissionings will encourage growing "professionalism" in lay church service and undercut voluntary service and in turn, the universal priesthood (p. 42). "A church which does not acknowledge the universal priesthood of all believers may find itself compelled to send ordained men, worker priests, into lay vocations for 'the church to be there'; ours doesn't" (p. 43).

[117] Transcript of the discussion, cited by Ohlekopf, "Ministry," LCA, p. 94.

81. A greater emphasis can be seen on the *authority of the pastor* and of *the national church* in the LCA documents, compared with those of the other two Lutheran bodies. Miss Dagny Ohlekopf sees the former in the fact that "the LCA documents accord the pastor a role in the direction and administration of congregational affairs which considerably exceeds that of an ALC or LC-MS pastor" — e. g., he is normally president of the church council and has voice and vote on all congregational committees. The latter point she sees exemplified in the fact that the LCA puts its ordination requirements not only in its model constitution for congregations (as ALC does) but also in the By-laws (II, 1) of the Constitution for the national church.[118] As in other Lutheran bodies, it is assumed that only the ordained ministers will administer *the Lord's supper;* this is implicit in the careful regulation provided in a 1964 statement on "Communion Practices" (intended to "liberalize" provisions in some areas but also to regulate any existing "abuses"):

> "A lay person may assist in the distribution of the elements by administering the cup, but this privilege must be carefully guarded. Whenever a lay person so assists, with the exception of a seminarian when approved by the church council, he must be a communicant member of the parish, be approved by the church council for this purpose, be instructed by the minister, and be commissioned for this ministry only in his own congregation and his appointment must be renewed annually by the church council." [119]

82. One point in the LCA Constitution where a *difference between ordained ministers and laymen* comes to the fore is in the matter of *membership in secret societies.* Article VII, section 4 provides, ". . . no person, who belongs to any organization which claims to possess in its teachings and ceremonies that which the Lord has given solely to His Church, shall be ordained or otherwise received into the ministry of this church. . . ." Clergy are thus forbidden to join such societies, though there is no statement forbidding laymen to do so. The background is the "lodge issue," especially the strong feeling against the Masons, found in many nineteenth century immigrants

---

[118] *Ibid.,* p. 112 and p. 100. She is not correct in saying, however, that the choice seems to be having the pastor as president *ex officio* or electing him to the office. Some congregations have a long tradition of lay presidents for the council.

[119] LCA *Minutes,* 1964, p. 676.

during the period of Confessional Revival and many Lutheran groups thereafter in the U. S. The provision is also found in the church's "Standards" for the ministry ("no minister . . . shall become a member of a group which because of its oath of secrecy makes it impossible for the church to determine if its 'teachings and ceremonies' are consistent with what 'the Lord has given solely to His Church' ").[120]

83. The *laity* are not frequently referred to in the LCA documents. "Church vocations," a term which, as noted, has received much emphasis in recent times, is understood as a collective term, used to unite "the ordained, the set-apart, the commissioned, the certified, and elected, and so forth, into a multiple yet ordered ministry"; "calling," as a term, is here used of all Christians, "vocation" (in this parlance) of a specific task or occupation.[121] "Lay readers" can be designated in synods. There have been proposals to "put into more effective practice the Christian doctrine of the priesthood of all believers," even for a "department of lay ministry," and study of the laity's role in worship. In synods and on boards, while the principle is equal representation, the specific provisions and actual results are usually weighted on the clergy side. Miss Ohlekopf has been led to conclude that by and large "the LCA presently offers the laity a lower standing than do the other two major Lutheran bodies," [122] though constitutional statements may be misleading compared with actual situations.

84. Related to these constitutional reflections of Lutheran understanding of the ministry is actual *liturgical practice at the ordination service*. W. A. Ewing, in working out this analysis, finds that the "duality" of "divine institution and the human appointment" appears throughout the "Order for Ordination." [123] In particular, in the order

---

120 Ohlekopf, "Ministry," LCA, pp. 109 f. At the 1966 convention, the chair ruled that the pertinent paragraph ("n") of the "Standards of Acceptance into and Continuance in the Ministry of the Lutheran Church in America," is "procedural" and does not establish a cause for discipline other than that in Article VII, Section 4 of the Constitution; *Minutes*, p. 827.

121 Ohlekopf, "Ministry," LCA, pp. 116 f.; 1964 *Minutes*, pp. 518 f.

122 Ohlekopf, "Ministry," LCA, p. 117, cf. 118 f. On lay readers (not "lay preachers") cf. 1964 *Minutes*, p. 313. Contrast the opinion of Otto W. Heick, s. v. "Lay Activity," Enc. Luth. Ch., p. 1277: "In American Lutheranism, too, the autonomy of the local church is fully accepted and the laity is in complete charge of all the affairs of the church." (!)

123 Ewing, LQ 16 (1964), p. 215. Text in *The Occasional Services* (1962), pp. 90-99, and *Service Book and Hymnal* (Text Edition, 1967), pp. 563-572. He does not go into the order employed in The Lutheran Church – Missouri Synod.

provided in the occasional services of the LCA and The ALC (1962), the whole is set in the context of the gospel and of the service, emphasizing worship and devotion (so that there cannot be just an "ordination service"). "Nothing is here directly said, either of a special function or office within the congregation of Christ which separates that office from the prophetic, apostolic, and divine mandate laid upon all persons within range of this Word." [124] Yet the office is not thereby "derivative from the priesthood of believers," for there are ample references to "this holy office," "the holy ministry of the Word and sacraments," and "the office and work of a minister in the church of God"; rather, the intention is to see this ordained ministry, here given authority to minister publicly, within the context of the church's total ministry. Here "the congregation of Christ takes upon itself the responsibility" to minister, and here gives to the ordinand "the *authority* to minister," which can be withdrawn when not exercised.[125] The rubrics, incidentally, provide that the order for ordination "shall be conducted by the President of the Synod or District, or by a Minister whom he shall appoint," and that only ministers, one or more, participate in the laying-on of hands.

B. Recent Discussions

85. What other ways exist for examining how Lutheranism looks at the ministry? Portraits of the clergy in *fiction* and *short stories* might be revealing of attitudes, but I have found little of significance for our purposes.[126] *Sociological surveys* on how laymen look upon the

---

[124] Ewing, *ibid.,* p. 217 (italicized in his article).

[125] *Ibid.,* p. 221.

[126] Cf. Gilbert P. Voigt, "The Protestant Minister in American Fiction," in LQ 11 (1959), 3-13. The general finding: these ministers "minimize liturgy, organizing ability, pulpit oratory, and, on the whole, even theological learning; they magnify sincerity, unselfish concern for the poor and outcast, fearless denunciation of evil from the pulpit, and wise, sympathetic counsel to the erring and perplexed" (p. 13). Among novels about Lutheran clergy are O. E. Rolvaag, *Giants in the Earth,* on an itinerant Norwegian minister in the Dakotas, revered by his people; James K. Paulding, *Koningsmarke,* a humble, unselfish, benevolent pastor among the Swedes in colonial Delaware, in contrast to his dour predecessor; and Christopher Morley, *Swiss Family Manhattan,* on a Swiss minister who goes to work for the League of Nations and ends up tending a gas station on Long Island. Add John Updike's short story reflecting a catechetical class in Eastern Pennsylvania, in *The Same Door,* "Pigeon Feathers" in *Pigeon Feathers and Other Stories,* and Pastor Fritz Kruppenbach in *Rabbit, Run,* and Conrad Richter, *A Simple*

ordained ministry would also be helpful, but I do not find any study like that compiled about Methodists in 1947, or even like an analysis in Lund, Sweden, which showed that "lay people showed more esteem for the minister than ministers showed for themselves." [127] One suspects, however, that a similar regard would show up for the clergy in American Lutheranism. Lutheran clergy probably continue to see many of the roles traditionally connected with the ministry, such as preaching and the leading of worship, as basic, but increasing value is no doubt assigned to newer roles such as counseling, administration, and community activity; for many, however, clergy and lay alike, there is probably an identity crisis about what the ministry is today in its ordained form.[128] One relevant study, by Ross P. Scherer, in 1959, of 572 Missouri Synod clergymen, concluded that ministers tended to look on themselves often very much in the way Synodical literature ideally pictures them, e. g. as primarily "mediator of the Word and sacrament," thus disputing the picture of the ministry as

---

Honorable Man, about a pastor in Central Pennsylvania. W. E. Mueller, "Protestant Ministers in Modern American Novels, 1927-1958: The Searcher for a Role" (diss. Univ. of Nebraska, 1961), was not available to me. I suspect that motion picture portrayals of clergymen would add little to help us. In the classification of ministers employed by R. S. Michaelsen, "The Protestant Ministry: 1850 to the Present," in *Ministry in Historical Perspective,* pp. 250-288, I find few categories in which to place Lutherans ("urban and rural" is rather obvious); the closest classification is "immigrant," but this category, according to Michaelsen, is but "similar to the place of the minister in the Negro community," i. e., as community leader, p. 269.

[127] Cf., on Methodists, M. H. Leiffer, *The Layman Looks at the Minister* (New York: Abingdon-Cokesbury, 1947); Berndt Gustafsson, "People's View of the Minister and the Lack of Ministers in Sweden," in *Archives de Sociologie des Religions,* 22 (1966), 135-144, as cited in *Ministry Studies,* 1, 3 (October, 1967), p. 28. Edgar W. Mills, of the Ministry Studies Board of the National Council of Churches, writes me, September 9, 1969, that he knows of no studies dealing directly with Lutheran views of the difference between clergy and laity.

[128] Cf. R. E. Sommerfeld, "Role Conceptions of Lutheran Ministers in the St. Louis Area" (diss., Washington Univ., 1957), summary in *Dissertation Abstracts of Research,* edited by R. J. Menges and J. E. Dittes (New York: Nelson, 1965), p. 94. Further, the dissertation by H. J. Bertness, Univ. of Minnesota, 1955, on "Interests of [ALC] Lutheran ministers as measured by the Strong Vocational Interest Blank" (*Dissert. Abstr.,* 15 [1955], pp. 2094-2095; *Psychological Studies,* p. 24).

disintegrating, then being given in the popular press. The ministers polled think "laymen would disagree with ministers most in wanting a minister who was primarily a 'generalist' (skilled in many things), had a pleasing personality, and sacrificed his own convenience for his members," and that ministers would clash with laymen most when the minister wants to be "an independent-thinking theologian, an expert in only a few pastoral functions, a go-getter for new Synodical programs, or to take additional university work." Sons of clergymen who enter the ministry seem to provide proportionally more occupants of leadership positions than sons of laymen; "apparently there is a kind of indelibility which is stamped on an individual by the parsonage or teacherage which clings to him throughout his life." [129] There is some evidence to suggest that Protestant and Catholic attitudes about the ministry are often similar in a given locality and can influence each other.[130]

86. It is chiefly to *periodical literature* and *recent books* that one must turn to find Lutheran views today. First of all, let it be noted that the *characteristic Lutheran views on the ministry* which we have noted *continue to be expressed*. In the United Lutheran Church in America, for example, the first of the "Knubel-Miller Lectures," in 1945, by the then secretary of the ULCA, set forth a popular summary, in succinct terms, on the Lutheran position as commonly understood.[131] The second set of lectures in the same series also dealt with the ordained ministry and reflected the high

---

[129] "The Lutheran Ministry: Origins, Careers, Self-Appraisal," in *The Cresset* 26 (1963), 9-17, also in *Information Service* 42 (1963), 1-8, summarizing a dissertation at the University of Chicago, 1963, "Ministers of the Lutheran Church – Missouri Synod: Origins, Training, Career-lines, Perceptions of Work and Reference." Phrases below come from pp. 13 and 15 of the *Cresset* article.

[130] Cf. W. W. Schroeder, "Lay Expectations of the Ministerial Role: an Exploration of Protestant-Catholic Differentials," in *Journal of the Scientific Study of Religion* 2 (1963), 217-227 (summary in *Psychological Studies*, pp. 93 f.). There are some statistics for twelve Lutheran congregations on how parishioners think ministers spend their time in C. Y. Glock and R. Stark, *Religion and Society in Tension* (Chicago: Rand McNally, 1965), pp. 141-150, but no comparative data from clergymen or from the past.

[131] Walton Harlowe Greever, *The Minister and the Ministry*, Knubel-Miller Lectures, 1 (Philadelphia: Board of Publication of the United Lutheran Church in America, 1945).

opinion of a layman, and of thirty other laymen responding to a survey, about the pastor: the minister is "God's unique representative," he is "as Christ going about and among his flock . . . an ambassador of the Most High God." [132]

87. Let it also be said that some of the *tensions* we have noted over the centuries continue to be displayed and some of the same characteristic differences of opinion. Thus in the same encyclopedia, one article avers that "the ministry is not derived by transfer of function from a general priesthood of all believers but it is derived from the authority of the keys," while another states, "Believers delegate and transfer the public exercise of this office to called servants of the Word." [133]

88. As a further example, we may note different points of view in *two treatments* of ministry, each *by Swedish churchmen*. (Both of them, it may be noted, frame their statements against traditional Roman Catholic understandings.) Ruben *Josefson* [134] emphasizes that the ministerial office is basically one office, of proclamation of word and sacraments, established by God, in Christ, and sustained by the Spirit. He insists it is never based on "the concept of sacrifice," either in the Roman sense (since "the office of sacrifice is abolished in Christ") or in the pietistic sense (the priest "offers his heart to God"). But he then goes on to add that this office, really a "divine order," "a God-given order," is "antecedent to the faith," "the fulcrum by which [God's redemptive] work exercises its continuing effectiveness," and thus is "one of the church's constitutive factors," and is of its *esse*. Per Erik *Persson*, on the other hand, poses the issue as whether gospel or ministry is central: "Either salvation is provided through the ministerial office, and therefore word and sacrament are provided, the presence of Christ being dependent on his presence in the bearer of the office, or else salvation comes through the gospel in word and sacrament, and on this account there is a ministry in the

---

132 Clarence C. Stoughton, *Set Apart for the Gospel,* Knubel-Miller Lectures, 2 (Philadelphia: Muhlenberg, 1946), pp. 1, 40.

133 R. P. Roth, "Ministry," p. 1581, and the article, "Keys, Office of" (reprinted from *Lutheran Cyclopedia*), p. 1207, in Enc. Luth. Ch.

134 Josefson, in *This Is the Church,* pp. 268-280, especially pp. 270, 276 for the five points he stresses; p. 273 on sacrifice; p. 277 on the ministry as a "divine order" (cf. also pp. 278, 279). It is when Josefson gets to his final points, on the ministry as "the fulcrum" and "a God-given order," that his citations from Luther cease.

church." [135] Thus two views are contrasted by Persson: the Roman, where the ministry represents Christ, there is a differentiation between priests and laity which is constitutive of the church (so that proper consecration and succession are vital), and what is said christologically also applies to the ministry — there is cooperation of the human with the divine; and the Evangelical, where ministry exists so the gospel may function, Christ's presence in the Lord's supper is not by virtue of the ministerial office but by the word, and there is no redemptive significance to ordination or a valid succession — "cooperation" between man and God is here an impossibility in the sense presented in the other view.

89. Secondly, however, we must note that, for all these characteristic assertions and tensions, the present is *a time of change,* as most writers on ministry are aware. Symptomatic of this change and the questions it raises is the fact that four Lutheran periodicals have devoted major space or an entire issue to the question of the ministry in the present decade: the *American Lutheran,* in its "Symposium on Authority," in 1963; *Lutheran World,* with an issue on "The Ministry Today" (dealing with the pastor, not the laity) in 1964; *The Lutheran Quarterly* in 1966, "Ministry and Ministries," focusing especially on ordination, LCA discussion, and the place of women in the ministry; and *Dialog,* on "Ministry as Vocation and Profession," 1969 (ordination and women).[136] None of these is oriented to clergy/laity as chief topic, however.

90. Periodicals of *The Lutheran Church-Missouri Synod* particularly exhibit a growing discussion over ministry. The centennial year of that church (1946) emphasized "royal priesthood." Articles about that time examined the theme of general priesthood and the pastor.[137] A report to the Synodical Conference in 1948 continued to stress the local congregation, but there were differences of opinion on points of

---

[135] Per Erik Persson, *Roman and Evangelical. Gospel and Ministry: an Ecumenical Issue,* trans. E. H. Wahlstrom (Philadelphia: Fortress, 1964), especially p. 89, and pp. 61-79 and 80-89 on the Roman and Evangelical views of ministry.

[136] *American Lutheran* 46, 1 (1963), 12-15; 46, 2 (1963), 12-14, 25; 46, 3 (1963), 14-15, 24; 46, 4 (1963), 14-16, 23-24 (N. B. the phraseology of the topic!: "Symposium on Authority – The Authority of the Ministry in Relation to the Laity"). LW 11 (1964), 389-462. LQ 18 (1966), 98-184. *Dialog* 8 (1969), 166-208.

[137] Richard R. Caemmerer, "The Universal Priesthood and the Pastor," in *Concordia Theological Monthly* (= CTM) 19 (1948), 561-582.

application — study on which was encouraged — as to whether the public ministry is divinely instituted "on its own," so to speak, or is to be viewed in light of the *Übertragungstheorie,* and whether Christ instituted simply the *genus* of the ministry, "in the abstract," the *Predigtamt,* or more specifically the *species,* or pastorate in the local congregation, the *Pfarramt.*[138] We have already noted how LC-MS church commissions began to take up the questions in the late 1950's. Sometimes individual treatments sought to transcend traditional hang-ups — e. g., by speaking, in biblical terms, of "the ministry of reconciliation" which belongs to all the saints (instead of "universal priesthood"), and, with criticism of the "transfer theory," by stressing a "ministry to the ministers" in the manner of Ephesians 4:8-13.[139] This type of language was at times reflected in the *American Lutheran* symposium, where there also appeared protests against "clerical domination" in The LC-MS, reaffirmation of the "ministry of the laity," and assertions that the church of the writer in this case has the answer — but one layman saw this "definite answer" in the universal priesthood; another in obeying the minister, who is God's intended ambassador, with authority "from God down, and from the Royal Priesthood on up." [140]

91. Is there, amid such change and debate, any *"image"* today *of the Lutheran clergyman?* Yes, one pastor wrote in 1961, in spite of rapid change, decline in the prestige of the ministry and the church, expanded duties for the clergy, and the often unflattering image in the mass media; there is an "image that seems to go without saying" of the clergy "as men of God, dedicated to their tasks, specialists from personal experience in the things of the spirit . . . the embodiment of compassion." The picture here is of the clergyman as "the keeper of the keys of morality, the comforter of the bereaved, friend of lonely and sick, the ear open to trouble, the pocket open to the way-

---

138 H. G. Brueggemann, "The Public Ministry in the Apostolic Age," in CTM 22 (1951), 81-109, favors the *Übertragungstheorie;* E. J. Moeller, "Concerning the Ministry of the Church," *ibid.,* pp. 385-416, the alternate view sketched above. On the study of the ministry by commissions in The Lutheran Church – Missouri Synod, cf. above, note 97.

139 Walter J. Bartling, "A Ministry to Ministers: An Examination of the New Testament *Diakonia,"* in CTM 33 (1962), 325-336.

140 Cited above, note 136. The examples noted are from Wayne C. Rydburg (M. D.), Vernon R. Schreiber (parish pastor), Harold Midtbo (layman), Oscar T. Doerr (attorney), and Fred A. Schurmann (layman) respectively.

farer." [141] Absent here seems any central stress on proclamation. An article the next year in the same periodical by a layman (!) takes the position that "laymanship" is not confined only to laymen and that there is a *"lay perversion* of the church": the danger that we lose sight of "the primary function of the church: to preach the Word and administer the sacraments through which God speaks, not man."[142]

92. Certainly we live in a time when *the role of the laity* has been *rediscovered*. It is commonplace to regard the clergy as "enablers" of the "real ministry," the laymen out in the world. Sometimes the analogy is employed of the clergy as "commissioned officers with special training" in comparison with the rest of the troops; other times it is said, "the distinction between clergymen and laity cannot be sharply drawn." [143] It is perhaps typical that the LCA Manifesto, "God's Call to the Church in Each Place," drafted by the "Commission on the Nature and Mission of the Congregation" and approved at the LCA's 1966 convention, speaks mostly of the laity ("to equip its members . . . to perform their ministries") and little of the clergy, except that, as the Study Guide to the Manifesto says, "the traditional image [whose?] of the role of the clergy" must change.[144]

93. *Exegetically*, as part of the current changes, there have been reexaminations of biblical bases traditionally cited in discussions about the ministry. A dissertation by a Lutheran New Testament scholar, for example, challenged the traditional use of *I Peter 2:5, 9,* on the "royal priesthood," to support the idea of a "universal priesthood of

[141] William Horn, "The Image of the Ministry," LQ 13 (1961), 193-210; quotation from p. 207.

[142] Robert E. Huldschiner, "The Lay Perversion of the Church," LQ 14 (1962), 217-229; quotation from p. 222. Cf. the comments of President Fry of the LCA, quoted above in section 80.

[143] As example of this concern for the laity, I have quoted from a Lutheran, Frederick K. Wentz, *The Layman's Role Today* (Garden City: Doubleday, 1963), cf. pp. 28 f., 163-166. Cf. also Wentz's article, "What Public Role for the Clergy?" in LQ 18 (1966), 148-154. In the Knubel-Miller lecture series of the LCA (see above, notes 130-131) the emphasis in the first two on the "set-apart" ministry has been followed by emphasis on the lay ministry: cf. nos. 13 and 18 in the series, *The Christian's Calling*, by Donald R. Heiges (1958), and *The Militant Ministry: People and Pastors of the Early Church and Today,* by Hans-Ruedi Weber (1963).

[144] LCA *Minutes*, 1966, pp. 556 f.; Donald R. Pichaske, *A Study Book on the Manifesto* (Philadelphia: Board of Publication of the LCA, 1967), especially pp. 166-174.

believers" (dear to the Reformers but also to recent Catholic theologians), by claiming the verses refer to election and holiness, eschatologically, of the community, and its witness to the world, not to priesthood — Levitical, spiritual, or otherwise — individually. But the author adds that Luther and others may well be correct on universal priesthood, even though not on the basis of this passage.[145] The *Old Testament* too has been invoked at times to provide perspective on ministry. One article, avowedly championing the "special priesthood" or ministry against the erosion of "classical Lutheranism" in America, argues, invoking recent Old Testament insights, that "as a priest, the clergyman alone" has the right to "absolve sins . . . or to excommunicate" and "to celebrate the Eucharist" — all Christians may "forgive one another," but the clergy have the "gift of absolution." [146] In reply, others deny the applicability of this Old Testament priest-

---

[145] John Hall Elliott, *The Elect and the Holy: An Exegetical Examination of I Peter 2:4-10 and the Phrase basileion hierateuma.* Supplements to *Novum Testamentum,* 12 (Leiden: Brill, 1966). See especially pp. xiii f. and 1-15 for connections with the general problem, pp. 219-226 for Elliott's conclusions, and pp. 225 f., note 3, on the relation to Reformation and other subsequent interpretations of universal priesthood. For a favorable Catholic reaction to the general position that I Peter 2:4-10 does not support "universal priesthood," cf. R. Schnackenburg's review in *Biblische Zeitschrift* 12 (1968), pp. 152 f.; for somewhat more critical but generally favorable comments, cf. F. W. Danker in CTM 38 (1967), 329-332, and C. F. D. Moule, *Journal of Theological Studies* 18 (1967), 471-474. Elliott himself makes application of his findings in "Death of a Slogan: from Royal Priests to Celebrating Community," in *Una Sancta* 25 (1968), 18-31, emphasizing that the passage has nothing to do with universal priesthood or with "baptism as ordination" or with the individual; rather the community is stressed, election and holiness, and public proclamation of God's saving deeds (2:9) as witness to the world. But is this not close, after all, to the emphasis which some have seen in this "slogan" on the priestly witness and service of the whole community, in the sense of Romans 12, "our reasonable service"? "Celebrating community," especially if it is made to refer to celebrating eucharist, is something of an extrapolated phrase, in light of what I Peter itself says or fails to say (Elliott's dissertation, pp. 186-188, finds no connection between 2:5, 9 and a celebration of the eucharist; *hierateuma* refers rather to the response of believers: a holy life of obedience and well-doing before God and for men). Some of Elliott's remarks seem directed at an individualized concept of priesthood oriented to the local congregation, devoid of much feeling for the larger church or people of God; but this concept which he attacks is scarcely what all have meant by "general priesthood."

[146] Horace D. Hummel, in LQ 18 (1966), especially pp. 104-106, 113, 116 f., 119.

hood idea to the New Testament or to present-day ministry.[147] The *New Testament* evidence, in its variety, charismatic setting, kerygmatic emphasis, and tendency toward order but not orders, undergirds — though here there is enormous difference of opinion — the general picture which has kept recurring in this paper, of variety, centered in the gospel, with some sort of public office and a general ministry for all believers.[148]

94. The *debate* goes on. The *traditional Lutheran emphasis* on the ministry as a functional office continues to be reasserted; ordination is a conferring of "the authority publicly to proclaim the gospel and administer the sacraments on behalf of those who call a man to do this," not "the most vital of the sacraments," without which "there is no sacrifice of the mass, and . . . the flow of grace . . . is cut off." [149] Others want *"other answers."* [150] Such answers are proposed. One younger writer wants a view of ministry not only "in conformity with the Word of God" but also *"relevant to the present cultural situation."* [151] He seeks it, however, by going back to orders of *creation* (as understood from "the sphere of Christ") — which turn out to be two divinely established orders in the church, the ministry and the laity, which correspond to the proclamation of, and response to, the word, in the priesthood of all believers. However, it is also asserted that the parish is scarcely the only or the "primary valid formation of Christ's body," "there is no primary valid form of the church"; and laymen, although placed in a different order from ministers, are nonetheless allowed to be included in "task forces of ministers" and indeed ought to have "consecration" (annually?) as a parallel to ordination for ministers. (It *is* rather difficult, it appears, to get away from the two points we've seen constantly: universal priesthood and a public office of ministry!)

95. One other recent article proceeds more radically, however,

---

[147] Peter L. Kjeseth, p. 179, and Gerhard Krodel, pp. 198 f., note 78, in *Dialog* 8 (1969).

[148] See especially Krodel's survey in *Dialog* 8 (1969), 191-202, perhaps the best survey article currently available in English.

[149] Martin J. Heinecken, "The Ministry, a Functional Office," in *Lutheran Church Quarterly* 20 (1947), 432-441; "What Does Ordination Confer?" in LQ 18 (1966), especially pp. 126 and 131.

[150] Edgar Brown, LQ 18 (1966), pp. 275 f.

[151] H. Paul Santmire, "An Introduction to the Doctrine of the Ministry," in LQ 16 (1964), 195-210 (his own summary on pp. 209 f.). Phrases quoted above are from pp. 195, 198, 206 f.

and takes up the "universal priesthood" side. It is argued that "the ordained ministry" is *not* essential to the life of the people of God, laymen can do everything without clergy; hence, *baptism* really amounts to *ordination for every believer*, it is his initiation and his commissioning. "Baptism as Ordination" is thus seen as the watchword for A. D. 2000.[152] Meanwhile, *news dispatches* report other proposals and events: it was proposed that laymen in Norway be authorized to administer the Lord's supper, and vicars in Germany have refused to accept ordination until any ceremony in the rite which suggests sacramental misinterpretation is omitted and until overstress on the pastorate in comparison with other ministries is omitted.[153]

96. In this welter of reports and ideas I single out two more which appear in recent discussion. (1) The notion of the Lutheran ministry as a *"presbyteral succession"* has appeared in several of the historical references above — i. e., that ministers are regularly ordained by other ministers. It reappears in current discussion, based on the confessions.[154] (2) Peter Brunner's view that the *"apostle"* in the early church was to the *charismatic ministries* there as the *"ordained ministry"* today is to the *layman*.[155]

97. According to Brunner, in the early church clearly there was an apostolic ministry, appointed by the Lord, in living confrontation after Easter through his word of command *(jure divino)*, to proclaim the gospel. It had priority temporally as well as in its eye-witness character. Proclamation of the gospel goes back to this ministry in a way that it cannot to the charismatic ministries. These *apostles* served

---

152 Peter L. Kjeseth, "Baptism as Ordination," in *Dialog* 8 (1969), 177-182. Kjeseth alludes to, and agrees with, the position expressed by J. Duss-von Werdt, on "What Can the Layman Do Without the Priest?" in *Concilium,* 34, *Apostolic Succession,* edited by Hans Küng (New York: Paulist Press, 1968), p. 112: "in virtue of the universal priesthood, in principle, 'laymen' can do everything without priests."

153 Lutheran Council News Bureau, 69-41, p. 6, on the Lutheran World Federation conference at Cartigny, Switzerland, on "The Structures of the Congregation in Mission" (3/28/69); and 69-91, p. 4, on the Evangelical Church in Württemberg (8/18/69). (Both proposals stem from regions where pietist emphasis on the universal priesthood has been strong.)

154 *Dialog* 8 (1969), in the "Symposium," p. 172, alluding to the Treatise on the Power and Primacy of the Pope, 62 and 67. On "presbyteral succession," cf. above, sections 22, 25, 40, 43, 45, 51, 55.7, 56, 58, 63.18, 67, 73, and 84.

155 Brunner, LQ 15 (1963), 99-117 (cited above, note 20).

as "missionary messengers" (*apostello = mitto*, send forth), and it is from their *missionary office* (Matthew 28:19f.) that the *pastoral office* developed. After this apostolic-missionary-pastoral office, charismatic ministries might flourish. But while every Christian has the Spirit and his own *charisma* and must have a part in the church's ministry and the extension of the apostolic message, preservation of the gospel "dare not be left to the charismatic ministries by themselves," and "to do justice to the Lord's apostolic commission," the church "must select, call, authorize, and send out individuals as bearers of the office of preacher." [156] Thus, *Predigtamt (Pfarramt)* succeeds the apostolic ministry and continues its work of preserving and spreading the gospel; the *laity*, under the Spirit too, continue to carry out all sorts of ministries for which they are charismatically equipped. In Brunner's presentation, the ministry is free to structure itself with all sorts of "helpers" and offices, *de jure humano*, but celebration of the Lord's supper is one of the functions of the ministerial-pastoral office. Thus we have the office of public ministry, fitted into the ministry of all Christians, the twin concerns of Lutherans through the centuries. Brunner's is a presentation favorably regarded in several recent articles. [157]

---

[156] *Ibid.,* p. 111.

[157] Cf. *Dialog* 8 (1969), in the "Symposium," p. 168, where the view is attributed to Schlink; Roloff, in LW 11 (1964), pp. 405-407. Roloff compares this position with that sketched in the section on ministry in *The Fourth World Conference on Faith and Order. The Report from Montreal* 1963, edited by P. C. Rodger and L. Vischer, Faith and Order Paper No. 42 (London: SCM, 1964), pp. 61-69, and contrasts the manner in which Montreal derives the "special ministry" from the ministry of all. Further, on reactions from a biblical standpoint on Küng's views in *The Church* (1967), that a church faithful to the New Testament need not be conditioned on ordination and that the reality of the eucharist in non-episcopal churches is a distinct probability, cf. M. M. Bourke, "Reflections on Church Order in the New Testament," in *Catholic Biblical Quarterly* 30 (1968), 493-511.

TRENT AND THE QUESTION: CAN PROTESTANT MINISTERS CONSECRATE THE EUCHARIST?

By Harry J. McSorley

In order to answer the important ecumenical question posed in the title of this article we shall divide it into three sub-questions: (1) Who, according to the Council of Trent, is the competent minister of the sacrament of the altar? (We take "minister" here to mean the consecrating minister or the celebrant, not the minister who distributes the eucharist, since this minister can be a deacon or, if need be, a layman.) (2) What does Trent say about other Christians who preside over the eucharist but who are not regarded as competent ministers? (3) Does Trent say anything — implicitly or explicitly — about the reality of the eucharist celebrated by Christians of the Reformation churches?

As was indicated in another article,[1] Trent said nothing about the minister of the eucharist in its October 1, 1551 decree concerning that sacrament (Session XIII). Canon 10 of Session VII (March 3, 1547), pertaining to the sacraments in general, rejects the view that "all Christians have power *(potestatem)* in the ministry of word and all the sacraments."[2] Here Trent is defending the indisputable biblical teaching of I Corinthians 12 that not all Christians have the same gifts or roles in the church. This much is clear. What is not clear is the sense in which "power" is to be understood.

As we stressed in our above-mentioned article, the term "power"

---

[1] "The Roman Catholic Doctrine of the Competent Minister of the Eucharist in Ecumenical Perspective," see above, pp. 120-137, esp. pp. 129-133.

[2] Denzinger-Schönmetzer, *Enchiridion Symbolorum,* 33rd ed. (= DS) (Freiburg: Herder, 1965), 1610. This is also the concern of chapter 4 of the doctrine on order from Session XXIII (1563): DS 1767. We have already commented on this canon on p. 130 of the article mentioned in note 1.

(potestas, exousia, dynamis) is highly ambiguous. Among the several senses of the term, we shall consider two of the more basic meanings.

(1) Power can be understood as the physical or radical ability to do something (e. g. to walk, to see, to heal sickness: Mark 3:15) so that without this power one simply cannot perform the commensurate act.[3] While *dynamis* tends to be confined to this first sense, *exousia* is frequently used in both of the senses we are discussing.[4] Even here there can be ambiguity. Bonaventure, for example, says that, even though a blind man cannot see *(videre non potest)*, he nevertheless has the power to see *(potentia visiva)*.[5] Ordinary use of the term "power" makes it possible for us to say: The blind man has lost his power of sight. But Bonaventure's technical usage requires him to distinguish, with other scholastic theologians and canonists, between power *quantum ad esse* and *quantum ad executionem*. This terminology helped the scholastics to distinguish between the power of order and the power of jurisdiction or *executio ordinis*. It is important to note that canon 10 of the Tridentine decree on the sacraments in general (DS 1610) does not indicate precisely in which sense *potestas* is to be taken.

(2) *Potestas* (or *exousia* in the church documents composed in Greek, such as canon 6 of Nicaea [6]) can also mean moral, social, political, or ecclesial authority or authorization to do something of which one is physically or radically capable even without such authorization or empowerment. This is the distinction between what one *can* do physically and what he *may* or can do legally, morally, socially, or canonically.

In the light of the ambiguities connected with the term "power" (and with the terms "valid" and "licit" even into the scholastic period [7]), one should proceed with extreme caution in interpreting

---

[3] Cf. W. Grundmann, *dynamai, etc.* in R. Kittel, *Theological Dictionary of the New Testament* (= *TDNT*) II (Grand Rapids, Michigan, 1966), 284-317, esp. 284-286; 310-313.

[4] Cf. W. Foerster, *exousia* in TDNT II, 562-575; *A Patristic Greek Lexicon*, ed. G. W. H. Lampe (Oxford, 1962), 389-391; 501-502.

[5] *In librum IV Sententiarum*, d. 19, a. 2, q. 2, ad I-3, ed. Quaracchi, (Florence, 1889) t. 4, 506.

[6] *Conciliorum Oecumenicorum Decreta* (= COeD) (Freiburg, 1962) p. 8.

[7] Cf. G. Fransen, "The Tradition in Medieval Canon Law" in *The Sacrament of Holy Orders* (Collegeville, Minn., 1962), 203, and the excursus on the terms "valid and invalid," "licit and illicit" in my essay (note 1 above), pp. 121-125.

ecclesiastical documents which use these terms. Such caution seems to have been lacking, for example, in Francisco Suarez and Robert Bellarmine, followed by a host of post-Tridentine theologians, when they used a parenthetical remark of canon 18 of the Council of Nicaea — deacons do not have the *exousia* to offer the body of Christ [8] — as an *assertio de fide certa* that a deacon effects nothing *(nihil efficiat)* if he attempts to offer the eucharistic sacrifice.[9] These authors overlook the fact that canon 6 of the same council clearly uses *exousia* in the sense of ecclesial authority, not in the sense of radical or physical capability. They have no textual or contextual basis for assuming a shift of meaning when the same term appears again in canon 18. The ambiguous term *exousia* in canon 18, therefore, cannot be used as evidence for an alleged *assertio de fide certa* that "nothing happens" when a deacon attempts to lead the eucharist. The "nothing happens" opinion of Suarez, Bellarmine, and others can be traced back at least as far as Bonaventure,[10] but it should be recognized for what it is: a widely held opinion — not an article of faith defined by Trent or any council before or since Trent.

Since the scholastic period it has been customary in Catholic theology and canon law to distinguish between the power of order and the power of jurisdiction. All Catholic theologians would see the power of jurisdiction as belonging to the second category of power we have discussed. Concerning the understanding of the power of order, however, two opinions can be distinguished.

The first opinion holds that the power of order is so absolutely necessary for consecrating the eucharist that "nothing happens" sacramentally if others who lack the sacrament of the priesthood lead the eucharist, regardless of whether they have sufficient reason and the ecclesial circumstances are otherwise proper. This opinion has been widely held by Catholic theologians since the scholastic age. Although it is a tenable opinion today, it carries with it obvious negative ecumenical consequences. It is important to remember, however, that it is nothing more than a widely held theological opinion. It is not part of the official faith commitment of the Roman Catholic church and it has never been affirmed by Trent or any other ecumenical council.

---

[8] COeD, 13.

[9] Cf. Suarez, *Opera Omnia,* ed. Vivès (Paris, 1861) t. 21, 693; Bellarmine, *Opera Omnia* (Naples, 1858) t. 3, 431.

[10] *In lib. IV Sent.,* d. 13, a. 1, q. 2, concl: *soli sacerdotes possunt conficere, et si alii conficiunt nihil omnino faciunt,* ed. Quaracchi (Florence, 1889) t. 4, 305.

A second tenable Catholic opinion does not agree that the power of order is such that, without it, the consecration of the eucharist is absolutely impossible regardless of circumstances.[11] Unlike the first opinion, which understands the power of order in terms of the first category of "power" that we distinguished above, this opinion places both the power of order and the power of jurisdiction in the second category of "power" we have outlined. In this view the power of order is seen as conferring a basic ecclesial *authorization* or *empowerment* to administer the sacraments, while the power of jurisdiction enables the ordained/authorized minister to *exercise* his sacramental ministry validly or licitly as the case may be. Such a concept of the powers of order and jurisdiction is by no means new. At the Council of Trent the distinguished Carmelite theologian, Eberhard Billick, put it this way: "Order is divided into sacramental and hierarchical; the first is authority, the second is the execution of the power. For the doorkeeper has power, but he cannot exercise it without a hierarchical order, or mandate. So it is also with the lector, exorcist, acolyte, deacon, subdeacon, and priest." [12]

It should be noted that if a sacrament is judged to be invalid, either because the required authorization (power of order) or the proper jurisdiction is lacking, one should not simply say that it is *no* sacrament, but that it is not a sacrament canonically or officially recognized by the church.

This second opinion is completely faithful to the essential content of the defined teaching of the Roman Catholic church on the sacrament of order. The opinion firmly maintains that the conferral of the authority to administer the sacraments is of such importance for the church that the very rite in which the church hands on the ministry is a sacrament that bestows grace for the faithful exercise of that ministry.[13] But this does not mean that the church could not recognize or establish ways in which the "power of consecrating" might

---

11 See my essay "Protestant Eucharistic Reality and Lack of Orders," *The Ecumenist* 5 (1967), 68-75, esp. 74.

12 *Ordo enim dividitur inter sacramentalem et hierarchicum; primus est auctoritas, secundus est executio potestatis. Nam ostiarius habet potestatem; eam tamen non potest exercere sine ordine hierarchico, si ei scil. mandatur. Ita lector, exorcista, accolitus, diaconus, subdiaconus et presbyter. Concilium Tridentinum. Diariorum, actorum, epistularum, tractatuum nova collectio.* Ed. Societas Goerresiana (Freiburg, 1901-) 7.410:18-22 [=CT, vol. 7, p. 410, lines 18-22].

13 Cf. K. Rahner, *The Church and the Sacraments* (New York, 1963), pp. 105-106.

be conferred other than through episcopal, sacramental ordination. Implicit in this opinion, therefore, is the thesis that the "power to consecrate" is included in, but is not restricted to, the power of order conferred by the sacrament of priestly order.

THE APOSTLES AND THEIR SUCCESSORS
IN THE PRIESTHOOD

The only other places where Trent addresses itself to the questions we are asking is in Session XXII (September 17, 1562) where it presents the Catholic doctrine on the sacrifice of the mass and in Session XXIII (July 15, 1563) where it treats the sacrament of order.

Chapter 1 and canon 2 of Session XXII along with chapter 1 and canon 1 of Session XXIII simply affirm that Jesus constituted the apostles priests of the New Testament and that they and their "successors in the priesthood" have been given the power of consecrating, offering, and administering the body and blood of Christ.[14] All that we have noted in the above remarks on "power" is to be taken into account in interpreting this teaching. Trent does not tell us in what sense it is using the term power here any more than Vatican II defines its understanding of the frequently used term "spiritual power." [15]

A similarly ambiguous use of "power" occurs in chapter 4 of the doctrine on the sacrament of order. There we are told that bishops "can confer the sacrament of confirmation, ordain ministers of the church, and perform many other functions over which those of a lower order have no power." [16] But it is quite clear from the history of the sacraments that priests have "had power over" the sacrament of confirmation and even the ordination of priests.[17] Trent cannot mean, therefore, that priests in no way or under no circumstances "have power over" the sacraments of confirmation and order.[18] The most

---

[14] DS 1740, 1752, 1764, 1771: *potestatem . . . consecrandi et offerendi.*

[15] Cf. K. Rahner in *Commentary on the Documents of Vatican II,* vol. I (New York, 1967), pp. 188-189.

[16] DS 1768: *potestatem . . . nullam habent.*

[17] Cf. P. Fransen, "Orders and Ordination" in *Sacramentum Mundi* IV (New York, 1969), 316-317; Rahner (note 15 above), 194-195. At Trent one bishop said that, in case of necessity, any priest could administer any sacrament: CT 6.312:15. Another, in the same discussion, said it was *perhaps (forsan)* false to say that priests could ordain: CT 6.312:26-29.

[18] Not accepted at Trent was a request by nineteen bishops to make this sentence from chapter 4 even more restrictive, so that it would read: "only [the bishops] can confirm, ordain," etc. CT 9:45:27-28.

plausible interpretation of this sentence is that only bishops have *ordinary* power to confirm [19] and to ordain.[20] Since the discussions by the Tridentine fathers and theologians make it clear that the distinction between the power of order and the power of jurisdiction was widely accepted at the council, one may assume that the "power of consecrating" mentioned in chapter 1 and canon 1 refers to the power of order.

What cannot be concluded from Trent or claimed to be part of Trent's teaching, is that the "power" that is handed on to the ministerial priests of the church in the sacrament of order (1) can be conferred in no other way except through the sacrament of order; (2) is so absolutely necessary for consecrating the eucharist [21] that without it, regardless of circumstances, "nothing happens" if one attempts to offer the eucharist.[22] Trent simply does not address itself to the questions: Is there any way other than the sacrament of order by which a Christian can be empowered to offer the eucharist when circumstances urge it? If, in case of need, and free from any spirit of temerarious usurpation, one who does not have the "power of order" attempts to offer the eucharist, is it true that "he does nothing whatever," as Bonaventure, Bellarmine, and Suarez would say? [23] Catholic theologians have given answers to these questions. But at the Council of Trent these questions were not even asked, let alone answered.

The point could indeed be made that, had such questions been raised at Trent, the fathers would have answered them along the lines of Bonaventure. But we must not confuse the historically conditioned theological assumptions of the Tridentine fathers with their explicit or clearly implicit dogmatic teaching, the formulations of which, to be sure, are also historically conditioned. What the council expressly taught as definitions of faith are binding for Catholics; the theological opinions presupposed by the theologians and bishops are not. Theologians after Trent are therefore free to question those presuppositions

---

[19] This was Trent's previous explicit teaching: DS 1630.

[20] This was the teaching of the Council of Florence: DS 1326.

[21] "Power" would thus be understood in the first of the two senses discussed above.

[22] Cf. CT 9.16:20-25 where Peter de Soto O.P., a leading council theologian, calls such an event "illegitimate" — not a non-event. This is the language that prevailed in the final formulation of canons 7 and 8 on order: DS 1777, 1778.

[23] For references see notes 9 and 10 above.

and to propose new ones, as long as they do justice to scripture and to the church's defined commitments concerning the minister of the eucharist.

THE DISCUSSIONS AT BOLOGNA: 1547

In the previous section we have arrived at the clear response of Trent to the first of the three questions posed: the competent ministers of the eucharist are the apostles and their successors in the "visible and external priesthood." In this section we wish to present the background at Trent of those aspects of the doctrine on order that relate to the second question.

The only part of Trent's teaching on order that touches upon the ministry of the Reformation churches or the celebration of the eucharist by Christians other than those who belong to the "visible and external priesthood" is found in chapter 4 and canon 7. The relevant portion of chapter 4 reads: "The holy synod . . . decrees that all those who are called and instituted only by the people or by the secular power and magistrature and then proceed to exercise these ministries [of bishop, priest, and the other orders], and who by their own temerity take these ministries upon themselves, are not to be regarded as ministers of the church but as 'thieves and robbers who have not entered by the gate' (cf. John 10:1)." [24]

Canon 7 says: "If anyone says . . . that those who have neither

---

[24] DS 1769. For centuries the church had forbidden the usurpation of ecclesial offices. The rationale was not that the usurper absolutely lacked "power" (in the first of our two senses) to perform a sacramental act, but that he lacked authorization, having been called neither by God (Hebrews 5:4 is invoked) nor by the church. Usurpation of the ministry is not censured because the usurper lacks the *potentia physicala* to offer mass as a widespread contemporary Catholic theology would have it (cf. E. Doronzo, *De Ordine* [Milwaukee, 1962] III 246), but because he thereby disrupts the order *(taxis)* of the church. This order, which the sacrament of order is obviously intended to serve, is not simply a juridical reality but a deeply theological one that is intimately related to church unity. Cf. I Corinthians 12 and 14:40; I Thessalonians 5:14; II Thessalonians 3:6; Colossians 2:5; Council of Antioch (341 A.D.) canon 13; Council of Constantinople I (381) canons 4 and 6. The *Apostolic Constitutions* (about 400) III, 10, for example, teach that if a layman performs the functions of a priest — including baptism! — he stands liable to the punishment that was meted out to Uzziah (II Chronicles 26:17-21) for his usurpation of the priestly office. Usurpation of the sacramental ministry is thus seen to be just as reprehensible in the early church as it was at Trent, but not on the grounds that "nothing happens" sacramentally if the minister is unauthorized.

been duly ordained nor sent by ecclesiastical and canonical power but come from some other source *(aliunde veniunt),* are legitimate ministers of the word and the sacraments, let him be anathema." [25]

An awareness of the genesis of the above teaching of 1563 is necessary for comprehending it. When the council fathers and theologians meeting at Bologna in 1547 turned to the sacrament of order, they were presented with four "articles of the heretics." Articles 3 and 4 read: "All Christians are equally priests, but for the use or exercise [of the priesthood] the call of the ruler *(maior)* and the consent of the people are required." "A bishop does not have the right *(ius)* to ordain; therefore an ordination performed by him is invalid *(irritam)*." [26]

In the discussion of the third article by the theologians (April 29 to May 7, 1547) some arguments against the *equal* priesthood of all Christians were: women cannot "confect" the eucharist because Paul commands that they keep quiet in church;[27] not all Christians can forgive sins, which is the primary office of the priests;[28] to offer sacrifice is the role of the priest, but *"Hoc facite . . ."* (Matthew 26 [*lege* I Corinthians 11]) was spoken only to the apostles and to priests;[29] furthermore, women cannot be priests because Paul forbids women to pray without a hat; but it is necessary for a priest to have tonsure; therefore. . . . [!] [30]

The discussion of the fourth article is of little substantive interest to us, since it mainly involves a defense of the right of Catholic bishops to ordain, a point that is uncontested today. It is of major importance, however, to note that this "defensive" posture about the legitimacy of Catholic bishops was more pronounced at Trent than any "offensive" assault against the legitimacy of the ministry in the Reformation churches.[31]

---

25 DS 1777.

26 CT 6.97:19-20; 6.98:3.

27 CT 6.110:12-13; a second theologian argues the same way: 6.116:25-27.

28 CT 6.118:10-15.

29 CT 6.118:15-16.

30 CT 6.112:20-21.

31 DS 1778 reflects the "defensive" emphasis, 1777 the "offensive." As late as December 1562, Cardinal Hosius had to remind the fathers that they were not at Trent to engage in questions disputed among Catholics nor even to deal with the question: are bishops instituted *iure divino,* but with the question: are the bishops who are appointed by the pope "true" bishops?

After the "articles of the heretics" [32] had been discussed by the theologians the substance of the matter was shaped into five canons proposed to the fathers for examination on July 21, 1547. The actual discussion lasted only two days, July 27-29, 1547.

Canon 3 reads: "If anyone says that all Christians are equally priests or that those who are to be legitimate priests need not be ordained according the keys of the church, but that for the use, exercise or function of the priesthood only the call of the governor (*maior* [33]) is needed, a.s." [34]

Canon 5 is also relevant to the question of the competent minister of the eucharist: "If anyone denies that there is a gradation of order in the church or says that every priest has the same or equal jurisdiction and authority, and therefore that any priest can absolve all Christians from all sins or can administer all the sacraments to any of the faithful, and not just the priest who has ordinary or delegated authority to do so, a.s." [35]

What catches our attention in canon 3 is the term "legitimate." Neither in the immediate nor in subsequent discussions does anyone offer a definition of this term. Yet it is an operative modifier both here and in the final formulation of the doctrine on the sacrament of order.[36] How is the term to be understood? The bishop of Majorca equates "legitimate" with "true." [37] In the revision of the canon of Aug. 18, 1547 *both* terms are used, [38] but, again, neither is ex-

---

CT 9.202:34-203:2; 215:1-4. Hosius, however, could not resist advocating a debatable point. Having given an affirmative answer to the above question — here he agreed with all the fathers — he went on to assert: . . . *si qui aliter quam a summo Pontifice instituuntur, non sunt veri episcopi:* 9.215:6-7. The fathers at Bologna were much more sensitive to the Greek church than was Hosius. Cf. CT 6.385:34-37. Again, however, everything hinges on what Hosius understands by *veri episcopi.* Cf. below notes 54 and 69, and pp. 294-295.

[32] We set aside here any effort to evaluate the accuracy and/or fairness of the work done by those who drew up the *"articuli."*

[33] The term *maior* was unclear to several fathers — one of whom was the bishop of Majorca *(Maioricensis!)* — and was subsequently replaced by *potestas saecularis.*

[34] CT 6.308:15-309:2.

[35] CT 6.309:7-11.

[36] DS 1777. Cf. note 22 above and pp. 297-298.

[37] CT 6.312:33-34.

[38] CT 6.378:11: *non . . . veros et legitimos sacerdotes.* Both terms are also found in the revision of August 20, 1547: CT 6.384:25. They are retained in DS 1778 but not 1777.

plained. The term "legitimate" surely has first of all a juridical meaning. The Tridentine doctrine about the need for "proper ordination according to ecclesiastical and canonical power," to use the language of the final definition,[39] means at least that one who is not so ordained has violated church law and discipline and that his ministry is therefore not legitimate. Our investigation has uncovered no evidence that would show that Trent certainly intended anything beyond this in referring to the ministers in question as not legitimate. There have been many Catholic theologians who have held that ministers "not ordained according to ecclesiastical and canonical power" have absolutely no capability of consecrating the eucharist. But they cannot correctly invoke Trent to support this position.

The above-mentioned canon 5 and the discussion of it tend to substantiate our interpretation. The proposed canon itself implies that a simple priest, with delegated authority, can — validly and licitly — administer all the sacraments, including confirmation and order! During the debate on canon 5 the influential [40] bishop of Accia, Benedetto de Nobili, called for the addition of the phrase "except in case of necessity." "Any priest," he argued, "can administer all the sacraments to anyone in case of necessity." [41] When the bishop of Fiesole asked that the canon be changed so as not to imply that a priest can ordain, even with delegated power, he did so on the grounds that such an implication "is perhaps false" (our emphasis).[42] Several other bishops did not agree with the latitude of the bishop of Accia's position.[43] It is surely not the case that Trent endorsed the position of the bishops of Accia and Bertinoro. But it is just as clear that Trent did not judge unorthodox the opinion that, even without delegated authority, a simple priest could ordain other priests in case of need.[44] In actual

---

[39] DS 1777.

[40] H. Jedin, A History of the Council of Trent II (St. Louis, 1961), 193.

[41] CT 6.312:15-16: et in fine addatur excepta necessitate, quia sacerdos quilibet posset in casu [neccessitatis] ministrare omnia sacramenta omnibus. The Dominican bishop of Bertinoro seems to have shared this view: CT 6.316: 25-26.

[42] CT 6.312:26-29: falsum forsan est.

[43] CT 6.314:35-39; 316:11-12; 319:2. It should be noted once again, however, how ambiguously the term "posse" is used in these discussions. We are told, for example, that neither deacons nor priests can preach (possunt praedicare) unless they are sent by bishops or by the apostolic see: CT 6.316:7-8; cf. 6.311:14-15; 321:9-10.

[44] The definitive chapter 4 rejects the legitimacy of those who enter the ministry "by their own temerity" (DS 1769). It says nothing whatsoever

fact Trent abandoned any attempt to state explicitly what sacraments a simple priest could — or could not — administer with delegated authority.[45] The question was simply left open and it is still open today.

An intervention during the discussion of the reformed version of canon 3 tends further to strengthen our interpretation of Trent's teaching on order. The revised canon presented for discussion on August 20, 1547 reads: "If anyone . . . denies that only those are true and legitimate priests who are rightly and canonically ordained by bishops, a.s." [46] Thomas Stella O.P., bishop of Lavello, proposed that the word "only" *(solos)* be deleted.[47] This would have left open the possibility of there being other "true and legitimate" ministers who were not ordained by bishops. Stella's intervention did not carry the day nor was it taken into account in the definitive canon. But it should be noticed that the definitive canon does not speak of ordination by bishops, but "by ecclesiastical and canonical power." [48] This suggests all the more, it seems to us, that Trent is asserting the canonical or juridical illegitimacy (illiceity) of Lutheran [49] ordinations — not their invalidity in a widely held modern sense.[50]

---

about those who do so in case of necessity. It is to be recalled that the Lutheran reformers argued that a case of necessity had arisen: the Catholic bishops refused to ordain priests for a given (reformed) congregation; therefore the pastor of that congregation, himself an ordained priest, can validly ordain priests for that congregation. *The Book of Concord,* ed. T. G. Tappert (Philadelphia, 1959): "Treatise on the Power and the Primacy of the Pope," 63-67. Trent would not consider such a ministry "legitimate," but it nowhere says or implies that the ordained pastor who ordains others "does nothing."

[45] This was evident as early as August 24, 1457 when a reformed version of canon 5 was presented in which penance is the only sacrament mentioned: CT 6.397:1-4.

[46] CT 6.384:24-25.

[47] CT 6.386:13.

[48] DS 1777. The revised canon 3 of August 26, 1547 also spoke of ordination "by bishops."

[49] Several interventions make it clear that the fathers did not want to dispute the legitimacy of Orthodox ordinations, but only those of the Lutherans: CT 6.385:27-28; 34-37; 39-41; 45-47.

[50] Even were one to argue that the judgment of *Apostolicae Curae* that Anglican orders are "absolutely null and utterly void" applies *a fortiori* to Lutheran and other Protestant ordinations, leaving aside recent re-evaluations of that encyclical, one could still point out that *"nullitas"* in canon law does not mean "nothing." Cf. K. Mörsdorf, *"Nichtigkeit," Lexikon für Theologie und Kirche* VII, 943.

THE DISCUSSIONS OF 1551-1552 AT TRENT

When the council reconvened at Trent in 1551 the fathers began to consider anew a set of six "articles" pertaining to the sacrament of order taken from the works of the reformers. The articles are substantially the same as those presented in 1547. Two points from the discussion of the theologians (December 7-29, 1551) are of interest. First, the refusal by several to deny without qualification that all Christians are equally priests as canon 3 maintained.[51] Second, the ambiguous way in which the term *potestas* is used. According to Eberhard Billick o. carm., those holding the office of doorkeeper, lector, or priest receive "power" from the sacrament to perform their ministry. But they cannot exercise this power [52] unless they are called to do so by the hierarchical order. This is the view of a representative theologian at Trent. What does it mean? It means that an ordained lector without a call — or jurisdiction — *cannot* read during mass even though he may *actually* read and may actually be a ministerial means of grace for those who are moved by his reading of God's word. It means that a man who has not been ordained a lector not only cannot read the epistle during mass — even when he does so — but that he does not have the *power* to read it — even though he does it and even though he, too, might be a means of grace for his hearers. It would be ludicrous to subject the "power" of the doorkeeper to a similar analysis. The interesting thing is that Billick applies the same principles to a priest as he does to a doorkeeper.

Actually Billick's rather standard position is not ludicrous once one realizes that he equates the power of the sacrament with *authority*,[53] not with a *sine qua non* capacity or power without which it would be impossible for a layman to open the church doors, read the epistle, or lead the eucharist. For Billick, a Christian layman who does such things without ordination would be doing them without *authorization*. This is his explicit teaching. Even though he does not advert to it, Billick's position seems to imply that the layman who exercises these ministries without sacramental authorization indeed does them and there is no reason to suppose that, under certain con-

---

[51] See CT 7.377:22-23 and 6.91:3-4 for the related canons and 6.312:8-10; 313:7; 7.413:25-26; 410:32; 412:3-5; 413:37-38; 415:43 for the statements of theologians who in some way held to the priesthood of all Christians.

[52] CT 7.410:22-23: *nullam potestatem exercere possunt.*

[53] CT 7.410:18-20. See note 12 above.

ditions at least: necessity, manifest ecclesial concern and responsibility, etc., these unauthorized or canonically illegitimate ministers can consecrate the eucharistic bread and wine. There is nothing in Trent's definitive teaching that excludes this interpretation of the meaning of the sacrament of order.

In the light of the discussion of the Protestant "articles" by the theologians, eight canons on order were drawn up and presented to the fathers on January 20, 1552.[54] Interesting is the fact that in contrast to the canons on order drawn up during the 1547 period of the council, these canons are purely "defensive." They simply defend the legitimacy and validity of Catholic ordinations but say nothing whatever about the ministries of the Protestant churches.

On January 21, 1552 the fathers received copies of the schema on the "Doctrine on the Sacrament of Order."[55] This schema was never discussed in a general congregation. Ten years later the council began again *de novo* when it dealt with the sacrament of order. Missing in the later formulations is the dubious historical affirmation found in the schema of 1552: ". . . Certain eminent functions always belonged to the bishops alone, not to priests. . . . The administration of the sacraments of order and of confirmation . . . always pertained to bishops alone, never to simple priests, for whom it would be invalid *(irritus)* and a vain effort if they began to exercise these functions *(munera)*."[56]

THE FINAL PERIOD AT TRENT

During Trent's final period (1562-1563) the sacrament of order was discussed intensively, but almost exclusively with reference to the questions: are bishops superior to priests *iure divino?* what is the origin of episcopal jurisdiction? — neither of which was definitively settled by the council. During the debate 219 fathers expressed their views, but scarcely an utterance is to be found concerning the question: can ministers other than those "properly ordained by canonical and ecclesiastical power" be regarded as leaders of the sacrament of the body and blood of Christ?

Chapter 4 of the definitive doctrinal statement teaches that "all those who are called and instituted only by the people or by the secular power and magistrature and then proceed to exercise these ministries

---

[54] CT 7.460-461.

[55] CT 7.483-489.

[56] CT 7.488:15-21.

[of bishops, priests, and the *other orders:* note that what follows applies to the ministry of doorkeeper and lector as well as to the bishop], and who by their own temerity take these offices upon themselves, are not to be regarded as ministers of the church, but as 'thieves and robbers who have not entered by the gate.' " [57]

The text of the definitive canon 7 reads: "If anyone says that bishops are not superior to priests; or that they do not have the power to confirm and ordain, or that the power which they have is common to them and to priests; or that the orders conferred by them without the consent or call of the people or the secular power are invalid *(irritos);* or that those who have neither been duly ordained nor sent by ecclesiastical and canonical power, but come from elsewhere, are legitimate *(legitimos)* ministers of word and sacraments: a.s." [58]

In chapter 4, the words "who are only" down to "exercise these ministries" were added only at a very late date and were subjected to no discussion.[59]

In considering the teaching of the chapter, it is surely germane to ask: are there in fact any Lutherans — or other Protestants — who hold that, for the exercise of the eucharistic ministry, a Christian needs only the call and consent of the people or the secular authority? Is it not true that at least the Lutheran and Calvinist confessions insist that a Christian believe he is divinely called to the ministry and that he also be ordained by the laying on of hands with invocation of the Holy Spirit? Are there any Christian churches who say that someone can be a minister of the church who temerariously takes the ministry upon himself? Nowhere in the Tridentine discussions on order of any of the three periods do we find an accurate statement of the Lutheran or Calvinist confessions pertaining to the ministry. This aspect of Trent's teaching on orders reminds us of a basic principle in interpreting Trent: because Trent condemns something, do not conclude that the Reformers were teaching it.[60]

Concerning canon 7, as was already noted,[61] such an influential

---

[57] DS 1769. Trent did not accept a proposal of some Roman theologians to have the chapter read: "They are *not* ministers but are to be regarded as thieves and robbers," etc. Cf. CT 9.233.32-33.

[58] See pp. 291-292 above.

[59] CT 9.235:14-20. Cf. CT 9.227:28-30 and 239:3-5.

[60] For elaboration of this point see my essay: "Luther, Trent, Vatican I and II," *McCormick Quarterly* 21 (1967), 95-104, esp. 96-97.

[61] See note 31 above.

figure as Cardinal Hosius wanted Trent to teach not only that the bishops appointed by the pope are true bishops [62] — over against some polemical utterances of Luther's *Babylonian Captivity* of 1520 — but also that *only* those bishops appointed by the pope are "true" bishops. This the council did not teach.

Nowhere in the *acta* of Trent do we find a definition of the phrase "ordained by ecclesiastical and canonical power." All we can find is that this broad term was used in preference to "ordained according to the keys of the church," [63] "duly and canonically ordained by bishops," [64] "according to the rite of the Roman church," [65] and other formulations. In the light of the discussion surrounding the latter two terms, it is difficult to see that what Trent said in canon 7 really touches the Lutheran confession concerning ministry.[66]

The important term "legitimate" is likewise given no explicit clarification during the council's deliberations.[67] The only intervention on canon 7 that sheds any light on it came from the Superior General of the Franciscan Conventuals who noted that "bishops consecrated among heretics according to the form of the church are true bishops, and yet they are not from the pope; but they are not legitimate and they are without jurisdiction." [68] "Not legitimate" here clearly

---

[62] This was taught in canon 8: DS 1778.

[63] CT 6.378:29; cf. 379:22-24; 45-46.

[64] CT 6.384:25.

[65] CT 6.385:10; 22-23.

[66] The proposal by the bishop of Verona to add *secundum ritum s. Romanae ecclesiae* was opposed by Ambrose Pelargus O.P. *ne excludantur sacerdotes ordinati apud Graecos et alias nationes eorum more etc.* CT 6.385: 27-28. He was immediately supported by two other bishops. Verona then explained that he had made his proposal because he thought *rite et canonice* did not touch the Lutherans. If the fathers are offended by his proposal, he said, let it be omitted "as long as something is added that would hit *(feriantur)* the Lutherans." CT 6.385:45-47. The phrase was eventually changed from *rite et canonice ab episcopis ordinantur* to *ab ecclesiastica et canonica potestate rite ordinati nec missi sunt.* The bishop of Verona died in 1548. It is therefore doubly difficult to say whether he would have thought that, as a result of this change of 1562/63, the Lutherans would now be "hit."

[67] CT 9.88:22-24; 28-29: The opinion of the synod is that "the legitimate minister be ordained by ecclesiastical and canonical power." Cf. note 22 above and pp. 291-292.

[68] CT 9.219;28-30: . . . *episcopi consecrati apud haereticos secundum formam ecclesiae sunt veri episcopi et tamen non sunt a Papa, sed non sunt legitimi et sunt absque jurisdictione.*

seems to mean canonically illicit but valid ("true"). The burden of proof is on those who would maintain that the term means something else in the definitive form of canon 7.

The very history of canon 7 during Trent's third period is evidence that the council gave practically no attention to the question of the minister of the eucharist in the Reformation churches other than to declare them at most "illegitimate." The original version of canon 7 at the third period (October 13, 1562) was quite similar to the final version of July 15, 1563. It contained both an "offensive" thrust — against the legitimacy of ministers "not duly ordained nor sent by ecclesiastical and canonical power" — and a "defensive" thrust — on behalf of Catholic bishops not elected by the people who were therefore accused of having been invalidly ordained. Canon 7 was altered three times prior to the final version. In each case the "offensive" thrust was missing.[69] During the greater part of the discussion [70] on canon 7, therefore, the text the fathers had before them did not refer in any way to "other" ministries.[71]

Thus, in response to the second question we posed at the outset, it can accurately be said that Trent teaches only that ministers of word and sacrament other than those properly ordained by ecclesiastical and canonical power are not legitimate — in the sense of illicit. Trent does not even say specifically that Lutheran — or any Protestant — ministries fall into this category. Surely no Protestant churches would regard as their own the concept of ministry and ordination described in chapter 4 on order. Furthermore, by refusing to say that by *divine law* bishops are able to ordain other priests, whereas by *divine law* presbyters cannot, Trent did not exclude the concept of ordination by priests defended in the Lutheran *Book of Concord,* a concept that was used to validate, if not legitimate, Lutheran ministers of the eucharist.[72]

As far as our third question is concerned, we can say without qualification that there is nothing whatever in the Tridentine doctrine on the sacrament of order concerning the reality of the eucharist cele-

---

[69] CT 9.107 (November 3, 1562); 9.228 (December 6, 1562); 9.239 (January 31, 1563). See note 31 above.

[70] November 3 to December 9, 1562, CT 9.110-225.

[71] We have discussed above the reference in chapter 4 to those ministers who are to be regarded as "thieves and robbers." Cf. note 24 above.

[72] Cf. "Treatise on the Power and Primacy of the Pope," *Book of Concord,* ed. T. G. Tappert (Philadelphia, 1959), 63-67.

brated by Christians of the Reformation churches. Catholic theologians who have maintained that there is no sacrament of the body and blood of Christ in Protestant churches because Protestant ministers are radically incapable of consecrating the eucharist are incorrect if they think this opinion is necessitated by the teaching of Trent.

ROMAN CATHOLIC THEOLOGY AND "RECOGNITION OF MINISTRY"

By George H. Tavard

"Recognition of ministry" is one of the major problems that stand in the way of a reconciliation between the churches which believe in "apostolic succession" through episcopal consecration and ordination and those which, having lost this mode of ordination, interpret apostolic succession differently. I propose to survey one aspect of this problem from the standpoint of Catholic theology today. Does contemporary Catholic thought hold that there are still sufficient reasons to deny the validity of the orders of non-episcopally ordained ministers?

To this question I see three general types of answers.

I. *First type*

The precedents of Counter-Reformation theology already constitute such reasons. The Catholic polemicists of the sixteenth century and the apologists of more recent times did deny the validity of Protestant eucharists and orders. This fact cannot be erased from the ledger. As one cannot start from the principle that the Counter-Reformation theologians were certainly and uniformly mistaken, their position provides a traditional reason (even though the tradition may be fairly recent) to deny the validity of Protestant eucharists and orders.

Such a denial, made today for this reason of historical precedent, may represent two distinct attitudes:

1. A merely conservative stance, refusing to revise former opinions when these may be considered as having been the "common theology" of a period.

2. A conviction that the church has committed itself to this denial, a reversal of which would amount to admitting that the church may make a mistake in an important doctrinal matter (or about a fact which is closely connected with important doctrines). This would

throw doubt on the very basis of the Catholic faith, namely the belief that the church cannot be positively in error, since it is guided by the Spirit.

II. *Second type*

Although precedent does constitute a reason, this is not, by itself, a compelling reason. The decision made by the Counter-Reformation theologians rested on arguments that must be examined before we can endorse or abandon the former negative judgment about Protestant orders and eucharists. Even though no final statement was made on these matters by the magisterium, the negative line was commonly adopted as the standard in cases involving the "ordination" of a convert who had himself been ordained to a Protestant ministry.

In the polemics of the sixteenth century, the chief argument was the lack of episcopal consecration and ordination in continental Protestantism (the case of the church of Sweden may be left aside for it raises a different problem) and break of continuity in England. Whatever may have been the practice of medieval and patristic times in regard to presbyteral ordination, the church had, by the end of the Middle Ages, adopted episcopal consecration as the standard method of perpetuating its ministry. It had no intention then of recognizing a presbyteral line of succession as sufficient. This intention of the sixteenth century church was manifested in canonical legislation, as also by the negative judgments passed on Lutheran and other Protestant or Anglican orders by the magisterium and the theologians. These orders were considered invalid because of defect of form.

An additional argument was lack of intention of perpetuating the priesthood, as manifested (1) in the indifference of the leaders of the continental Reformation to episcopal consecration (here, defect of intention is based on defect of form, and we are back in the preceding argument), and (2) in the shifts of emphasis which the Reformation imposed on eucharistic theology: these are interpreted as having effected a rupture in the continuity of sacramental faith, which in turn implies a defect of intention concerning orders and the eucharist.

Facing these two arguments, contemporary Roman Catholic theology can adopt four attitudes:

A. It can endorse their value and conclusion, both for the sixteenth century and for today.

B. It can recognize their value for the sixteenth century, but deny it for today, on the ground, either (a) that Lutheran thought has

302

evolved, thus becoming more Catholic, or (b) that Roman Catholic theology has evolved, thus being now able to see as valid what sixteenth century theologians could not so see.

C. It can suspend judgment as to the value of these arguments for the sixteenth century, on the ground that the theological situation was then too confused to admit of clear solutions to the sacramental problems raised by the Reformation; and deny this value for today, on the same grounds as in (B), plus the ecumenically-oriented consideration that our problem is not to judge the past, but to prepare the future by trying to open new theological avenues.

D. It can deny the value of these arguments even for the sixteenth century, on the ground that the Catholic position was then based, (a) on inadequate theological conceptions (e. g., about the matter and form of the sacrament of orders), (b) on insufficient evidence and on misunderstanding concerning Protestant intentions and conceptions. Current sacramental reflection makes (a) a plausible line of thinking, while recent re-assessments of Luther go in the direction of (b).

III. *Third type*

The above position II.C forms actually a third type of answer. This can be expressed in another way. We need not examine the past, for the past, in such a matter of fact as the validity of Protestant eucharists and orders, cannot normatively determine the position we should take today. We may simply examine Protestant doctrines and ministries today, sizing them up in the light of contemporary Catholic theology. The problem then becomes: In the light of what Catholic theological principles could the validity of Protestant orders and eucharists be recognized?

Let me recall briefly several principles that have been put forward recently as sufficient ground for a recognition of a non-episcopally ordained ministry:

1. The traditional concept of extraordinary minister of a sacrament. The Protestant minister would be seen as an extraordinary minister of the eucharist, episcopal ordination being necessary for the ordinary minister.[1] With van Beeck, this goes with his conception that eucharist and orders are already somehow included in the sacrament of baptism; any one who has been baptized may, if cir-

---

[1] Edgar Bruns, in *The Ecumenist* 3 (1964-65), 21-23; Frans Josef van Beeck in *Journal of Ecumenical Studies* 4 (1966), 57-112.

cumstances warrant it, become extraordinary minister of all the sacraments.

2. The plurality of ministries in the New Testament can justify a similar plurality today. While Roman Catholics have preserved the institutional ministry, Protestants, in the sixteenth century, revived the charismatic ministry. Protestant eucharists and orders can then be recognized as being, at least *in voto*, the true eucharist and order of the gospel.[2]

3. The term *Ecclesia*, which is applied by Vatican II to the "separated communities of the West," or at least to some of them, implies that these communities have all the essentials of a church, including the validity of orders and eucharists.[3]

4. Several applications of the principle *Ecclesia supplet* to the question of Protestant orders have been attempted.[4] For Tillard, such an application of the principle *Ecclesia supplet* is justified by St. Thomas's theology, for which baptism includes a "desire for the eucharist." Protestant baptism being recognized by the Catholic church, the desire for the eucharist included in it is by the same token recognized. Logically, this should be followed by an official application of the principle *Ecclesia supplet*, expressing the Catholic church's wish to supply what may be missing in these eucharists in order to validate them. In this line of thought, the actual validity of Protestant orders would seem to depend on the Roman Catholic church's official recognition that the principle applies.

5. The position I have taken [5] is also based on the principle *Ecclesia supplet* and on the corresponding Orthodox notion of "economy." But it assumes that the principle applies and works, regardless of official recognition, as soon as some conditions are fulfilled. These conditions may be expressed as amounting to a recognizable continuity of eucharistic faith between the pre-Reformation (biblical, patristic, medieval) tradition and the Reformation positions. Or, if one prefers a less historical concern, these conditions may be seen as the existence of a recognizable analogy (in the strict sense of pro-

---

[2] Hans Küng, *The Church* (New York: Sheed and Ward, 1968).

[3] Robert Adolfs, in *New Christian* (4 May, 1967), 11-12.

[4] E. g., by Maurice Villain (*Concilium*, vol. 34, pp. 87-104), J. M. R. Tillard (*Miscellanea Liturgica in onore di S. E. il Card. Lercaro* [Rome, 1967], pp. 143-194).

[5] *Journal of Ecumenical Studies* 5 (1967), 629-649; *Continuum* (1968), 260-269.

portional correspondence, not in the metaphorical sense of more or less remote similarity) between the Catholic and the Protestant eucharistic faiths. The term "recognizable" does not mean that orders or eucharists within the context of such an analogy must wait for Roman Catholic recognition in order to become valid. It implies, on the one hand, that the Protestant community in question recognizes its sacrament as that of the New Testament, and on the other that, pending an official stand by the Catholic magisterium, theologians do recognize the Catholic tradition and faith in the confessional formulae, the theological explanations and the liturgical practices of the community in question. For instance, the agreement reached by the Catholic-Lutheran colloquium in the U. S. A. concerning eucharistic doctrine[6] seems to me sufficient to warrant the opinion that the principle *Ecclesia supplet* is at work at present in the Lutheran churches. Similar joint studies of eucharistic doctrines ought to be made with other churches.

6. Taking account of the fact that there is some evidence that both the early centuries and the Middle Ages did entertain a concept of presbyteral succession, I would be prepared to go further, and to admit that episcopal succession is not absolutely required for valid ordination. Presbyteral succession suffices, for these two successions are of one and the same kind, episcopacy and priesthood constituting one sacrament only. This conclusion is tied to a theology of the priesthood which sees no essential difference between priests and bishops as far as orders go, the difference lying in the order of jurisdiction, authority and mission. Although this corresponds to the doctrine of St. Thomas, it has been a minority position in more recent times. It remains so today. Vatican II would seem to go in the other direction, although I do not think it had any intention of ending the discussion of this matter. At any rate, this line of argumentation could only serve as collateral evidence showing the possibility of presbyteral ordination. The main problem, in our ecumenical context, does not lie in evaluating historical lines of succession, but in appreciating the catholicity of Protestantism today.

---

[6] Cf. *Lutherans and Catholics in Dialogue III: The Eucharist as Sacrifice,* 1967, pp. 187-198.

THE CONCEPT OF "CHURCH" IN THE DOCUMENTS OF VATICAN II AS APPLIED TO PROTESTANT DENOMINATIONS

By Kilian McDonnell

The phrase "churches or ecclesial communities" is used of Protestant denominations both in the Constitution on the Church and in the Decree on Ecumenism. What is of special interest is the application of "church" to Protestant groups. Was the word "church" used as a polite form of address, accepted in ecumenical circles but without theological content, as when a Roman Catholic bishop refers to the Lutheran church or the Methodist church? A similar situation would arise were a curial official to address Arthur Michael Ramsey as "archbishop." No one would take this as a repudiation of the bull *Apostolicae Curae* and therefore a recognition of Anglican orders by a member of the Roman curia. One could ask whether "church" is used as a kind of phenomenological description of Protestant denominations which is void of either theological intent or content. Is this the kind of language one meets in the two documents, or is the term "church" used in a specifically theological sense?

Neither of the first two drafts of the Constitution on the Church apply the term "church" to Protestant denominations. Indeed the first preliminary draft explicitly restricted the word "church" so that it would not apply to Protestant denominations: ". . . that is why rightly only the Catholic Church is called (the) Church." Article 9 of the second draft of the Constitution, which was discussed in the council from 30 September 1963 to 31 October 1963 did not use the term "church" when talking of groups separated from the Roman church: "They lovingly believe in Christ, Son of God and Saviour, they are signed with an indelible baptism, indeed they recognize and receive all or at least certain of the sacraments, and many of them foster faith in the holy eucharist and cultivate devotion toward the Virgin Mother of God." [1] In the final draft of 1964 this section (which becomes article 15) introduced the word "church" into the text: "They lovingly believe in God the Father Almighty and in Christ, Son of God and Saviour. They are consecrated by baptism, through which they are united with Christ. They also recognize and receive other sacraments within their own churches or ecclesial communities. Many of them rejoice in the episcopate, celebrate the holy eucharist, and cultivate devotion toward the Virgin Mother of God." [2]

The *relatio* for article 15 explains unambiguously the reason for the introduction of the terms "churches or ecclesial communities." "The elements which are enumerated apply not only to separated Christians as individuals but also to their communities." [3] Up to Vatican II the Roman church recognized that there were individual non-Catholic believers, but, with regard to what were considered the dissident groups of the West, did not attribute any theological or ecclesial reality to the denominations as such. In the pre-Vatican framework they were not, and could not, be called "churches." In the pre-Vatican framework there was no official Roman recognition of the ecclesial

---

[1] *Cum omnibus illis qui, baptizati, christiano nomine decorantur, integram autem fidem vel unitatem communionis sub Romano Pontifice non profitentur, Ecclesia, pia omnium Mater, semetipsam scit plures ob rationes coniunctam. Amanter enim credunt in Christum, Filium Dei Salvatorem, baptismo indelebili signantur, imo omnia aut saltem quaedam sacramenta agnoscunt et recipiunt, et plures eorum fidem erga Sanctissimam Eucharistiam necnon pietatem erga Deiparam Virginem fovent. Schema Constitutionis De Ecclesia* (Typis Polyglottis Vaticanis 1964), 36. This edition gives both the *textus prior,* which is the second draft, and the *textus emendatus,* which is the third draft. The Latin texts are included here because they are not so readily available.

Care should be taken in using article 9 of the second draft or article 15 of the third draft. Though largely concerned with non-Catholic groups of the West they apply also to the Orthodox groups of the East.

[2] *Sacram enim Scripturam ut norman credendi et vivendi in honore habent zelumque apostolicum ostendunt, amanter credunt in Deum Patrem omnipotentem et in Christum, Filium Dei Salvatorem, baptismo signantur, quo Christo coniunguntur, imo et alia sacramenta in propriis Ecclesiis vel communitatibus ecclesiasticis agnoscunt et recipiunt. Plures inter illos et episcopatu gaudent, Sacram Eucharistiam celebrant necnon pietatem erga Deiparam Virginem fovent. Ibid.,* 36-37.

[3] *Elementa quae enumerantur non tantum individuos respiciunt, sed etiam communitates. Ibid.,* 51.

nature of Protestant denominations. The *relatio* to this section, however, rightly declares that the recognition of the ecclesial nature of groups other than the one to which one belongs is the operating principle of the ecumenical movement: "It is precisely in this supposition that the underlying principle of the ecumenical movement is to be found." [4] In other words where elements of the church are to be found, such as love of scripture, belief in the Fatherhood of God, Christ as Son of God and Saviour, baptism and possibly other sacraments, in some cases episcopacy, eucharist and devotion to the Blessed Virgin, there one finds not only true Christians but there one finds what can be truly called a church in the theological sense.

One must not use this passage to institute a quantification of ecclesiology. The recognition in article 15 of the presence of a number of ecclesial elements in other churches must not lead one to add up what elements are found in what churches and on this basis to arrive at a quantified estimation of a denomination's ecclesiological worth. The difference between the Roman Catholic church and the other Protestant churches is not to be found in a quantitative and measurable number of ecclesial elements, but by the mode in which they are present.[5] Further, one should not use the terms "churches or ecclesial communities" to postulate quantitative differences between Protestant groups, as though ecclesial communities were quantitatively inferior in the ecclesiological sense to those groups one would designate as churches. The purpose of the council was not to introduce quantitative categories but simply to accommodate those denominations who refuse to apply the term "church" to themselves, and would find it offensive to have themselves so designated in a conciliar document.

It is also evident from both the Constitution on the Church and the Decree on Ecumenism that the framework is that of full incorporation and less full incorporation into the church which Christ founded. For example article 14 of the Constitution states: "They are fully incorporated into the society of the church, who, possessing the Spirit of Christ. . . ." [6] In article 3 of the Decree the question is more precisely of a full manifestation of the church which Christ founded and a less full manifestation: "For it is through Christ's Catholic

---

[4] *In hoc praecise situm est principium motionis oecumenicae. Ibid.*

[5] Heribert Mühlen, *"Der Kirchenbegriff des Konzils," Die Autorität der Freiheit,* ed. Johann C. Hampe, vol. I (München: Kösel Verlag, 1967), 305.

[6] *Illi plene Ecclesiae societati incorporantur, qui Spiritum Christi habentes . . . Schema Constitutionis De Ecclesia,* 36.

Church alone, which is the all-embracing means of salvation, that the fullness of the means of salvation can be obtained." [7] A true but incomplete manifestation of the church which Christ founded is an ecclesial reality and can be called a "church." "The brethren divided from us," reads article 3 of the Decree, "also carry out many of the sacred actions of the Christian religion. Undoubtedly, in ways that vary according to the condition of each church or community, these actions can truly engender a life of grace and can be rightly described as capable of providing access to the community of salvation." [8]

Though the council did not want to introduce quantitative categories, it did give at least the appearance of introducing a species of quantification when it adopted the categories of full or less full manifestation of the church, and complete or less complete incorporation into the church which Christ founded. Unfortunately even the appearance of quantification will lead to an operative quantification. It must in all honesty be said that the use of full, less full, complete and less complete are not to be understood as referring to measurable numbers of elements but to the mode in which these elements are present. Modality here has to do with an operative presence of a whole series of interrelated signs of the kingdom. Modality is a category of presence, not of mathematics.

The ecclesial nature of the separated groups can be seen clearly in article 8 of the Constitution. In the second draft after speaking of the mystical body of Christ and the church which Christ founded as a visible society, article 7 identifies this church as the Roman Catholic church. "This church, the true mother and mistress of all, constituted and founded as a society in this world, is the Catholic Church, governed by the Roman pontiff and the bishops in communion with him, although many elements of sanctification can be found outside of her visible structure which as realities (*res*) proper to the church of Christ, possess an inner dynamism toward Catholic unity." [9] This

---

[7] *Per solam enim catholicam Christi Ecclesiam, quae generale auxilium salutis est, omnis salutarium mediorum plenitudo attingi potest. Schema Decreti De Oecumenismo* (Typis Polyglottis Vaticanis *1964*), 6.

[8] *Non paucae etiam christianae religionis actiones sacrae apud fratres a nobis seiunctos peraguntur, quae variis modis secundum diversam condicionem uniuscuiusque Ecclesiae vel Communitatis, procul dubio vitam gratiae reapse generare possunt atque aptae dicendae sunt quae ingressum in salutis communionem pandant. Ibid.*, 5.

[9] *Haec igitur Ecclesia, vera omnium Mater et Magistra, in hoc mundo ut societas constituta et ordinata, est Ecclesia catholica, a Romano Pontifice et*

text was changed in the last draft to read: "This church, constituted and organized in the world as a society, subsists in the Catholic Church, which is governed by the successor of Peter and by the bishops in union with that successor, although many elements of sanctification and truth can be found outside of her visible structure. These elements, however, as gifts properly belonging to the church of Christ, possess an inner dynamism toward Catholic unity." [10] Note carefully the transition from the clear text of the second draft: "This church . . . is the Catholic Church," to the unclear text of the third draft: "This church . . . subsists in the Catholic Church." When a conciliar document moves from a clear, unambiguous text to an unclear, ambiguous text this has meaning in terms of the theological intent of the council. It is undoubted that the word *subsistit* was carefully chosen for its ambiguity.

Before the final redaction thirteen of the fathers asked that the text of the second draft be restored which made a simple identification between the church which Christ founded and the Roman Catholic church by using *est*. Nineteen other fathers asked that the text read "subsists in an integral manner in the Catholic Church" (*subsistit integro modo in Ecclesia catholica*) while still another group of 25 fathers wanted the text formulated to read ". . . by divine law subsists" (*iure divino subsistit*). However the theological commission decided to retain the *subsistit in*. These suggestions and their final rejection by the theological commission are important for the interpretation of the text. What a council explicitly rejects is a manifestation of its intention as related to doctrinal formulations. The council approved the action of the theological commission which rejected the formulations tending to weaken the force of *subsistit in* and also tending to weaken the ecclesiological evaluation of Protestant denominations. It is significant that the suggested formulations which were rejected tended to reintroduce an oversimplified identification between the Roman Catholic church and the church which Christ founded.

Episcopis in eius communione directa, licet extra totalem compaginem elementa plura sanctificationis inveniri possint, quae ut res Ecclesiae Christi propriae, ad unitatem catholicam impellunt. Schema Constitutionis De Ecclesia, 15.

[10] *Haec Ecclesia, in hoc mundo ut societas constituta et ordinata, subsistit in Ecclesia catholica, a successore Petri et Episcopis in eius communione gubernata, licet extra eius compaginem elementa plura sanctificationis et veritatis inveniantur, quae ut dona Ecclesiae Christi propria, ad unitatem catholicam impellunt. Ibid.*

The clear identification between the church which Christ founded and the Roman Catholic church in the first and second draft was a faithful reflection of the teaching of Pius XII in number 23 of *Mystici Corporis*. As in all pre-Vatican II official documents there is no question of recognizing the ecclesial nature of Protestant denominations. And the identification between the Roman Catholic church and the church which Christ founded is complete and exclusive. Protestants are addressed only as individual believers, never as corporate ecclesiological entities. Speaking of those separated from Roman communion Pius said: "From a heart overflowing with love we ask each and every one of them to be quick and ready to follow the interior movements of grace, and to look to withdrawing from that state in which they cannot be sure of their salvation. For even though unsuspectingly they are related to the mystical body of the Redeemer in desire and resolution, they still remain deprived of so many precious gifts and helps from heaven, which one can only enjoy in the Catholic Church." [11] The whole problem of belonging to the church which Christ founded was defined in terms of being a member of the mystical body of Christ, which makes degrees of belonging clumsy at best. "Only those are really (*reapse*) to be included as members of the church who have been baptized and profess the true faith and who have not unhappily withdrawn from body-unity or for grave faults been excluded by legitimate authority." [12] With such an ecclesiological conception it is not possible to speak of Protestant denominations as true though incomplete manifestations of the church which Christ founded.

Though the mystical body theology is incorporated into the text of the Constitution on the Church, the text does not build the theological relationship of persons to the church which Christ founded in terms of member. The member vocabulary was consciously set aside. The *relatio generalis* stated that "the status of Catholics, Christians

---

[11] *Quam quidem sollemnem adseverationem Nostram per Encyclicas has Litteras, quibus "magni et gloriosi Corporis Christi" laudes praedicavimus, imploratis totius Ecclesiae precibus, iterare cupimus, eos singulos universos amantissimo animo invitantes, ut internis divinae gratiae impulsionibus ultro libenterque concedentes, ab eo statu se eripere studeant, in quo de sempiterna cuiusque propria salute securi esse non possunt. Acta Apostolicae Sedis,* Series 2, 10 (1943), 242-243.

[12] *In Ecclesiae autem membris reapse ii soli annumerandi sunt, qui regenerationis lavacrum receperunt veramque fidem profitentur, neque a Corporis compage semet ipsos misere separarunt, vel ob gravissima admissa a legitima auctoritate seiuncti sunt. Ibid.,* 202.

and non-Christians are described without the terminology of 'members,' which (terminology) is full of difficulties." [13]

In setting aside the word *est* of the second draft and substituting the word *subsistit* the council was able to express the identification between the church which Christ founded and the Roman Catholic church, without making the absolute claim of being the only manifestation of that church. The move from *est* to *subsistit* is clearly a move to loosen up the exclusive claim of the Roman church to be the one and only manifestation of Christ's church.

Those who have been acquainted with the classical scholastic theology will recognize the good uses to which scholasticism can be put in an ecumenical age. While *esse* quite simply means "to be" and is used to express identification, *subsistere* means "a determined mode of existing." [14] Therefore in this context *subsistit* means "to be there," "to be present," "to exist concretely," "to exist in this particular mode." Though it admits of a degree of identification it is not an absolute identification. The *relatio* for this article states specifically that the substitution of *subsistit* for *est* was introduced "so that the whole statement may be more in accordance with the affirmation of the ecclesial elements which are to be found elsewhere." [15] Speaking of the more general intent of this section the *relatio* for specific articles elaborated in some detail:

"The intention was to show that this church here on earth is concretely to be found in the Catholic Church. This empirical church manifests Christ's mystery, albeit in darkness, until the time when it shall be made manifest in the fullness of light. Thus Christ himself endured humiliation before entering into his glory. In this way it will be possible to avoid any impression that the description of the church offered by the council is purely unreal and idealistic. For the sake of clearer understanding the matter was subdivided and the following points dealt with in order:

---

[13] *Describitur enim status catholicorum, christianorum et non-christianorum sine terminologia de "membris," quae difficultatibus plena est. . . . Schema Constitutionis De Ecclesia,* 56.

[14] *Subsistere autem dicit determinatum modum essendi.* St. Thomas Aquinas, *Commentum in Quatuor Libros Sententiarum,* Sent. I, Dist. 23, q. I. a. I c. (*Opera Omnia,* Petrus Fiaccadorus Parma, 1856, vol. 6, 193).

[15] *Quaedam verba mutantur: loco* "est," *dicitur* "subsistit in," *ut expressio melius concordet cum affirmatione de elementis ecclesialibus quae alibi* adsunt. Schema Constitutionis De Ecclesia, 25.

a) The mystery of the church is present and manifests itself in a concrete society. But the visible society and the spiritual element are not two things but *one* complex reality embracing the divine and human, the means of salvation and also the fruits of salvation. This is illustrated by a comparison with the Word made flesh.

b) The church is one and unique and she subsists here on earth in the Catholic Church, even though ecclesial elements are to be found outside the Catholic Church.

c) The manifestation of the mystery of the Catholic Church is made at one and the same time in strength and in weakness, even in the circumstances of poverty, persecution, sin and purification, so that the church may become like Christ, though he was without sin. The theme of poverty was somewhat developed according to the wishes of the fathers.

d) But the church overcomes all these difficulties through the power of Christ, and through love, through which it reveals his mystery — albeit in darkness — until the time when it shall be made manifest in the fullness of light." [16]

Lest the attempt to loosen up the identification between the church which Christ founded and the Roman Catholic church should

---

[16] Intentio autem est ostendere, *Ecclesiam, cuius descripta est intima et arcana natura, qua cum Christo Eiusque opere in perpetuum unitur, his in terris concrete inveniri in Ecclesia catholica. Haec autem Ecclesia empirica mysterium revelat, sed non sine umbris, donec ad plenum lumen adducatur, sicut etiam Christus Dominus per exinanitionem ad gloriam pervenit. Ita praecavetur impressio ac si descriptio, quam Concilium de Ecclesia proponit, esset mere idealistica et irrealis.*

Ideo magis dilucida subdivisio *proponitur, in qua successive agitur de sequentibus:*

a) *Mysterium Ecclesiae adest et manifestatur* in concreta societate. *Coetus autem visibilis et elementum spirituale* non sunt duae res, *sed una realitas complexa, complectens divina et humana, media salutis et fructus salutis. Quod per analogiam cum Verbo incarnato illustratur.*

b) *Ecclesia est* unica, *et his in terris adest in Ecclesia catholica, licet extra eam inveniantur elementa ecclesialia.*

c) *Manifestatio mysterii in Ecclesia catholica fit simul* in virtute et debilitate, *scilicet etiam in conditione paupertatis ac persecutionis, peccati et purificationis, ut Ecclesia assimiletur Christo, qui tamen fuit sine peccato. Thema de paupertate, secundum desideria Patrum, aliquatenus evolvitur.*

d) *Ecclesia autem omnes illas difficultates devincit* per virtutem Christi et caritatem, *qua mysterium licet sub umbris revelat, donec ad plenam lucem perveniat. Ibid.,* 23-24.

result in an image of the church which is without concrete visible realization, Bishop A. M. Charue of Namur, who gave the *relatio* for the whole of chapter one, stated that "the mystery of the church is not an unreal or idealistic image, but exists in the concrete Catholic society under the guidance of the successor of Peter and of the bishops in his *communio*. There are not two churches, but only one, which is both of heaven and of earth, and which manifests God's eternal decree by becoming like her Lord both in his humiliation and in his glorious victory." [17] This makes it impossible to imagine that the ideal form of existence of this church is in some transhistorical sphere where it exists in purest potentiality, a sort of super-essence which pre-exists its historical manifestation, a Platonic image which always inadequately reflects its pre-existent prototype. The radical historicity of the church, with all the notes of an unmitigated particularity, are still very much in evidence. The documents leave no doubt that the church which Christ founded has a real, historical existence.

Also unmistakably clear is that this manifestation of the church is found in a fullness which is not a negation of its historicity. Article 8 of the Constitution reads: "But the society furnished with hierarchical agencies and the mystical body of Christ are not to be considered as two realities, nor are the visible assembly and the spiritual community, nor the earthly church and the church enriched with heavenly things. Rather they form one interlocked reality which is comprised of a divine and a human element." [18] While the text does not affirm a distinction between a supposed super-essence and its historical manifestation, there is maintained a distinction between the historical mystical body of Christ and its concrete form of existence in the Roman Catholic church. The substitution *subsistit* for *est* is clearly a blurring of the simple identification between the mystical body of Christ and the church which Christ founded, an identification clearly found in Pius XII's encyclical. As seen in the early sections of article 8 just quoted, the immediate context for the *subsistit* passage is the theology of the church as the mystical body of Christ. Though the Roman church

---

[17] *Relatio Super Caput I Textus Emendati Schematis Constitutionis De Ecclesia* (Typis Polyglottis Vaticanis 1964), 3.

[18] *Societas autem organis hierarchicis instructa et mysticum Christi corpus, coetus adspectabilis et communitas spiritualis, Ecclesia terrestris et Ecclesia coelestibus bonis ditata, non ut duae res considerandae sunt, sed unam realitatem complexam efformant, quae humano et divino coalescit elemento. Schema Constitutionis De Ecclesia, 14-15.*

is not a distinct reality from the mystical body of Christ, neither are the two by an absolute identification coterminus.

The whole vocabulary of belonging to the church fully or less fully has an interesting development in the documents. The second draft, which is the 1963 text, took over the vocabulary of *Mystici Corporis* and spoke in terms of those who "really" (*reapse*) belong to the church. Article 8 of the second draft said that "only those are really (*reapse*) and simply incorporated into the society of the church who. . . ."[19]

If the language of being incorporated into the church *reapse et simpliciter* had been maintained in the third and last draft, then incorporation into the church could not have been thought of in terms of degrees. Incorporation would have been an indivisible category and the only way non-Catholics could be related to the church would be by means of a *votum*, that is by intention or desire. This would have been to remain satisfied with the position of Pius XII in *Mystici Corporis*, or an approximation of Pius' position.

Some of the fathers of the council objected to speaking of being incorporated *reapse et simpliciter*, saying that it was obscure and in fact not correct. Besides no one uses this manner of speaking consistently. Other fathers proposed that in place of *reapse et simpliciter* either *plene* or *plene et perfecte* or some similar phrase be used.[20] To give support to this view the allocution of Pope Paul VI to the second session on 29 September 1963 was quoted, in which Paul uses the phrase *vinculo perfectae unitatis* ("bond of perfect unity"). It was pointed out that if Paul could speak of a bond of perfect unity there must also be an imperfect or less full bond of unity. One father regretted that there was no express mention of "members" when speaking of who was incorporated into the society of the church, which objection found some support among the fathers. Others however wanted to avoid the term "members" because it would not really solve the question at hand.[21] The *relatio generalis* for chapter 2 of the Constitution records why some of the fathers of the council (*iuxta Patres suadetur*) desired that the new chapter on the people of God be inserted into the schema on the church. One of the reasons given

---

[19] *Reapse et simpliciter loquendo Ecclesiae societati incorporantur illi tantum. . . . Ibid.*, 35.

[20] Cf. *Relationes de singulis numeris, ibid.*, 49-50.

[21] *Ibid.*

was that such an insertion would enable one to talk about the status of Catholics, Christians and non-Christians without using the terminology of members, a terminology which presents many problems.[22]

The final draft took over the vocabulary of fullness and degrees, leaving aside the vocabulary of member. Article 14 reads in part: "They are fully incorporated into the society of the church, who possessing the Spirit of Christ, accept her entire system and all the means of salvation given to her, and through union with her visible structure are joined to Christ, who rules her through the supreme pontiff and the bishops." [23]

When discussing the Decree on Ecumenism and the Constitution on the Church one is faced with some problems of chronology. The first draft of the Constitution was introduced in 1962 and was discussed in assemblies 31-36 of December of that year. The second draft of the document was discussed from 30 September to 31 October 1963. In May 1963 the first draft of the Decree on Ecumenism was sent to the fathers of the council and during the following months they communicated their first comments to the General Secretariat of the council. From 30 September to 31 October 1963 the council went back to discuss the second draft of the Constitution on the Church. On 18 November 1963 the council began the general discussion on the Decree on Ecumenism. The discussion of the various chapters ended on 2 December 1963. A second draft of the Decree was prepared and on 27 April 1964 Pope Paul VI ordered that it be sent to the fathers. During May, June, and July of that year the fathers sent in their views in written form on the new text. On 16 September 1964 the fathers took up the final text of the Constitution on the Church. During October and November of that year the fathers were at different times discussing both the second draft of the Decree on Ecumenism and the third draft of the Constitution on the Church and the final vote on the Decree was taken on 20 November 1964, while that of the Constitution was taken the next day, November 21. This means that there is some overlapping, and even repetition of the discussion on the

---

[22] *Sic melius videtur quomodo opus et vita Christi in mundo continuatur. Describitur enim status catholicorum, christianorum et non-christianorum sine terminologia de "membris," quae difficultatibus plena est. Ibid.*, 56.

[23] *Illi plene Ecclesiae societati incorporantur, qui Spiritum Christi habentes, integram eius ordinationem omniaque media salutis in ea instituta accipiunt, et in eiusdem compage visibili cum Christo, eam per Summum Pontificem atque Episcopos regente, iunguntur, vinculis nempe professionis fidei, sacramentorum et ecclesiastici regiminis ac communionis. Ibid.*, 36.

two documents in those areas where there is a common theological concern.

The first draft of the Decree on Ecumenism did not apply the term "church" to the communities which in a generic way owe their origins to the events of the 16th century. The first draft entitled chapter three "Concerning Christians Separated from the Catholic Church" *(De Christianis ab Ecclesia Catholica Seiunctis)*. The second section of this chapter, which deals specifically with Protestant denominations, contented itself to speak of "communities." This section was entitled "Concerning the Communities which Arose in or after the Sixteenth Century" *(De Communitatibus inde a Saeculo XVI Exortis)*. One of the *modi* suggested that in four places in this article the word *"communiones"* be used instead of *"communitates,"* because *"communitates"* does not come out of a specifically Christian vocabulary and does not have any theological content.[24] One father asked that the positive elements preserved in Protestantism be more explicitly recognized and that their missionary activities among the pagans be praised.[25] The *relatio* on the whole Decree also mentions the missionary activity of Protestant groups as something worthy of praise.[26]

When the specific question whether or not "church" could be applied to communities separated from the Catholic church (such are the categories) many said that the church of Christ is one, and indeed Catholic and Roman, while others pointed out that the expression "Eastern churches" is a quite customary usage, being found even in the documents of the holy see.[27] It was further asked whether in a given schism, even though many Christians are separated from the Catholic church, it is not possible that the church as such remains perfect and undivided, or whether in this division, which is against the will of God, the church is not in some sense divided, as the Council of Trent seems to affirm when it speaks of the church being "torn in many and various parts."[28]

On 26 November 1963 Archbishop Gabriel Manek of Endeh, Indonesia, speaking in the name of 29 Indonesian bishops, spoke in

---

[24] *Emendationes a Concilii Patribus scripto exhibitae super schema Decreti De Oecumenismo* (Typis Polyglottis Vaticanis 1963), 28.

[25] *Ibid.,* 7.

[26] *Relatio super schema Decreti De Oecumenismo* (Typis Polyglottis Vaticanis 1963), 16.

[27] *Emendationes a Concilii Patribus scripto exhibitae super schema Decreti De Oecumenismo,* 8.

[28] *Ibid.*

the council aula and said that the ecclesial elements found in the Protestant communities entitled them to be called "churches." "These communities are groups of baptized persons, united with us through the virtues of faith, hope, and charity. They accept the creeds of the early councils. Thus they are really particular Christian churches, and the elements which they share with us are a manifestation of church unity. They also have sacred actions which signify grace. The Holy Spirit does not refuse to use these communities as instruments of salvation. If they *can* be called churches without any damage to faith, then they *should* be given this title. The dialogue we are encouraging must take place not only between individuals but also between churches and their representatives. The first beginnings of this dialogue are in recognizing these groups as churches, not only in the sociological but in the theological sense." [29]

Three days later Bishop Charles Helmsing of Kansas City-St. Joseph criticized the first draft on the floor of the council because of its failure to recognize the ecclesial character of Protestant denominations. "The text as it stands, with its unwillingness to recognize the term 'church' as applicable to non-Catholic communities, will certainly be an obstacle to any effective ecumenical action. Reasons for this (application of 'church') would be: 1) Ordinary decency and politeness, because in daily life, Catholics and non-Catholics alike use the term 'church' to designate such Christian communities. 2) The word 'church' does not have a strictly univocal meaning but can be used analogically. 3) In the Old Testament when the Northern part of the Kingdom of Israel was cut off by schism it nevertheless continued to belong to the people of God, was moved by the Spirit of God, and had prophets. 4) The elements of imperfect union referred to in the text are found not merely in individuals but likewise in these communities considered as groups. Many of them have an admirable sense of the ministry and have also had martyrs. We cannot deny them communion in the sense of *koinonia*." [30]

These voices and the discussion which had already taken place on the Constitution on the Church brought about changes in the Decree on Ecumenism. The section which had been entitled "Concerning

[29] *Concilio Ecumenico Vaticano II, Ufficio Stampa,* News Bulletin no. 39, General Congregation no. 75, November 26, 1963. This bulletin service gave summaries of speeches rather than verbatim documentation.

[30] *Ibid.,* News Bulletin, no. 42, General Congregation no. 78, November 29, 1963.

Christians Separated from the Catholic Church" became "The Separated Churches and Ecclesial Communities in the West" (*De Ecclesiis et Communitatibus ecclesialibus in Occidente seiunctis*). The text of article 19 in the first draft spoke of the Catholic church and the other Christian communities (*illae Communitates christianae*) which are bound together by a special affinity and necessity because of the long ecclesiastical communion in ages past before the break. In the second and final draft the word "churches" was introduced: "The churches and ecclesial communities (*Ecclesiae et Communitates ecclesiales*) which were separated from the Apostolic See of Rome during the serious crisis that began in the West at the end of the Middle Ages, or during later times, are bound to the Catholic Church by a special affinity. . . ." [31]

Archbishop (now Cardinal) John Heenan of Westminster, England, presenting the Decree for its final discussion, remarked that the western communities separated from the Roman see are not only a sum of individual Christians but that they show church-forming elements which they have preserved from the common inheritance. These elements give these communities a truly ecclesial character. He noted that the text itself does not attempt to indicate which groups are to be called churches and which ecclesial communities.

The final draft of the Decree did apply the word "church" to the groups which in one way owe their origin to the events of the sixteenth century. Further, the term "communion" was applied to these groups. Early in the document the problem of ecumenical relationships is presented in the framework of "communion," a theological category heavy with ecclesiological and eucharistic content. St. Augustine had used the term *communio* to refer to both the Catholic and the Donatist churches. It was especially through the influence of Yves Congar that it found its way into the Decree.

Speaking of the friendly confrontation between experts from the various "churches and communities," article 4 of the Decree continues: "This dialogue involves on the part of each participant an explanation at a deeper level of the doctrine of his communion. . . . It enables everyone to acquire a truer understanding and a fairer esti-

---

[31] *Ecclesiae et Communitates ecclesiales, quae vel in gravissimo illo rerum discrimine, quod in Occidente iam ab exeunte medio aevo initium sumpsit, vel posterioribus temporibus ab Apostolica Sede Romana separatae sunt, cum Ecclesia catholica peculiari affinitate ac necessitudine iunguntur ob diuturnam populi christiani vitam praeteritis saeculis in ecclesiastica communione peractam. Schema Decreti De Oecumenismo*, 16.

mate of the doctrine and life of the other's communion. Another good effect is the fuller collaboration that the communions achieve. . . ." [32] To indicate that this usage is not taken over from popular usage without any specific theological content, article 20 indicates its Christological basis. "We rejoice to see the separated brethren looking to Christ as the source and center of ecclesiastical communion. Inspired by longing for union with Christ, they feel compelled to search for unity ever more ardently. . . ." [33]

It is through baptism that one is incorporated into the crucified and glorified Christ, who is the source and center of ecclesiastical communion. However, baptism is oriented toward full communion in faith and sacraments and toward complete participation in eucharistic communion. Article 22 states: "Baptism is thus oriented toward a complete profession of faith, a complete incorporation into the system of salvation such as Christ himself willed it to be, and finally, toward a complete participation in eucharistic communion." [34] And it is at this point that the document indicates that communion is not yet complete in the ecclesiological and eucharistic sense. According to the Decree, the communion is not a full expression of the sacramental reality of Christ in the sacrament of orders and of the eucharist and therefore not a full expression of ecclesiastical communion. "The

---

[32] . . . *dein, in conventibus Christianorum ex diversis Ecclesiis vel Communitatibus in spiritu religioso ordinatis, "dialogus" inter peritos apte instructos initus, in quo unusquisque suae Communionis doctrinam profundius explicat eiusque characteres perspicue praesentat. Per hunc enim dialogum veriorem utriusque Communionis doctrinae vitaeque cognitionem et magis aequam aestimationem omnes acquirunt; tum etiam illae Communiones eam consequuntur ampliorem collaborationem in quibusvis officiis. . . . Ibid.,* 6.

[33] *Laetamur tamen videntes fratres seiunctos in Christum tamquam fontem et centrum communionis ecclesiasticae intendere. Desiderio tacti unionis cum Christo compelluntur ad unitatem magis magisque quaerendam. . . . Ibid.,* 17. It should be noted that in those places where the first draft had *fratres separati* the final draft has *fratres seiuncti.* The change was made because the word *separati* might have a pejorative connotation, while *seiuncti* merely states the fact that a separation exists. This change in the Latin text is not always clear in the English translations as *fratres seiuncti* is generally translated "separated brethren."

[34] *Attamen baptismus per se dumtaxat initium et exordium est, quippe qui totus in acquirendam tendit plenitudinem vitae in Christo. Itaque baptismus ordinatur ad integram fidei professionem, ad integram incorporationem in salutis institutum, prout ipse Christus illud voluit, ad integram denique in communionem eucharisticam insertionem. Ibid.,* 18.

ecclesial Communities separated from us (*Communitates ecclesiales a nobis seiunctae*) lack that fullness of unity with us which should flow from baptism, and we believe that especially because of the lack of the sacrament of order they have not preserved the genuine and total reality of the eucharistic mystery." [35] Given the fact that in the Roman church the only way to authenticate ministry is by ritual validation, in which the role of a bishop is essential, the council could not have declared otherwise and Pope Paul could not have considered any other position. The Decree maintains that as long as the ecclesial communities lack the sacrament of orders they lack the fullness of the eucharistic mystery, or, in other words, the validity of the sacrament depends on the validity of the ministerial office.

One would not want to quarrel with the principle that an authentic or valid eucharist depends on an authentic or valid ministry. I know of no Protestant theologian who would reject this as a principle. But one could argue that there is more than one avenue of access to the mystery of Christ and to the ministerial realities to which that mystery gives expression. Orders conferred by a bishop, which is one avenue of access, is not the only one. Elsewhere I have argued that one cannot tie valid ministry or valid eucharist to the possession of episcopal orders in the communion.[36] I have argued that besides authenticating orders by a process of ritual validation (conferral of orders by a bishop) there are other styles of ministry possible which are validated ecclesiologically (where there is a true though incomplete manifestation of the church, there one has a true ministry) or validated charismatically (if the Corinthian church order was authentic and valid in New Testament times, could it not be authentic and valid today?). The text of the Decree suggests the possibility of discussion on the whole matter of ministry. "Dialogue should be undertaken concerning the true meaning of the Lord's Supper, the other sacra-

---

[35] *Communitates ecclesiales a nobis seiunctae, quamvis deficiat earum plena nobiscum unitas ex baptismate profluens, et quamvis credamus illas, praesertim propter Sacramenti Ordinis defectum, genuinam atque integram substantiam Mysterii eucharistici non servasse. . . . Ibid.,* 18. It was Pope Paul who changed the second draft from *plenam realitatem Mysterii eucharistici* to *genuinam atque integram substantiam Mysterii eucharistici* (from "full reality of the eucharistic mystery" to "genuine and total reality of the eucharistic mystery"). This makes clearer the differences between Catholics and Protestants in terms of the eucharist and the sacramental basis of ministry (the sacrament of orders).

[36] Kilian McDonnell, "Ways of Validating Ministry," *Journal of Ecumenical Studies* 7 (1970), 209-265.

ments, and the church's worship and ministry." [37] These would seem to include the episcopacy, the sacrament of orders, an authentic ministry and an authentic eucharist, in a word, the whole question of order in the church and the nature of the church itself.

It would be to go beyond the text of the conciliar documents to suppose that in recognizing the Protestant denominations as true manifestations of the church which Christ founded, they thereby wished to make a direct statement confirming the theological authenticity of Protestant ministry in general or Protestant eucharist in particular. Clearly this was not the intention of the council as article 22 of the Decree specifically states that Protestant churches lack the genuine and total reality of the eucharistic mystery.

However in a theological process one can go beyond the text; indeed one must do so. It does not seem possible to posit a true but incomplete manifestation of the church and then assert that the eucharist is without authenticity. Many are tempted to say that a true but incomplete manifestation of the church leads to a true but incomplete ministry and that the deficiency of the ministry is to be found precisely in the want of the genuine and total reality of the eucharistic mystery. This seems to be postulated on the assumption that the ultimate, irreducible, ministerial moment is eucharistic action (the consecration), a stand which would find no support in the New Testament.

It has been suggested [38] that the text wishes to emphasize the common and positive aspects of the Protestant celebration of the Lord's supper: "When they commemorate the Lord's death and resurrection in the Holy Supper, they profess that it signifies life in communion with Christ and they await his coming in glory." [39] It is undoubtedly true that the intent of the text is to say something ecumenically significant and positive but at the same time not to compromise the basic assertion that they "have not preserved the genuine and total reality of the eucharistic mystery." A close look at the text

---

[37] *Quapropter doctrina circa Coenam Domini, cetera sacramenta et cultum ac Ecclesiae ministeria obiectum dialogi constituat oportet. Schema Decreti De Oecumenismo,* 18.

[38] Johannes Feiner, "Commentary on the Decree," *Commentary on the Documents of Vatican II,* ed. Herbert Vorgrimler, vol. 2 (New York: Herder & Herder, 1968), 154-155.

[39] *. . . tamen, dum in Sancta Coena mortis et resurrectionis Domini memoriam faciunt, vitam in Christi communione significari profitentur atque gloriosum eius adventum expectant. Schema Decreti De Oecumenismo,* 18.

shows that what is said is nothing more than that when Protestants gather for a eucharistic celebration, *"they* profess *(profitentur)* and it signifies life in communion with Christ." Obviously this is to say very little. And because these denominations lack the sacrament of orders and have not "preserved the genuine and total reality of the eucharistic mystery," therefore the application of the term "communion" to Protestant denominations is positive in its theological content but incomplete in its full realization. Until the eucharistic question and the whole question of the order of the church is worked out in its ecumenical implications, the term "communion" as well as the term "church" will be without its full eucharistic and ecclesiological content.[40]

One should not, however, minimize the importance of recognizing the ecclesiological quality and nature of Protestant denominations. This is a development of major importance for ecumenical relations in general and the problem of ministry in particular. For the first time the Roman church has recognized that Protestant denominations are more than sociological groupings, but are true churches in a true theological sense and, as article 3 of the Decree declares, the sacred acts they celebrate are "capable of providing access to the community of salvation." Anyone who knows how jealously the Roman church has guarded her exclusive identification with the church which Christ founded cannot fail to see that the council's use of "church" in referring to Protestant denominations, a use which is specifically theological and ecclesiological in intent, is truly a historic event which opens up yet unexplored ecumenical possibilities.

---

[40] L. Hertling, *Communio und Primat — Kirche und Papsttum in der christlichen Antike," Una Sancta* 17 (1962), 91-125.

PARTICIPANTS

Catholic Participants:

The Most Rev. T. Austin Murphy, Auxiliary Bishop of Baltimore, Maryland

Dr. Thomas E. Ambrogi, Professor of Religious Studies, University of the Pacific, Stockton, California*

The Rev. Msgr. Joseph W. Baker, Vice-Chairman of the Ecumenical Commission of the Archdiocese of St. Louis, Missouri

The Most Rev. William W. Baum, Bishop of Springfield-Cape Girardeau, Missouri

The Rev. Raymond E. Brown, S. S., Professor of Sacred Scripture, St. Mary's Seminary, Baltimore, Maryland

The Rev. Walter J. Burghardt, S. J., Professor of Patristics, Woodstock College, New York, New York

The Rev. Godfrey Diekmann, O. S. B., Professor of Patristics, St. John's Abbey, Collegeville, Minnesota

The Rev. Maurice C. Duchaine, S. S., Professor of Dogmatic Theology, St. Mary's Seminary, Baltimore, Maryland

The Rev. John F. Hotchkin, Associate Director, Bishops' Committee for Ecumenical and Interreligious Affairs, Washington, D. C.

Professor James F. McCue, School of Religion, University of Iowa, Iowa City, Iowa

The Rev. Kilian McDonnell, O. S. B., Executive Director, Institute for Ecumenical and Cultural Research, Collegeville, Minnesota

Dr. Harry J. McSorley, Professor of Ecumenical Theology, St. Paul's College, Washington, D. C.

The Rev. Anthony T. Padovano, Professor of Dogmatic Theology, Immaculate Conception Seminary, Darlington, New Jersey

The Rev. Jerome D. Quinn, Professor of Old and New Testament, The St. Paul Seminary, St. Paul, Minnesota

The Rev. George H. Tavard, A. A., Visiting Professor, Methodist Theological School, Delaware, Ohio

---

* Participated in first two sessions only

Lutheran Participants:

Dr. Paul C. Empie, General Secretary, U. S. A. National Committee of the Lutheran World Federation, New York, New York

Dr. Kent S. Knutson, President, Wartburg Theological Seminary, Dubuque, Iowa

Dr. Fred Kramer, Professor of Systematic Theology, Concordia Theological Seminary, Springfield, Illinois

Dr. George A. Lindbeck, Professor of Historical Theology, Yale University Divinity School, New Haven, Connecticut

Dr. Paul D. Opsahl, Associate Executive Secretary, Division of Theological Studies, Lutheran Council in the U. S. A., New York, New York

Dr. Arthur Carl Piepkorn, Graduate Professor of Systematic Theology, Concordia Seminary, St. Louis, Missouri

Dr. Warren A. Quanbeck, Professor of Systematic Theology, Luther Theological Seminary, St. Paul, Minnesota

Dr. John Reumann, Professor of New Testament, The Lutheran Seminary at Philadelphia, Pennsylvania

Dr. Joseph Sittler, Professor of Theology, University of Chicago Divinity School, Chicago, Illinois